# COPING WITH A BAD GLOBAL IMAGE

*Human Rights in the People's
Republic of China,
1993-1994*

John F. Copper
Ta-ling Lee

University Press of America, Inc.
Lanham • New York • Oxford

University Press of America,® Inc.
4720 Boston Way
Lanham, Maryland 20706

12 Hid's Copse Rd.
Cummor Hill, Oxford OX2 9JJ

Copublished by arrangement with the East Asia Research Institute

**Library of Congress Cataloging-in-Publication Data**

Copper, John Franklin.
Coping with a bad global image : human rights in the People's
Republic of China, 1993-1994 / by John F. Copper and Ta–ling Lee.
        p.    cm.
Includes bibliographical references and index.
1.  Civil rights--China.  2.  Human rights--China.  I. Lee, Ta–ling, II.
Title.
JC599.C6C69   1997   323'.0951'09049--dc21      97-18988 CIP

ISBN 0-7618-0788-8 (cloth: alk. ppr.)
ISBN 0-7618-0789-6 (pbk: alk. ppr.)

# Preface

This biennial "update" is a survey and analysis of human rights events, issues and trends in the People's Republic of China (PRC) during 1993 and 1994. It is the sixth update the authors have written since the publication of *Human Rights in the People's Republic of China* (Boulder: Westview Press, 1988), a comprehensive study of human rights in the PRC that we wrote in collaboration with four other scholars.

The other surveys were: *Reform in Reverse: Human Rights in the People's Republic of China, 1986/87* (Baltimore: University of Maryland School of Law, 1987); *One Step Forward, One Step Back: Human Rights in the People's Republic of China, 1987/88* (Baltimore: University of Maryland School of Law, 1989); *Failure of the Democracy Movement: Human Rights in the People's Republic of China, 1988/89* (Baltimore: University of Maryland School of Law, 1991); *Tiananmen Aftermath: Human Rights in the People's Republic of China, 1990* (Baltimore: University of Maryland School of Law, 1992); *The Bamboo Gulag: Human Rights in the People's Republic of China, 1991–1992* (Baltimore: University of Maryland School of Law, 1994).

Like previous updates, this book considers changes in the political and legal systems and Communist ideology (more correctly, its demise) in its appraisal of the human rights condition in the PRC. These, the authors contend, are causative factors of human rights abuses and need to be understood to put the human rights situation in its proper perspective. Again, such matters as crime, forced labor, and executions are examined in detail to delineate the worst kinds of the human rights abuses as well as current trends. Dissidents, religious advocates, and intellectuals are also a focus of attention. Like the last update, but not previous ones, this book examines the PRC's human rights situation as a foreign policy issue–which it has become in recent years.

The authors wish to express their appreciation to the Chinese Association for Human Rights in Taipei for its support and for providing and sharing information and data. We are also grateful to a host of other organizations and individuals too numerous to cite for their encouragement and moral support.

*John F. Copper and Ta-ling Lee*
May 1996

# Table of Contents

Preface

Chapter 1    Introduction

Chapter 2    Chinese Politics and Human Rights

Chapter 3    Political Dissidents and Human Rights

Chapter 4    Freedom of Speech and Human Rights

Chapter 5    Criminal Justice and Human Rights

Chapter 6    Foreign Policy and Human Rights, I

Chapter 7    Foreign Policy and Human Rights, II

Chapter 8    Conclusions

Appendixes

Bibliography

Index

About the Authors

# Chapter 1

## Overview and Scope of Study

Since the Tiananmen Massacre in 1989, the human rights condition in the People's Republic of China has been the subject of considerably more attention and scrutiny.[1] In fact, much more. But this only in part compensates for the fact that China's human rights abuses were largely ignored in the past, that there was a gross difference in terms of abuses reported in China compared to other countries in the world, and that the People's Republic of China had what some called a "human rights edge" in that its government could abuse more and fewer people knew about it or seemingly cared.[2] In fact, China still attracts less attention for human rights abuses than most other countries if one takes a measure of the number of people whose rights are abused compared to what is written about them.

In fact, there are a number of areas where human rights abuses in China clearly do not get sufficient attention considering their scope. Even in areas that have been of concern, such as executions and political prisoners, there is a lack of good statistics. In addition, there are few reports that have analyzed China's political system for indications of the causes of human rights abuses. Nor have many scholars considered China's human rights situation as a problem or a factor in Beijing's foreign policy making.[3] In this work, the authors endeavor to cover the areas not covered or not covered thoroughly or systematically enough, and make some connections to domestic and foreign policies.

In Chapter 1, the authors examine China's political system for clues to its human rights abuses. They note that expectations were raised in the 1980s by China's leaders scrapping the nation's communist political system. But, during the period under review this created false expectations because a succession crisis troubled leaders from the top down in the Chinese Communist Party, which still ruled the nation without challenge, and in the government. Top officials did not want to appear soft or weak in the context of the scramble for position and advantage in what was thought by those involved to be a pending political vacuum due to Deng Xiaoping's declining health and his anticipated death. Nor did they invite any challenge to their authority since demands for expanded political and civil rights were seen to invite political instability. Meanwhile, traditional communist ideology and Maoism, were being replaced by Deng Xiaoping's ideas.

All of this transpired in the milieu of a more acute struggle between right and left in the Communist Party and the government. In the past, such contests for power and influence resulted in the leadership ignoring human rights matters while seeking any means possible to weaken and undermine their opposition, including the persecution of them or their friends and supporters. During 1993 and 1994, this constituted a serious cause of human rights abuses.

Even though to many observers Jiang Zemin seemed to assured of inheriting Deng's mantle of power, and the political right (which sought to promote capitalism and more political freedoms) where both Deng and Jiang found their support, appeared to be dominant, the succession process was not transpiring without difficulty. The left's challenges, criticism, and obstruction- ism all caused Jiang to tread slowly, make concessions and keep tough policies and even ideology in place. Even among his supporters there was concern expressed that Jiang was assuming too much power and that he and others who supported the economic reforms which many have long assumed would perforce bring political reform, may be putting themselves in a position to deny human rights if they so chose. Patently they were trying to increase their political power. To some it seemed possible that Jiang's bid for power would be blocked by those who feared a strong leader (as happened several times in the Soviet Union and in China's past) and that the succession process and its consequent political paralysis might last a long time.

While the succession issue evoked both apprehension and uncertainty, the political system itself was undergoing change that did not exactly help the cause of human rights. The political system was, as part of a long-term modern- ization process, being downsized. China was getting rid of its immense Communist-built bureaucracy. Its leaders as well as the public realized that communism was antiquated. More important still they understood that China had to compete (and was) in the world economy and that the government had to be streamlined to do this. This had already paved the way for expanded political liberties by virtue of a smaller and less intrusive polity. But the way in which this was done had also hurt the cause of human rights. And this continued to be a serious problem.

During 1993 and 1994, much of the downsizing, in fact, was done for very "partisan" political reasons. Opponents of top leaders in power were fired or dismissed from their jobs. Others were dismissed for challenging decisions by those above them. Many lost their jobs because they lacked "connections." The process, in fact, resembled party purges of the past. In addition, much down- sizing was done without regard for getting employees to retire or finding other jobs or transferring them into the private sector.

In some other realms, there were systemic problems. The household registry system, which many felt should have been a casualty of reform, was retained to control the population. This meant that reducing the size and functions of government did not create greater freedoms of movement as some expected. Legal reform took the form mainly of increasing the percent of convictions in China's courts. Meanwhile, reform of the legal process had little to do with an expansion of civil or political rights or improving due process. Neither situation helped the cause of improved human rights. The same was true of new rules for Communist Party control over the press, which many top leaders saw as getting too free. Under the guise of preventing instability and preventing the influx of Western "spiritual pollution" and pornography, the press was subjected in several ways to more controls. The media also experienced several periods of the government "sending them a message" not to assume greater press freedoms and that the media had to heed the party "line."

An even bigger problem was concern expressed at the top hierarchy of the Party that economic decentralization had caused the "center" to lose authority, that the provinces were running the country, and that even fragmentation of the country was a real threat. If economic decentralization was creating problems, certainly there could be no more political decentralization of power. During the period under study there were frequent orders from the top that officials must "rein in" the provinces and local government. In this context, of course, there was little hope for expanding political rights as a result of less government.

Worsening corruption also posed an impasse to an increased concern about human rights. Corruption, which was already very bad in China, got even worse during 1993 and 1994. Corrupt officials certainly did not want to draw attention to procedures for guaranteeing human rights or any other rights. They were concerned about more money and favored a system that lacked guarantees of any form because they benefitted from the arbitrariness and personal nature of such a system. When crackdowns were called for, and they were periodically, human rights were ignored in the process of punishing those guilty of corrupt activities. In fact, many were harshly punished for economic crimes to set an example. Security and police agencies meanwhile were given expanded authority to deal with crimes of corruption since they were more difficult to investigate than ordinary crimes.

Corruption was especially rampant in the military and agencies of government involved with big projects. This engendered cries of outrage by concerned leaders and citizens. It, in fact, created a widespread feeling that the government did not care about its people and that privilege was all important. It was also antithetical to a system wherein obeying the rules was important and in that context of the government granting rights and guaranteeing their practice.

Another very discouraging sign during the period was the government's and the Chinese Communist Party's disregard for rural China and the peasants. This was so serious and so blatant, in fact, that it gave rise to riots in several places in China and in some cases involved thousands of protesters. The riots were violent and so were the government's efforts to quell them. And punishments followed, without much regard for due process or the rights of the accused. Although obviously concerned about the open opposition to the government, the authorities did little to stop the corruption and the over-taxation that caused the riots. They attacked the result of the problem rather than the causes. Specifically, little was done about the declining comparative advantage facing agricultural goods or the general lack of concern for education, hospitals and the like in the countryside, while the lives of city residents improved.

Since China is still, by population, a nation of peasants—80 percent of the population—this had a very serious impact upon China's human right situation. Those who lived in rural China felt alienated and ignored. Those who sought to move to a city found themselves among China's estimated 50 million "floating population" that became victims of China's brutal law enforcement. Many were sent to labor camps for years or worse.

China's treatment of dissidents, which is the subject of Chapter 2, also mirrored both the political leadership's attitudes about human rights and trends in the human rights condition in the People's Republic. The easily observable fact that the fate of political dissidents generally worsened during the period under study is instructive. So too was the fate of certain dissidents and the fact some were released and then rearrested, while almost all were treated in many ways reminiscent of the totalitarian political and social systems that existed under Mao. Clearly political leaders in the People's Republic of China seemed yet unprepared and unwilling to accept dissent.

Wei Jingsheng and Wang Dan were the most well-known cases. Wei had been imprisoned since 1979. He had been an activist at the time of the Democracy Wall movement when Deng Xiaoping came to power. Deng used the broad public support for democracy and those who led the charge, to divert the attention of his adversaries while he confused them and weakened and undermined their authority. Then he turned his back on democracy and punished those who demanded it. Wang had been a student leader of the Democracy Movement, some said the brains behind this movement that provoked widespread calls for political reform that preceded the June 1989 Tiananmen Massacre. He went into hiding and after appearing on China's most wanted list for some time was finally arrested and jailed.

Wei was released from incarceration just days before the International Olympic Committee was scheduled to decide on the site for the Olympic games to be held in 2000. China had applied to host the games. Wang's release was timed to coincide with China's application to the General Agreement on Tariffs and Trade. Both were subsequently rearrested—some would say because they had served their purpose or that because China failed to get what it wanted from their release. The moral of the story, of course, is that Chinese leaders will treat its dissidents (and presumably its citizens) with greater respect in human rights terms if it suits their political interests to do so, either domestic (to send a message the government is kind and lenient) or international (that China has made progress in political modernization and democracy in order to get something).

Perhaps just as meaningful in terms of elucidating the chimerical nature of China's human rights situation is the fact that Wei and Wang were abused when in jail and that Herculean efforts were made by top authorities to erase the memory of what they did and stood for and make them non-persons. After their releases they were followed and harassed and pressured to not engage in their earlier pursuits and to express guilt and remorse for what they had done. When they did not they were jailed again. All of this resembled in many ways how the government treated dissent under Mao. In short, the question arose: Had anything changed?

The fate of other dissidents was not too much different. As usual they were treated worse than those that were well known in China and especially abroad. One such person was Xu Yiruo, who was accused of being an anti-communist at a time when communism as an ideology or political philosophy had come to mean very little in China, though the Communist Party could not formally abandon it as it still underpinned its legitimacy—or many top leaders apparently so thought. Xu was released when it was convenient, for show. But he was not allowed to have a job. His hopes for greater rights for Chinese citizens and for the expansion of basic freedoms in China were not realized. His release came to mean very little.

Others were released before President Clinton was to decide whether to extend most-favored-nation status on trade to China. Many were rearrested, signalling that China was not really grateful. Many others were arrested on charges that had no basis, at least by the standards practiced in most democratic countries. Many were discriminated against in various ways: being denied jobs, being removed from important positions, being transferred to isolated areas of China, not being allowed to live in a city, and so on.

China's control of dissent also extended to those residing abroad. The State Council in the fall of 1993 established a regulation barring the return of eight categories of Chinese citizens, including those who had engaged in any anti-government activities or who had accepted financial help from "hostile foreign sources." The other categories were almost as broad, vague or ill-defined. Chinese leaders obviously did not want its "best and brightest" back if there was any chance they had been tainted by their stay abroad or if they were going to cause trouble.

Numerous stories meanwhile circulated in China and among China watchers of dissidents who had formed anti-government organizations, who had made daring escapes from detention or while under surveillance, and special cases that came to the attention of foreign governments, especially the United States government. Chapter 2 contains some sagas and some detailed documentation on some of these cases.

Dissidents were also maltreated as a matter of course or precaution during the days and weeks leading up to the anniversaries of the Tiananmen Massacre in 1993 and 1994. The government desperately sought to head off any new demonstrations or protest. But the government succeeded only in part. Many preemptory arrests were made; yet there was still protest. What happened in June 1989 was obviously not forgotten and recalling it could not be stopped. In fact, governments in this realm seem to have created more desire on the people for rights that citizens of other countries enjoy.

Other dissidents were cautious and made their protest in other ways. Many organized, but stayed underground. It thus was difficult to assess the scope of underground dissident movements, but they were clearly there. Information on some of them is provided in Chapter 2, together with the government's response. It too is quite revealing.

Chapter 3 assesses the issue of freedom of speech and how in 1993 and 1994 this particular freedom related to the human rights condition in general in China (it being such an important facet of civil and political freedoms). It was also an important barometer of human rights trends in view of the fact that the government has expanded certain freedoms, including freedom of movement, in order to ensure the success of the economic reforms. Freedom of speech likewise seemed to benefit for a while as a result, but whether it was really becoming institutionalized or whether it would be expanded any further as the economy continued to grow was indeed uncertain.

During the period under study, while the freedom of citizens to speak out was broadened, it was in many ways still severely restricted and in some realms diminished a right given by the government or allowed by law enforcement authorities than in the past. One of the main reasons for this was the perception by government and Communist Party leaders that there was a danger of foreign plots against China. Frequent mention was made by top leaders of "American hegemonists" that were attempting to "infiltrate, sabotage or encircle China." Official publications mentioned this regularly. Chinese leaders, in fact, seemed preoccupied, even paranoid, about the so-called U.S. threat, saying at times that the United States regarded China as its main adversary.

To deal with this "threat" the State Council passed by-laws to the National Security Act in mid-1993 that defined "hostile groups" and set forth activities that would be severely punished. These activities included "distorting facts, expressing opinions that endanger national security, instigating disputes between nationalities and illegally meeting with foreigners." The government and the controlled press continued to harp on the theme of "hostile forces"—even relating them to China's failed bid to host the Olympics in 2000. Chinese citizens were jailed for meeting with foreigners, including several that met foreign reporters, for allegedly passing on secrets (even though they had never had access to state secrets). Foreign magazines were banned and Voice of America was jammed based on this perception of a threat. In addition, satellite dishes to receive television programs from abroad were confiscated.

The government, apart from this concern, also made efforts to stop the publication of stories about top leaders, radio call-in shows (which had become very popular and were an important avenue of free expression), and magazines that published pornography and violence. The Party Propaganda Department was very busy during the period under study while new government directives and laws helped them in their crackdowns.

The most widely known case of censorship during the period under study occurred in 1993 when the government banned the first Chinese film ever to win the coveted top award at the Cannes International Film Festival. The film was *Farewell, My Concubine*. It was apparently put on a list to be condemned because it contained themes about homosexuality and political persecution. It was also reported that one or more members of the Party Politburo personally did not like the film. The Film Bureau of the Ministry of Radio, Film and Television later said it would ban films that contained "attitude problems" and put the Communist system in a bad light.

Because of the ban against *Farewell, My Concubine* and some other movies, some films that were begun and were being worked on were canceled. And some that had been under consideration for production in China were instead started elsewhere.

A well known book was also banned: *A Third Eye Observes China*. This book was attacked by censors in 1994, even though it had been once praised by Communist Party General Secretary Jiang Zemin. The problem was that it warned about dire consequences of China's rapid economic development and pursued other themes that were not in step with current policy. Several other noted books were banned allegedly for sensationalism and inaccuracies. Some books were also banned for criticizing Deng Xiaoping or for portraying Chinese society in a negative light.

Not only were films and books banned, but the government increased its promotion of Deng Xiaoping's works—which some saw as connected to the banning of other books and increasing censorship. Promoting one book would demote another, Chinese leaders apparently thought. Alternatively the government and the party sought to promote Deng's ideas as China's new "ideology." Promoting an ideology would tell people what to think and what not to think. Clearly Deng's writings were being lauded and pushed in many ways as Mao's works were in the 1960s. Some patriotic songs and books were also promoted in ways reminiscent of the Mao era when the Chinese Communist Party not only dictated what Chinese citizens could read, but what they must read, see and hear.

Chapter 5 discusses criminal justice in China during 1993 and 1994 and how it fostered human rights abuses. The central problem from the point of view of the government was the increase of crime throughout the country, including almost every kind of crime. This was ironically a product of expanding economic and civil and political rights especially the right to travel granted by Deng in association with China's economic reforms. But it also seemed it was as much caused by the affluence and disparities in income and wealth produced by Deng's reforms. In any event, to Chinese Communist Party and government officials the solution was stricter law enforcement and harsher punishments.

In the realm of severe punishments, very long jail terms (usually in labor camps) and capital punishment became more common and sentences were meted out in an almost administrative fashion. Large numbers of sentences were handed down on or before the Lunar New Year holiday or on other specific occasions. When crime waves became a matter of concern the government ordered the police, security agencies or the military to crack down, and the enforcers were rated and promoted according to the numbers of criminals apprehended and punished. This was particularly the case following the various announcements of drug eradication campaigns or efforts.

However, the tough attitude toward crime had another face. It seemed not only intended to control crime, but to produce profit for the government. In fact, most of those punished were sent to labor camps where they were put to work producing goods that could be sold domestically or exported. During the period under study there was more available documentation of prison-made goods being sold both in China and abroad, including goods made specifically for export to Western countries and in many cases for certain stores or chains. Harry Wu, Human Rights Watch/Asia and other individuals and organizations provided both proof and estimates of these practices—which were truly astounding in terms of the numbers of people affected and the scope of the human rights abuses caused. Though one can only guess the number of working prisoners in the labor camps or the number of political prisoners or prisoners of conscience among them (often indistinguishable since China labels troublemakers and vagrants as criminals and arbitrarily makes many lesser crimes serious offenses punishable by assignment to a labor camp when officials deem it necessary or profitable), it was certain that both the numbers of prisoners and the profits they produced increased during 1993 and 1994.

Windfall profits were made from still another source during this period: from selling the organs of executed criminals. While this has been common practice since the late 1980s, much more has been learned about it in recent years. It also become more and more clear that many executions were timed according to the need for organs and that China was in the business of providing organs for foreigners who could not get them elsewhere and that it was even advertizing their freshness (became they came directly from the execution grounds to the patient) and their quality (because they came from young people). Chinese citizens, with the exception of high party and government officials, could generally not get transplants as they could not afford them. Also organ donation was not voluntary and in most cases relatives were not consulted. Most astonishing to some observers, often the donating individual was not even told he or she would be an organ donor.

This helped explain the fact that China accounted for a very large portion of the total executions done in the world, certainly more by a large margin than any other country, and that the number increased during the period under study. Many were executed for what would be considered minor crimes in other countries. Also many were executed at one time (in what appeared often to be a celebration or mass execution to frighten citizens, sometimes in advance of a holiday or a visit by a foreign leader) or for some other reason that did not relate to the operation of the justice system. While no reliable statistics or lists of criminals executed were available, this chapter provides details on a number of cases—enough to provide a good picture of the widespread use of capital punishment in China.

In Chapters 6 and 7 the authors delineate the foreign criticisms of China's human rights abuses and its bad record on human rights, which have been troubling to top leaders in the Chinese Communist Party and the government. This consisted of both comments by foreign leaders and by reports written abroad on China's human rights condition. Greater foreign scrutiny has been the case since the Tiananmen Massacre in 1989 riveted world attention on the plight of those who demanded more democracy in China and caused world attention to focus on China's human rights situation as never before. Clearly thoughts of Tiananmen have not been erased abroad.

The U.S. Department of State annual reports on China's human rights situation as well as publications by Amnesty International, Human Rights Watch/Asia, and the Tibet Information Network were of special concern during the period under study. So were statements by U.S. officials, including a number of members of Congress and the Dalai Lama. All documented special problems, including the persecution of minorities, advocates of certain religions and women. Tibet attracted considerable concern.

These two chapters likewise contain information on and an analysis of China's response to human rights criticism that was linked to the granting of most-favored-nation trade status by the United States. Chinese leaders at times tried to give the impression that they did not care whether MFN was extended or not. At other times they took actions to improve conditions for prisoners, released dissidents and made other improvements in their human rights condition. Clearly many political prisoners were literally saved and many more, including probably many that were not apprehended or bothered by the government, helped by the U.S. linking the granting of MFN with human rights abuses in China.

On the other hand, linking trade privileges to improvements in the human rights condition was not as effective as it might have been, the authors state, because of China's political influence (in the United Nations, in restraining North Korea and on other matters) and due to China's attraction to and influence on the U.S. business community which hoped for profits in the China market and did not want to be shut out or discriminated against because of their leaders making trouble over human rights issues.

China's human rights record was also linked to its buying and selling arms and its alleged transfer of nuclear technology. Though not generally related to human rights violations, China's bad behavior in both realms caused these issues to be linked or connected at times. And Chinese leaders seemed to adopt policies to deal with criticisms about both that were similar.

Finally, while Chinese leaders have responded with denial and anger over human rights criticisms, they more and more took the offensive. That is, they criticized the critics (almost exclusively Western nations) for their own human rights problems, often mentioning problems in the United States such as lack of freedom of movement due to dangerous streets, the plight of the aged, homelessness, the number of people in jail, recidivism, and other problems. Chinese policy makers also took to promoting China's policies on human rights and soliciting support from Asian and Third World countries for a redefinition of human rights that gives greater emphasis to economic rights over political rights and which considers cultural and other differences in setting human rights standards. China, in fact, as these two Chapters reveals, made noted headway in winning support for its human rights views.

## Endnotes

1. See the author's other books listed in the preface and the bibliographies in the recent ones. For a recent study that provides background analysis, see Marina Svensson, *The Chinese Conception of Human Rights: The Debate on Human rights in China, 1898–1949* (Lund, Sweden: Lund University Press, 1996).

2. See Roberta Cohen, *The People's Republic of China: The Human Rights Exception* (Baltimore: University of Maryland School of Law, 1988) and John F. Copper et al, *Human Rights in Post Mao China* (Boulder, CO: Westview Press, 1985).

3. See the author's most recent update. Also see John F. Copper, "The Human Rights Factor in Peking's Foreign Policy," *Issues and Studies*, October 1994.

# Chapter 2

## Chinese Politics and Human Rights

"...as long as a despised corrupt official stays in good with his superiors, the sky's the limit to his power and the money just rolls in."

*—Hong Kong Economic Journal*[1]

"The scale of corruption in China is beyond description."

—Chinese Communist Party Central Discipline Commission[2]

The human rights condition in the People's Republic of China (PRC) during 1993–1994, as has been the trend in the recent past, reflected the general political situation, political trends and political instability in China. A power struggle in the top leadership, in anticipation of the demise of paramount leader Deng Xiaoping, diminished concern about human rights among China's political leaders. In addition, changes in the political system both belied serious political insecurity and allowed human rights abuses in some areas to proliferate. In short, human rights interests were pushed into the background not only by succession troubles but also by a resurgence of the political Left (which demanded greater adherence to communist ideology and more central power) and concessions by fearful rightist reformists. Corruption, rampant in China in recent years, which worsened during 1993 and 1994, was likewise a cause for reduced concern about human rights, especially political and civil rights. Meanwhile, venality produced a situation wherein respect for justice and political liberties meant very little. Money increasingly translated into power and influence and defied efforts to institute standards of proper conduct. Finally, difficulties in the countryside mirrored the depth of the instability, while revealing a callous lack of concern about the rights of the vast majority of Chinese citizens—the peasants. It was almost as if the rights and even the living conditions of peasants could be ignored or trampled upon freely.


### The Political Leadership

During 1993-1994 China continued to scrap its Communist economic system. A more capitalist economic system, in fact, caused the population to expect political change in the direction of democracy and to hope for expanded political and civil rights. At the same time, however, legitimacy in the context of economic change for China's top leadership became a more serious problem. These two trends collided. Meanwhile, questions about Deng's health underscored the succession problem, adding to political anxiety—a milieu in which human rights have been given short shrift in the past. In short, Chinese politics and human rights, which are intimately linked, focused on Deng and his heir(s) apparent.

In January 1993, the Chinese Communist Party launched a major campaign to promote Deng Xiaoping's writings and ideas. Quotations from his 200,000-word book were published with great fanfare in nearly all of China's major newspapers. Most quotations underscored the theme that the Chinese government and the Chinese Communist Party had provided the populace with vast economic freedoms, but in the realm of politics tight controls were to remain.[3] The publication of Deng's works suggested that, even though pragmatic rightists still dominated the top leadership, in the context of a pending power struggle, they would not hesitate to use ideology to preempt leftist hard-liners who sought to restore their influence. In other words, a cult of Deng seemed to be growing and taking precedence over Deng's sometimes-heard calls for more political freedoms and rights.

The publication of Deng's writings also coincided with a revamping of the party's propaganda machine. Subsequently it was announced that this would ensure social and political stability.[4] In fact, a plan initiated at the 14th Party Congress in late 1992 was made official at this time in a document entitled "Step Up Management of the Publishing Industry and Press, Keep a Close Watch Over Political Quality," drafted by the Communist Party's Propaganda Department and approved by the Secretariat of the Central Committee. Widely disseminated to party and government organs, the document declared that as long as China is led by the Communist Party, propaganda will "never be neglected" and "bourgeois freedom of the press will never be allowed." In this context it mentioned the "erroneous orientation" of the media leading up to the events at Tiananmen Square of June 1989. The document went on to criticize those writing history who "vilify proletarian revolutionaries" in the name of "giving history its true face" and called for more control over religious publications and the careful inspection of the news by party schools.[5] *People's Daily* came out in support of these efforts to tighten political control under the leadership of the Chinese Communist Party and suppress dissent; in fact, the paper (the PRC's most important official newspaper) seemed to want even stricter controls, saying that the Communist Party had failed to uphold the basic organizational principle of democratic centralism.[6] All of this signaled both internal dissension and a shift to more hard-line leftist policies.

In the face of a leftist upsurge, Deng and the rightist reformists tried to further consolidate their power in March 1993 when the eighth National People's Congress (NPC) "voted" (with only one candidate on the ballot) Jiang Zemin president of the People's Republic of China to replace Yang Shangkun. This made Jiang not only the head of state (as president), but also head of the party and the military, marking the first time since 1959 (when Mao was removed from the presidency) that one person held the top positions in all three centers of power. Deng ostensibly orchestrated the decision, hoping to prevent a power struggle when he dies.[7]

Although Jiang is generally categorized a rightist reformer and has not, compared to other Chinese leaders, taken a hard line on human rights, his "election" was nevertheless seen in the West as ominous for several reasons. First, his "election" was in reality an appointment probably made at the 14th Party Congress in 1992 and simply confirmed at the NPC meeting. Thus, the assumption that the cause of democracy was advanced by a shift of power to the National People's Congress was probably wrong. (Qiao Shi's appointment as chairman of the Standing Committee of the NPC, on the other hand, might suggest that a division of power is evolving.) Second, although the political Right seemed to have enhanced its strength with Jiang's appointment and one could speculate that human rights might be expected to improve, with political development being linked to economic development, there was evidence to suggest that this was not really the case; rather, China seemed to be moving to the right economically, but not politically. Supporting this view was the fact that Li Peng (a leftist hard-liner and the person considered responsible for the Tiananmen Massacre) remained premier and head of the government. Third, recent leadership changes, including the ones made at this meeting, indicate a growing overlap between the party and the government, reversing the trend of a separation of party and state power that had marginally helped democratize the system over the past few years. Fourth, the military seemed to have more authority in the new lineup.[8]

As the Congress closed, the nation's Constitution was amended to expunge Mao's thought and collectivist ideals and enshrine Deng's concept of a "socialist market economy." Observers interpreted this move together with the leadership changes to represent more extensive and probably more aggressive Communist Party and government efforts to ensure a smooth transition from the

Deng era.[9]  Noticeably, however, nothing was said about advancing political or civil rights or about human rights in any form in connection with the constitutional changes.

In July 1993, the impending power struggle seemed to take on a personal slant. This turn of events raised warning flags to observers who recognized that vicious power struggles between and among party factions have led to various forms of persecution in China's past as many recalled, including during the Cultural Revolution in the late 1960s. It was reported in Hong Kong that President Jiang Zemin had accused Premier Li Peng and his wife of supporting a commercial enterprise that had collapsed, resulting in massive fraud. The company in question was the Great Wall Machinery and Electronics High-Technology Industrial Group Corporation, which had sold bonds worth 1 billion *yuan* (U.S. $174 million) that had become nearly worthless.[10]  It was also reported that Li was being made the scapegoat for China's overheated economy and that his plight mirrored the fact that Deng had made no genuine provisions for political debate or for the use of democratic processes following his death when crucial leadership issues will have to be decided.[11]

Several other factors evoked serious questions about China's post-Deng leadership and consequently about stability in China. For one Li Peng's future was in doubt especially since he is still regarded as China's most hated person because of his role in the Tiananmen Massacre (which, incidently, was not mentioned when questions arose about his political future). Second, Jiang Zemin seemed to lack the support of the military. Third, Jiang was regarded in some quarters as representing a Shanghai "mafia" lacking firm commitments from any other power base—causing some to recall warlord rule in China in the 1920s.

Complicating matters still further, some party elders reportedly favored a "Jiang-Li" (Jiang Zemin and Li Peng) balance of power after Deng's death even though there were serious doubts about the survivability of this kind of "collective" leadership. This idea then evoked speculation about a Qiao-Zhu (Qiao Shi and Zhu Rongji) leadership eventually emerging—Qiao having the support of the military and security organs and Zhu being in charge of the economy.[12]  All of this, of course, strongly suggested that China's political leadership was not stable and that a power struggle should be expected soon. In this context one could not anticipate any improvements in political and civil rights, but rather more rigid controls over the population.

Reflecting fears of a future shakeup that would result in demotions, if not purges, top party and government officials scrambled to place their dependents, and no doubt much of their money, overseas. Eight thousand such individuals were reported living in Hong Kong. As a result, Hong Kong's and Macao's Chinese-owned institutions and joint-venture companies were 95 percent staffed by the relatives of top party and government officials in Beijing.

Similarly there were 1,500 family members of those with influence in China living in the United States and 1,800 in Europe.[13]

In the fall of 1993, various bits of evidence surfaced which indicated that Deng Xiaoping was again exerting pressure to ensure that Jiang Zemin would be his successor and that Jiang would be able to consolidate power before Deng's death. These efforts, however, only fostered increased apprehension about a stable leadership transfer. In mid-August *People's Daily* printed an article by Deng's daughter, Deng Rong. Entitled *My Father Deng Xiaoping*, it contained a quote from Jiang about Deng's retirement: "I will certainly devote myself body and soul to the affairs of state until my very last breath." (Incidentally Jiang's quote was copied from the words of a famous statesman of the Three Kingdoms period in the third century B.C.)[14]

On August 22, 1993, Deng's eighty-ninth birthday, the Jiang family was invited to Deng's residence. No other leaders were invited. Several weeks later, Jiang took China's top leadership to a meeting of the Chinese Welfare Fund for the Handicapped—chaired by Deng Pufang (Deng Xiaoping's son). Some said Jiang wanted to convince Deng Xiaoping that he would respect and take care of his children after his death—a move designed to assure Deng's continued support (as if there may be some question about this).[15]

The Central Committee of the Chinese Communist Party published a new edition of *The Selected Works of Mao Zedong* in September to commemorate the 100th anniversary of Mao's birth later in the year. This looked like an effort by the Left to resurrect Mao and perhaps change the course of the political debate in the PRC. But the event was given little fanfare. Rather, greater attention was given to the second publication of *The Selected Works of Deng Xiaoping* with a special focus on Volume 3. The Communist Party sponsored several meetings at this time to study the work—with Jiang Zemin giving a major speech about Deng's writings. These events seemed to indicate another concerted effort by Deng and/or Jiang to make Jiang Deng's heir and to build a cult of Deng that Jiang might use to enhance his power.[16] Meanwhile, rumors circulated to the effect that Zhu Rongji had fallen out of favor with Deng. Zhu issued a 16-point plan for stabilizing the economy, only to be contradicted by Deng who advocated rapid, unrestricted growth.[17]

All of this evoked serious speculation, especially about whether Deng had really solved the question of China's post-Deng leadership. Deng's references to Jiang as the "core" of the third generation leadership reminded observers of what had happened to the second generation: Hu Yaobang and Zhao Ziyang. Both, previously Deng's heirs, were purged as result of apparently irresistible opposition from party leftists that despised Deng's rightist reforms (most notably his political reforms) and his appointed successors. Pundits could not help but wonder, therefore, about Deng's current efforts to promote Jiang and give him all of the titles and accolades that he might need to consolidate power after Deng's death. They mentioned and the press, still under the sway of the Left, reported openly and repeatedly that Jiang was brought into the top hierarchy at the time of the Tiananmen Massacre from a much lesser position and that he did not have the confidence of the military and many top party officials. In other words, they asked, could Jiang survive? One had to recall also (and this was discussed in the press) Deng's 1992 criticism of Jiang. Had Deng forgiven Jiang? Was Deng again desperately trying to ensure he had a viable successor? Or was Jiang manipulating Deng? Clearly there was cause for puzzlement, and, if one hoped for political stability in China, doubt.

The one hundredth anniversary of Mao's birth brought to the fore the party's assessment of Mao and the right-left struggle still permeating the party and government at all levels. Jiang Zemin's position was that Deng Xiaoping had already given his so-called 70-30 evaluation of Mao (meaning that Mao was 70 percent correct), and thus there should be no more debate. Meanwhile, the Central Committee's Propaganda Department issued a declaration that sounded like a warning: "Don't exceed propaganda specifications, don't force unanimity, don't force participation, and don't engage in debate." Apparently there was widespread concern that the party Left would use the occasion to push its agenda and criticize or oppose Deng's reforms. There may have been fear of a rightist backlash as well. According to a secret internal report issued at this time, 65 percent of the members of the Chinese Communist Party felt that Mao should be denounced and that his views and actions on population control, social classes, and the Cultural Revolution should be condemned.[18] If this poll was accurate, and it probably was, Jiang should have had little to fear. Yet the Left was still strong and determined to share political power which meant keeping Jiang in check.

Leftists, in fact, subsequently called for an evaluation of Deng, specifically because of his involvement in the Anti-Rightist Campaign (during which time Deng, at Mao's behest, condemned many rightists to horrible suffering and death). Also cited were his role in the decisions to purge Hu Yaobang and Zhao Ziyang, Deng's view of the Tiananmen Massacre (when Deng sided with hard-line leftists and suppressed the Democracy Movement), and his involvement in party and government corruption. Some speculated that Jiang Zemin would not be able to wield power after Deng's death and that the Left would make a comeback, reviving Maoism, and causing further setbacks for human rights.[19] In any case, in the milieu of such a debate no near-term progress in allowing the practice of civil and political rights seemed likely.

In early 1994, it was revealed that a number of elder politicians, supposedly forced into retirement when the Central Advisory Commission was abolished in 1992, had in fact not really retired and had kept offices and office staffs. Some of these—Peng Zhen, Yang Shangkun, Bo Yibo, and Song Ping—were also reported to have issued various kinds of official (or at least regarded as official) communications. They sent congratulations to military units and sent investigating teams to various enterprises. They even used their offices to issue several proposals to the Politburo, such as one entitled "A Six–Point View of the Socialist Market Economy," and another called "Central Macro-economic Control Is the Foundation for Stabilizing the Healthy Development of the National Economy."[20] Clearly they seemed to possess real political power and authority. In fact, many recalled their backstage role in ending the Democracy Movement in 1989. The question then was: Could they block Jiang's ascendancy or influence a pending leadership struggle?

According to watchful observers, this situation mirrored the reality that a factional struggle between Deng Xiaoping and Chen Yun (often described as China's second "strongman" after Deng and the leader of the Left who opposed Deng's reforms) was still raging and that many party elders opposed Deng's reforms and might at any time interfere with or block Deng's policies (as they had done in 1989 before the Tiananmen Massacre) or his effort to transfer power to Jiang Zemin. They also seemed to ensure that the party at the provincial level could not bring in new blood or promote reform by transferring authority to younger party members.[21]

Chen Yun's ability to block Deng's reforms and push China to the left politically (or prevent a further shift to the right) was demonstrated vividly by his "Fifteen-Point Opinion," published by the Secretariat of the Central Committee at this juncture. Chen made a number of highly critical points: the party lacks political work and policies are devoid of content; Marxist theory is being ignored; anti-Marxist inclinations are apparent; ideological work has been abandoned; socialist morality and work style have been neglected; the spirit of struggle has been damaged; party discipline is at its lowest ebb; regionalism and individualism have ballooned; anarchism and liberalism are rampant in the ranks of the cadres; plutolatry and capitalism have pervaded the party; there is a "problem" in education; corruption has weakened the leadership; an in-depth rectification of the party is needed; and good cadres should be picked to improve inspection and discipline. Chen concluded that an "Office of Corruption Eradi-cation" should be established in the Politburo.[22]

This and the fact that ultra-leftist Deng Liqun at this juncture launched a movement to "remember Mao" on his 100th birthday and to "praise Mao and oppose Deng." This probably prompted Deng (who was largely in retirement) to make an unexpected trip to Shanghai to deal with leftism there. Observers wondered at the time why Deng could not have sent someone there to speak for him. Was he afraid to do this? Did he think the Left would attack Jiang if he went? In any case, while in Shanghai Deng Xiaoping warned against "isms and ideology" (pointedly aimed at the party Left) and called for party building and support for Jiang Zemin.[23] Shortly after this, in April, Zhu Rongji made an inspection tour to Northeast China where he reportedly fired Heilongjiang Party

Secretary Sun Weiben on the spot. This move was unprecedented inasmuch as Zhu ranked only third or fourth in the Chinese Communist Party hierarchy and Sun was a member of the Central Committee.[24] It seemed to indicate that Zhu had become very powerful, that Jiang was not, or that there was political instability and factional fighting at the top of the party.

Later in the spring apparently mirroring fears that political instability might follow in the wake of Deng Xiaoping's impending death, Jiang Zemin, in a secret speech, reportedly warned the Chinese Communist Party that "national calamity hangs over our heads." The People's Liberation Army and security organs at this time received orders to remain on a high state of alert to prevent disorder, and the Communist Party and the government took special actions to guarantee that officials, especially in provincial and local governments, remained loyal to the center.[25]

At this juncture it was revealed that the Central Research Office of the Chinese Communist Party had conducted a public opinion survey of cadres asking a number of questions including leading ones about the Deng era and Deng's leadership. Though the report was secret, some parts of it were leaked. The document indicated that although 88 percent of cadres generally approved of the Deng "line" and his rule, 62 percent expressed concern about the political situation and about stability in the post-Deng era.[26] Party General-Secretary Jiang Zemin subsequently expressed serious concern and called for party unity. Bo Yibo, an elder statesman in the party and Politburo "adviser," stated, ostensibly in connection with this, that "people at all levels, overseas compatriots and foreign friends, are all concerned about…the political situation in China after the passing of Comrade Deng."[27]

A party meeting in September 1994, focusing on political issues and party construction, drew further attention to the succession issue, though, it was not broached per se. That this issue was not discussed seemed to indicate that it was too sensitive to talk about openly. Jiang Zemin, who by this time had nine official positions in the party, government and military (member of the Party Central Committee, Politburo, and Politburo Standing Committee; general secretary of the Central Committee; chairman of the Military Commission of the Central Committee; chairman of the State Military Commission; state president; head of the Central Financial and Economic Group; and Head of the Central Taiwan Work Group), seemed comfortably in command. Yet, as some party members were quick to point out, Jiang was merely secretary of the Shanghai Municipal Party Committee before the Tiananmen Massacre and was only a local official before that. He had moved up fast (as had a number of other leaders who subsequently fell from power) and his support in the military was weak. Then, some recalled a number of heirs named in the past had failed to grasp power, including Liu Shaoqi and Lin Biao under Mao; Hua Guofeng after Mao's death; and Deng's heirs Hu Yaobang and Zhao Ziyang. Furthermore, some apprehension, if not opposition, was expressed because Jiang appointed a number of other Shanghai people to top positions. The term "Shanghai mafia" was even used publicly to describe Jiang's "clique." Some felt Jiang had assumed too many positions and had appointed cronies in a blatant bid for power. The old guard seemed especially unhappy with some of Deng's reforms, especially political and economic reforms (which are also Jiang's) and Jiang's leadership.[28]

Meanwhile, reports from the provinces reflected a concern about nepotism and the misuse of personnel connections in the new leadership, the role of the military in supporting Jiang (in return for special favors and privileges), the re-centralization of political power in the party (away from the government) with all of this leading to a less democratic system with decreased concern for civil and political rights.[29]

### Changes in the Political and Legal Systems

Early in 1993, Chinese leaders engaged in intense debate about whether the government needed downsizing. Some felt the political system had ossified. In addition, political leaders elsewhere in the world were streamlining their governments, prompted in large measure by the need to compete in the global economy. Paring down the size of the government and the Chinese Communist Party, however, could not be done without bias and discrimination—thus purges, layoffs or forced retirements.

Throughout the history of Communist rule in China, personnel cuts and purges have been used to punish those with unorthodox or dangerous ideas and to maintain control or win power struggles. Job cuts and/or dismissals have likewise inevitably dampened political and other types of expression and have resulted in the loss of political and civil rights of those expelled from employment. They have also often been followed by much more serious human rights abuses. During 1993 and 1994, extensive personnel reductions were made in the name of efficiency. Many reductions were in actuality purges. An analysis of these cuts is revealing. Although the human rights situation in China may be advanced by China's having a smaller and less intrusive government, the downsizing itself involved human right abuses.

Following the eighth National People's Congress in early 1993, Premier Li Peng issued a report on streamlining the administration of government and separating politics and business while combatting crime and improving social order.[30] According to Premier Li's plan, the 86 ministries, commissions, and other government units under the State Council were to be reduced to 59 and personnel downsized by 20 percent.[31] This report was discussed widely in the government and party and reported in the Chinese media. Some commentators charged that the system was too bureaucratic and hence totalitarian. Moreover, it was much too costly. The party had 34 million cadres and 40 percent of the cost of government was administrative.[32] Some related the size of the government and the Communist Party to corruption. A few even pointed out that the mere size of government led to difficulties in promoting democracy and political and civil rights. Others, especially those representing the political left, focused on the unemployment problems faced by those released from their government jobs. In an effort to prevent the purges from going too far, they advocated a larger government to maintain better and more thorough control in view of concern over political instability and rapidly increasing crime rates.[33]

The reformists might have created a better human rights situation with the reduction in the size and scope of government had it not been for the fact that their intent was almost exclusively to make government work more efficiently and reduce the power of the Left. They did not seek to improve political and civil rights, to reduce bureaucratic barriers to the practice of individual freedoms, or to lessen government intrusiveness or controls. In addition, they did very little for those left jobless and often used the purges against "enemies" with different ideological views or those with different "mentors" at the top.

A related "hot" topic that caused dissent in political leadership circles concerned the household registration system (a system used to keep a record of the population of cities, countries and other political districts). This system, used for centuries to control China's population and continued in use by the Communists, was being challenged by reformers as anti-market and as a source of corruption. It was criticized by others as a tool used to discriminate against those who did not support the government and caused trouble, or spoke out too much. Eliminating it, however, meant reducing the power of the party, whose authority was already being undermined by the decentralization of power and the market economy. Thus, party leaders, essentially rightist reformers who wanted to revamp the system, declined to abolish what many citizens regarded a hereditary and corrupt system of assigning people to living areas. Their reason: They feared alienating members of the party and losing control.[34]

Still another problem during 1993–1994 involved legal reform. Clearly, the antiquated, Communist legal system of the Mao era has long been an impediment to both economic and political change. But little was done during the heyday of Deng's rightist reform to improve or change the system. The reformists were too busy with other matters. Thus, a recent rapid increase in court cases presented a serious problem. The most popular solution, rather than pursuing legal reform, was simply to keep the rate of convictions high—only 0.4 percent of the defendants are found not guilty—while increasing administrative litigation (up 35 percent annually in recent years).[35] But this arrangement did little for human rights; in fact, it generally had a negative impact because it led to more arbitrary arrests and trials. Meanwhile, because of the money-making opportunities for members of the party and government officials embedded in the system, there has been strong internal resistance to change. This was another hotly debated issue during 1993.[36]

Related to the issue of corruption, a report issued by the Communist Party's Central Discipline Inspection Commission declared that a single-party dictatorship lies at the heart of China's political system and that the government lacks democratic supervision. This is the cause, stated the report, for horrendous corruption and a system that "eliminates all value on human life." The report went on to assert that "as long as a despised corrupt official stays in good with his superiors, the sky's the limit to his power and the money just rolls in." The report also assailed the system of public ownership, whereby it makes sense to "give up a mountain of gold" (of public funds) for a "precious ring" (some personal gain). Supporting the concern for corruption in the political and legal systems in China, it was revealed that one in ten cases of criminal activity in China (in the first three quarters of 1993) involved part and state officials and of these twenty percent were in the legal organs of government.[37]

The cure, it suggested, is a system of private ownership where expenditures and earnings are "placed in the same order" and whereby there would not be so many people "stuffing their own wallets at the expense of the nation and the common good." The report also cited the absence of both a viable legal system and rule by law in China as causing this situation.[38] In September, the Central Committee of the Chinese Communist Party issued a long document on party building that supported virtually all aspects of one-party rule thus sending a signal that there would be no change from party dominance. In the context of mobilization campaigns and worse human rights abuses, one observer saw this response as reflecting a "bunker mentality" as the nation "prepares for the succession."[39]

In November, the Chinese Communist Party convened its third plenary session of the 14th Central Committee. Work at the meeting centered on passage of a fifty-article resolution on establishing socialist market economic reforms. A leading newspaper in Hong Kong (where there was the most concern about political change in China) reported disappointment in the meeting because of the "complete disregard of the need for political reform."[40] *People's Daily*, the mouthpiece of the Chinese Communist Party, in fact, said essentially the same thing in referring to the decisions taken—which mirrored, it said, changes launched at a similar meeting in 1978.[41]

Coinciding with this meeting, the third volume of *The Selected Works of Deng Xiaoping*, was published and widely excerpted and quoted in the Chinese press.[42] This work contains more than one hundred speeches and writings covering the period from 1982 to 1992. It includes pieces on China's policy toward Hong Kong and Taiwan (mostly about the "one country, two systems" formula for incorporating these areas) and international problems. Most of the work, however, focuses on (defines, promotes, and more) Deng's ideas about "socialism with Chinese characteristics." In other words, Deng (who allegedly spent four months going over each article) sought to set forth blueprints for continued reform in China—reform that would survive the Deng era. The book promotes the market system and explains how socialism and a free market could be combined. However, it says almost nothing about political reform, which was obviously viewed as virtually impossible given the disagreements in the top ranks of the party at this time and the leadership struggle. One could assume that democratizing the political system or expanding on political freedoms in this context would be extremely unlikely.

The inability or unwillingness of top Chinese Communist Party leaders to democratize was also very evident at meetings of the National People's Congress (constitutionally the highest organ of the Chinese government) and sessions at the Chinese People's Political Consultative Conference (a high level advisory branch of the government) in March. Chinese Communist Party officials expressed concern that these organizations had been corrupted by bureaucratism. Meanwhile, provincial and local governments and citizens demanded more democracy. Politburo member and head of China's security, Qiao Shi, making reference to the National People's Congress, declared that the party must exercise more control, that "mobilization and interpretation" of work "must be completed prior to the meeting," that opinions must be expressed through channels, and that accusations against individuals must be stopped.[43] In other words, an orchestrated rather than spontaneous democratic agenda was preferred. Others critical of the fact that elections were won only by "official" candidates charged that the election process itself was flawed because the elected bodies of government were too large and party influence was too strong.[44]

Questions also arose about the functions and significance of the Chinese People's Political Consultative Conference, which had been designed to promote democracy through political consultation, democratic supervision, and participation in politics. (In fact, these functions are given to it in China's Constitution.) At its March meeting, however, it was not plain that any of this was happening—bringing into question once again whether Chinese leaders were at all serious about creating government organizations that were in any way democratic. Some observers continued to call this body a "rubber stamp" organization and a "beautiful vase" (meaning something good to look at but with no useful function).[45]

At this same time it was learned that the Secretariat of the Chinese Communist Party Central Committee had issued a classified report of a speech by Jiang Zemin about ideological education. In this speech, Jiang addressed twelve problems that underscored his concern that party control was weakening and that promoting civil and political rights and democracy was a mistake. The report prompted a return to a hard-line position on the party's relationship with the government and democratization and called on party committees to take action.[46]

Top Chinese Communist Party leaders late in 1993 ordered a "rectification of the press" to strengthen party control over the media. Coincidentally (or not), the Propaganda Department of the Central Committee established a task force to investigate—on a daily basis—important articles in newspapers and magazines. The move was particularly aimed at "leisure" publications, which were thought to have been "deficient" in recent months.[47] At this same time, the party also strengthened controls over movies, both Chinese and foreign and television programs. This action was apparently taken in response to the film *Farewell My Concubine* that won America's Golden Globe Award. The film, which was described by a Chinese Communist Party publication as "glorifying homosexuality and enemy puppet rulers," had reportedly angered Jiang Zemin.[48] In late January 1994, the National Ideological Propaganda Work Conference was held in Beijing, with Jiang Zemin and other top party leaders in attendance. Jiang demanded that the party "grasp with both hands" to deal more effectively with propaganda work.[49] (See Chapter 4 for further information on this topic.)

There was also serious disagreement at various levels of government and between the government and the party about the economy. At the second session of the eighth National People's Congress, Premier Li Peng declared in his government work report that the rate of economic growth must be held at 9 percent. Local governments, however, had planned for much higher growth in their budgets. In fact, in some of the coastal provinces economic development plans projected over 20 percent growth. Subsequently there were reports that leaders in the central government and the Chinese Communist Party had threatened provincial leaders over economic growth issues as well as political authority and that serious fractional and centrifugal tendencies were evident.[50] There were also reports that provincial and local governments were collecting tariffs or fees on goods coming into their areas and that many were practicing what the central government called protectionism. These practices, it was said, were undermining the state's financial discipline and causing tension between the center and provincial and local governments.[51]

In connection with the friction over economic development plans, economic crime constituted an important issue that affected political decision making as well as the system itself. In the spring, Ren Jianxin, on behalf of the Supreme People's Court, issued a report calling for more severe punishments for economic crimes which were rapidly increasing and causing social and political unrest. Shortly after, Tao Siju, minister of public security, called on the National People's Congress to pass laws to strengthen the "Regulations for Controlling and Punishing Public Offenses" by criminalizing "disturbing public order and damaging people's health through religious activities, stirring up conflicts between nationalities, [and] hurting the unity of nationalities..."[52]

These provisions were so vague, however, as to give police and the courts the authority to deal with almost any kind of non-approved behavior. (See also Chapter 5.) Clearly, individual rights were damaged in this process.

Reflecting the systemic nature of the controversy over economic issues, articles in the *Liberation Daily* and *People's Daily* railed against allowing too much decentralization of political power to accompany the process of implementing the free market and against giving local governments too much authority. The former lamented about the lack of social order; the latter using language reminiscent of Mao cited "contradictions" between central authorities and local officials. Both advocated, directly or indirectly, the reestablishment of more central control at the expense of economic development and the broadening of political and human rights.[53]

At the eighth session of the National People's Congress Standing Committee in July, more talk was heard about democratic centralism—indicating that Chinese authorities were still grappling with the problem of the evolution away from a totalitarian system to a simple authoritarian one. Deng's works were cited, but the emphasis was on economic growth ("socialism with Chinese characteristics") and order and stability. Qiao Shi subsequently spoke about the differences between socialist democracy and capitalist democracy, which he described as analogous to the difference between socialist democracy and "ultra-democracy" or even anarchism. As a means of preserving the former, he advocated a strong socialist legal system, though he did not define exactly what this meant.[54]

In September 1994, at the Fourth Plenary Session of the 14th Central Committee of the Chinese Communist Party, the focus of debate was on party construction. Documents published at the meeting, in particular one entitled "Resolutions of the Central Committee of the Chinese Communist Party Regarding Several Significant Questions on the Strengthening Party Construction," reflected serious concern about the capacity of the party to control its 54 million members and to deal with corruption, crime, and other problems. At the meeting a motion was passed to declare democratic centralism fundamental to the party's leadership. This, of course, meant that civil and political liberties and democracy were not the order of the day. The party's attention to morale, security concerns, and instability suggested the same thing.[55]

At year's end, the Chinese Communist Party made several other efforts to reform and strengthen the party. *Liberation Daily* declared that problems with party authority could cause China to devolve into a "heap of loose sand." General Secretary Jiang Zemin addressed a national conference on organizational work in early December and, in desperation, called for reforming the cadre system, improving the quality of party officials, launching a "prolonged war" against corruption, and correcting ideological attitudes.[56]

### The Issue of Corruption

Corruption was regarded as an extremely serious problem threatening social and political stability during 1993-1994. It engendered wide disparities in wealth and caused people to distrust the government and the Chinese Communist Party and even engage in protest. This situation evoked human rights concerns as citizens' protests were not duly heeded, or, even worse, regarded as dangerous and citizens involved persecuted. The government also meted out punishments for corruption to stop the complaints, but the punishments reflected favoritism and at times were very harsh.

Actions to do something about corruption were manifold and far-reaching during the period under study. In May 1993, both the Central Committee of the Chinese Communist Party and the General Office of the State Council issued stern directives prohibiting party and government officials from accepting money or securities. This came shortly after Jiang Zemin made several exhortations to party members and government workers to reduce corruption and end the "mentality of money fetishism."[57] Party leaders subsequently linked corruption to difficulties in fulfilling economic plans and condemned those people who diverted funds from agriculture, engaged in property speculation, and established illegal monetary institutions. Party leaders who were pressured to adopt policies to deal with the problem suggested self-examination and more emphasis on democratic centralism.[58]

In mid-1993, China's top law enforcement official, Procurator-General Zhang Siqing, spoke out strongly against graft and corruption and demanded that the law be applied strictly to punish the guilty. He noted that between January and April law enforcement officials had dealt with 13,729 cases of these kinds of crime. He said this reflected the "appearance of unbridled avarice—the flowering of plutolatry." But he also observed that the number of those not charged was 44.2 percent and that in some areas more than half of such cases were dropped, reflecting how corruption, in fact, prevented the enforcement of laws against corruption.[59] He demanded more law enforcement and stricter penalties. This resulted in a huge increase in the number of people sentenced to long terms in jails and even executions for economic crimes. (See Chapter 5 for additional details.)

Party General Secretary Jiang Zemin subsequently issued another warning about the seriousness of corruption that was given broad play in the media. He declared that the "struggle" against corruption was an important task in party construction. But he also warned against mass movements and said there would be no litmus tests—apparently fearing that an anti-corruption campaign might be used by his opponents on the Left to attack Deng's reforms and to bring back Maoist ideology and totalitarian rule. He asserted that the issue should be handled by the Central Commission for Discipline Inspection.[60]

Forthwith, the Commission for Discipline Inspection issued a directive that referred to the "five forbiddens." Cadres were told that they were not to operate a business or enterprise, work in an economic entity, trade in stocks, accept gifts, or use public funds for lavish entertainment.[61]

Publicity about corruption widened after this. Some even charged that it had affected China's security system. Citizen's complaining of security police involvement in various kinds of criminal activities, however, were rebuffed by the authorities, who simply said that criminals were using police uniforms. Confirming these charges, Hong Kong and Taiwan Chinese visiting the PRC said that security agencies (meaning real officers) frequently asked for bribes and fees for protection and were involved in criminal activities ranging from covering up murders to receiving bribes and gun running.[62]

The security police system in China was also criticized for misusing investigative detention laws, employing brutal means in interrogating suspects, and operating temporary "holding cells" that in reality were work prisons. Cases of people being held in cells for long periods of time, bringing to question alleged progress in establishing fair legal procedures, were widely published in the Hong Kong media.[63]

Others claimed that the party was selling memberships and that the People's Liberation Army sold promotions and ranks. Apparently a significant number of party members and soldiers had acquired their positions through bribery and were collecting salaries, pensions, and other benefits this way. They also used their authority to demand bribes and engage in other "profiteering" activities.[64] An American scholar even suggested that military secrets were for sale and that more than 20,000 economic enterprises were under the military's control.[65]

Some figures were leaked that reflected the vastness of the corruption: 100 billion *yuan* had been spent on official entertainment of guests in 1992. In one part of China, 80 percent of the "class A" cigarettes were purchased by the government. One writer noted that this kind of behavior goes on while 200 to 300 million children do not have book bags, and suggested that these people who "wine and dine" have no consciences.[66]

Later, Jiang Zemin, speaking to students at the National Defense University, attacked corruption and called for help in dealing with the problem. This was followed by the publication of a report written by the State Council entitled "Corruption, Degeneration and Unhealthy Tendencies Have Engulfed Party and Government Departments and Every Sector of Industry." According to the report, in some areas of China party membership can be bought for 5,000 *yuan* and an appointment to a party committee can be purchased for 10,000 to 20,000 *yuan*. Positions in factories and diplomas were said to be for sale virtually anywhere for similar amounts or to individuals bringing in large amounts of foreign investment.[67]

A subsequent report of the Party's Central Discipline Inspection Commission said the seriousness of corruption in China was "beyond description." It reported that more than 733,000 party members had been investigated and gave details on the large amounts of money involved (citing one case of U.S.$30 million being sent abroad by a single person).[68]

Some party members and government officials were suspected of using government funds to purchase automobiles for personal use. According to figures released by the State Commodity Control Office, public funds spent on autos increased 137 percent during the early part of the year with the average price per car increasing 22 percent. In addition, it said, the total amount spent for autos had increased 430 percent over the period five years earlier. Some officials, it was said, were even on record complaining that they had to use a Chinese-made car.[69]

A number of officials were also suspected of colluding with organized crime or criminal or underground merchants to commit trademark falsification, which the government feared would lead to bad publicity abroad.[70] Still others were charged with the misuse of government and party travel funds. In October, the government issued its third anti-corruption edict in three days. This one banned junkets. One province had reported at this time that 11,472 government and party people had traveled abroad between October 1992 and April 1993 and the "vast majority" had no official business.[71]

Other kinds of evidence surfaced concerning the scope of corruption in China, which was nothing less than mind boggling. According to a Beijing source, during a thirteen-year period the total of state property lost was 500 billion *yuan*, or 100 million *yuan* a day.[72] Another source put the amount of taxes evaded during the period 1985-1992 at 98.27 billion *yuan*. Confirming this, an official government publication estimated that the rate of tax evasion was 50 percent in state-owned enterprises, 60 percent in village enterprises, 80 percent in individual businesses, and 95 percent for individuals. Fourteen provinces and regions were under investigation for massive tax cheating.[73]

Corruption had broad and serious side-effects. In some areas of China, it was said to have affected in flood control, which, it noted, could result in catastrophe.[74] Elsewhere it created public outcries and outrage especially when grave robbing (100,000 incidents—20,000 involving ancient tombs—in the past seven to eight years) became rampant. In some cases, these robberies were organized and involved the use of weapons.[75]

In mid-October, five government officials from Guangdong Province were executed in an anti graft campaign. In one newspaper story about the executions, entitled "Execution Ode," the writer said: "I think the sound of gunshots that felled these guys sounds a lot better than Beethoven's famed Ode to Joy."[76]

During the last ten days of October, the Standing Committee of the National People's Congress met and discussed the matter of public order and corruption. Mention was made of the successful use of telephone hot lines to get information on corruption. It was reported at that time that 8,063 "major" cases of bribery, graft, misuse of public funds, and other economic crimes had been heard in the past two months. A total of 40,209 cases had been handled since the beginning of 1993. Some representatives asserted that party cadres were often not responding to directives or were involved in corruption themselves. Still others expressed concern about the increase of youth involvement in drugs and prostitution for profit.[77]

Articles in the press late in the year, acknowledged top-level concern about military personnel pulling strings for private companies and engaging in other kinds of influence peddling. One investigation revealed that 19 percent of soldiers were *guanxi*, or "influence" soldiers.[78] Elsewhere it was reported that military personnel were often found carrying large sums of money and using bribes to get special privileges, thereby destroying the military's morale and reputation. The term "moneybags" had, in fact, become commonplace to describe soldiers who had outside interests or were engaging in corrupt activities.[79]

The gravity of the problem was reported in the January 1994 issue of *China Digest*, which stated—in an article entitled "Corruption as Fierce as a Tiger"—that corruption "was out of control." The magazine noted that the public had no confidence in the government or the party—seeing both replete with dishonesty, deceit, and venality. Other articles in this popular magazine linked corruption to the "loss of China's soul," to questions about China's greatness, and to social problems such as divorce. *China Digest* cited public comments about the government that revealed that few people had confidence in the honesty of officials.[80]

Procurator-General Zhang Siqing said in February that corruption cases had increased threefold or fourfold in 1993. Chinese Communist Party General Secretary Jiang Zemin added that the "corruption phenomenon" remained widespread and that the ongoing anti corruption campaign had met with only mixed results.[81]

At the second session of the eighth National People's Congress and at a meeting of the Chinese People's Political Consultative Congress, both held in March, a number of motions were passed to deal with official corruption. The president of the Supreme People's Court Ren Jianxin and Procurator-General Zhang Siqing both cited major cases and suggested quick actions to deal with this serious problem.[82] Independent analysts, however, declared that the anti-corruption talk was aimed at economic and not political corruption and that until efforts were made to sincerely deal with the latter, the situation would not improve.[83]

Deng Xiaoping addressed the issue in the summer of 1994. He said corruption was one of the most pressing problems facing the country and that curing it demanded "party work at the top." Party General Secretary Jiang Zemin met with Deng to discuss what do to about this "serious issue." Outside analysts, however, suggested that mechanisms were already in place to deal with the problem, but nothing was happening—indicating that corruption was more deeply embedded and pervasive than it was assumed. In short, anti-corruption efforts were not working because those responsible for enforcing the laws were themselves corrupt or were profiting from corrupt practices.[84]

Corruption, in other media reports, was linked to "interest groups" in the Central Committee, where "cliques" had formed—not as before, on the basis of ideology or mentors, but upon corrupt ties with enterprises and among individuals. These cliques, it was said, amounted to mutual support groups engaging in corruption.[85] As a result, among other problems, the accuracy of economic and other data and statistics had seriously deteriorated.[86]

### Problems in the Countryside

Human rights in China improved after Mao's death in large part because of Deng's rural reform (the first of the "Four Modernizations"), which gave the peasants increased economic opportunities and freedoms. The fact that the reforms produced a new prosperity, thus relieving the grinding poverty of rural China, was a real plus and was even more important than other changes that China experienced at this time. In fact, Deng deserves much praise for improving the livelihood of the vast majority of Chinese. The reforms were later described by the Chinese media as a particularly Chinese solution, since they emphasized economic rights and led to improvements in standards of living.

The fact that rural reforms have been ignored or even reversed in recent years is regarded as serious both by the Western observer and by the Chinese. In fact, the lot of the majority of China's population (80 to 85 percent) did not improve and in many respects deteriorated during 1993–1994. Thus, it appeared that the government had lost its concern for the peasants and in some ways felt a need to repress rural China to maintain political stability. Rampant corruption also played a role, but an unstable leadership and other factors seemed to bear even more on the situation.

There was an attention-riveting event in June 1993 that made observers understand the gravity of the situation. Thousands of peasants rioted in Sichuan, Deng's home province in west central China, beating officials, blocking traffic, and destroying property. In the single worst incident, 10,000 rioters attacked government offices, threw rocks at army troops, and burned vehicles. The protest, accompanied by strikes and other incidents, reflected serious peasant unrest that could be traced to lack of commitment on the part of the government and the Chinese Communist Party to continuing rural reform together with increased taxation and other oppressive government actions and policies.[87] The party and the government expressed alarm over the situation and enunciated a need for more strict political controls.

This situation was typical of rural China, though the violence was not ordinary. The crisis was precipitated specifically by the government issuing notes or "white slips" instead of money for farm products purchased by the state. This occurred because of corruption and because so much money had been diverted to urban construction and other infrastructure projects. This put the government in arrears to the tune of tens of billions of *yuan*. In many areas of rural China peasants were unable even to buy food and other basics. Believing that the government was spending huge amounts of money in the cities and that officials were syphoning off large amounts of money for their personal use, the peasants became restive and angry.[88]

Some writers saw the situation as more complicated, reflecting a host of government policies discriminating against rural China. They said the central government was using rural China to "house" China's massive unemployment (by preventing the free movement of people into the cities or coastal areas of China that were prospering). In addition, property laws and utilization rights regarding agricultural land were too fuzzy, the government had lowered comparative prices of agricultural products (especially grain) to benefit city residents, heavy and burdensome regulations had been imposed, the free market in rural China was distorted, funding for village development had been diverted or "lost," and science and technology funding  barely included anything for the agricultural sector.[89]

The seriousness of the situation, on top of the peasants revolts, was underscored by an alarming number of resignations among rural cadres. Reasons mentioned included: safety concerns, low pay, low quality of colleagues, and the difficulty of the work. Party leaders vowed to do something to rectify the situation, but after the passage of several months it was uncertain what  the results were,  if any.[90]

In late June, after the riots, provincial authorities sent work teams and security forces to several troubled areas to deal with corrupt cadres and to either punish or placate angry peasants. Peasants were punished. This caused further unrest. Subsequently, Minister of Agriculture Liu Jiang took a concessionary kind of action: He abolished thirty-seven types of "burdensome" "contributions, charges and fees" collected by various departments of the central government in rural China.[91]

Notwithstanding concern by party and government officials and their actions just mentioned, unrest in the countryside remained at a critical level. Farmers complained of falling wages, being looked down upon by city people, not having the opportunity to live in the cities (because of the household registration system), and other problems. They described China as having a "dual social structure" and said the government and the party had stopped trying to improve the lot of the peasants. They felt both had abandoned the "revolution" that in the early years had erased the barriers between workers and peasants and between rural and urban China.[92]

Peasants and others continued to complain also that the government collected too many rural fees and taxes and did not use the money properly.[93] A Hong Kong source revealed that although the government had promised that taxes and fees would not exceed 5 percent of a peasant's net income, in many places it was 30 percent. Meanwhile, state investment in agriculture was only 5 to 6 percent, compared to over 10 percent in the past. And government-run markets remained backward and inadequate.[94]

A government source revealed that the urban-rural income gap had increased to 4:1 (from 2.2:1 in 1964) and that the "social insurance" (meaning the total services provided by the government) gap between cities and the countryside was 30:1. Further, primary school attendance was 99 percent in the cities and only 80 percent in rural China and 50 percent in grazing areas, and 69 percent of city students went on to high school compared with only 10 percent in the countryside. One-third of villages had no sanitation facilities, and only 5 percent had medical care, while these things are available to almost all city residents.[95]

These revelations evoked grumbling from peasants who compared their situation to the peasants plight under Mao, when, because of his mistakes in agricultural planning, 40 million people died—99 percent of them peasants. Many also complained of the inequities between rural and urban China that were reappearing after the advances produced by Deng's reforms in 1979–1985. They noted that there was no tax on city residents unless they had very high incomes, but peasants were heavily taxed.[96] Official statistics confirmed that the peasants had cause for grievance. Between 1989 and 1991, peasant incomes increased only 0.7 percent annually—much below the rate of inflation. In 1991, rural incomes increased 2 percent while city incomes increased by 12 percent. Although no similar statistics were published for 1993–1994, it was obvious that the gap remained or was getting worse. Clearly rural incomes were, in terms of buying power, declining owing to low increases negated by inflation.[97]

All of this caused Deng Xiaoping to express grave concern and even speculate that if economic problems were to become serious in the 1990s, agriculture would likely be the main cause. Peasants meanwhile began to swarm into the cities in various parts of China and create problems. Rural Chinese residents continued to complain not only about high and unfair (and unpublicized) taxes, but also about disruptive and lazy cadres, and the serious and worsening income and wealth gaps between the cities and the countryside.[98] Some even said China's peasants were being treated worse than peasants in the Soviet Union under Stalin and worse than blacks in South Africa under apartheid. Comments appeared in the Chinese press to the effect that the peasants were being "cheated" and "exploited" in order for city people to maintain their relatively high standards of living—a system that resembled China's past.[99]

In December 1993, at the third plenum of the 14th Central Committee of the Chinese Communist Party, a "decision" was made recognizing serious problems in the countryside. Mention was made of declining comparative advantage in agriculture, faster price increases in industrial products than in agricultural ones, and low rural wages. It was proposed that the government invest more in agriculture, stabilize prices, and promote industry in rural areas.[100] But no immediate actions were taken.

Chinese Communist Party General Secretary Jiang Zemin, at a meeting of the Central Commission for Discipline Inspection in February 1994, revealed that bribery cases in the countryside during September through December 1993 had risen seven-fold. He lamented that efforts to eradicate corruption had not been very successful.[101]

At about this time it was revealed that the government's promise to limit taxes and fees to no more than 5 percent had not been carried out. Little, in fact, had been done other than to make a false promise. In some cases taxes had been raised directly or through overvaluing peasants' incomes. Meanwhile, less was being spent on water conservancy. All of this, it was reported, was causing market forces to fail.[102] It was also prompting peasants to refuse to contract for crops and causing the harvests of grains and cotton to decline.[103] Even worse, it was said that the gap between rural and urban income continued to increase and was now greater than before Deng's reforms.[104]

Minister of Agriculture Liu Jiang drew attention to price fluctuations in farm products, the low rate of increases of rural incomes, the lack of investment, high rural unemployment, and other problems. He cited as a very important problem the "negative growth" in real terms of state investment in agriculture, the increasing disparity between agricultural and industrial prices, and an absence of good rural management.[105]

It was reported in April 1994 that additional "peasant disturbances" had occurred, arousing grave concern on the part of the government (after fifty such incidents had taken place in 1993). Most happened in impoverished regions, and inflation was cited as the major cause.[106]

The Public Security Leading Group and the General Office of the State Council (China's cabinet) held a teleconference in May at which time it was disclosed that there were "hostile elements" (to the government) in thirty-three cities and seven districts in seventeen different provinces and autonomous regions. These "elements," the report said, aimed at subverting the government. Foreign businessmen working in inland provinces were also said to have engaged in activities intended to discredit or undermine the government.[107] Whether these warnings mirrored an official concern about rural unrest, or the government and the Chinese Communist Party wanted to stop demonstrations and anti-government activities leading up to the fifth anniversary of the Tiananmen Massacre, was not certain.

Difficulties in rural China had still other ramifications. The large number of rural residents flocking into the cities presented a serious problem. Security and police organizations attempted to keep them out or force them back to the countryside and often employed force or coercion. Officials were reported to be commonly taking bribes for city residency permits. Some 70,000 people were coming into the capital city, Beijing, from rural China per year, and this figure was apparently increasing.[108] To stem the tide and prevent bribery to obtain city residency permits or "green cards" that were reportedly going for between 10,000 and 100,000 *yuan* in the summer of 1994, the city standing committee of the National People's Congress passed a bill entitled "Regulations for the Collection of Beijing Accommodation Fees."[109] This solution to the problem, as reflected in the new regulations, amounted to decreasing rights of free movement in China which had improved since the death of Mao.

It was reported in September that "large agricultural provinces" were falling behind the rest of the nation in terms of economic growth and that economic expansion mainly depended upon secondary industries. One source noted that in agricultural counties in Jiangsu Province, per capita incomes were below 1,000 *yuan* whereas per capita income in the commercial counties in that province were over 4,000 yuan—a disparity of more than fourfold. These figures, in fact, were probably an understatement, since there were much worse disparities elsewhere. In any case, it was evident that there was some official concern.[110] At this same time it was reported that peasants were failing to deliver grain to government grain purchasers and putting it on the market elsewhere or hoarding it. This brought to question whether land should remain even theoretically owned by the state and/or whether it should instead be privatized. The peasants were flouting laws and regulations and tension was developing between peasants and the government because of low grain payments together with high (and illegal) taxes and fees.[111] Meanwhile, China's public security organs published figures on the number of security personnel killed in the line of duty, noting a large increase which reflected that the situation was especially bad in the country-side.[112]

Minister Liu made some very dire predictions in the fall. He spoke of a "setback" in agriculture that would require a three-to-five year recovery period. He mentioned 50 million "floating peasant laborers"—20 million of whom were moving from province to province—and again noted that investment in the agricultural sector was negative. He added that expenditures on agricultural science and technology had been cut by a third between 1992 and 1993.[113]

**Endnotes**

1. *Hong Kong Economic Journal*, September 2, 1993, p. 2.

2. Cited in *Hong Kong Economic Journal*, September 2, 1993, p. 25.

3. "Government Seeks U.S. Friendship," *Asian Bulletin*, March 1993, p. 71.

4. Ibid.

5. For details, see Tian Zhen, "Beijing's Stranglehold on Press Freedom," *Cheng Ming*, February 1993, pp. 42–44.

6. *People's Daily*, February 4, 1996, cited in "Quarterly Chronicle and Documentation," *China Quarterly*, June 1993, p. 391.

7. See "Eighth NPC Charts Courses," *Asian Bulletin*, May 1993, p. 77.

8. See Xia Taining, "A Sneak Peek at Top CCP Personnel Changes," *United Morning Daily* (Singapore), March 5, 1993, cited in *Inside Mainland China*, May 1993, pp. 7–10.

9. "Eighth NPC Charts Courses," p. 78.

10. See "Austerity Plan Unveiled to Cool Overheated Economy; U.S. Opposes Missile Sale," *Asian Bulletin*, September 1993, p. 84.

11. See, for example, Zi Xin, "To the Man at the Top Goes All Glory and Blame," *Economic Journal* (Hong Kong), p. 18.

12. See, for example, comments and analysis in *Open Monthly* (Hong Kong), August 1993, pp. 44–45.

13. Zong Lanhai, "Nearly Ten Thousand Cadre Dependents Live in Hong Kong and Macao," *Cheng Ming* (Hong Kong), October 1993, pp. 16–17.

14. See *The Nineties* (Hong Kong), December 1993, pp. 27–29.

15. Ibid.

16. See *Pai Hsing Semi-Monthly* (Hong Kong), December 1993, pp. 62–63.

17.   David Backman, "China in 1993: Dissolution, Frenzy, and/or Breakthrough? *Asian Survey,* January 1994, p. 34.

18.  See *Ming Pao Daily*  (Hong Kong), January 4, 1994, p. 10.

19.  See *The Nineties*  (Hong Kong), January 1994, pp. 36–37.

20.  See *Cheng Ming* (Hong Kong), January 1994, pp. 13–16.

21.  Ibid.

22.  See *Cheng Ming*  (Hong Kong), February 1994, pp. 13–14.

23.  See *Pai Hsing Semi-Monthly* (Hong Kong), February 1, 1994, p. 9.

24.  See David Backman, "China in 1994: Marking Time, Making Money," *Asian Survey*, January 15, 1995, p. 38.

25.  *Open Monthly* (Hong Kong), May 1994, pp. 10–12.

26.  *Cheng Ming* (Hong Kong), August 1994, pp. 16–17.

27.  Ibid.

28.  For details, see Wu Anjia, "Will Collective Leadership Hold in Post-Deng Era?" *Central Daily News* (Taipei), August 23, 1994, p. 3.

29.  See *The Nineties* (Hong Kong), December 1994, cited in *Inside Mainland China*, February 1995, pp. 5–6.

30.  "Quarterly Chronicle and Documentation," *China Quarterly*, June 1993, p. 386.

31.  Ibid., p. 389.

32.  "Why Is Reform of Government Agencies Inevitable?" Xinhua News Agency, April 13, 1993, cited in *Inside Mainland China*, June 1993, p. 4.

33.  See "Where Do Problems with Agency Reform Lie?" *Ta Kung Pao* (Hong Kong), April 13, 1993, p. 19.

34. See *Present Era* (Hong Kong), July 15, 1993, pp. 28–30.

35. "Quarterly Chronicle and Documentation," *China Quarterly*, June 1993, p. 389.

36. See "No Slack in Strengthening Attainment of Clean Government," *Ta Kung Pao* (Hong Kong), June 20, 1993, p. 2.

37. Backman, "China in 1993," p. 36.

38. *Hong Kong Economic Journal* (Hong Kong), September 2, 1993, p. 2.

39. Backman, "China in 1994," p. 39.

40. "Third Plenary Session Neglects Political Reform," *Ming Pao Daily* (Hong Kong), November 16, 1993, p. A2.

41. Cited in Ibid.

42. *Ming Pao Monthly*, December 1993, pp. 56–57.

43. See *Trend Magazine* (Hong Kong), March 1994, pp. 6–7.

44. See *Ming Pao Daily* (Hong Kong), March 18, 1994, p. A9.

45. See *Ming Pao Daily* (Hong Kong), March 31, 1994, p. A2.

46. See *Cheng Ming* (Hong Kong), March 1994, p. 20.

47. *Prospective Monthly* (Hong Kong), February 1994, pp. 49–50.

48. *Open Monthly* (Hong Kong), February 1994, pp. 10–11.

49. *Perspective Monthly (Hong Kong), February 1994, pp. 49–50.*

50. *See Pai Hsing Semi-Monthly* (Hong Kong), April 1, 1994 , cited in *Inside Mainland China*, June 1994, pp. 4–5.

51. See *Guangming Daily* (Beijing), March 9, 1994, p. 3.

52. "Quarterly Chronicle and Documentation," *China Quarterly*, September 1994, pp. 859–860.

53. Ibid., pp. 861–862.

54. "Quarterly Chronicle and Documentation," *China Quarterly*, December 1994, pp. 1222–1223.

55. See *Wen Wei Po* (Hong Kong), October 7, 1994, p. A2, for further details.

56. "Quarterly Chronicle and Documentation," *China Quarterly*, June 1993, pp. 266–267.

57. "Quarterly Chronicle and Documentation," *China Quarterly*, September 1993, p. 631.

58. Ibid.

59. See *Outlook Weekly* (Beijing), June 29, 1993, pp. 9–10.

60. *People's Daily* (Overseas Edition), August 23, 1993, p. 1.

61. *Ta Kung Pao* (Hong Kong), August 6, 1993, p. 1.

62. See Shao Li, "Decay in the Public Security System," *Trend Magazine* (Hong Kong), August 1993, pp. 30–31.

63. See *Contemporary Monthly* (Hong Kong), August 15, 1993, pp. 57–60.

64. See Ding Cheng, "Army Ranks and Party Memberships Up for Sale," *Ta Kung Pao* (Hong Kong), August 19, 1993, p. 21.

65. Backman, "China in 1993," p. 36.

66. See *Economic Weekly* (Hong Kong), July 12, 1993, cited in *Inside Mainland China*, November 1993, pp. 17–18.

67. See *Cheng Ming* (Hong Kong), September 1993, pp. 30–31.

68. See *Hong Kong Economic Journal* (Hong Kong), September 2, 1993, p. 25.

69.  See Fang Xiangming, "HK$14.5 Billion of Public Funds Spent in Five Months to Purchase Cars," *Front-line Monthly* (Hong Kong), October 1993, pp. 44–45.

70.  See "Corrupt Phenomenon Reaching Critical Proportions," *Wen Wei Po* (Hong Kong), October 29, 1993, p. 3.

71.  "Nuclear Tests Bring International Criticism; Measures Taken to Curb Corruption," *Asian Bulletin*, December 1993, p. 86.

72.  See "Erosion of National Assets Must Not Continue," *Outlook Weekly* (Beijing), October 1993, pp. 17–18.

73.  Yang Yu, "A Memorandum on the Loss of State Tax Revenues," *Workers Daily* (Beijing), September 28, 1993, p. 3.

74.  Mei Xiaojing, "Who Will Come to the Defense of the Yellow River? *Front-line Monthly* (Hong Kong), October 1993, pp. 58–59.

75.  See several citations in *Wen Wei Po* (Hong Kong), October 14, 1993, p. 3.

76.  *Asian Bulletin,* December 1993, p. 86.

77.  "Quarterly Chronicle and Documentation," *China Quarterly*, March 1994, pp. 295–296.

78.  From a broadcast from Central Broadcasting Station in Beijing, November 28, 1993, cited in *Inside Mainland China* , February 1994, pp. 64–65.

79.  See *Ta Kung Pao* (Hong Kong), December 2, 1993, p. 7.

80.  See Xinhua News Agency broadcast of January 10, 1994, cited in *Inside Mainland China*, March 1994, pp. 23–25.

81.  "Quarterly Chronicle and Documentation," *China Quarterly*, June 1994, p. 571.

82.  See *Hong Kong Economic Journal*, May 4, 1994, p. 26.

83.  *Cheng Ming* (Hong Kong), May 1994, pp. 49–51.

84.  See *Economic Journal* (Hong Kong), August 12, 1994, p. 25.

85. See *Contemporary* (Hong Kong), August 1994, pp. 6–8.

86. *Ming Pao Daily* (Hong Kong), August 15, 1994, p. A13.

87.   "Tiananmen Quiet as Rural Peasants Revolt over Inequalities," *Asian Bulletin*, August 1993, pp. 73–74.

88. See *Ming Pao* (Hong Kong) June 21, 1993 and *Asian Wall Street Journal*, May 24, 1993, cited in "Quarterly Chronicle and Documentation," *China Quarterly*, June 1993, p. 636, and *Economic Journal* (Hong Kong), June 17, 1993, p. 24, cited in *Inside Mainland China*, August 1993, p. 40.

89. See *Outlook Weekly*, April 12, 1993, pp. 4-6, cited in *Inside Mainland China*, August 1993, p. 58.

90. See "Why Are Large Numbers of Village and Organizational Cadres Asking to Resign?" *People's Daily*, May 11, 1993, cited in *Inside Mainland China*, August 1993, pp. 64–66.

91. "Quarterly Chronicle and Documentation," *China Quarterly*, September 1993, p. 635.

92. See, for example, Yu Zhongcheng, "The Oppressed Agrarian Sector," *Farmers' Daily* (Beijing), July 28, 1993, p. 1.

93. See Shen Wen, "Difficulties Facing Rural Cadres," *Legal Daily* (Beijing), July 24, 1993, p. 3.

94. "Agricultural Warning Lights Flashing Again," *Wide Angle Monthly* (Hong Kong), October 1993, pp. 62–63.

95. "Urban and Rural Differences in China," *Study, Research and Reference* (Beijing), No. 6, p. 9, cited in *Inside Mainland China*, December 1993, pp. 40–41.

96. See *Open Monthly* (Hong Kong), January 1994, pp. 29–31.

97. Ibid.

98. See, for example, *Contemporary Monthly* (Hong Kong), December 15, 1993, pp. 76–78.

99.  See *Open Monthly* (Hong Kong), January 1994, pp. 29–31.

100.  "Quarterly Chronicle and Documentation," *China Quarterly*, June 1993, p. 380.

101.  "Quarterly Chronicle and Documentation," *China Quarterly*, September 1993, p. 591.

102.  See *Hong Kong Economic Journal*, March 21, 1994, p. 23.

103.  *Wen Wei Po* (Hong Kong), March 28, 1994, p. A3.

104.  Central News Service, April 5, 1994, cited in *Inside Mainland China*, June 1994, pp. 50–51.

105.  "Quarterly Chronicle and Documentation," *China Quarterly*, September 1994, p. 868.

106.  Chen Li, "Mainland Hit with Critical Price Rises," *Pai Hsing Semi-Monthly* (Hong Kong), May 1, 1994, pp. 48–49.

107.  *Cheng Ming* (Hong Kong), June 1994, p. 10.

108.  *Ming Pao Daily* (Hong Kong), September 10, 1994, p. B13.

109.  Ibid.

110.  See *Quest on Economic Problems* (Beijing), No. 7, 1994, pp. 18–20.

111.  See *People's Daily*, August 18, 1994, p. 2.

112.  See *Contemporary Monthly* (Hong Kong), September 1994, pp. 78–80.

113.  "Quarterly Chronicle and Documentation," *China Quarterly*, December 1994, pp. 1226–1227.

# Chapter 3

## Political Dissidents and Human Rights

People from the top to the bottom of the society have a strong desire for democracy and freedom. . . In the past 15 years, people's thinking has changed a lot and that's why the political situation must be changed.

—Wei Jingsheng, China's most famous political prisoner.[1]

The Western notion of serving your time doesn't apply in China.

—Robin Munro[2]

This time his testicles were smashed.

—Li Jingfang (speaking about her husband's torture)[3]

The fate of political dissidents in China worsened in 1993 and 1994 as relentless pressure by the government to prevent open dissent by its citizens continued. Four years after the military crackdown in Tiananmen Square, trials of political dissidents from the 1989 pro-democracy movement were still being held and stiff sentences for "counter-revolutionary" activities were being handed down. Several well-known prisoners of conscience were released in 1993 and 1994 for political gains or under foreign pressure, among them Wei Jingsheng, Wang Dan, and Wang Juntao. But they were freed either at a time when China needed to polish its international image in a campaign to host the 2000 Olympic Games or just before Washington was about to make its annual decision on extending trade privileges to China. (For further details, see Chapters Six and Seven.) Once again, there was proof that China does bow to foreign pressure. When the released political prisoners refused to follow the ways prescribed by the government and the political gains had been made, however, they were quickly arrested again. Furthermore, even as well-known dissidents were being released, new arrests were made, especially of college instructors and students who were charged with forming underground "anti-government" groups. And, despite government repression, intellectuals, including many senior scholars, continued to speak up. The most significant development in this respect was an appeal issued in March 1994 by seven prominent scholars, including a respected 74-year-old member of the Academy of Sciences who is a leading authority on Albert Einstein.

### Release and Rearrest of Wei Jingsheng and Wang Dan

Among the most prominent political dissidents released in 1993 were Wei Jingsheng and Wang Dan, the former jailed since 1979, the latter a top student leader of the 1989 Tiananmen democracy movement. They were released essentially as well-timed political moves. However, the releases were only the first step; what was to take place after the release was a matter of grave concern to the Beijing authorities. Beijing's options were obviously limited to either granting them true freedom or keeping them under surveillance so that they would not stray from the prescribed political line. Given the reasons for their arrest in the first place, the latter was Beijing's clear choice. Wei and Wang were kept under close watch and were allowed only limited freedom concerning their residence, travel, and contact with others. And any time when they stepped out of bounds, swift actions were taken by the authorities. Wei Jingsheng was arrested again in April 1994 and later sentenced to fourteen years on counterrevolutionary charges; Wang was also rearrested.[4]

The stock-in-trade treatment of a prominent political dissident includes condemnation as a criminal on trumped-up charges, prolonged incarceration and total silence about the person, in the hope that if the "silent treatment" lasts long enough, people will eventually forget him and his influence. Wei Jingsheng's misfortune provides a classic example of all this. A forerunner of the democracy movement in post-Mao China, he was active during the Democracy Wall events in 1978, a heady period similar to the brief and ill-fated Prague Spring before Alexander Dubcek was banished. Deng Xiaoping, newly rehabilitated after the dark days of the Gang of Four, needed help to bolster his image as an economic and more so as a political reformer. Political reform, holding out the hope of China moving away from Communist dictatorship and the promise of freedom of speech, fired the enthusiasm of a generation of educated young people, among them Wei Jingsheng, the son of a ranking party official. Together with a few like-minded young people, Wei started a magazine, *Tansuo* (Exploration), and became its editor and principal writer.

In a series of sharply worded essays, Wei focused attention on the top leadership, urging genuine political reform to lead China down the road of democracy. In addition to the Four Modernizations—agriculture, industry, military, and science and technology, first enunciated by Zhou Enlai in the early 1970s and now continued by Deng—Wei in a widely hailed essay urged a "fifth modernization"—political modernization for freedom and democracy. Seeing through Deng as a leader who lacked genuine desire for political reform but was merely using the young people to support his political comeback, Wei in a blistering essay questioned Deng's real intention, suggesting that Deng was only consolidating power to achieve dictatorship.[5] *Tansuo* became an instant best-seller. Consisting of mimeographed sheets cranked out on an old duplicator and stapled together in Wei's pint-sized apartment, the magazine was sold at Democracy Wall, a corner in a Beijing park that was designated as a place for free airing of views. There, the walls were plastered with posters and young people, mostly students from colleges and universities in Beijing, among the best in the nation, would gather and hotly debate issues of common concern. Issues of *Tansuo*, snatched up by those enthusiastic college students the moment they were hand-carried there, were making an impact on the minds of the nation's best and brightest.

Precisely as Wei had predicted, Deng, a hard-line dictator at heart, had little stomach for dissent and a mortal fear of any challenge, real or imagined. Before more damage was done to his rule, Deng ordered Democracy Wall torn down and put an end to the brief Beijing Spring. Wei was arrested, a show trial was conducted, and he was sentenced to fifteen years in prison for disclosing military secrets to a foreign reporter concerning China's brief border war with Vietnam in 1979. The charge was patently false, for Wei merely quoted information readily found in the newspapers.[6]

Once he was in jail, Wei's name hardly appeared in the press in China. For many years, he was much better known abroad than at home, thanks to the tireless campaign by human rights groups in the West. He was switched from one labor camp to another, spending years in solitary confinement and working in the desolate Qinghai Province, virtually as a non-person. Occasional reports would reach the outside world from underground sources pointing to his failing health but unbroken spirit. After more than a decade, a whole generation of young Chinese, now in their twenties, hardly knew his name, despite Wei's fame as China's leading democracy advocate and the fact that he was arguably the most respected political prisoner, a reputation he continued to enjoy abroad.[7]

The release of Wei from prison in September 1993, six months before the completion of his fifteen-year prison term, came as a surprise. The Chinese government had repeatedly rejected appeals from foreign governments and leaders for his release. In fact, Deng Xiaoping once bragged that the imprisonment of Wei not only did not hurt China's image but in fact enhanced its international standing. "We put Wei Jingsheng behind bars, didn't we? Did that damage China's reputation? We haven't released him, but China's image has not been tarnished by that; our reputation improves day by day," Deng said before the Tiananmen Massacre.[8]

Wei was released on September 14, 1993, ten days before the International Olympic Committee (IOC) was to decide on the site for the Olympic Games in 2000. For some time, Beijing had been mounting an all-out campaign to host the games. The city was awash with banners and signs greeting the games in the year 2000, an event that was seen as a much-needed boost for China's international image from the low point of the post-Tiananmen years. As the IOC was near its final decision on the widely reported close race between Beijing and Sydney, the timely release of Wei was seen as a last-ditch effort to put Beijing on top. To the dismay of the Chinese government, Beijing lost out and Sydney won the nod to host the 2000 Games, but Wei Jingsheng did win his freedom, however briefly.

In a statement greeting the release of Wei, the New York–based Human Rights in China organization made public the names of sixteen other political prisoners awaiting trial on charges of "counterrevolutionary" activities. The trials were scheduled to take placed after the IOC meeting. Human Rights in China condemned the sinister use of prisoners of conscience as a "bargaining chip" of the state for political purposes. Pointing to the fact that the release of one political prisoner was accompanied by the incarceration of many more, representatives of the organization Human Rights in China said that the Chinese government, instead of improving its human rights performance, was actually stepping up its abusive practices.[9]

Although Wei's release made headline news abroad, it was barely mentioned in the controlled domestic press and the actual act of letting him out of prison was shrouded in mystery. Two days after the official announcement of his release, Wei was taken to a government hostel in the suburbs of Beijing, where police allowed Wei's younger brother and sister to see him only briefly. In a handwritten note, Wei said he was resting and would return to Beijing in a few days and thanked all his friends for their concern.[10]

A few days later, at his parent's tiny apartment in Beijing, Wei met reporters for the first time. Confessing to a heart ailment and the loss of a dozen teeth as a result of the harsh treatment he received during his long imprisonment, Wei demonstrated sharp mental faculties and unbent spirits. Carefully choosing his words, Wei vowed that he would not give up his "struggle" for democracy in China but would be forced to restrain his activities during the period of probation, which would run for three years. "I will continue to carry forward political activities, but not for the present time," Wei said.[11] He explained that under Chinese law, his three-year probation would mean that he could not vote or join any organization, and that he would have little freedom of expression.

These broad and vague restrictions were apparently designed to allow the government maximum latitude to clamp down on him at will.

At the time of Wei's release, human rights groups pointed out that the following prominent political dissidents were still in prison:

**Wang Juntao**, thirty-four, journalist, sentenced to thirteen years in 1990 for supporting the Tiananmen democracy movement;

**Chen Ziming**, forty, journalist and social science researcher, also serving a thirteen-year term for the same "crimes" as Wang;

**Liu Gang**, thirty-two-year-old student, sentenced to six years for participating in the Tiananmen democracy movement;

**Ren Wanding**, forty-eight-year-old accountant and veteran human rights campaigner who had been in and out of prison since 1979, sentenced to seven years for participating in the Tiananmen democracy movement;

**Bao Tong**, sixty, personal secretary to Zhao Ziyang, deposed former party general secretary, sentenced to seven years in 1992 as a victim of a high-level power struggle;

**Zhang Xianliang**, a forty-eight-year-old worker, sentenced in August 1993 to three years of labor reform for trying to commemorate the fourth anniversary of the June 1989 Tiananmen Massacre;

**Fu Shenqi**, a worker in his forties, convicted of the same "crime" as Zhang. Both Fu and Zhang had been in prison before.[12]

Reflecting on the years he had spent in prison, Wei said he had no regrets. He smiled at a question about whether there had been any conditions set for his release, saying, "You don't know me very well. If there is any pre-condition, I would not accept it."[13] During his long imprisonment, much of it in solitary confinement, his reading had been limited to official propaganda like the *People's Daily* and therefore he knew little about the outside world. He displayed his undiminished sharpness of mind, however, when responding to a question on whether the Chinese authorities should trade the release of political prisoners in hope of hosting the Olympics. "The Olympics, after all, are a kind of sport which should not be mixed with politics," he said. If the games were changed into a political trade, then it would be "very dirty and abnormal." He said he felt it would not be compatible with the "feelings of the people and the whole nation" to bargain for the Olympics.[14]

Wei's comments echoed those of Robin Munro, director of Asia Watch, who saw sinister designs behind Beijing's moves to release political prisoners and postpone the trials of others. Pointing to the upcoming IOC vote on Beijing's bid to host the 2000 Games, Munro said: "The Chinese leadership appears to be deliberately postponing these trials until after the decision of the International Olympic Committee is announced."[15] Commenting on Wei's release, Munro, a veteran observer of the Chinese human rights scene for many years, was blunt: "They have waited fourteen and one-half years to release Wei. To wait so long and then to release him at this eleventh hour, it is just so obvious what they are trying to do."[16] Munro said there were 4,000 or more political and religious prisoners in China. "We have a whole new generation of Wei Jingshengs in prison," he asserted.[17] Munro gave two examples: Chen Lantao, a marine biologist who criticized the government for the Tiananmen Massacre four days after the bloodbath and was given an eighteen-year sentence; Tan Yuanjuan, a worker from the No. 1 Automobile Factory in Changchun in the northeast who organized a memorial ceremony for the students killed in Tiananmen and got twenty years.[18]

Wei refused to be silenced while observing the probation rules. He spoke out in March 1994 in protest of the imprisonment of a Chinese citizen for his opposition to the government's failed bid to host the 2000 Olympic Games. In an op-ed page article in the *New York Times*, Wei called for the release of Qin Yongming, who was arrested and illegally put in a labor camp. Wei said that although he supported China's Olympics bid himself, he was thoroughly against the use of force to suppress those who opposed the bid. Wei pointed out that the fact someone was arrested and given a prison term for expressing his views about the Olympics was an indication that the spirit of the movement had deteriorated. Wei reminded the world that one case of this deterioration, overlooked deliberately in the 1930s, "gave rise to Nazism," which caused "the biggest setback to the history of the modern Olympic movement."[19] As an ordinary sports fan, Wei said, he called on members of the IOC and the IOC's member countries and all sports fans to intervene in the case.[20]

Wei stood as a symbol of the indestructible spirit of many Chinese in their quest for freedom. He said his jailers had repeatedly told him that he was a hopelessly stubborn counterrevolutionary from the very beginning. Describing his long ordeal in China's gulag, he said during the first eight months of imprisonment he was put in a small cell together with prisoners condemned to death. In the small cell, there was nothing but a wooden bed for each prisoner and a communal latrine with an unbearable stench. There was hardly any fresh air. In the ensuing years, he was mostly under solitary confinement and suffered from mental torment. The prison food was very poor and he was allowed virtually nothing to read. He went on a hunger strike several times, demanding better treatment. In 1982, after his request for a pen and some paper was granted, he said, he began writing letters to Deng Xiaoping and other leaders. "I felt I had a responsibility to warn them that they were wrong," Wei said, adding with a touch of humor: "Of course, nobody bothered to reply to my letters."[21] Wei said that during his last three years in a Qinghai labor camp, in the late 1980s, he received considerably better treatment than before. He believed that it was ordered by then Party General Secretary Hu Yaobang after an inspection tour to the province. Hu, however, was later forced out by hardliners, and died in early 1989.[22]

After his release, Wei was followed daily by plainclothes police. He was hardly a free person. He said he planned to do some traveling in order to better understand the country, which he literally had not seen for nearly fifteen years. As part of his parole conditions, he needed permission from the police to travel beyond Beijing, and he was not allowed to publish or engage in activities the authorities regarded with disfavor. He would consider foreign travels, Wei said, but only if the government would guarantee his return, so that he would not be banished from his own country like some other dissidents.[23]

In the first few weeks of his freedom, Wei, although under surveillance, already was busy speaking out against the Communist leadership because he sensed that "people from the top to the bottom of the society have a strong desire for democracy and freedom."[24] After a fifteen-year seclusion from the real world, Wei said he was struck by the change of thinking among common Chinese. "I talked with farmers about what they need most at present. . . and I talked extensively with factory workers. In the past fifteen years, people's thinking has changed a lot and that's why the political situation must be changed," he said.[25]

In the letters he wrote to Deng Xiaoping while in prison, Wei was blunt in telling Deng that he was too old and should step aside to allow others to run the government. He particularly criticized Deng for being the architect of China's "hopeless" position on human rights. By advocating different standards for different countries, Wei argued, Deng had played into the hands of "Fascist" and "Nazi" thinkers who would have the world believe that concepts of human rights of white people in the West should not be applied to the Chinese and other "inferior nationalities."[26]

In an interview with the BBC in late November 1993, Wei said he was treated poorly compared with other prisoners during most of his fourteen and a half years of imprisonment. Once, he said, a big electric saw was placed next to his prison cell and the loud noise around the clock made it impossible to sleep. When he developed serious dental problems because of malnutrition and poor sanitation, he was denied medical care. His face was swollen for years and he had difficulty eating and drinking. He said the two things that impressed him the most after his release from prison were the "high political awareness" of the general public and the "serious corruption and disorder" in the Chinese Communist Party.[27]

Wei acknowledged that there had been considerable improvement in living standards over the past fifteen years, but he disagreed with the notion that the people were satisfied and therefore had no use for democracy. Citing the rising prices that accompanied recent economic growth, Wei pointed out that most wage earners had a hard time coping with inflation and that there was a good deal of disaffection in society. He also forcefully refuted the popular argument used by the authorities that democracy would cause chaos, as in post-Communist Russia. Chaos was caused not by democracy, but precisely by the lack of democracy with its legal institutions and systems, he argued.

On another commonly heard argument that China lacked a democratic tradition, he pointed out that before modern democratic systems were firmly established, nobody had any experience, including Great Britain and the United States. He asserted that China today probably already has more experience than many Western countries did when they started out and, besides, China has the advantage of being able to follow their examples. The key was action instead of talk, and the first act down the road of democracy must be to abolish the present one-party dictatorship.[28] Wei showed remarkable consistency and foresight, for his advocacy of abolishing the one-party dictatorship was precisely what got him in trouble back in 1979 when an enraged Deng Xiaoping threw him in jail.

Wei severely criticized the leadership's attitude toward democracy and human rights in an op–ed piece in the *New York Times* November 18. He accused the Chinese leaders of refusing to listen to reason in favor of using political dissidents in a "hostage transaction" in which freedom for the prisoner was a bargaining chip in an economic poker game. Exposing the true face of the government, he said that although the present leaders in China shouted their support for human rights and democracy before they ascended to power, "their subsequent dictatorship made clear that they had no intention of making good on the promises they once made to the masses."[29] The limited tolerance of the authorities for Wei's activities was quickly reached. After the appearance of the essay in the *Times*, public security officials warned him that such writings were a violation of his parole and should not be repeated.[30]

Despite efforts by the police to muzzle him, Wei continued his free speech campaign, giving more interviews to foreign journalists on issues concerning democracy and human rights. Only through the foreign press, he and other dissidents long ago learned, can their message be spread and eventually fed back into China through such channels as the VOA, the BBC, and the free press of nearby Hong Kong. A tiny but potent population of free-thinking opponents of Communist rule, even in a sea of 1.2 billion Chinese, Wei thought, could potentially form the nucleus of a new democracy movement in China and Tibet. In Mao's often quoted prophetic words recalling his earlier role as a guerrilla fighter, "a single spark can light up the prairie."

The human rights challenge, however, as Wei knew is one that the Beijing leaders are most reluctant to accept because they fear that doing so could set themselves on a path of extinction. In late January 1994, Wei said that in the absence of the rule of law, China could easily roll back any concessions it had made on human rights. Commenting on the upcoming debate on trade and human rights, Wei urged the Clinton administration to be alert so as not to be cheated. "If you do not exert continuous pressure, the Chinese government will soon take back what it has said," he warned.[31]

Wei continued his activities undaunted and on February 27, 1994, he met secretly with John Shattuck, U.S. assistant secretary of state for human rights affairs, who was visiting Beijing. Shattuck agreed to take a message from Wei to President Clinton urging him to maintain economic pressure on Beijing as the best way to win the releases of political prisoners.[32]

For the Chinese government that was the last straw. Soon after his meeting with Shattuck, Wei was sent away from Beijing and later arrested by the authorities along with six other dissidents. The arrest came at a particularly sensitive time, for Secretary of State Warren Christopher, after Shattuck's visit, had spent a week in Beijing to review the human rights situation there in preparation for the congressional debate on the renewal of most–favored-nation (MFN) trade status for China. In Washington, President Clinton criticized the arrests. Expressing his dismay, the president said: "We strongly disapprove what was done and it obviously was not helpful to our relations."[33]

Beijing was apparently very annoyed that Wei continued his campaign despite repeated warnings from the authorities. But the fact that Beijing decided to arrest him despite his international fame and mounting pressure from the United States clearly showed the authorities' deep concern and fear for the impact of his activities. Wei's brief freedom and subsequent arrest show the crude way in which the authorities manipulated the treatment of political prisoners for political purposes.

Wei was cited for violation of rules of his parole, according to which he was not allowed to meet foreign journalists or to publish abroad. He had done both. The clear intention of the government was to silence him as a political dissident of great stature. Through his interviews with foreign journalists which were beamed back into China in foreign radio and television broadcasts, and through essays published abroad, Wei had quickly developed a formidable new international profile as China's leading democracy campaigner. Beijing leaders' increasing discomfort with his activities and their fear of his domestic impact was unmistakable. In the eyes of the government authorities, whatever "merit" they had earned in granting him freedom was now outweighed by the damage he had caused, and he must be muzzled for good. After the arrest, the Beijing Public Security Department announced a new investigation because Wei was suspected of having committed "new crimes" while on parole.[34]

Wei's secretary, Tong Yi, who first brought news of Wei's arrest to foreign journalists, was also arrested. Human rights workers were stunned and incredulous. John Kamm, a Hong Kong–based American businessman who has advocated friendly persuasion as the way to approach the Chinese government on behalf of political prisoners, asked in exasperation: "How in the world can the Chinese expect Bill Clinton to extend China's trade privileges with this kind of behavior?"[35] Pointing to the fact that Wei was merely exercising the universal right to freedom of opinion and expression as set forth in Article 19 of the Universal Declaration of Human Rights, one Western diplomat said in Beijing: "They seem to be setting a new standard on the denial of political rights, and it is disturbing."[36] Wei was once again silenced. Beijing had every expectation that the world would soon forget him once again.

Wei's second arrest may have been precipitated by his alleged ties to a new dissident organization aimed at stirring up support among disgruntled workers. Known as Labor Alliance, the new group, although run by intellectuals, as were the student organizations of the Tiananmen days, departed sharply from the past in its strategy. Instead of working among students and faculty on university campuses, it aimed to mobilize workers in fields and factories. This struck fear into the minds of the present leadership, for it was this strategy that half a century ago helped bring the Communists to power in China. And the slogan of the Labor Alliance sounded disturbingly familiar to those in power who were once dedicated revolutionaries: an end to special privilege, a limit to excessive powers, protection for human rights, and a fair division of wealth. Wei, who was seen as a spiritual leader of the alliance, said bluntly before his arrest: "Of course the government is afraid of workers and peasants. It would be good for the government to make friends with them, but it just cannot do it. So it has to take the path of crushing them."[37]

The Alliance, which modeled itself on Poland's Solidarity Movement, claimed a hard-core membership of 300 people and widespread support among the popu-lation. Beijing was apparently more apprehensive about its potential than its size, as its formation had come at a time of widely reported workers' discontent. Reflecting this apprehension, Ren Jianxin, a ranking judicial official, said in May that "the public order situation throughout China has become extremely grim."[38] The leadership of the alliance was already decimated under government crackdown. Two of its founders, Yuan Hongbing and Zhou Guoqiang, had been arrested; a third, Wang Jiaqi, was arrested but escaped and fled the country. Liu Nianchun, the leader of the alliance, was last known to be on the run. Liu claimed that despite the crackdown, the alliance was growing. "Give us until the end of the year, and we will have established a national framework," he said.[39]

Earlier, in February 1993, another leading dissident, Wang Dan, was released from jail. Wang's release was timed to the upcoming discussion of China's membership application to the General Agreement on Tariffs and Trade (GATT) in March and Washington's renewal of MFN status to China in June. The release also came just before the opening of the rubber-stamp National People's Congress, an annual political meeting held to demonstrate China's democracy at work.

Wang was a prominent leader during the student protests that ended in the Tiananmen Massacre in June 1989. A senior history major at Beijing University, he was regarded as the brains behind the democracy movement. After the bloody suppression, he became a fugitive, the first name on a list of twenty-one most-wanted people issued by the police. In a nationwide manhunt, his picture was posted in public places. Wang was in hiding for a while, but he was soon captured by the police as he tried to flee the country. He was under detention for more than a year without formal charges and then put on a show trial in early 1991 on charges citing "counterrevolutionary propaganda and incitement." The entire trial lasted only three hours and was closed to the public. Only Wang's immediate family attended the proceedings, which included Wang meekly reading a prepared statement of confession. His government-appointed lawyer, who came to the courthouse in a police car, made a pleading for mercy. At the end of his prepared statement, Wang is said to have asked the court: "How was my performance?" One of the three presiding judges replied: "O.K., not bad."[40] Wang's meek and compliant attitude apparently won him a relatively light sentence of only four years for "counter-revolutionary crimes." A conviction for such crimes would normally would have carried a much stiffer penalty. This interpretation was confirmed by Timothy A. Gellat, a professor of Chinese law at New York University, who said, "The court places a great deal of emphasis on the compliant attitude of the defendant."[41]

With much fanfare, Wang was released from jail in February 1993, a year ahead of time, ostensibly for good behavior while in prison. A Xinhua News Agency dispatch said Wang was released early because he observed "prison regulations." With Wang's release, Xinhua said, all students who were jailed in connection with the 1989 democracy movement had been freed. However, human rights organizations gave Beijing's claim little credence. Asia Watch pointed out that the release of one prominent dissident was often accompanied by the arrests of many others. Between May 1992 and the time of Wang's release, it said, at least forty political dissidents in Beijing and around the country were detained, including workers, intellectuals, and students who allegedly were involved in underground pro-democracy activities, such as putting up posters and forming a loose network of democracy movement supporters. Calling the release of Wang part of a smile offensive, Robin Munro of Asia Watch said, "It is a calculated show of lenience to certain well-known figures, but at the same time proceeding with business as usual in suppressing dissent."[42]

Wang, who incurred the ire of the authorities by organizing "democratic salons" on the campus of Beijing University before the Tiananmen Massacre, said upon his release that his political views had not changed in the past and would not change in the future, vowing that he would continue the fight for democracy. "I hope that someday I will be able to make more contributions. I don't regret a thing," he declared.[43] His immediate plans were to seek readmission to Beijing University (he was automatically expelled from the school after his arrest) and to continue working for democratization. He was destined to be thwarted in both: He was never readmitted and was kept under close police surveillance.

Wang perceived his release from prison as an indication that the "gerontocrats" in Beijing were beginning to realize that they could no longer go against the broad trends of the times. "This is a smart move by the Chinese government," he said, adding, "They have learned the direction the world is heading."[44] Wang said that in the first four months following his arrest he was kept in solitary confinement. Afterwards, he shared a cell with three common criminals. "They were very nice to me," he told foreign journalists, explaining: "In China, people especially respect political prisoners."[45] He was also allowed to read the *People's Daily* and even watch news programs on television in the evening.

Wang praised the market economy but felt there was little done in the realm of political reform during the years of his imprisonment. Refusing a direct comment on Beijing's human rights record, he said, "China's human rights situation is well-known."[46] If the government would allow him to travel outside the country, he said, he would like to go to Hong Kong and Taiwan to see democracy at work among Chinese. Fearing exile, he stressed that he would not leave China if his return was not assured.[47] In an open letter, Wang thanked those at home and abroad for their support and concern and urged their continued concern for other prisoners of conscience. He pledged that he would persevere as a member of "open opposition under the law" in China.[48]

Wang soon found out that "open opposition under the law" was a role not welcome to the authorities, who continued to view it as a source of trouble. In March, during the annual session of the National People's Congress in Beijing, he was sent south to Hainan on an expenses-paid "vacation" under a false name in the company of his brother-in-law, so that he would not be able to send petitions or give press interviews during the NPC meeting.[49]

In late April, however, when Wang wanted to go south to treat a case of chronic throat infection he suffered while in prison, the Beijing Public Security Bureau denied his request, presumably trying to limit his contact with others. "When I wanted to return to Beijing last time, they kept me in the south until the conference was over. Now I want to visit the south, they won't let me. This is illegal," Wang protested but to no avail.[50] Meanwhile, there were other forms of intimidation. Ma Shaofang, a student leader released earlier, was arrested on April 22 because he was too close to Wang. Ma and Wang had published a series of "dialogues" abroad in which they touched on a number of sensitive political and social issues.[51]

## Ordinary Dissidents in the Provinces

The strategic release of some political dissidents and jailing of others when deemed necessary, a kind of two-pronged tactic, was repeated in less well-known cases in 1993 and 1994. While famous dissidents like Wei Jingsheng and Wang Dan walked out of prison with much publicity, there were thousands of "ordinary" dissidents whose suffering both in and out of prison was virtually unknown to the public. The experience of one such political prisoner, Xu Yiruo from Qingdao in Shandong Province, who had the courage to tell his story to a foreign journalist, reflects the special vulnerability of thousands of political prisoners in the provinces.[52] Anonymous at home and abroad and absent from the lists of prisoners compiled by human rights groups, these prisoners of conscience languished in jail and continued to suffer as non-persons after their release without any public knowledge.

Xu was a twenty-three-year-old former student at Qingdao University, where he was caught up in the 1989 democracy movement. In July 1993 he took the risk of agreeing to talk with a foreign journalist even though the last time he tried to contact a foreigner by phone, he found out, not surprisingly, that the line was tapped, and he was arrested and imprisoned for nineteen months. During the interview he boldly expressed his desire to go abroad. Having been in and out of prison three times, he told of the hopeless life of an ostracized non-person under surveillance. He could not get back into the university and could not find a job. "They call me an 'anticommunist and anti-socialist reactionary' and so I can't get a job. I would take a job as a laborer but I can't get one," he said. Leaving prison meant little real freedom for him.

Xu's first prison experience came after the military crackdown in June 1989, when he was arrested as a student leader at his university. He was arrested and spent seven weeks in jail. After his release, he was sent back to his university on probation. In March 1991, for fear of arrest in a new wave of crackdown, he stowed away to Hong Kong in a container ship. Held incommunicado by the Hong Kong immigration authorities and refused political asylum, he was later sent back across the border and was handed over to Chinese police. He spent the next few months in a labor camp and was released just before the second anniversary of the Tiananmen Massacre. Back on the Qingdao University campus, Xu posted two poems in memory of the tragic day, beginning with the following verses:

> It is two years since that bloody June Fourth,
> Today I think back and my heart shrivels.[53]

He was quickly taken into custody, interrogated, and put under house arrest while the police prepared its case. Then, evading police surveillance, he slipped out of Qingdao at night and fled to Beijing, where he tried to make telephone contact with human rights groups such as Amnesty International and Asia Watch in Hong Kong. One day, after one such call, he was arrested while walking out of the telephone booth. Obviously, overseas phone lines were tapped. For the next three months, he was locked up in Qingdao No. 1 Prison, sharing an 8 x 10 foot cell with eleven common criminals and sleeping on the floor at night. Xu said they worked every waking moment, sometimes up to twenty hours a day, assembling Christmas tree lights. He was later transferred to a labor camp for two years of "education through labor," working in a mine to produce fine clay. "It was exhausting, heavy work, with long hours in unsafe conditions," Xu said, recalling that the prisoners worked twelve–hour shifts in narrow tunnels several hundred feet under-ground. "Some prisoners wanted to commit suicide, to hang themselves, but they couldn't. The guards were always watching."[54]

Xu was released from the camp in February 1993 along with a number of other political prisoners when Beijing was trying to improve its image in its bid to host the 2000 Olympic Games. Though out of prison, he was unable to find a job. "The Western notion of serving your time doesn't apply in China," said Robin Munro of Asia Watch, the same person Xu telephoned before his arrest in 1991. Even after serving a sentence, Munro explained, "you are stigmatized as a political criminal and therefore have to be monitored continually."[55]

Referring to his hope to flee abroad, Xu said if he were optimistic about China's changing, he would not choose that path. Since ordinary people did not care much about human rights and democracy, Xu said, the Communist Party was very successful in refocusing the attention from the democracy movement to making money. Xu realized the danger of speaking to a foreign journalist, but he said he had thought about it long and hard before agreeing to the interview. "There are so many things that foreigners don't know about China. If I don't speak out, then none of this will be known," he said. Xu stated emphatically that he wanted to get the word out in order to encourage the world to put pressure on the Chinese government to stop violating human rights.[56]

Another example is the case of Fu Shenqi, a veteran democracy campaigner from Shanghai who has been in and out of jail since the late 1970s. He was last detained in late June 1993, during Australian Prime Minister Keating's visit to Shanghai. He was taken into custody by several policemen who stopped him in the street the night before Keating's arrival as a suspect for stealing a pedicab which belonged to his wife. The reason for his arrest was that he broke the official ban and gave an interview to reporters of Australian Broadcasting Company who accompanied Keating on the visit. It is all the more ironic that the arrest was made at a time when Keating was praising Beijing for the "improvement" of human rights conditions in China.[57] He was held until

July 10, when his wife, Li Liping, was summoned to the police station and told that Fu had been sent to an undisclosed labor camp for three years. His crime was to disclose Shanghai dissident activities to foreign journalists.[58] Fu's jailing, which was without trial, came after the arrest of four other protesters in Shanghai in six weeks, suggesting a possible reversal of an earlier trend of tolerating low-level protests while releasing selected well-known or famous dissidents. Mrs. Li was told by the police that she could not visit her husband and that she should not tell "outsiders" about his imprisonment.[59]

As the arrest of Fu shows, dissidents can still be sent to jail on any trumped-up charges. In Canton, three dissidents were arrested on charges of smuggling and gambling in April, according to the Hong Kong *South China Morning Post* on July 7, 1993. The three, Li Guohan, Liang Weimin, and Wu Songfa, were arrested at the airport when they tried to board a flight for Shanghai to distribute flyers urging more democracy and less controls. The paper reported that according to the Canton Public Security Bureau, the three had already signed confessions and would probably be sentenced to three to five years. The bureau denied the use of torture to extract confessions, but one of the dissidents, Li Guohan, was known to have asked his wife to bring him medication for a bone fracture during a jail visit.[60]

On May 26, 1993, just days before President Clinton's decision on extending trade benefits to China, Xu Wenli, a prominent pro-democracy campaigner who had spent twelve years in solitary confinement, was released from prison. A forty-nine-year-old former editor of an underground magazine and a contemporary of Wei Jingsheng, Xu was paroled three years before the completion of a fifteen-year sentence. He was arrested in 1981 and spent the first three years in a tiny punishment cell in Beijing's main prison, where he was known as "special prisoner No. 1."[61]

Xu was jailed for his role in the 1979–1980 Democracy Wall movement, the first major political protest in China calling for democracy. He was the editor of *April 5th Forum*, an influential magazine. At first, Deng Xiaoping encouraged the movement. At that time Deng was consolidating his power against the Maoist ultra-leftists who had been in power since the Cultural Revolution in the 1960s. By 1980, when Deng had succeeded in his political comeback and was firmly in power, he pulled down the Democracy Wall and sent most of the campaigners to prison. Xu was a moderate at the time; he advocated the separation of powers and an independent judiciary. He regarded himself as a Marxist trying to improve the system rather than a rebel trying to overthrow it. He went to prison nevertheless. Commenting on Xu's release three years before his term was up, John T. Kamm, the Hong Kong-based American businessman who helped lobby for the release, gave two reasons: MFN and 2000 Olympics. Kamm said that as of the end of March 1993 there were 3,501 "counter-revolutionaries" still in prison or labor camp.[62]

In 1985, while in prison, Xu wrote a long description of the prison conditions that was smuggled out and published in the West. As a punishment, he was moved from a six square meter single cell to a three square meter single cell, in which he was kept in solitary confinement for the next four years.[63]

As the case of another dissident demonstrates, attempts to help dissidents in detention can make matters worse. Yu Zhuo, a graduate student at the Wuhan Polytec College in Hubei Province, was detained in June 1992 when in an open letter marking the third anniversary of the Tiananmen Massacre he urged the authorities to reverse the verdict (pingfan) on the 1989 student movement, which had been condemned as "counter-revolutionary" in nature. In May 1993, after nearly a year under detention, he was formally arrested on charges of "counterrevolutionary propaganda and incitement." Yu's father, Yu Minchu, petitioned judicial authorities and spoke to the media about his son's plight. He felt that the authorities at the Wuhan Public Security Bureau may have made the serious charges against his son in anger because of his efforts to have him released. "Yu Zhuo has been under 'detention and investigation' (shourong shencha) only a few months and you are making appeals (gaozhuang) all over the place. Others have been here for years and have kept quiet," Yu's father quoted an angry public security official as saying.[64]

As another case indicates, mentioning the use of torture in prison only brought more pain. Liu Gang, a thirty-one-year-old physicist serving a six-year sentence at the notorious Lingyuan Labor Reform Camp in Liaoning Province for participating in the Tiananmen demonstrations smuggled a letter out of prison in early 1993. In it, he wrote that each time he told visiting family members about being mistreated, he was punished with further beatings. The beatings left him with a prolapsed anus, psoriasis and swellings all over his face. "This is the dictatorship of the proletariat, the meat grinder," a prison commander, Wang Shijun, told Liu during one of the torture sessions, according to the smuggled letter. "If you refuse to bow your head, we'll grind you slowly to death," the prison commander said.[65] When he went on a hunger strike, he was force-fed by prison guards, who also arranged to have him beaten by fellow inmates.[66]

In addition to intimidation and arrest, another effective way of silencing dissent is through exile. On August 21, 1993, Chinese officials in Hong Kong revoked the passport of Han Dongfang, a dissident labor leader, barring him from returning to China and effectively rendering him stateless. He was told by Chinese officials in Hong Kong that he had broken Chinese law by engaging in subversive activities abroad. Han was on his way home to Beijing from the United States, where he was treated for the tuberculosis that he had contracted while in prison in China. Nevertheless, he slipped into China through a small border post where immigration officials did not know who he was. After reaching Canton and checking into a hotel, he was discovered by alert security agents who routinely examine hotel registers. He was dragged from his room, pummeled, and expelled to Hong Kong.[67]

Han, a railroad worker, organized China's first free labor union during the 1989 Tiananmen pro-democracy demonstrations. After the protests were crushed, he spent twenty–two months in prison without trial. There he was tortured and kept with prisoners who had tuberculosis.[68] Released in 1991 under strong pressure from Western governments and human rights groups, Han came to the United States for eleven months of treatment, during which part of his lung was removed. While in the United States, he met President Clinton and American labor leaders. Han vowed to return to China to continue his campaign for free unions. Apparently, Beijing was angry about his activities abroad and did not want him back as a potential troublemaker. Beijing accused the West of trying to use Han to spread unrest in China and to deprive China of its chance to host the 2000 Olympics Games. "Through the performance of this anti-China tool, we can see the vicious intentions of the 'international hegemonists' who hate China," declared *Wen Wei Po*, a pro-Beijing newspaper in Hong Kong. "He is entirely a pawn controlled by Western forces specifically to make troubles in China."[69]

After he was exiled, Han said, "I have become someone existing alone in this world." If the international community accepted China's decision, it would legitimize Beijing's power to expel any one of 1.2 billion people, he said, adding: "This is a humiliation for the Chinese people." The Hong Kong government in a statement said China had violated international law, and the U.S. government criticized Beijing for violating Han's human rights.[70] But Han was effectively silenced and disappeared from the public view. Asia Watch's Robin Munro put it succinctly: "It was actually a policy to export the problem, to exile the dissidents on a one-way ticket."[71]

Another possible exile was Zhang Weiguo, a dissident journalist who was allowed to leave China in February 1993. Arriving in San Francisco where he would be a visiting scholar at the University of California at Berkeley, Zhang said that freedom of the press was essential to China's reform but that he was pessimistic about the prospect of having real freedom of the press in China. Zhang was formerly a reporter of the influential *World Economic Herald* in Shanghai, which was ordered closed down just before the June 1989 Tiananmen Massacre by Jiang Zemin, then the Communist Party boss of Shanghai. Zhang was soon arrested and spent twenty months in prison for "instigating turmoil." He was arrested again in the summer of 1991 and later released on parole. He credited his release to Beijing's desire to improve its image by responding to international pressure, particularly from the United States. He recalled during his parole hearing a public security official saying, "It doesn't matter whether Bush or Clinton will be U.S. President. You will be released anyway. We have no other choice."[72]

According to the Hong Kong magazine *Cheng Ming,* the State Council in October 1993 issued orders barring eight types of Chinese citizens abroad from returning to China. This would seem to confirm the suspicion that the government indeed tried to exile political dissidents. *Cheng Ming,* which has a solid record in obtaining confidential information from China, said the decisions were based on recommendations of the Public Security Ministry and the National Security Ministry. Labelling such people was clearly meant to permanently exile those who were opposed to the government. The eight "categories" are:

1. Holders of Chinese passports abroad who are engaged in plotting to overthrow the Chinese government and socialism;

2. Leaders of groups abroad engaged in anti-government activities in collusion with foreign political forces and accepting financial support from hostile foreign sources;

3. Key members of hostile exile groups abroad dedicated to the overthrow of the Chinese government and opposed to socialism and the Constitution;

4. Those who are on the most-wanted list for advocating or participating in plots to overthrow the government;

5. Holders of expired Chinese passports or those whose passports have been confiscated for anti-government activities abroad in collusion with anti-China foreign forces;

6. Those who had been punished for or warned against engaging in anti-government activities who resume such activities after they have gone abroad;

7. Hostile anti-China elements and ringleaders in Hong Kong; and

8. Ringleaders in Hong Kong and Macao plotting to split up China in collusion with foreign anti-China forces.[73]

Those who had "previous records" always lived in fear, even if cleared of past "wrongdoing." Li Sanyuan, a Chinese student–turned–entrepreneur in the United States related his personal experience. He had briefly run a radio station after the June 4, 1989, Tiananmen Massacre that was known as the Voice of June 4. The station had beamed its broadcasts to China. The station soon went bankrupt, however, and Li decided to turn his energy from political activism to business. He rose to the position of president of the Chinese Student-Entre-preneur Association in the United States. Inspired by a science park in Taiwan with heavy participation by overseas Chinese entrepreneurs, he approached the Chinese government with the idea of a similar science park in China to tap talents from among tens of thousands of Chinese students abroad, particularly in the United States. The idea appealed to the Chinese authorities and was given a big play in the official media. Li went back to China on a five-month home visit as a born-again "patriot." He toured many big cities and was accorded VIP treatment. On June 29, he when he went through security check before boarding a flight to return to the United States, he saw customs officers checking the name list of the tour. At the Shanghai airport, going his papers against a two-page name list in alphabetical order. They stopped at "L," where presumably his name appeared. The agent's face turned solemn, Li said, and he ordered Li to proceed to a small room where he called his superior for instructions. Li was held and interrogated for more than three hours before he was allowed to leave. "Apparently, the blacklist was a bit outdated," Li said later.[74]

A similar experience was reported by Wang Xizhe, who was released from prison in early 1993 after serving more than twelve years for criticizing the government. By then a middle-aged man with a ruined career, Wang, like many other dissidents, turned to business, hoping to start anew. On July 3, 1993, he was suddenly led away by security police, who prevented him from meeting some American businessmen. Wang's wife later found out from the police that Wang was taken to an undisclosed location to attend a week-long "study session."[75]

Bao Zunxin, who served time for involvement in the Tiananmen democracy movement, also received continued persecution. Released from jail in November 1992, Bao, formerly a senior fellow at the Institute of History at the prestigious National Academy of the Social Science, found himself without a job. The academy had earlier expelled him and refused to reinstate him. He had written letters to senior officials, including the head of the National People's Congress and the minister of justice but received no reply. With his background, Bao said, "no unit would dare to hire me until there is a nod from the central authorities."[76]

### Releases of Prisoners in 1994 Coupled with New Arrests

Two significant releases of political prisoners were made, both under considerable U.S. pressure, in 1994 and took place just before President Clinton's decision to renew the MFN trade status for China. This time Wang Juntao and Chen Ziming, both serving thirteen-year prison terms for their role in the 1989 Tiananmen democracy movement were the ones chosen for release. Wang was seriously ill with a heart ailment and hepatitis. He was one of five political prisoners with serious medical problems singled out in appeals by U.S. lawmakers to Chinese leaders in February. These five were also mentioned in subsequent talks with Chinese officials by John Shattuck, U.S. assistant secretary of state for human rights affairs. After his release from prison, Wang was immediately put on a flight for the United States where he was to receive medical treatment. At the airport, he saw his mother for the first time since his arrest in 1989.

By sending Wang out of the country, the leadership rid itself of a major figure from the Tiananmen period just before the fifth anniversary of the military crackdown. His release was also timed as a gesture to Washington as the U.S. government approached the annual decision on China's trade status. Chinese authorities might also refuse to allow Wang to return to China after treatment, thus ending his influence in China. "It has all the earmarks of an exile," observed John Kamm, the Hong Kong-based U.S. business-man experienced in negotiating with the Chinese government on human rights.[77] Wang and his colleague, Chen Ziming, who was paroled a month later, were co-directors of the Beijing Social and Economic Sciences Research Institute. The institute published the *Economic Weekly*, a journal advocating political reform and democracy that strongly influenced the demonstrating students during the 1989 democracy movement.

In addition, Beijing released three other political prisoners jailed in connection with the 1989 Tiananmen democracy movement. Among them was Xiao Bin, a forty–six-year-old Beijing resident, who in an interview he gave ABC News soon after the military crackdown said as many as 20,000 people may have been killed by tanks and machine guns. He was arrested, forced to recant on television, and sent away for "vilifying the righteous acts of martial law troops."[78] The other two were Ding Junze, a university philosophy instructor who took part in the 1989 demonstration, and Liao Yiwu, a poet who had made an art video that the police judged too sympathetic to student demonstrators. Linking the releases with the upcoming U.S. trade decision, John Kamm, who negotiated the releases, said, "It is a step in the right direction, but let's not overstate it." He added, "There are still hundreds if not thousands of prisoners of conscience."[79]

The month of March was a sensitive time in China because it was when the National People's Congress opened its annual session. In the past, dissidents often took the opportunity to file petitions to the rubber-stamp parliament to make their cases known. The government does not take such acts kindly. Regarding such moves as anti-government and counterrevolutionary, it often reacts harshly, arresting dissidents for speaking out boldly. The year 1994 was no exception. On the day before the opening of the NPC session, the Beijing Public Security Bureau announced that it had arrested three dissidents for "unlawful acts in inciting turmoil and disrupting social order." The three were Zhou Guoqiang, a labor leader and lawyer; Yuan Hongbing, a law professor; and Wang Jiaqi, a legal worker. According to the government-controlled China News Service, Zhou had been discovered making plans to distribute T-shirts bearing slogans of dissent. He was charged with illegal use of a fax machine, presumably to disseminate messages that the government disliked, and with meeting foreign journalists. All three dissidents planned to circulate petitions during the meeting protesting government corruption and violation of civil rights. One petition called on the people to use their legal rights to fight against civil rights violations and corrupt activities. Though outwardly an innocuous exhortation to political action, the petition and others like it were considered counter-revolutionary threats to the government. The *New York Times* was given a copy by a sympathizer apparently seeking to make the petition public.[80] With the domestic media under government control, dissidents have long learned that the only way to make their cause known is through foreign journalists whom they are forbidden to contact.

It became known by late May that Yuan and Zhou might be charged with the very serious crime of "plotting to overthrow the government" because of their efforts to organize a civil rights group (incidently a right guaranteed by the Constitution).[81] The full story did not come to light until late June, through the miraculous escape from prison of Wang Jiaqi, a fellow organizer of the alleged "underground labor union." Wang, thirty-four, a candidate for the master's degree in law at Beijing University at the time of his arrest in early March, along with Yuan, Zhou, and several other pro-democracy workers, had planned to establish the Alliance for the Protection of Workers' Rights, or the Workers' League for short. Since the organizers were all lawyers or legal workers familiar with the law, they took meticulous care to announce their plans openly. They framed their activities as an exercise of rights guaranteed by the Constitution. Wang said that by doing so, they naively hoped to prove that China was marching down the road of democracy and rule of law. However, after the news appeared in the foreign press, the government concluded that the group was a dangerous "underground organization" that must be eradicated. In ensuing weeks, security police were out in force to search for all those who were connected with the planned organization, about 120 people in all. Over a dozen were arrested.

Emerging in New York in late June, Wang related a hair-raising story of his arrest and escape. Wang was kidnapped on the night of March 2, eight days before he was to marry his fiancee, an instructor at the Beijing college of Economics. Wang said he was accosted by six or seven burly men when he was just about to call a client from a public phone in the hallway of the college. Two men held Wang's arms while a third put his hand on his mouth to prevent him from crying for help. Wang was a policeman for six years before entering Beijing University to study for his law degree, but he said he was powerless against the overwhelming physical force. As he was dragged past the door of his fiancee's dormitory, Wang said, he struggled and managed to yell out her name. Stopped at the door by the police, she saw Wang being taken away.

Wang was forced into a waiting car on campus and blindfolded. The car sped away taking him to a government guest house, where nobody would tell him why he was arrested. When he went on a hunger strike, he was told by the guards that his protest would be of no use because his coconspirators, Yuan Hongbing and Zhou Guoqiang, were also arrested. Because he was a former policeman with friends in many police facilities, he was later transferred to another guest house instead of a detention house. On March 27, he evaded his guards while going to the men's room, walked out of the gate, and jumped onto a slow-moving truck. In the city, he disappeared into a crowd. With the help of an underground rescue group, he got to Hong Kong in mid-April. From there he proceeded to a European country before he was granted political asylum in the United States. He arrived in New York in June to take the position of visiting scholar at Columbia University.[82]

One of the other organizers, Zhou Guoqiang, was sent to a labor camp for three years of education through labor. The sentence did not begin until November 15, some eighteen months after his arrest. According to the New York-based group Human Rights in China, the government announced that Zhou was guilty of "organizing a hostile group to engage in anti-government activities in and out of China." Believing that he had acted within the law, Zhou sued the government, to no avail.[83] Nothing was known of the fate of Yuan Hongbing.

At least seventeen organizers or leading affiliates of dissident groups such as the Workers' League and the Shanghai Association for Human Rights were rounded up by police between March and August 1996. The detentions were either unacknowledged or denied by police, Human Rights in China reported. Released dissidents came under such close surveillance by the government that they lived virtually like prisoners. Wang Dan said that for three months his home was besieged by police officers who followed his every movement. Chen Ziming, one of the two pro-democracy journalists released from prison just before the U.S. government renewed China's MFN trade status, was confined to his tiny Beijing apartment, with public security agents camping out in the hallway and ringing his doorbell frequently to verify his presence.[84]

Seven leading intellectuals issued an appeal to government leaders in March 1994 to end human rights abuses in China and release all imprisoned political dissidents. They timed their actions for just before the opening of the NPC meeting and before the arrival of U.S. Secretary of State, Warren Christopher. The petition was the first by a group of eminent intellectuals since the Tiananmen military crackdown in June 1989. It urged the government to end China's long history of "punishing people for their ideas, speeches and writings and release all those incarcerated because of their ideas and speeches." (For full text of the petition, see Appendix 2.) The group was led by Xu Liangying, a seventy-four-year-old physicist at the Academy of Sciences who was famous for his translation of Albert Einstein's collected works into Chinese.

The appeal noted the recent waves of arrests in Shanghai and Beijing. It said intellectuals "who are concerned about the fate of the nation and dedicated to the modernization of our country are shocked and deeply disturbed and worried."

Tracing the development of the awareness of inalienable rights in modern history, the statement quoted an expression in classical Chinese to warn that to talk about modernization without mentioning human rights was like "climbing up a tree to look for fish."

Other signers of the petition were Ding Zilin and Jiang Peikun, both professors at the People's University in Beijing whose only son was killed during the Tiananmen Massacre; Shao Yanxiang, a poet; Zhang Kangkang, a writer; Liu Liao, a physicist; and Professor Xu's wife, Wang Laidi, a historian. Professor Xu's reputation among the Chinese was also based on the persecution he had suffered for many years because of his criticisms of Mao and his break with Marxism in 1974. After his rehabilitation by Deng Xiaoping in the late 1970s, he formed an alliance with other intellectuals to champion the cause of "science and democracy,"[85] an ideal of the May Fourth Movement of 1919.

After the appeal was made public, Xu and other signers were immediately put under surveillance and subjected to police harassment. Plainclothes agents literally camped out at the door of their apartments and followed their movements. They were visited by party officials and called in for long interrogations by security police. Only their stature prevented them from being arrested. During Secretary of State Christopher's brief stay in Beijing, Xu said, "police were ordered to block the door and not to allow me to go out or to let my friends and relatives come in," in order to prevent any possible contact with Christopher. "We made a reasoned appeal for improvements of the human rights situation and, as a result, we immediately experienced flagrant violations of our own rights," Xu said, calling this "the official version of human rights with Chinese characteristics."[86] Professor Ding Zilin reported that she and her husband, both signers, were repeatedly harassed and followed all the time by police. Their phone line was cut, making it impossible to summon medical help when her heart condition worsened on the night of March 10.[87]

Not long after President Clinton renewed the MFN status to China and announced that future extensions would no longer be linked to human rights, Beijing began the trial of fourteen dissidents, most of them arrested in 1992 and held for nearly two years. The trial had been repeatedly postponed, most likely in a deliberate move to have them occur after the trade decision.[88] The dissidents were charged with "counter-revolutionary" activities linked to underground pro-democracy and labor groups. Some were involved in writing and printing leaflets that were to be distributed in June 1992 during the third anniversary of the massacre in Tiananmen Square. "Reactionary publications" were found in the homes of several dissidents, according to the government indictment. Liu Jingsheng, a thirty-eight-year-old chemical plant worker, was named "chief conspirator" in organizing and leading a "counterrevolutionary group," presumably of workers. Among the others were Wang Guoqi, thirty-one, a printing plant worker; Wang Tiancheng, twenty-nine, a law lecturer at Beijing University who was arrested just as he was about to leave for Germany as a visiting scholar; and Hu Shenglun, thirty-eight, a lecturer at the Beijing Foreign Language Institute,[89] an elite school for training diplomats.

At least three leaders of the Shanghai Human Rights Association, Yang Zhou, Bao Ge, and Yang Jingsheng, were sentenced to three years of "education through labor" in mid-October. Yang Zhou was charged with "inciting turmoil" and "distributing reactionary material," while Bao Ge incurred the ire of the authorities by organizing a campaign demanding reparations from Japan for aggression against China. The government's policy was not to offend Japan, which had extended huge loans to China for economic development.

"Education through labor" is a peculiar form of punishment in China that does not involve trial by court. It is a police action, with a maximum term of three years plus a one-year extension. It can be swiftly dispensed by the public securities. Inmates perform hard labor at camps just like other criminals. Many political dissidents were quietly sent away for "education through labor" in 1994, according to Human Rights in China, which called attention to the increasing use of this convenient form of punishment.[90]

By year's end, nine political dissidents were tried and sentenced to prison terms of up to twenty years for "counterrevolutionary" crimes in one of the largest trials since the crackdown after the June 1989 Tiananmen Massacre. Among the sentenced were Hu Shigen, a thirty-nine-year-old professor at the Beijing Foreign Language Institute, who drew twenty years for leading a "counter-revolutionary group" and "distributing counter-revolutionary propaganda;" Kang Yuchun, a thirty-year-old physician, who was convicted of the same crime and given seventeen years; Liu Jingsheng, a forty-year-old worker at a chemical plant, who received fifteen years for the same crime; and thirty-two-year-old Wang Guoxing, unemployed, who was given eleven years for leading a "counter-revolutionary group." Others included several law school professors and students charged with "distributing counterrevolutionary propaganda" and "joining counterrevolutionary groups."[91] In an editorial, the *New York Times* noted that although the roots of the new crackdown was domestic, its severity reflected Beijing's perception that it could now ignore international pressure. Reminding its readers that the trials were postponed from early 1994 when President Clinton was weighing extension of China's low-tariff access to the U.S. market, the editorial said: "Extending trade access without human rights conditions reduced the outside world's leverage."[92]

## Two Tiananmen Anniversaries: Brutal Repression

The anniversary of the 1989 Tiananmen Massacre remained a time of tension and heightened security as well as a time of sad memories and new revelations in 1993 and 1994. In late May 1993, during the run-up to the event's fourth anniversary, the authorities were particularly jittery about possible disturbances by students and workers because of the declining health of paramount leader Deng Xiaoping and the rumored deterioration of the condition of Premier Li Peng, who had earlier suffered a heart attack. Deng ordered the 1989 military crackdown and Li, known as the butcher of Tiananmen, enforced the martial law decree. Ten students from Beijing area colleges were arrested, including Zhou Shaowu, of Qinghua University, who had been imprisoned in 1990 and again in 1991, in connection with Tiananmen observances. Also arrested was a twenty-four-year-old "red rock star," Huang Jingang, who used Marxist language to sing protest songs against government corruption. Huang, a political science major at the China Youth Political College, sang the following tune on the campus of Beijing University before his arrest:

> Why the poor people are so poor
> And the rich people so rich?
> We need to struggle!
> We need to struggle![93]

At Beijing University, students played a cat-and-mouse game with the security police who cordoned off the campus. At midnight, with security police patrolling outside, lights in the graduate students' dormitories were suddenly turned off and students began to throw bottles from windows, shout slogans, and sing protest songs. The activities attracted foreign journalists, who were kept at a distance. Smashing little bottles had become a June 4 protest ritual because in Chinese, the word for "little bottle" sounds exactly like Deng Xiaoping's name. When police rushed to the scene to chase away foreign journalists, students were heard to yell, "Bad guys are coming!"[94]

In Shanghai, three factory workers were arrested for planning a commemoration of the anniversary, according to the Associated Press (AP). In Canton, three passengers were arrested when they boarded a flight to Beijing because they were found carrying a twenty-foot-long banner with the message "Reverse the Verdict on Tiananmen Movement."[95]

On October 12, 1993, an AP dispatch from Beijing reported that a college student, Yu Zhou, was sentenced to two years in prison for putting up posters commemorating the 1989 democracy movement. (Any public display of sentiments in memory of the 1989 tragedy remained a crime.) He was convicted of spreading "counter-revolutionary propaganda," according to his mother. Yu took part in the 1989 student movement in Wuhan and spent eight months in jail after the military crackdown. He was arrested again in September 1992.[96]

In anticipation of the Tiananmen anniversary in June 1994, security measures in Beijing were tightened to prevent problems. Scores of dissidents were either put under house arrest or sent away from the capital, and international news broadcasts were interrupted. In Tiananmen Square, there were more uniformed and plainclothes security police than strollers. The plainclothes police, easily recognizable by their dark glasses and two-way radios wrapped in copies of the *People's Daily*, shadowed all foreigners and quickly broke up any gathering of more than five people. Virtually all group activities were banned, including art exhibits, softball games, and parties. The authorities also ordered work units to tell their employees to stay away from the square and go home early at night.[97]

The capital's university district, birthplace of the 1989 movement that sent millions into the streets of Beijing and other cities, was cordoned off like an army camp with a heavy security presence to prevent renewed protests. International hotels and even housing compounds for foreign diplomats, journalists, and businessmen were ordered to pull the plug on satellite reception of CNN to prevent file pictures of the massacre on Chinese television screens. The effort to keep the capital quiet reflected a deep unease in the aging Communist leadership and indicated that the military crackdown, and the democracy movement that prompted it, remained a grave concern. It also mirrored Chinese leaders' uncertainty about China's international image and support at home for the government as people were still grumbling about double-digit inflation and rampant official corruption, ostensible causes of the 1989 protests.[98]

Outwitting the government security apparatus, ingenious protesters moved from the streets to the information highways in 1994. Using international computer networks accessible in China, Chinese students and professionals on several continents published an electronic file of personal reminiscences of the fateful night when tanks rolled into Tiananmen Square facing unarmed students. In the electronic bulletin, one student recalled the experience of being run down by a tank on Changan Avenue west of Tiananmen. The tank driver, possibly blinded by a cloud of tear gas, rushed the students on the side of the avenue. "Since I was in the front row, I found no way to run," the student wrote in the electronic file. He said he was bumped onto the ground and passed out. When he came to and tried to sit up, he could not move his left thigh. "It was lying on the ground, strangely shaped," he said, describing his mangled and blood-smeared thigh. By his side, he said, "there were seven to ten mashed bodies, too terrible to look at."[99]

Highlighting the subdued observances of the fifth anniversary of the Tiananmen Massacre in 1994 was a particularly poignant story in the *International Herald Tribune* of a courageous mother campaigning on behalf of all victims of the massacre in memory of her seventeen-year-old son who was killed in the military suppression. Ding Zilin, the fifty-seven-year-old mother and an aesthetics professor, remembered how she begged her high school sophomore son, Jiang Jielian, not to go out on that fateful night in June 1989. She bolted the front door of the apartment, but her son locked himself in the bath-room and jumped out the window. "I remember saying to him, 'What can you do? You are only a high school student,'" the mother recalled, fighting back tears. "He said, 'If all parents were as selfish as you, there would be no hope left for our country.'"[100] About thirty minutes later, the boy was shot and killed by Chinese soldiers. The bullet hit him in the back and ripped through his chest.

The death of her only son launched Professor Ding on a one-woman campaign to locate the families of those killed and wounded by the army. Defying government harassment, she tried to contact the families and give them money she raised from donations abroad. "I want the real truth to be known. I want to know how many were killed by the government," Ding said, believing that the government knew but withheld the information from the public while calling the killed civilians "counterrevolutionary rebels" and "thugs" while offering no compensation.[101]

Ding said she had located eighty-four families of those killed and nearly fifty other families of people seriously injured. She went public with her case in 1991 to counter a claim by Premier Li Peng that families did not want an accounting of the dead and injured. At first, she said, it took months to get in touch with victims' families because people feared reprisal, but gradually the numbers multiplied. Ding came under close government surveillance because of the campaign and because of her connections with human rights groups abroad. With money raised in the United States, Japan, and Germany, she was able to send donations to the victims' families twice a year.

Ding's accounts of the army attack underscore its indiscriminate nature. The victims included onlookers as well as protesters—students, teachers, office and factory workers, old men and women, and children. She recorded the story of a nurse killed by a bullet in the throat as she lifted her head while treating the wounded. A university professor was killed while trying to persuade his students to return to the campus. She found no instance of any victims having used violence against the soldiers, as the government claimed. Her campaign, however, also revealed the deep fears of the survivors. Families of those killed were afraid to acknowledge the deaths, and several had refused to see her or accept her donations, Ding said.[102]

Confirming Ding's chronicles, Amnesty International issued a report on the eve of the fifth anniversary of the Tiananmen Massacre, documenting details about seventy-five victims, including a seventy-eight-year-old woman and a nine-year-old boy who died under army gunfire. The report said that the woman was shot on the night of June 3 near the window of her thirteenth floor apartment in the western suburbs of Beijing, when tanks rumbled by the building with guns blaring. At the same time, a journalism student, Lin Keqin, was killed in the street while trying to rescue wounded civilians. The report also said that a group of soldiers shot the nine-year-old boy in the head near

Tiananmen and killed another journalism student-intern working for a government news agency while he was taking pictures on the roof of a nearby building.[103]

Amnesty International also published a letter from some forty prisoners in a labor camp in central China for their involvement in the Tiananmen demonstrations. The letter, received by Amnesty International in 1994, recorded many cases of savage beatings and torture of political prisoners at the camp in 1990 and 1991. In one case, a writer named Lin Ziyang and a student named Jiang Pingchao were beaten with electric baton and whip for four hours and then made to stand with their hands raised above their heads for three hours until they collapsed. Then they were dragged on the ground with their hands tied behind their backs until their legs and feet were covered with blood and dirt. Another inmate was beaten for six hours for refusing to do hard labor. When he continued to resist, he was beaten with an electric baton and a whip for several hours.[104]

## Many Dissidents Go Underground

Since open dissent is so dangerous, dissidents often operate underground or form illegal groups. Such groups are in all probability very small and only loosely organized, but they are enough to cause concern to the authorities. Their members, when caught, are treated as counter-revolutionaries. Information on the existence and operation of such groups is hard to come by, and what little is known to the outside world is at best fragmentary and hard to verify. The official press does not report news of this type, except when sentences are announced after secret trials. Even then, few details are released. But enough reports have come out of China through different channels over time to lend credence to the existence of some groups, formed largely by young intellectuals who are critical of the government and who advocate democracy out of patriotic idealism. Though their goals are far from insurrectionary, they are often thrown in jail for merely exercising what amounts to their freedom of speech by Western standards (a right that is also guaranteed by the Chinese Constitution).

According to the Hong Kong newspaper *South China Morning Post* on August 20, 1993, security police in Shanghai discovered a dissident group in April 1992. Three members of the group were arrested and sentenced to prison terms from one to five years. The underground group was known as China Alliance Society (Zhongguo Tongmenghui) and the three imprisoned members were Zhou Yuan, Liu Kai, and Tang Weihua, the Hong Kong newspaper reported. All three were charged with counterrevolutionary crimes. One, Zhou Yuan, appealed the sentence to the Shanghai Supreme People's Court but was rebuffed.[105]

United Press International (UPI) reported on October 18 that trials of members of underground dissident groups were beginning in several major cities, including Shanghai and Wuhan in central China. According to a secret court document obtained by UPI, the Wuhan Intermediate People's Court sentenced the leader of a dissident group to five years for advocating multiparty democracy in China. The dissident, Zhang Mingpeng, was secretly tried on sedition charges. In the sentencing document, Zhang was named the alleged leader of a heretofore unknown Republican Party (Gonghe Dang). Twelve other members of the party were also named and were thought to be charged with the same crime. Zhang, thirty-seven, is said to have more than thirty followers scattered over China. According to the document, Zhang was sentenced to five years in prison and stripped of his civil rights for two additional years for "organizing a counter-revolutionary group."[106]

Apparently a hardened dissident intellectual, Zhang was first sent to a labor camp in 1980 for three years of "education through labor" for publishing a magazine without a permit. He was arrested again in July 1992, according to court documents, which charged that his anti-government activities began in 1991 and continued for sixteen months until the time of his arrest. In Beijing, according to UPI, trials of sixteen other dissidents on counterrevolutionary charges, first postponed because of concerns about their possible adverse impact on China's bid to host the 2000 Olympic Games, were also under way. No information was available, however, to verify whether the defendants were connected to Zhang's group. The new wave of trials, said UPI, clearly indicated that Beijing was determined to suppress any opposition despite Western efforts to engage the government to improve human rights in China.[107]

Arrests continued into mid-November, when the authors of the now widely circulated "Peace Charter" (see Appendix 1) and several others associated with the document were arrested in Beijing and the city of Xian in northwest China. On November 14, Qin Yongming and Yang Zhou, two authors of the charter, which urged a multiparty political system in China, were arrested in Beijing hours after they unveiled the document. The same day, a group of democracy campaigners gathered in Xian and issued a statement asserting that "human rights conditions in China are deplorable" and urging the people to make a "concerted effort to uphold human rights." Many of the signers of the statement were survivors of the June 1989 Tiananmen Massacre, including Zheng Xuguan, who was among the twenty-one student leaders included on the most-wanted list and who served a two-year sentence after his arrest in August 1989.

The gathering was billed as the most important meeting of dissidents since the 1989 Tiananmen suppression of the democracy movement. The group in its statement called for "rational, nonviolent means" in an effort to improve human rights conditions in China. Zheng hailed from Xian and was a student leader at the Beijing College of Aeronautics at the time of the 1989 military crackdown. According to one source familiar with the democracy movement, Zheng's group in Xian did not fully agree with the point of view in the Peace Charter, indicating that the democracy movement, if it was a movement at all, encompassed many diverse views. However, Zheng was later arrested when he traveled to Beijing, where he allegedly met with people from the Peace Charter group.[108] The arrests of the authors of the Peace Charter and the Xian student leader took place when German Chancellor Helmut Kohl was visiting Beijing and only days before President Clinton and Chinese President Jiang Zemin were to meet at the Asian-Pacific Economic Cooperation (APEC) meeting in Seattle. "All this once again indicates that while pushing economic reform, the Chinese government has no intention to carry out political reform at the same time," observed a veteran Western diplomat in Beijing.[109]

After more than three months in detention, in January 1994 Qin Yongming, one of the two authors of the Peace Charter, was sentenced to two years of "education through labor." His crime was "de-stabilizing society and attempting to create turmoil."[110] Serving the two-year term in "Hewan Labor Camp" in Wuhan, Qin was tortured by camp guards and possibly crippled, according to Qin's wife Li Jingfang, who appealed to the authorities for permission for her husband to receive medical attention outside the camp.

In an appeal to the National People's Congress, Li said after she filed papers with the Wuhan People's Court in March 1994 to appeal her husband's sentence, Qin began to receive "special treatment" at the camp. He was locked up in a room on the second floor and not allowed to talk to anyone, to listen to the radio, or to go downstairs, and all his mail was intercepted. During jail visits, Li said, security guards searched her in an offensive way and did not allow her to bring her son. Referring to her appeal to the courts, the guards told her, "If you continue to do this, you had better arrange to have someone care for your son," a not-too-subtle threat that she might be thrown in jail. During a visit on July 15, Li said she learned that Qin was savagely beaten on June 8 and he was still bleeding from the lower parts of his body. On July 20, when Qin asked for medical attention as the injuries turned worse, he received more beating. This time, his testicles were smashed, Li said in her appeal.[111]

The human rights group Asia Watch issued a report in March 1993 on certain underground groups in China and their immediate suppression by the authorities. They were identified as the Freedom and Democratic Party, the Chinese Socialist Democratic Party, the China Free Labor Union, the China Progressive Union, and the Federation of Chinese Civil Groups. These groups, though small and suppressed by the government, were scattered widely over China. Their members, mostly young and educated, advocated changes by peaceful means and claimed constitutional guarantees of their rights to free speech and association. The Freedom and Democratic Party, for example, issued a statement on human rights conditions in China at the time of then U.S.

Secretary of State James Baker's visit in 1991. The group also petitioned the National People's Congress in 1992 for freedom of the press and release of political prisoners. The China Free Labor Union, suppressed in June 1992, advocated workers' inherent rights to form their own unions and contacted the International Labor Organization in Geneva for support of its cause. Though many groups were based in Beijing, others were found elsewhere. The Chinese Socialist Democratic Party, according to the Asia Watch report, was based in Lanzhou in the northwest, and the Federation of Chinese Civil Groups was formed in Hunan in central China and claimed to have members in other provinces.[112]

The government was especially nervous about political dissidents from other cities traveling to Beijing where they would presumably meet with locally based democracy groups. Although far-fetched, this worry would recall in the mind of the aging leaders the specter of the so-called "link-ups" (chuanlian). Link-ups occurred during the heyday of the Cultural Revolution in the 1960s, when millions of rampaging Red Guards from others parts of China egged on by Mao as his little rebels, traveled to the nation's capital to "exchange revolutionary experiences." The Red Guard "link-ups" got completely out of hand, causing national chaos. Eventually, the army had to be called in to restore order. It subsequently banished the radicalized Red Guards to the countryside. The authorities clearly did not want to see a recurrence of that, however remote the likelihood. To forestall any such development, political dissidents in other parts of China were barred from the nation's capital. The Xian group, later known as the Group to Protect Chinese Human Rights, is a case in point. Despite its non-violent goals and its professed differences with the Peace Charter group in Beijing, its members were arrested or quietly disappeared when they reached Beijing.

The rigid, hard-line position of the government on political freedom stood in sharp contrast to the seemingly free-for-all scene in other areas, abetted by the economic reform. Ma Shaohua, one of the leaders of the Xian group, told a Western journalist in Beijing on December 29 that China must respect human rights and carry out democratic reform "before it is too late." Ma took part in the 1989 Tiananmen democracy movement and spent eighteen months in prison after the military crackdown. In a secret interview with the Agence France Presse (AFP), Ma said the reason the Chinese government would not tolerate a single dissident was that "they know that the situation in China is increasingly unstable and it is also because of this that they are arresting dissidents." Ma stressed that he was not opposed to the Chinese Communist Party. "We don't advocate violent overthrow of the government; we merely want to reform the Party before it is too late," he said.[113]

Speaking of the mood among intellectuals, the twenty-five-year-old democracy campaigner said many people in China today favored modern capitalism, meaning "democracy and market economy." "We hope to change the present system according to popular will through a bloodless way," he said. He paraphrased a familiar Mao quotation during the early days of the Communist movement in China ("A spark can light a prairie fire.") to warn that "the situation in China is serious today and a breeze can turn into a tempestuous storm through the land."[114] Taking issue with Beijing's official line that it is more important to provide 1 billion Chinese people with food, clothing, and shelter than with human rights, Ma said, "Of course, the economy is changing and millions are living better," but the vast majority of the Chinese people had neither power nor money. "The economic reform in large part benefits only the families of high government officials and corrupt cadres," he said. Ma disappeared soon after the interview.[115] He was later reported to have been arrested in Tianjin, a city east of Beijing.

## Endnotes

1. Cited in Patrick E. Tyler, "A Dissident's Letter from Prison," *New York Times*, October 24, 1993, Section 1, p. 8.

2. Cited in Nicholas D. Kristof, "Chinese Dissident's Odyssey: In and Out of Prison, Now Trying to Flee Abroad," *New York Times*, July 19, 1993, p. A9.

3. Cited in "Qin Youngming's Wife Appeals Prison Torture to NPC," *Shih-chieh Jih-pao*, August 28, 1994, p. A18.

4. Wang was rearrested in May 1995 and in October 1996 was sentenced to eleven years in prison. See Patrick E. Tyler, "Chinese Verdict Points to an Era of Harsh Rule," *New York Times,* October 31, 1996, p. A1.

5. Wei Jingsheng, "Democracy or New Dictatorship?" *Freedom Appeal* (New York), No. 1, September-October 1979, p. 11.

6. For further details, see Ta-ling Lee and John F. Copper, *Reform in Reverse: Human Rights in the People's Republic of China, 1986/87* (Baltimore: University of Maryland School of Law, 1987), pp. 96–98.

7. Through the 1980s, Ta-ling Lee, one of the coauthors of the book, interviewed many young Chinese, both in China and among Chinese students in the United States, and found that many had never heard Wei Jingsheng's name. Wei, rearrested in April 1995, has been nominated by many U.S. lawmakers and European parliamentarians for the Nobel Peace Prize. See "58 U.S. Lawmakers Nominate Wei for Nobel Peace Prize," *Shih-chieh Jih-pao* (World Journal) (New York), October 19, 1994, p. A2. On November 17, 1994, he was awarded, in absentia, the Robert F. Kennedy Human Rights Award, along with another jailed Chinese human rights campaigner, Ren Wanding. See "Wei Jingsheng, Ren Wanding Receiving RFK Human Rights Award," *Shih-chieh Jih-pao*, November 18, 1994, p. A20.

8. Ta-ling Lee and John F. Copper, *Failure of Democracy Movement: Human Rights in the People's Republic of China, 1988-1989* (Baltimore, MD: University of Maryland School of Law Occasional Papers/Reprints Series in Contemporary Asian Studies, 1991), p. 9.

9. "Human Rights in China Welcomes Release of Wei Jingsheng," *Shih-chieh*

*Jih-pao*, September 16, 1993, p. A2.

10. "Wei Secluded in Hostel After Release," *Shih-chieh Jih-pao*, September 16, 1993, p. A1.

11. Patrick E. Tyler, "Chinese Dissident Emerges, Still Unbowed," *New York Times*, September 21, 1993, p. A1.

12. "Many More Are Still in Prison," *Shih-chieh Jih-pao*, September 15, 1993, p. A1. Wang Juntao, Chen Ziming, and Liu Gang were released in 1994 and Bao Tong was released in June 1996. See the latter part of this chapter.

13. Tyler, "Chinese Dissident Emerges."

14. Ibid.

15. Ibid.

16. Patrick E. Tyler, "China Says Dissident Is Freed, but Family Waits," *New York Times*, September 15, 1993, p. A3.

17. Ibid.

18. Ibid.

19. Wei Jingsheng, "A Hostage to the Olympics," *New York Times*, March 1, 1994, p. A23.

20. Ibid.

21. "Wei Jingsheng: Fighting Spirits Undiminished by 15 Years of Imprisonment," *Shih-chieh Jih-pao*, October 3, 1993, p. A3.

22. "Wei Vows to Continue Democracy Movement," *Shih-chieh Jih-pao*, October 23, 1993, p. A2.

23. Ibid.

24. Patrick E. Tyler, "A Dissident's Letters from Prison to Beijing Will Appear in China," *New York Times*, October 24, 1993, p. 8.

25. Ibid.

26. Ibid.

27. "What Is Wei Jingsheng Thinking?" *Shih-chieh Jih-pao*, December 6, 1993, p. D18.

28. Ibid.

29. Wei Jingsheng, "The Wolf and the Lamb," *New York Times*, November 18, 1993, p. A27.

30. Patrick E. Tyler, "Chinese Dissident Warned by Beijing," *New York Times*, December 12, 1993, p. 7.

31. Patrick E. Tyler, "Crossroads for China," *New York Times*, January 29, 1994, p. 1.

32. Patrick E. Tyler, "Highest U.S. Rights Official Meets with Leading Chinese Dissident," *New York Times*, February 28, 1994, p. A2.

33. Patrick E. Tyler, "China Arrests Leading Dissident Despite U.S. Warning on Rights," *New York Times*, March 5, 1994, p. 1.

34. Patrick E. Tyler, "Chinese Dissident Faces Possibility of New Charges," *New York Times*, April 7, 1994, p. A12.

35. Ibid.

36. Ibid. Wei remained under detention for nearly two years after his rearrest, with no official charges filed. Chinese criminal law requires the release of a suspect from detention if no official charges are filed within 90 days. This provision, however, is routinely ignored by the authorities.

37. "Seeds of Subversion," *The Economist*, May 28, 1994, p. 32.

38. Ibid.

39. Ibid.

40. For details of the trial, see John F. Copper and Ta-ling Lee, *Tiananmen Aftermath: Human Rights in the People's Republic of China, 1990* (Baltimore, MD: University of Maryland School of Law Occasional Papers/Reprints Series

in Contemporary Asian Studies, 1992), pp. 90–92.

41. Ibid.

42. Sheryl WuDunn, "China Frees Top Dissident of '89 Protests," *New York Times*, February 18, 1993, p. A2.

43. Ibid.

44. "Wang Dan Shows No Regret," *Shih-chieh Jih-pao*, February 18, 1993, p. 2.

45. Ibid.

46. Ibid.

47. "Wang Dan Hopes to See Democracy at Work in Hong Kong and Taiwan," *Shih-chieh Jih-pao*, February 19, 1993, p. 2.

48. "Wang Dan Dedicates Himself to Democracy Movement," *Shih-chieh Jih-pao*, March 4, 1993, p. 2.

49. "Wang Dan 'Vacations' in Haikou," *Shih-chieh Jih-pao*, March 20, 1993, p. 18.

50. "Wang Dan Barred from Traveling South," *Shih-chieh Jih-pao*, April 24, 1993, p. 18.

51. "Ma Shaofang, Student Leader, Arrested," *Shih-chieh Jih-pao*, April 29, 1993, p. 18.

52. Nicholas D. Kristof, "Chinese Dissident's Odyssey: In and out of Prison, Now Trying to Flee Abroad," *New York Times*, July 19, 1993, p. A9.

53. Ibid.

54. Ibid.

55. Ibid.

56. Ibid.

57. "Three Shanghai Dissidents Seized," *Shih-chieh Jih-pao*, June 29, 1993, p. A18.

58. "Shanghai Dissident Fu Shenqi Gets 3-Year Reform-Through-Labor," *Shih-chieh Jih-pao*, July 12, 1993, p. A2.

59. Nicholas D. Kristof, "Signaling New Hard Line, China Jails a Dissident," *New York Times*, July 12, 1993, p. A9.

60. "Canton to Try Three Dissidents," *Shih-chieh Jih-pao*, July 8, 1993, p. A18.

61. Sheryl WuDunn, "Chinese Dissident Released; Bow to U.S. Is Seen," *New York Times*, May 27, 1993, p. A5.

62. Ibid.

63. "Xu Wenli Holds Fast to Democratic Ideals," *Shih-chieh Jih-pao*, May 27, 1993, p. A2.

64. "Yu Zhuo Arrested on Counterrevolutionary Charges," *Shih-chieh Jih-pao*, June 23, 1993, p. A18.

65. Nicholas D. Kristof, "4 Years After Tiananmen, the Hard Line Is Cracking," *New York Times*, June 1, 1993, p. A1.

66. "Liu Gang Tortured at Labor Camp," *Shih-chieh Jih-pao*, May 13, 1993, p. A2.

67. Nicholas D. Kristof, "China Raises a Great Wall: Can Dissident Scale It?" *New York Times*, August 20, 1993, p. A4.

68. On his imprisonment, see Ta-ling Lee and John F. Copper, *The Bamboo Gulag: Human Rights in the People's Republic of China, 1991–1992* (Baltimore, MD: University of Maryland School of Law Occasional Papers/Reprints Series in Contemporary Asian Studies, 1994), p. 80.

69. Kristof, "China Raises a Great Wall."

70. "China Revokes Passport of Expelled Labor Leader," *New York Times*, August 22, 1993, p. 6.

71. Kristof, "China Raises a Great Wall."

72. "Zhang Weiguo, Dissident Journalist, Arrives in U.S.," *Shih-chieh Jih-pao*, February 12, 1993. p. 2.

73. "Government Bars 8 Types of Chinese from Abroad," *Shih-chieh Jih-pao*, December 1, 1993, p. A1.

74. "Li Sanyuan Confirms Beijing Blacklist," *Shih-chieh Jih-pao*, July 4, 1993, p. A2.

75. "Dissident-Turned Entrepreneur Constantly Harassed," *Shih-chieh Jih-pao*, July 4, 1993, p. A2.

76. "Bao Zunxin Fails to Get Job Back," *Shih-chieh Jih-pao*, July 21, 1993, p. A16.

77. Patrick E. Tyler, "China Releases Dissident and Sends Him to U.S. for Treatment," *New York Times*, April 24, 1994, p. 6.

78. "China Releases 3 Prisoners in Gesture to U.S.," *New York Times*, February 5, 1994, p. 5.

79. "Chinese Frees 3 Political Prisoners," *New Haven Register*, February 5, 1994, p. A10.

80. Ibid.

81. "Yuan Hongbing and Zhou Guoqiang Face Anti-Government Charges," *Shih-chieh Jih-pao*, May 18, 1994, p. 18.

82. "Wang Jiaqi, Labor Union Organizer, Escapes to U.S.," *Shih-chieh Jih-pao*, June 24, 1994, p. A2.

83. "Zhou Guoqiang, Given Three Years, Sues the Government," *Shih-chieh Jih-pao*, December 24, 1994, p. A18.

84. Patrick E. Tyler, "Abuses of Rights Persist in China Despite U.S. Pleas," *New York Times*, August 29, 1994, p. A1.

85. Patrick E. Tyler, "7 Chinese Intellectuals Appeal for End to Political Repression," *New York Times*, March 11, 1994, p. 1.

86. Xu Liangying, "Chinese Officialdom's Ridiculous and Unique Conception of Human Rights," *China Rights Forum* (New York), Summer 1994, pp. 10–11.

87. Ding Zilin, "Diaries, March 7 to March 16," *Beijing Spring* (New York), May 1994, pp. 7–10.

88. Philip Shenon, "Prison Sentences Seem Likely in Trial of 14 Chinese Dissidents," *New York Times*, July 24, 1994, p. 15.

89. Ibid.

90. "Zhou Guoqiang Given 3 Years Education Through Labor," *Shih-chieh Jih-pao*, December 24, 1994, p. A18.

91. "Nine Chinese Dissidents Sentenced to Prison Terms," *Shih-chieh Jih-pao*, December 16, 1994, p. A2.

92. "Hard Wind from Beijing," *New York Times* editorial, December 20, 1994, p. A22.

93. "Zhou Shaowu and Huang Jingang Disappear," *Shih-chieh Jih-pao*, July 15, 1993, p. A18.

94. "Beijing University Students Smash Bottles," *Shih-chieh Jih-pao*, June 4, 1993, p. A1.

95. "Security Tightened for Tiananmen Anniversary," *Shih-chieh Jih-pao*, May 29, 1993, p. A2.

96. "Tiananmen Figure Convicted," *New York Times*, October 12, 1993, p. A10.

97. "On Anniversary, Security Is Tight in Tiananmen Square," *International Herald Tribune*, June 4–5, 1994, p. 7.

98. Ibid.

99. Patrick E. Tyler, "China Tries to Blot Out Memories of 1989," *New York Times*, June 5, 1994, p. 16.

100. Lena H. Sun, "Tiananmen Recalled: A Son Lost, A Cause Born," *International Herald Tribune*, June 1, 1994, p. 1.

101. Ibid.

102. Ibid.

103. "Amnesty International Reveals Tiananmen Atrocity," *Shih-chieh Jih-pao*, May 31, 1994, p. A1.

104. Ibid.

105. "Shanghai Dissident Group Members Sentenced to Prison Terms," *Shih-chieh Jih-pao*, August 22, 1993, p. A2.

106. "Beijing Broadens Campaign Against Democracy Movement," *Shih-chieh Jih-pao*, October 19, 1993, p. A2.

107. Ibid.

108. "Xian Democracy Movement Leader Zheng Xuguang Arrested in Beijing," *Shih-chieh Jih-pao*, November 28, 1993, p. A16.

109. "Peace Charter Authors Arrested in Beijing," *Shih-chieh Jih-pao*, November 17, 1993, p. A2.

110. "Qin Yongming Sentenced to Two Years of Hard Labor," *Shih-chieh Jih-pao*, January 25, 1994, p. A18.

111. "Qin Yongming's Wife Appeals Prison Torture to NPC," *Shih-chieh Jih-pao*, August 28, 1994, p. A 18.

112. "Underground Groups Reported in Mainland China," *Shih-chieh Jih-pao*, March 3, 1993, p. 2.

113. "Ma Shaohua Urges Respect for Human Rights," *Shih-chieh Jih-pao*, December 1, 1993, p. A18.

114. Ibid.

115. "Ma Shaohua Disappears," *Shih-chieh Jih-pao*, December 2, 1993, p. A8.

# Chapter 4

# Freedom of Speech and Human Rights

The hostile forces outside our country have never stopped endangering the safety of our country. They take advantage of our policies of reform and openness to get hold of our political, economic, and scientific secrets through different channels and try all means to infiltrate, split, and damage us. If we lose vigilance and let them succeed, the safety of our country will not be assured.

—*People's Daily*[1]

We know they are listening. They give us our rice bowl, and we don't want it broken.

—A Shanghai talk show host referring to government censors[2]

## Introduction

Freedom of speech, as part of overall political reform, saw only limited improvement during 1993 and 1994. It is true that compared with the worst Maoist days of suppression and obscurantism in the past, people enjoyed a measure of freedom like never before in terms of what they could say and publish. When measured against the pace of economic development, however, freedom of speech lagged. This incongruity reflected a phenomenon evident since the beginning of Deng Xiaoping's reform in 1978: economic relaxation paired with political control. People were allowed to make money, but were not allowed to challenge the supremacy of the party.

For Deng's brand of "socialism with Chinese characteristics" to survive after the demise of communism else everywhere in the world, the leadership had to be especially jittery about losing control. Besieged by a rising tide of yearning for democracy, Beijing leaders, as the sole guardian of dying socialism, found themselves surrounded by "hostile" forces out to get China. These "hostile" forces, mainly Western democracies with their Chinese followers, were trying to promote "peaceful evolution" in China, meaning the end of Communist rule, or so Chinese leaders proclaimed. The leadership also believed, perhaps not completely without foundation, that many in the West both in and out of government, regarding a strong China as a threat, were trying to contain China and thwart its growth.[3]

Beijing leaders hoped that whipping up nationalistic sentiment amongst the Chinese would provide a new rallying point for all of China and would serve to replace the discarded, dead ideology—communism. To fight a "peaceful evolution," any remote indication of opposition to the Beijing authorities must be eradicated. To counter the "anti-China" plots by other nations, the government had to maintain vigilance and protect the people from undesirable outside influence. This attitude resulted in continued abuses of human rights, ranging from curbing freedom of speech and information to spying on foreign journalists in China and prosecution of those Chinese having contact with them, in the name of nationalism.

### Anti-China Plot by "American Hegemonists"

Standing members of the Party Politburo fanned out to the provinces to hold meetings with local leaders, urging greater vigilance against the "anti-China plot of American hegemonists," in April and May 1993. The leadership must have concluded, perhaps not without reason, that as the only superpower in the post-Cold War world, the United States was evolving a set of new global strategies, treating China as a potential future adversary. The United States, according to this view, was attempting to "infiltrate, sabotage, and encircle" China by ideological, economic, and military means. A confidential document prepared by the party propaganda department, entitled "Hostile U.S. Strategy Against China," was issued to the provinces and major military regions in May 1993. The document outlined the forceful argument that the United States was turning its attention to China as its main adversary in formulating its new global strategy after the collapse of the Soviet Union. It warned that the United States was plotting to "turn China into another Russia" in ten to fifteen years. According to the document, Washington planned:

1. to influence and instigate Japan and Korea to encircle China;
2. to arm Taiwan to further separate it from China;
3. to use trade as a means of interfering in China's domestic affairs;
4. to turn Hong Kong into an anti-China springboard for the United States and Britain;

5. to obstruct China's economic development by trying to keep China out of world trade organizations;
6. to instigate the Western allies to follow its policies of fomenting drastic changes in China;
7. to broadcast anti-China propaganda via the Voice of America;
8. to establish Radio Asia to step up anti-China propaganda;
9. to infiltrate Chinese religious groups to carry out anti-China activities;
10. to provide financial and political support to exiled anti-China groups abroad;
11. to help groups abroad return to China to infiltrate factories and rural areas for illegal activities; and
12. to support the Dalai Lama's campaign for Tibetan independence and anticommunist activities.[4]

To counter the threat of "foreign hostile forces" and their allies inside China, the State Council promulgated bylaws of the National Security Act on June 4, 1993, defining "hostile groups" and "activities endangering national security" which subjected violators to very severe penalties. According to the by-laws, "hostile groups" broadly covers all groups "hostile to the Chinese government and its socialist system." "Activities endangering national security" include: (1) fabricating or distorting facts; (2) publishing writings, expressing opinions, or making audio or video broadcasts that endanger national security; (3) instigating disputes and splits between nationalities; and (4) illegally meeting with foreigners if under suspicion of engaging in anti-government activities.[5]

A conference on state security was held in Beijing in early October 1993. The main theme of the conference was how to protect China against "hostile foreign forces." Underscoring the importance of the five-day conference, top leaders, from President Jiang Zemin and Premier Li Peng on down, including most standing members of the Party Politburo, were present to urge heightened vigilance. A feeling of insecurity, whether genuine or as a pretext for increased control, permeated the conference. That feeling was perhaps best summed up in a commentary in the official *People's Daily* that coincided with the conference:

> The hostile forces outside our country have never stopped endangering the safety of our country. They take advantage of our policies of reform and openness to get hold of our political, economic and scientific secrets through different channels and try all means to infiltrate, split, and damage us. If we lose vigilance and let them succeed, the safety of our country will not be assured.[6]

*People's Daily* did not point fingers. Yet it blasted the U.S. Congress for sabotaging its bid to host the 2000 Olympic Games by unjustifiably bringing up human rights issues and China's nuclear tests. Thus the reader understood that "hostile forces" meant the United States.

Fallout included punishment of Chinese citizens making contact with foreign journalists. On July 29, 1993, the Beijing Intermediate People's Court sentenced Bai Weiji, a former Foreign Ministry employee, to ten years in prison for "illegally providing national secrets to a foreigner." Bai's wife, Zhao Lei, received six years for the same crime.[7] Lena H. Sun, the Beijing bureau chief of the Washington *Post,* to whom Bai had allegedly passed national secrets, said the information she received related only to mundane matters.[8] A month later, the same court sentenced Wu Shisheng, a former editor of the official Xinhua News Agency, to life in prison for allegedly providing a "top secret" document to a correspondent. The top secret document turned out to be a political report Jiang Zemin delivered to the 14th Party Congress which had appeared in the Hong Kong newspaper. Wu's wife was given six years.[9]

Other measures were taken: censorship, jamming foreign broadcasts, and banning satellite dishes. The March 21, 1994 issue of *Newsweek*, featuring Wei Jingsheng, on its cover, was banned. China Books and Periodicals Import and Export Company, the general distributor of all foreign publications in China, said the issue "has some problems."[10] In July 1994, VOA Director Jeffrey Cowan reported "intense jamming of VOA," particularly broadcasts in Mandarin.[11] This violated conditions the U.S. had set to extend MFN trade status to China in 1993. However, President Clinton de-linked the renewal of the MFN and human rights issues in May 1994. The immediate result was the resumption of jamming. Still, Cowan reported that "millions of our listeners in East and S.E. Asia rely on VOA Mandarin broadcasts to provide an accurate and objective source of news and information about China, America, and the world."[12] Harrison Ford's *Fugitive* was banned in November 1994. Officials did not want U.S. film makers to "influence future generations of Chinese with Western thinking," according to the official *China Business Times.*[13]

A far more difficult problem for the "Beijing thought police" was Western television programs picked up in China by satellite dishes. Policing the information highway proved to be too daunting a task for government authorities. Despite efforts by hard-liners in the Ministry of Radio, Film, and Television to fight "spiritual pollution" from the West, it looked as though by late 1993, more than a decade after Deng Xiaoping had instituted his policy of opening to the West, the information explosion genie had already been out of the bottle too long for the authorities to ever be able to put it back in. Although foreign satellite programs were officially banned by the government, local authorities, particularly in southern China, were slow in carrying out Beijing's orders and few people paid attention to the ban. As a result, satellite dishes flourished and Western television programs, from CNN and BBC to Japan's NHK and Hong Kong's Star Television, were routinely seen in ordinary homes.

No one really knew just how many satellite dishes there were in China, but at the time the ban was reiterated in late 1993, it was estimated that there were more than 500,000. Because of numerous cable hookups in apartment buildings and in official compounds, however, subscribers to multichannel systems may have run into tens of millions. One estimate put the audience in southern China alone at well over 20 million.[14] After the Australian media tycoon, Rupert Murdoch, acquired satellite stations in Hong Kong in late 1993, with an eye to the vast market in China, the government issued new regulations, reiterating the previous ban on installing satellite dishes by private households. In January 1994, the Ministry of Public Security and the Ministry of State Security were ordered to help implement the ban, but the results were less than satisfactory.[15] Privileged government officials and retired public functionaries were often among the worst offenders. In the Fang Village neighborhood of south Beijing, for example, apartment buildings housing families of retired officers of the dreaded public security bureau were wired up for satellite programming from the United States, Britain, and Hong Kong. Government officials even used public funds to install satellite dishes for personal use.[16] In addition, satellite dishes were produced by state-owned companies, including the powerful People's Liberation Army factories, which recently had been converted to produce consumer products to cash in on this lucrative market.[17]

### Books and Movies Banned

At a three-day joint conference in March 1993, the Party Propaganda Department and the Information and Publication Administration under the State Council decided to ban unauthorized reporting on the personal lives of national leaders as well as "nude pictorials." Officials at the conference said some books on national and party leaders contained serious inaccuracies on policy matters, while others exaggerated aspects of their personal lives. Such publications "damage the image of leaders and the interest of the party and state," they asserted. They also called attention to the appearance of a number of "nude pictorials" aimed at the youth market containing "obscene and pornographic materials." These publications, put out by enterprising merchants for quick profits, were harmful to the mental and physical health of adolescents and should be banned, they said. The officials stressed the importance of "correct guidance" to the publishers to ensure "correct viewpoints and contents."[18] In a subsequent report, Xinhua counted thirty-seven pictorial books on national leaders put out by twenty-seven publishing houses in 1992 without approval. The news agency singled out *Mao Anlong, Son of Mao Zedong,* a book purported to be on one of

Mao's alleged illegitimate sons, published by the Inner Mongolia People's Publishing House. Xinhua accused the author of "serious distortion of facts" and "creating a myth around the national leader and spreading superstitious ideas" to satisfy the curiosity of the public.[19]

Meanwhile the Ministry of Culture clamped down on unauthorized cultural activities, particularly those involving cultural groups from foreign countries. In a May 1993 circular, the ministry said some organizations ignored government regulations when they held competitions, exhibits, or performances without approval. Some even organized international competition or invited foreign groups to perform in China, the ministry said, characterizing some groups as shoddy and motivated only by profit. The ministry reiterated a previous directive that all cultural activities must be first approved.[20]

Radio call-in shows suddenly exploded onto the Chinese news scene in a number of major cities in the Spring of 1993. In Shanghai, the newly launched Radio Orient was able to reach a potential audience of over 100 million in China's largest city and the nearby provinces. The station received 1,000 letters a day and operated four busy call-in lines, tackling topics from romance and marriage to business and careers. However, understandably there was nothing on democracy or human rights. In any case, there was a 14-second delay in the broadcast so that anything untoward could be easily censored.

Observers regarded talk show radio as a small step toward the building of a civil society in China. After four decades of producing mush, radio stations and newspapers were taking advantage of the opening to the West to test the new limits. But those who were doing the testing were realistic. "The leaders give us a lot of freedom," Zhang Qian, a Radio Orient host said, "but we also know they are listening." She then said bluntly: "They give us our rice bowl, and we don't want it broken."[21]

Yang Minghua, head of news programs at Radio Orient, suggested that evading the censors was easier for radio shows than for newspapers. If a reporter at *Wen Hui Bao* or *Liberation Daily*, two of Shanghai's biggest newspapers, wanted to write a critical story about a company, the reporter would first have to submit the story to the company, he disclosed. "Then the company [would] get to work and soon," he said sarcastically, "the critical article [would] be turned into a tribute." With radio, however, "we are on the air before they can stop us."[22]

During the first six months of 1994, according to Yu Youxian, director of the Press and Publication Administration under the State Council, several dozen newspapers, periodicals, and books were banned and several publishing companies were ordered to close. He cited reasons ranging from "leaking state secrets" to "playing up pornography and violence."[23]

Ding Guangen, a powerful member of the Party Politburo and Central Secretariat in charge of propaganda, reiterated the government views on freedom of the press in August 1994. Speaking to a press delegation from Hong Kong, Ding declared, "Freedom does not mean that a person can say what he thinks." Freedom can only be exercised within the framework of the law, which "each country establishes according to its conditions," he stressed. Underscoring Beijing's long-held position on freedom of the press, Ding called on all newspapers in the country to play their role essentially as a tool of the government: to foster solidarity and to promote stability. "It will not do if newspapers instigate people against solidarity everyday," he warned. Ding stressed that no newspapers in any country or region could enjoy absolute freedom; all newspapers must follow "the aspirations of the people and state interests," he declared.[24]

The Party Propaganda Department tightened censorship of the media in late September 1994 in an effort to promote stability and to silence "discordant voices." The stepped-up control followed a seminar on media attended by propaganda chiefs from many cities. There, Ding Guangen, who was also head of the Party Propaganda Department, laid down comprehensive guidelines for checking with government authorities before releasing "potentially destabilizing news." Editors were told to consult with the Propaganda Department when they had doubts about political stories. In addition, to help "unify the national will" in fighting inflation, the activities and speeches of liberal economists were kept off the official press. Efforts were also stepped up against "infiltration" by foreign publications and broadcasts, including the long-delayed implementation of the ban on satellite dishes by private households. The drafting of a press law, begun in 1985, was further delayed.[25]

The Party Propaganda Department and such government agencies as the Press and Publication Administration, the Ministry of Posts and Telecommunications, and the State Administration for Industry and Commerce promulgated many regulations in 1994 aimed at fighting what the authorities called "conspicuous problems" in the newspaper business. These regulations included the "Circular on Strengthening the Management of Internal Newspapers and Journals," the "Circular on Banning the Publishing and Distributing of Commercial Publicity Material in a Newspaper Format and Strengthening Management over Printed Advertisement Material," and the "Circular on Banning the Sale of Partial Pages of Newspaper." Xinhua provided a sample of what it regarded a "conspicuous problems" in the newspaper market: Some newspapers "blindly pursue" profit by carrying a "great quantity of items on murder and pornography cases"; some did not hesitate to "fool readers with fraudulent news items"; and some internal newspapers and journals (limited to party members or government employees) went on market openly and "engaged in advertising and other business activities."[26] It is well known that rampant commercialism, and degeneration of journalism as a profession have become a serious problem in

China brought on by the economic reform; still, the situation also provided a convenient pretext for curtailing freedom of the press.

Although the press remained very much under party control, given the scope of economic change, it was only natural that the authorities would find it increasingly difficult to continue the tight rein, according to Hu Jiwei, former head of *People's Daily*, the party mouthpiece. In the late 1970s and early 1980s, Hu, as director of the most important party newspaper in China, set in motion a series of measures at the newspaper in line with his understanding of Deng's reform policies. One of his best-known innovations was to add a letters to the editor page to the otherwise dull paper. He published letters from the public complaining about matters in everyday life ranging from poor garbage collection to corrupt cadres at the lower levels of government. This feature helped push the circulation of the paper to more than 7 million. After 1984, Hu also worked at the National People's Congress, where he was in charge of drafting a press law. He was dismissed from all his positions after the 1989 military crackdown in Tiananmen, when his reformist views came under criticism by hard-liners in power.

Partially rehabilitated in 1993, Hu was allowed to travel to the United States in July at the invitation of the American Enterprise Institute to study freedom of the press. Although there were signs of new vigor in the press after nearly two decades of economic reform, Hu said three "fundamental problems" remained in China in the years since the 1989 crush of the democracy movement. First, the official Xinhua News Agency was in control of all news releases, and newspapers were not allowed to print anything not released by Xinhua. Second, political commentary was controlled by *People's Daily* and all newspapers still had to follow its lead. Third, the Left remained in control of the media regarding ideological matters and there was only one voice: tolerate no dissent.[27]

The reimposition of control over major party newspapers cost them dearly, with the circulation of the *People's Daily*, for example, dropping from 7 million to 2 million. The loss of government subsidies added to the financial woes. As a result, enterprising editors at major newspapers came up with a novel idea: publishing tabloids to evade party control as a new way to subsidize the main papers. Hu claimed that since tabloids were not subject to stringent rules, and were more lively and appealing with their controversial and scandalous stories, they could, in due course, force change on the major papers.[28]

Party censors were alert to the trends. An internal circular in July 1993 ordered newspapers to cut down on negative reports about problems arising from reform, such as angry peasants and financial scandals. An official dealing with propaganda reiterated a journalist's duties this way: "to spread the ideas of Deng Xiaoping, to provide reliable and useful information," to educate readers about the "socialist market economy," and to disseminate a "correct outlook on life."[29]

Far from living up the official standards, however, journalists were corrupted by Deng's socialist market economy. Some wouldn't attend a press conference unless paid by the organizers, and others charged fees for writing flattering articles about enterprises. These ranging from a few hundred to tens of thousands of yuan.[30] Indeed, on July 31, the government issued a decree to prohibit the practice of *"youchang xinwen"* (news with compensation).[29]

Following the time-honored practice of making history serve present needs, an ingenious Shanghai scholar in an essay presented Marx in his early years as a journalist fighting for freedom of the press against the control and persecution by the Prussian government. Zhou Baoxin's article, entitled "Freedom Is Human Nature" appeared in the May 1993 issue of *Xueshu Yuekan* (Scholarship Monthly), published by the Shanghai Federation of Social Sciences Societies. He quoted Marx as saying, "Freedom is human nature and freedom of the press is its chief manifestation."[30] The monopoly of information was not a "sharp knife of reason" but a "dull knife of tyranny," Zhu quoted Marx as saying, with clear reference to the situation in China.[31]

### *Farewell, My Concubine*, Banned in China

Artists, as wayward free souls, were always a headache for government and party authorities in China who wanted them to walk the prescribed line. In July 1993, the government banned the first Chinese film ever to win the top prize at the Cannes International Film Festival. The film, *Farewell, My Concubine*, tells the story of the lives of two Peking Opera actors through five turbulent decades of recent Chinese history, including the years of the Cultural Revolution in the 1960s, when the worst turmoil occurred. It deals with such sensitive subjects as homosexuality and political persecution. Co-produced with Hong Kong film-makers, the picture shared the 1993 Palme d'Or, the "Oscar" at Cannes, with *Piano*, the acclaimed film from New Zealand. It also received the International Critics Prize for its "incisive analysis of the political and cultural history of China and its brilliant combination of the spectacular and the intimate."[32]

A censored version of the picture was earlier approved for release in China. After a few showings in Shanghai, however, the government abruptly reversed its decision and imposed the ban without offering an explanation. It was reported that Politburo members walked out in disgust during a private showing and the film was therefore doomed.[33]

Since the ban had no effect on the film's international release by its co-producers, an irony resulted: The picture was seen abroad from New York to Singapore, but Chinese in the People's Republic of China were barred from seeing it. Deeply hurt, Chen Kaige, the film's director, said his intention in the film was not to pass political judgment on the government. He noted that films like *The Godfather* and *Platoon* were not regarded as anti-American even though they depicted, respectively, violence by organized crime and the trauma of the Vietnam War. The ban had a chilling effect on other productions. Chen decided to put aside plans to film *Life and Death in Shanghai*, based on a book by Nien Cheng describing her suffering during the Cultural Revolution, and to make a movie on the early life of Jiang Qing, Mao's last wife and a former actress.

The government bowed to international pressure and allowed the film to resume public showing in China in early September 1993, but only after the censors had made further cuts. The Film Bureau of the Ministry of Radio, Film and Television meanwhile issued a directive that warned that it would continue to ban films that put the Communist system in a bad light. The bureau said its censors continued to find "attitude problems" in many films, with some "mixing up justice with injustice" while others contained violent and bloody scenes. "All of these things are contrary to the Party's principle on art and socialist spiritual civilization," the statement said. "If such trends appear again, the Film Bureau would deal with it seriously and ban the film," it warned.[34] Film Bureau officials indicated that the ban was lifted on *Farewell, My Concubine,* only because the international outcry was threatening to sour China's image during its campaign to bring the 2000 Olympics to Beijing. "We have no choice. We face a lot of pressure because some people abroad try to link the issue with China's human rights situation," the official said. Some even linked it with China's bid for the Olympics, "so we had to let it show."[35]

Beijing's censors were true to their warning. Two other Chinese films, both winners at the Tokyo Film Festival, were banned in China. The two films were *Blue Kite*, which depicts the suffering of a mother and a son from the Great Leap Forward in the late 1950s to the Cultural Revolution in the 1960s, and *Beijing Bastards*, featuring the nonconformist rock star Cui Jian portraying the life of a depressed Beijing youth. Both films were co-produced with foreign film-makers. The Chinese delegation pulled out of the competition in protest, claiming that the two films were entered without Chinese government approval.[36] The two films were among 13 finalists from 246 entries.

Co-production with film makers outside China became one way for Chinese directors to evade government censors. It was also a marriage of convenience between financially strapped Chinese film studios and foreign companies, under which the Chinese side supplied the crews, cast, and locations while the foreign partners would come up with the cash and ultimately own the completed negative. Edited abroad, it became possible for foreign co-producers to enter these films at international festivals even before they were sanctioned for domestic releases in China. *Blue Kite*, which was co-produced with a Japanese company, for example, was edited literally by "remote control." Forbidden to travel to

Tokyo to oversee post-production, Tian Zhuangzhuang, the film's director, dictated how it should be put together by telephone from China.

After the picture won the top prize at the Tokyo Film Festival, government authorities in Beijing in effect banned Tian from further filming and introduced new rules limiting future co-production to thirty a year, all of which must be edited and passed by the censors in China before release.[37] Zhang Yimou, another award-winning director, was banned from making any more international co-productions for five years when his picture *To Live* failed to pass the Chinese censors but won a prize at the 1994 Cannes Film Festival.[38]

Censors were toughening their stance not only toward movie production but toward books as well. In August 1994, a book once praised by Party General Secretary Jiang Zemin was banned because of "ideological problems." The book, *A Third Eye Observes China*, was purportedly written by a German scholar, with the name "Lo-yi-ning-ge-erh" (a Chinese transliteration). The Chinese version, "translated" by Wang Shan, was published by the Shanxi People's Publishing House in March 1994. Many believed that the German scholar was fictitious and that Wang was the real author.

Purporting to be the observation made by an impartial third party, the book covered China's recent history and analyzed political and economic developments. The author was critical of the fast pace of Deng's economic reform, pointing to the sharpening of contradictions between the industrial and agricultural sectors of the economy, between coastal and inland provinces, and between urban workers and peasants in the countryside. China, the author said, had been led into the "trap" of fast growth by Deng Xiaoping, with dangerous consequences. The author opposed privatization of state enterprises, felt that conditions were not yet ripe for China to practice democracy, advocated ideological control, and favored curbing personal freedom in order to prevent turmoil. Taken as a whole, the book sounded strangely similar to the "new authoritarian" approach favored by Jiang Zemin, who had already praised the book as early as January, several months before it came on the market. The fact that Jiang openly praised a book critical of the aging Deng, who had picked him in 1989 to replace Zhao Ziyang as the party's general secretary, was seen by many as a subtle sign of Jiang's attempt to placate party hard-liners in the context of a coming post-Deng power struggle. According to this view, the subsequent ban of the book therefore represented yet another turn in the power struggle. The official reason given for the ban, however, was that the book contained inflammatory passages such as the one in which the author described the 800 million disaffected peasants as "a live volcano, ready to erupt anytime."[39] (See Chapter 2 for further details on the power struggle and the lot of the peasants.)

According to the Hong Kong newspaper *Ming Pao*, several other books, including *Deng Xiaoping, Divining Post-Deng Era, Can China's Army Win the Next War?* and *China's Secret Wars*, were also banned for their sensationalism and inaccuracies. Two widely popular books published abroad were also banned in China. One contained the memoirs of Xu Jiatun, who as a member of the Party Central Committee and director of the Xinhua office in Hong Kong in the 1980s was the highest-ranking Chinese official to flee the country in the wake of the 1989 Tiananmen crackdown. Xu, a close associate of deposed former party boss Zhao Ziyang, once out-ranked Jiang Zemin in the party hierarchy. The other book was *Too Hard to Call Father*, by Ai Bei, purported to be a story by an illegitimate daughter of the late premier Zhou Enlai.[40]

The government also banned an ostensibly martial arts novel that obliquely criticized Deng Xiaoping and other leaders in early September 1994. The author of the book, which was entitled *Luanda Yuanyang Bang* (Indiscriminate Beating with a Mandarin Duck Cudgel), went into hiding, and six officials connected with the publication of the book were arrested. The novel was published by the Heilongjiang Arts and Literature Press. The heads of the Propaganda Department of the Heilongjiang Provincial Party Committee and the Provincial Publication Bureau were detained. The book was characterized as counter-revolutionary by President Jiang Zemin because it contained a chapter that bore an allusion to the Tiananmen Massacre, the main characters given derogatory names that resembled those of top party leaders, such as Deng Tuozi (Deng Xiaoping), Hu Peng (Li Peng), and Yang Xiakun (former president Yang Shangkun). "Although the book was not praised highly by literary critics, it vividly expressed the social consciousness of Chinese intellectuals," a source said. It also broke through the officially controlled publishing channels and was printed.[41]

A week later, another book, *93 Hasty Thoughts—Who Are the Ugly Chinese*, by the noted writer Liang Xiaosheng, was also banned. The book was a graphic expose of social problems accompanying economic reform and the opening to the West, including corruption, moral deterioration, human degradation, and the dangerously "de-stabilizing effect" on society of new, stringent standards issued by the Party Propaganda Department. In a sarcastic way, the book raised a number of questions, such as why the government worked so hard to host the 2000 Olympics and whether the gold necklace worn by the grand-daughter of an "authoritative old man in the country" was extravagant in the eyes of the peasants. Writing as the conscience of society, Liang said that when the Chinese Communist Party began to make revolution, its main objective was to solve the problem of unfair distribution of wealth. Citing corruption and the widening gap between the rich and poor, he asked, "Have not all efforts for socialism in the past 40 years and more been wasted?"[42] Liang, a Red Guard during the Cultural Revolution in the 1960s, gained notoriety as a writer of "critical reality" fighting injustices. His novels include *The Snow City, There Is a Snowstorm Tonight, A Showy City,* and *The Confession of a Red Guard*. While professing no fear for himself, Liang said he was concerned that the *Zhongshan Magazine*, which serialized his book, and the Shanxi Joint Publishing House for Institutions of Higher Learning, which published and distributed it, might be punished.[43]

In a somewhat similar incident, a lecturer in the Central Party School was charged with "leaking state secrets" in October 1994 for printing in his book a letter of self-criticism written by Deng Xiaoping to Mao in 1973. Yu Xiguang, thirty-seven, was secretly tried and sentenced to an undisclosed prison term after being detained for more than a year. His book, *Muse Fengyuan* (The Stormy Twilight), was banned as soon as the authorities discovered the letter in it.[44]

The letter in question was written when Deng was in political disgrace during the Cultural Revolution. He had been denounced as a "capitalist-roader" and exiled to the countryside by Mao. In the letter, Deng asked for rehabilitation, pledging that he would never reverse the course of the Cultural Revolution while admitting he had made serious mistakes in his career. Apparently because of his promise, Deng was rehabilitated in 1974 and soon rose to prominence. He served as vice premier at a time when premier Zhou Enlai was dying of cancer. In early 1976, however, Deng was again dismissed by Mao for allegedly masterminding an anti-Mao demonstration in Tiananmen Square that ostensibly was a memorial meeting for Zhou Enlai, who had died in January. After Mao's death and the fall of the Gang of Four in late 1976, Deng again wrote similar letters to the Party Central Committee and Mao's successor, Hua Guofeng, "repenting" his mistakes. Hua rehabilitated Deng but was soon himself pushed aside by Deng. Deng's letters, in short, reflected his chameleon-like character and his willingness and ability to lie and supplicate to remain in power, suggesting this is, in fact, how he became China's paramount leader. This was clearly embarrassing to Deng and to the Chinese Communist Party and the government and was something they did not want made public.

## Deng's "Works" become the New Orthodoxy

With the demise of communism in much of the former socialist world, China's leaders found it increasingly difficult to defend its new orthodoxy. That orthodoxy was based on Deng Xiaoping's recently published books and other writings which were a concoction that mixed some features of a market economy newly borrowed from the West with traditional practices of Leninist political control in order to prop up a tattered system in a perceived hostile world, to create a system known as "socialism with Chinese characteristics."

The perception of a hostile world was particularly important in creating this new ideological line, for such a perception can be an effective way of whipping up a hysteria of raw nationalism among the people against perceived foreign enemies. And China's recent history comes in handy in this connection: The aggression and humiliation China suffered at the hands of Western imperialism in the nineteenth century and of Japanese militarism in the first half of the twentieth century provided solid "historical proof" of foreign hostility against China. Indeed the Dengist ideologues, in working out a new ideological paradigm for mobilizing the Chinese people in the post-Communist era of cynicism and ideological vacuum, seem to draw both inspiration and power by deliberately fostering a "victimization" psychology in the people.

To uphold the new orthodoxy, however, party ideologues and thought police showed a remarkable lack of imagination in their propaganda campaign. Shying away from anything innovative, they resorted to a time-honored technique: flooding the market with Deng's writings the way China was deluged with millions of copies of *Quotations of Chairman Mao*, better known as Mao's "Little Red Book," during the Cultural Revolution in the 1960s. According to the Beijing *Information and Publishing Journal*, over a ten-year period from 1984 to 1994 more than thirty works by Deng were published, totaling more than 100 million copies printed. The third volume of Deng's *Collected Works*, for example, had more than 24 million copies in print within one year of publication. In addition, it was also published in several foreign translations, including English, German, and Italian.[45] The *Information and Publishing Journal* said "Deng Xiaoping Thought" must be studied because it was the "sole guide and motivating force" behind the policies of reform and opening to the West. The journal did not say, however, if the books were read. (It is interesting to recall that despite the fact that tens of millions of copies were printed, the once ubiquitous Mao's "Little Red Book," which was the "Bible" during the Cultural Revolution, has disappeared from view since Mao's death.)

Promoting "Dengism" continued unabated throughout 1994. In December, more than 250 key personnel in charge of ideological work from the party, the government, and the military gathered in Beijing at a "Seminar on Studying Deng Xiaoping's Works and Establishing Socialism with Chinese Characteristics." The seminar was jointly sponsored by the Party Propaganda Department, the Central Party School, the Social Sciences Academy, the State Education Commission, and the General Political Department of the PLA. Speaking before the seminar, Hu Jingtao, a standing member of the Party Politburo, stressed the importance of "arming the party with Deng's theory of building socialism with Chinese characteristics." Calling it a long-range strategic task, he urged the participants to work hard to make sure that officials from the county level up and intellectuals in all disciplines of the social sciences study and follow Deng's teaching in earnest. Party propaganda chief Ding Guangen called the seminar a major endeavor to combine theory and practice and to ensure that the current party line of building socialism with Chinese characteristics would "not change in the next 100 years."[46]

The celebration of Mao's birthday provided a special occasion for hailing the importance of Deng's thought by criticizing Mao's mistakes in his later years. On December 26, 1994, the *Guangming Daily* printed an article that bitterly attacked Mao for the calamities of the Cultural Revolution. The article, written by Liao Gailong, vice president of the Society on Party History, was based on Deng's criticism of Mao, thus elevating Deng's teaching to a still more authoritative position. Liao quoted Deng's words in 1980 that Mao in his later years had "unhealthy ideas" in that he behaved like a "patriarch with unquestioned authority in a feudal society." It was in that way Mao caused the nation great damage through the Cultural Revolution in which Deng himself was a victim. Liao further developed Deng's criticism of Mao, saying that Mao's "unhealthy ideas" were mainly manifested in two ways: Mao adopted an ultra-leftist position by denouncing the past, and yet at the same time he practiced the worst feature of past feudalism by behaving himself like a patriarch with unquestioned author-ity.[47] Deng, the "paramount leader" of China, without actually holding any government or party posts, has been referred to as "Da Jiazhang" (Great Patriarch) in China in recent years. (The term Da Jiazhang, literally "great family head," in this context is a cynical reminder of China's past when the Emperor often styled himself as the head of a large family—the Chinese nation.) Seen in this light, Liao's criticism of Mao would seem to take on a new significance.

In line with the efforts to combine Dengism with nationalism, the government in late 1994 ordered all nightclubs and karaoke parlors to buy and play a government-produced compact disc packed with fifty-five patriotic songs. The Ministry of Culture said the more than 200,000 such establishments had to purchase the CD by the end of the year or face lifting of their licenses. Xinhua said in a dispatch that the CD contained theme songs from movies applauding socialist reconstruction of the nation and Communist revolution. The news agency made no mention, however, of how these revolutionary songs were coolly received by nightclub patrons.[48]

Despite all the efforts at mind-control, it was clear that the government fought a losing battle during 1993 and 1994. Economic reform produced rising expectations, while opening to the West made it increasingly hard for the author-ities to filter out ideas it did not like. Affluence in urban areas and exposure to Western ideas resulted in popular demands for freedom, political rights, and a more responsive government, demands that were unheard of when China was under obscurant Maoist rule as late as the mid-1970s. Su Shaozhi, an exiled former top Marxist theorist who was once director of the Institute of Marxism-Leninism-Mao Zedong Thought under the Chinese Academy of Social Sciences, made the most direct observation. Su, who was fired from his job and expelled from the party for allegedly instigating the 1989 Tiananmen student demon-strations for democracy, said in early 1993 that despite the economic reforms, Deng Xiaoping would not end the Leninist one-party dictatorship and tolerate dissent. He characterized Beijing's ruling style, unchanged from Mao to Deng, as

"Stalin plus Qin Shi-huang," the latter being the worst despot in Chinese history, who ruled in 221–206 B.C.[49]

Commenting further on the incongruence between the economic reforms and the continued political repression, Su compared Deng's policies to a car signaling a right turn but actually turning left. "There will be a problem sooner or later," he said.[50] The Marxist–turned–dissident called the lack of democracy and rule of law the "greatest crisis" facing China. He urged the establishment of rule of law, not as a tool of the government to control the people but as a bulwark to secure the rights and freedoms of the people. As a first step toward political reform, he urged democratization within the Communist Party. As a result of the economic reform, Su pointed out, the political leadership in China was under increasing pressure for political participation from an awakened populace and the "contradiction" would only sharpen with Beijing's procrastination and cause domestic political instability.[51] Su Shaozhi's urging that political reform should begin with democratization within the party was echoed by a high party official at a National People's Congress session in March 1993, which heard a chorus of voices demanding greater democracy.

Liang Buting, former party secretary of Shandong Province, bluntly told the congress that one of the most serious shortcomings of the ongoing reform was the conspicuous lack of any attempt at political reform. Nobody dared to touch politics or talk about democracy, the former Shandong party boss said, speaking of those who "were in the saddle guiding China's reform in recent years." The former party boss, from an economically important coastal province that benefited enormously from Deng's reform, told the congress that people had needs in three areas, in this order: material, cultural, and political, the last meaning democracy. As the material needs of the majority of the Chinese people were being met, it was inevitable that people would demand political participation. By avoiding the mention of democracy and denying people's rights to supervise the government, "no leader, however great, and no party, however superior, can prevent corruption and decay," he warned bluntly.[52]

Liang was not alone in boldly expressing his opinion. A delegate from Hong Kong urged true election of the premier by the NPC from a slate of candidates rather than rubber-stamping the party's choice. And Xiao Yang, governor of Sichuan, China's most populous province (more than 100 million), urged election of provincial governors through direct balloting rather than by delegates to provincial people's congresses picking them. Scholars at the National Academy of Social Sciences did not find the cry for political reform from within the party surprising. With the quickened pace of economic reform, they pointed out, the leadership had become factionalized between the old guard and those favoring inevitable political reform.[53]

In a down to earth way, the demand for democracy—meaning greater participation in decision-making and more responsive government—was also expressed by the public. According to a survey conducted by the Public Opinion Research Institute of People's University in Beijing, nearly one-half of the residents of a major coastal city were not happy with their lives despite improved living standards. The survey, published in the Beijing *Financial Daily*, said that of 1,000 households in Qingdao, a prosperous city on the southern coast of Shandong Province, 43.5 percent of the people felt that there were no channels through which to "express views and grievances," while 37 percent were unhappy about the "relations between party and government officials and the people." Only 12 percent showed confidence in their work units and 17 percent showed confidence in the judicial system. Summarizing the survey results, the authors said: "People are not animals, satisfied with food and shelter. People demand justice, respect, and a role in their own affairs."[54]

Not surprisingly, the most pronounced failure of the thought police was among the young people, the future masters of a China that Mao and Deng successively tried so hard to mold in their images. According to a survey published in the official *China Youth Daily* in March 1994, only 7.7 percent of young people in China professed faith in socialism, and 14.2 percent said they had no faith in anything. The majority said they had some faith in something but felt lost. The survey was conducted between October 1992 and March 1993 among young intellectuals, including students, scientists and technicians, teachers, cadres of the Communist Youth League, and young professionals, ranging in age from eighteen to thirty-five.[55] The survey showed that graduate students were the most skeptical, with more than a quarter flatly saying that they did "not believe in socialism." They were followed by 9.3 percent of the young scientists and technicians and 5.4 percent of the college undergraduates who professed no faith in socialism.

Dissatisfaction with official corruption ran deep among young intellectuals, with 89.3 percent of those interviewed regarding corruption by party and government officials as "very serious." The market economy should be further strengthened, according to 42.5 percent of them, but 57.7 percent felt that political reform lagged behind economic reform. Nearly 42 percent believed that "social problems"—official corruption and privileges, inflation, low wages, poor housing, and the like—were behind student unrest, while only 7.5 percent attributed student unrest to patriotism. However, 27.4 percent believed that student movements were caused by "bourgeois liberalization," showing the effect of official propaganda.

While government efforts at mind control produced few desired results during the period under review, they represented continued human rights abuse. Whether it was in the persecution of those who had contacts with foreign journalists, the banning of books and motion pictures, or the stepped–up control of the media, human rights suffered. In this connection, the government moved in exactly the opposite direction from that of economic reform. And this divergence further exacerbated the problem: More economic reform brought in more outside influence, and greater efforts at keeping out outside influence resulted in more serious human rights violations. Moreover, affluence in the coastal areas brought about by the economic reform translated into rising expectations in all areas, including political awareness. As a result, there was not only a greater and bolder demand for human rights but also a greater awareness of the government's human rights abuses in the past, prompting a more harsh response by an insecure totalitarian regime. The vicious cycle probably will not end until the day when economic reform and political reform begin to move in the same direction.

## Endnotes

1. *People's Daily,* October 11, 1993, p. 1.

2. Cited in Nicholas D. Kristof, "Chinese Find Their Voice: A Radio Call-in Show," *New York Times,* April 26, 1993, p. A4.

3. For example, in a speech at the Foreign Policy Association in New York after his visit to India in January 1995, Defense Secretary William Perry said: "India wants to retain its nuclear capability to deter the Chinese military, which is superior to India both in nuclear and conventional capability." In New Delhi, Perry's words suggested Washington's encouragement for India's military growth as a counterbalance to China. See John F. Burns, "After Decades of Wariness, Forces of U.S. and India Begin to Cooperate," *New York Times,* June 11, 1995, p. 12.

4. "Leaders Urge Vigilance Against U.S. Plot Against China," *Shih-chieh Jih-pao* (World Journal) (New York) , June 5, 1993, p. A.2

5. "Bylaws of National Security Act Issued," *Shih-chieh Jih-pao*, July 13, 1993, p. A18. Under the last provision, foreign journalists contacting Chinese democracy campaigners or human rights advocates were put in jeopardy of violating Chinese law.

6. "Fear of Foreigners," *The Economist*, October 16, 1993, p. 37.

7. Nicholas D. Kristof, "Chinese Gets 10 Years for Giving Data to Foreigner," *New York Times*, July 30, 1993, p. A6.

8. Ibid.

9. "Xinhua Editor Given Life for Selling Secrets," *Shih-chieh Jih-pao*, August 31, 1993, p. A3.

10. *"Newsweek* Issue Banned by Beijing," *Shih-chieh Jih-pao*, March 22, 1994, p. A2.

11. "Chinese Still Jamming American Broadcasts," *New Haven Register*, July 10, 1994, p. A 10.

12. Ibid.

13. "'Fugitive' Canceled in China," *New Haven Register*, November 20, 1994, p. A2.

14. "Shenzhen Clamps Down on Satellite Reception of Foreign TV Programs," *Shih-chieh Jih-pao*, April 19, 1994, p. A14.

15. Ibid.

16. Patrick E. Tyler, "CNN and MTV Hanging by a 'Heavenly Thread,'" *New York Times*, November 22, 1993, p. A4.

17. Ibid.

18. "Control over Books and Magazines Stepped Up," *Shih-chieh Jih-pao*, March 15, 1993, p. 17.

19. "Censorship Increased to Protect Image of Leaders," *Shih-chieh Jih-pao*, April 14, 1993, p. 15.

20. "Ministry of Culture Tightens Control," *Shih-chieh Jih-pao*, May 21, 1993, p. A18.

21. Nicholas D. Kristof, "Chinese Find Their Voice: A Radio Call-in Show," *New York Times*, April 26, 1993, p. A4.

22. Ibid.

23. "Several Dozen Newspapers and Magazines Banned for Playing Up Pornography and Violence," *Ming Pao* (Hong Kong), July 12, 1994, p. A12, in Foreign Broadcasting Information Service (FBIS) CHI-94-149, August 3, 1994, p. 15.

24. Tsao Chi-yun, "Democracy and Freedom of the Press—Ding Meets the Hong Kong Press Delegation," *Ta Kung Pao* (Hong Kong), August 29, 1994, p. 1, in FBIS-CHI-94-179, August 15, 1994, p. 35.

25. Willy Wo-Lap Lam, "CPC Propaganda Department Steps Up Control over Media," *South China Morning Post*, September 26, 1994, p. 9, in FBIS-CHI-94-186, September 26, 1994, p. 29.

26. "State to Control Newspaper Publication Violations," Xinhua Domestic Service, October 12, 1994, in FBIS-CHI-94-201, October 18, 1994, p. 18.

27. "Former Head of *People's Daily*: Press Controls Remain," *Shih-chieh Jih-pao*, July 22, 1993, p. A2.

28. Ibid.

29. "Better Read than Dead," *The Economist*, July 31, 1993, p. 33.

30. Ibid.

34. Patrick E. Tyler, "China Censors Issue a Warning," *New York Times*, September 4, 1993, p. 11.

35. Ibid.

36. "Beijing Pulls Out of Tokyo Film Festival," *Shih-chieh Jih-pao*, September 29, 1993, p. A1.

37. "In the Censor's Toils," *The Economist*, November 12, 1994, p. 115.

38. "China Bans One of Its Own Films."

39. "Several Books Banned in China," *Shih-chieh Jih-pao*, August 12, 1994, p. A18.

40. Ibid.

41. Zhang Weiguo, "CPC Bans Novel Criticizing Deng," *South China Morning Post*, September 10, 1994, p. 10, in FBIS-CHI-94-176, September 12, 1994, p. 39.

42. "Noted Writer Liang Xiaosheng's New Book Banned," *Ming Pao* (Hong Kong), September 20, 1994, p. 2, in FBIS-CHI-94-188, September 28, 1994, p. 23.

43. Ibid.

44.  Amy Liu, "Lecturer Tried for Revealing Deng Letter," *Hong Kong Standard*, November 11, 1994, p. 6, in FBIS-CHI-94-219, November 14, 1994, p. 51.

45.  "More Than 100 Million Copies of Deng Works Printed," *Shih-chieh Jih-pao*, December 4, 1994, p. A14.

46.  "Seminar to Ensure Post-Deng Ideological Line," *Shih-chieh Jih-pao*, December 15, 1994, p. A18.

47.  "*Guangming Daily* Criticizes Mao with Deng's Words," *Shih-chieh Jih-pao*, December 27, 1994, p. A16.

48.  "Night Clubs Must Buy CD of Patriotic Songs," *Shih-chieh Jih-pao*, November 23, 1994, p. A18.

49.  "Su Shaozhi Hails Taiwan Experience in Democracy," *Shih-chieh Jih-pao*, March 4, 1993, p. 2.  Qin Shi-huang, or the First Emperor of Qin Dynasty in 221 B.C., who burned books and buried intellectuals alive to suppress dissent, is remembered as the worst despot in Chinese history.

50.  Ibid.

51.  "Su Shaozhi:  Demands for Democratic Reform Inevitable," *Shih-chieh Jih-pao*, March 2, 1993, p. 2.

52.  "Liang Buting: Nobody Dares to Mention Democracy," *Shih-chieh Jih-pao*, March 25, 1993, p. 16.

53.  Ibid.

54.  "Survey Shows Public Demand for Democracy," *Shih-chieh Jih-pao*, May 9, 1993, p. A14.

55.  "Only Seven Percent of Youth Believe in Socialism," *Shih-chieh Jih-Pao*, April 1, 1996, p. A16.

# Chapter 5

## Criminal Justice and Human Rights

Neither [Nazi Germany nor the Soviet Union] made use of slave labor so efficiently as China.

—Bao Ruowang, former labor camp inmate[1]

There is a price for everything. A price for getting a thief out of prison, a price for getting out a rapist. Even a price for getting out a murderer.

—*People's Police News*[2]

We must never underestimate the effect of rural unrest on our national situation and must understand these problems in terms of the overriding interests of the Party and state."

—Ren Jianxin, President of People's Supreme Court[3]

### Introduction

The years 1993 and 1994 saw a worsening of the "law and order" problem in China. Renewed efforts by the authorities to fight rising crime rates with stiff punishments, including wide use of the death penalty, produced few tangible results. Crime rates went up in various categories: armed robbery, rape, murder, drug-related offenses and the catchall category of "economic crime" (meaning such offenses as corruption, bribery, fraud, embezzlement, profiteering, and other money-related offenses). Drug-related offenses rose sharply. Despite seizures of large quantities of illicit drugs by government agents and well-publicized mass executions of smuggling ringleaders, drug trafficking continued to increase at an alarming rate. It became one of the most serious problems facing the law enforcement officials as the illegal activities expanded from southwestern China, the traditional drug-infested area near the "golden triangle" across the border, to other parts of the country, particularly major cities with international air connections.

Violent crime increased in scale and grew more violent, perhaps in part because guns were so readily available. Train robberies occurred frequently in the mountainous regions in the southwest, where groups of heavily armed bandits would stop trains at night between stations and terrify and rob hundreds of passengers of their cash and jewelry. Also common were highway robberies: long-distance buses were frequently ambushed in deserted areas by well-armed robbers, many of them former army soldiers. Overseas tourists, particularly those from Taiwan who made little attempt to hide their wealth from their poor cousins in China, became easy prey. In one particularly gruesome case in 1994, more than thirty tourists from Taiwan aboard a pleasure yacht on a lake were robbed and then doused with gasoline and burned to death before their boat was scuttled.[4] There were other types of major crimes, such as kidnapping and selling women and children into prostitution across provincial lines by large, well-organized criminal groups.

An increase in economic crime accompanied the growing affluence of the coastal provinces. This was brought about by the economic reform and its attendant rampant corruption in government that included top officials and their families as well as petty bureaucrats at the lowest level. The power of official positions was invariably abused for ill-gotten monetary gains. Periodic anti-corruption drives, launched with much fanfare by government authorities, often fizzled out without netting the big fish who were secure in their high positions in the party hierarchy. Instead, a few lesser officials would be punished. The public cynically said the drives aimed "not to catch tigers, but to catch mere flies."

To deal with the ever worsening crime problem, Beijing's policy was first to mete out severe punishment, meaning the wide and indiscriminate use of the death penalty, and this had obvious human rights implications. Death sentences were handed down swiftly, often at mass meetings with thousands or tens of thousands of people in attendance. The condemned prisoners were as a rule bound and paraded through the streets, then taken to the execution grounds where they were forced to kneel. Soldiers would then unceremoniously put a bullet in their heads at a point blank distance in direct view of the many people who were watching.

## Mass Executions Before Lunar New Year

The period just before the traditional Lunar New Year, now better known as the Spring Festival, has been a time for mass executions—a sort of year-end "cleanup" in order to usher in the new year. According to the Ministry of Public Security, between New Year's Day and the Spring Festival in February 1993, more than 29,600 criminals of all types were sentenced throughout China, of whom 2,552 were condemned to death and immediately executed. More than 18,000 people were sentenced to imprisonment of ten years or more. In a month, according to the ministry, more than 42,700 people were detained and arrested. Public security authorities and the armed police, in fact, initiated more than 25,000 actions, cracking and eliminating more than 630 crime syndicates of all types in the anti-crime sweep, the ministry said.[5] From January to July 1993, in Yunnan Province alone there were more than 2,300 drug trafficking cases reported, with the seizure of more than 1,870 kilograms of high-quality heroin, according to the Hong Kong-based China Information Agency.[6] In a dispatch issued on November 12 quoting official figures, the agency said more than 3,400 traffickers were prosecuted in the province, of whom 477 were given death, death with reprieve, or life sentences. In the two-year period ending in July 1993, more than 300 drug traffickers had been executed in Yunnan. In Guangdong Province, during the first five months of 1993, more than 900 drug-smuggling cases were reported, involving more than 1,000 traffickers and more than 8,000 addicts. Several scores of traffickers were sentenced to death.[7] Drug seizures in Yunnan totaled more than five tons in 1993, consisting mostly of opium and heroin, according to Colonel Si Jiuyi, commander of the armed police of the province. Drug traffickers were increasingly better armed, Si said. Guns and grenades were seized during drug raids and more than twenty of his men died during the year in those raids.[8]

In the first quarter of 1994, more than 2,000 drug trafficking cases were handled by police and more than 2,000 kilograms of narcotics were seized, according to the Ministry of Public Security. Yunnan alone accounted for more than 900 cases, involving over 700 kilograms of heroin, the ministry said.[9] On June 22, 1994, Bai Jingfu, vice minister of public security, told a national anti-drug conference in Beijing that Yunnan and Guangxi accounted for 82 percent of the heroin and 70 percent of the opium seized during the first quarter of 1994. His boss, Minister Tao Siju, added that while the bulk of the drugs came from the golden triangle areas, "illegal planting of opium poppies by individuals continues to exist in scattered regions" in China. Sounding a familiar theme, he pledged Beijing's full cooperation yet urged greater efforts on the part of the local governments to combat the drug problem.[10]

The *Liberation Army Daily* in early January 1993 carried a graphic report of a three-month campaign against entrenched drug bandits in the Yunnan mountains. In the Pingyuan region in southern Yunnan near the golden triangle, armed police, on orders from the State Council in Beijing and the Yunnan provincial government, fought the bandits for three months in what was described as a "large-scale campaign." At the end of the campaign, according to the army newspaper, 2 armed bandits were killed, 210 were captured, and more than 640 surrendered. The armed police seized from the rebels 964 guns of various types, more than 40,000 rounds of ammunition, 258 hand grenades, and 16 mines. More than 2,000 pounds of drugs were also confiscated.[11]

In the Guangxi autonomous region in southwestern China, which has become another drug-infested area because of its proximity to the golden triangle, the local government launched a so-called "double strike" campaign from July to October 1994 against both drugs and illegal arms. According to a China News Agency dispatch on December 2 from Nanning, capital of Guangxi, the four-month campaign cracked more than 1,000 drug-manufacturing and trafficking cases, including two international cases involving traffickers from Myanmar and Vietnam. The report listed the following results of the campaign: 1,401 drug-related offenders arrested, 196 drug manufacturing or trafficking groups smashed, 271.5 kilograms of opium and 60 kilograms of heroin seized, 145 gun-traffickers arrested, 16 gunrunning groups smashed, and 102 military firearms of various types and more than 5,000 rounds of ammunition seized.[12]

The sharp increase in drug-related cases in southern China reflected a nationwide trend in recent years. The large numbers of death sentences and seizures of huge quantities of illicit drugs suggest both tough measures taken by the government and its inability to cope with the problem. Nationwide in 1992, for example, more than 14,700 drug-related cases involving more than 28,000 traffickers were prosecuted, resulting in the seizure of nearly four and one-half tons (4,489 kilograms) of heroin alone, a 140 percent increase over the previous year. Between 1991 and 1992, a total of 2,220 traffickers were given death, death with reprieve, or life sentences.[13]

In advance of the International Anti-Drug Day observances on June 26, 1994, a wave of executions of condemned drug traffickers were carried out in many provinces. These included 46 in Guangdong, 51 in Shanxi, 7 in Fujian, 3 in Sichuan and 1 in Qinghai. Many more were sentenced to death but were given a reprieve or a long prison terms.[14] Harsh punishment apparently failed to stop the worsening situation and by mid-1994 it became known that even in remote Tibet, there was a drug problem. On June 26, with much fanfare, the Lhasa Intermediate People's Court sentenced one drug trafficker to death and three other offenders to long prison terms. A Xinhua dispatch from the Tibetan capital said Qamjig, the main offender, was executed immediately after the death sentence was handed down to him for buying more than 1,000 grams of narcotics in Yunnan and selling them at high profits in Tibet at the end of 1993. Another main offender, Dojie, was sentenced to life imprisonment, and two accomplices, Huang Tinghong and Losang Soinam, were sentenced to fifteen years each.[15]

Health Minister Chen Mingzhang said in Beijing in December 1993 that there were some 250,000 known addicts in China. The number, while small for a country of more than 1.2 billion people, was growing fast. The addicts were scattered in seventeen provinces, from the southwest to the northeast, affecting more than 700 of China's 2,000 counties. Chen told a conference in Beijing that the majority of the addicts were young people and that refined heroin had replaced the traditional opium as the preferred drug. He said that among the small number of AIDS patients, over 60 percent were addicts who were infected through the sharing of needles.[16]

Enterprising restaurateurs also cashed in on the easy availability of drugs to increase their profits. In many coastal cities as well as rural towns in inland areas, many restaurants were known to add opium-poppy shells to the foods in order to make patrons addicted to their tasty dishes. According to the Beijing *Legal Daily News*, in a citywide sweep, many restaurants in the coastal city of Qingdao in Shandong Province were found to have spiked their chicken soups with opium-poppy shells.[17] Addicted to the aroma, innocent patrons would keep coming back and fall into the "poppy trap," the paper said.

In his annual report to the National People's Congress in March 1993, Ren Jianxin, president of the Supreme People's Court, said courts at all levels in the country had handled more than 2 million criminal cases in the five years from 1988 to 1992, with an annual increase of 7.9 percent.[18] A grand total of 2,438,217 criminals were convicted, with 34.9 percent sentenced to death, life prison terms, or terms of over five years. Ren singled out violent crime, drugs, kidnappings (especially of women and children), and pornography as areas in which law enforcement authorities had concentrated their efforts.

He said that during the five-year period from 1988 to 1992, violent crime, including murder, armed robbery, arson and bombings, rape, "hooliganism," train and highway banditry, and sabotage of transportation, communication, and power facilities, totaled 750,744 cases, with 1,107,816 people convicted. Drug-related offenses, prostitution, kidnapping, and the sale of women and children and pornography accounted for 69,060 cases with 101,367 convictions, of which 24,879 occurred in 1992. Ren also spoke of serious corruption in government, saying thousands of government officials were involved in more than 169,777 cases of economic crime during the same period. Conviction rates among corrupt officials were rather low, however. In five years, only 638 officials at the county level and a mere four at the provincial or ministerial levels were convicted.[19] The situation apparently did not change in 1994. During the first four months of the year, the number of economic crimes soared to 19,000 cases, of which 12,000 involved corruption by public officials. Of the 7,130 people convicted, including 102 death penalties or life-term sentences, only one was an official of sub-ministerial rank and nine were directors or bureau heads.[20]

Ren told a forum on "Comprehensive Management of Social Security" in Beijing in May 1994 that "security problems [were] escalating enormously" in the rural parts of the country and the situation needed the urgent attention of Communist Party officials. Violent crimes, such as robbery, rape, and hooliganism, Ren warned, were so serious in the vast rural areas that China "must never underestimate the effect of rural unrest on our national situation and must understand these problems in terms of the overriding interests of the party and state."[21] Ren attributed the deterioration of law and order in rural areas to the erosion of the Communist Party's traditional control caused by the economic reforms. According to a China News Agency report from Taiwan in October 1994, of the 1,610,000 criminal cases recorded in 1993, 750,000 were in the rural areas. A survey of all prisons and labor camps showed that 57 percent of those convicted in 1993 were former peasants.[22]

The continued use of torture represented yet another seamy side of the Chinese criminal justice system. Despite the fact that China signed the U.N. convention against the use of torture in 1988 and a professed effort by the government to clean up the system, cases of torture were on the rise and became more cruel. Between 1988 and 1993, judicial authorities had investigated 1,687 cases of alleged torture by the police and other law-enforcement agencies, according to the supreme procurator's office.[23] According to *Henan Legal News*, between 1990 and 1992, in Henan Province alone as many as forty-one prisoners and suspects were tortured to death. Henan is one of thirty provinces and regions in China. In 1992, seventeen people died of torture in Henan, or 40 percent of the three-year total. Sixty-four cases of alleged torture were reported in the province in 1992, a 24 percent rise over 1991. The statistics clearly showed that torture was on the rise both in number and in severity. A report in the paper characterized a simple three-step formula widely used by the security police: arrest, interrogation, torture. According to the report, the most common forms of torture included suspending the suspects in midair and beating them, scalding them with boiling water, burning them with cigarettes, and whipping them. The criminal justice practice encouraged torture, the paper said, because those who cracked a case through the use of torture were often praised or promoted rather than reprimanded. In many areas, judges and prosecutors protected alleged torturers from police investigation. The paper even cited a case in which local officials attempted to burn the body of a torture victim before the arrival of investigators.[24]

Police and security officers are not always dedicated to crime prevention in the atmosphere of "everything goes" brought on by Deng Xiaoping's economic reforms. As public servants, their pay is low, about 200 yuan ($35) a month as of late 1993, when there was double-digit inflation. The *People's Police News* reported in November 1993 that the police in a district in Henan

Province were not paid for three months. In the end, each policeman was given 36 ducks as compensation. Given their positions, it is understandable that the police could easily supplement their incomes in other ways. "There is a price for everything," boasted a policeman. "A price for getting a thief out of prison, a price for getting out a rapist. Even a price for getting out a murderer."[25] Sometimes the police would act as little more than hired thugs. According to a report in the *China Youth Daily* on December 7, 1993, peasants in one village complained that local officials were siphoning off funds meant for poverty relief. The police went in to investigate the complaint and arrested the peasants.[26]

If the low pay of police and other law enforcement officials justified corruption, there was also another side to what otherwise looked to be a serious increase in crime and criminal activities: crime statistics and news reports about crime were routinely doctored for political purposes. The proliferation of crime reports and releases of crime figures had considerable to do with both a more sensationalist press and government officials anxious to show the results of their crime-fighting work. But, in some cases the exaggeration came from hard-line officials who sought to discredit or undermine Deng's reforms. There were also those who felt that publicizing crime statistics made China look bad when in reality China was a safe and stable place compared to many Western countries. Tao Siju, minister of public security, for example, while admitting to increases of serious crime with economic liberalization, insisted that the crime rate in China was still lower than that in rich countries.[27]

## Labor Camps Continue to Export Goods

In 1993 and 1994, the vast network of prisons, labor reform camps, and mental institutions in China remained a concern of international human rights groups. No one really knows just how many people are kept in these institutions where prisoners work to make large profits for the state by turning out consumer goods for both domestic and international markets. Writing about this not-so-secret part of China's economy in the winter 1993 issue of *China Quarterly*, published by London University's School of Oriental and African Studies, Jean Pasquallini (Bao Ruowang), who spent seven years in a Chinese jail during Mao's time, compared the vast Chinese system to those of Nazi Germany and the Soviet Union. Both of the latter used prisoners to benefit their economies. But... "Neither made use of slave labor so efficiently" as China, Bao contended.[28]

According to Harry Wu, executive director of the California-based Laogai Foundation, Chinese prisoner-made goods continued to come into the United States despite an agreement signed in August 1992 between Washington and Beijing to ban such goods. At a Washington press conference on May 18,

1993, Wu displayed a variety of prison-made goods he and members of his organization found on the market in the United States during a three-month investigation. Instead of stopping the exports, Wu said, Beijing merely changed the brand names and shipped the goods through companies in Hong Kong to hide their place of origin. The goods displayed at the conference ranged from hand tools to rubber shoes, many carrying American trademarks.[29] In September 1994, artificial flowers smuggled out of a prison factory near the south China city of Canton were shown to carry the brand name of "Ben Franklin Retail Stores," a popular chain store in the United States.[30]

Wu spent nineteen years as a political prisoner at various Chinese labor camps. Now a naturalized U.S. citizen, Wu has written a book on the labor camps and made clandestine trips back to China to secretly investigate and film the poor conditions in the camps. Disclosing what he learned from his most recent trip to China in videotapes and photographs, Wu said that in April of 1994 he entered China from the remote Xinjiang region in the northwest and in the next thirty-five days traveled through eight provinces and secretly visited twenty-six labor camps.[31] Wu and his organization then traced the origins of prison-made goods to prisons from Liaoning Province in northeastern China to Yunnan Province in southwestern China.

Wu said Chinese goods made with prison labor can be divided into two major categories. One consists of tools and industrial products such as lathes, which are relatively easy to identify. The other category, a broader one and bigger in terms of volume, include such varied goods as cotton textiles, chemicals, tea, and mineral products retailed through vast networks. These products are very hard to track down.[32]

Wu estimated that as much as 50 percent of Chinese rubber products may have come from chemical factories that employ forced labor. Human Rights Watch/Asia claimed that as late as January 1994 Beijing was still exporting prison labor-produced latex gloves used by doctors.[33] Beijing Jeep, a joint venture with Chrysler Corporation (58 percent owned by its Chinese partner Beijing Auto Works (BAW), is known to have links with two of China's biggest labor camps, Shayang in Hubei Province and Ya'an in Sichuan Province, which supplied auto parts to the company, including universal joints and transmission shaft assemblies.[34] Both Beijing Jeep and BAW were listed in 1994 as constituent enterprises of Beijing Auto Industrial Corporation (BAIC), which was known to have production links with Beijing's biggest labor camp. Chrysler denied any ties to BAIC, but a reporter for the Hong Kong-based *Eastern Express* discovered that the chairman of Beijing Jeep, Wang Mei, was the deputy general manager of BAIC. Wang's office said, "BAIC has an administrative role in Beijing Jeep." A bus factory run by the New Face Labor Camp was listed as an enterprise belonging to BAIC in the 1993 Beijing Industrial Yearbook.[35]

Reports on prison goods for exports were corroborated by the *New York Times*. Beijing bureau chief Nicholas Kristof said in July 1993 that a recently imprisoned Chinese student told him of his experiences in a prison factory that made Christmas tree lights. Former student leader, Xu Yiruo, confirmed this; he disclosed that during his imprisonment at the Qingdao No. 1 Prison, in the coastal city of Qingdao in Shandong Province, he and his inmates worked long hours—up to 20 hours a day when facing deadlines—assembling the lights. Christmas trees and Christmas tree lights were virtually unknown in China at the time so presumably, the lights they assembled were for export. Indeed, Xu Yiruo said officials at the prison had told him the lights were for export to Great Britain.[36]

Xu was later transferred from Qingdao to the Shandong Province No. 1 Reeducation Through Labor Camp at Zibo, where he and fellow inmates mined a fine clay for export. The clay, known as "jiaobaoshi" in Chinese, is used to make heat-resistant ovenware. When Kristof contacted the Shandong Province Metals and Minerals Import and Export Corporation, the government agency proudly acknowledged that the unique product was indeed from the Zibo labor camp and said the clay was exported to Japan and the United States. Officials at the company, anxious to do business, even asked the inquiring American journalist if he would like to buy a few tons for export to the United States.[37] Noting that American companies continued to buy prison goods from China in violation of U.S. laws, the *New York Times* urged the Clinton Administration to require importers to specify where they obtained their products.[38]

Human rights groups throughout the period under study put the total number of labor camp inmates in China at around 20 million, of whom perhaps 20,000 or more were political prisoners. The estimated number of political prisoners was understandably at variance with the official figure. According to Minister of Justice Xiao Yang, the total number of "counter-revolutionaries" in custody, meaning political prisoners, was around 3,700.[39] The real figure is impossible to discern because in China many political offenders are jailed for offenses not normally punished with prison terms in other countries.

If the figure of 20 million is considered accurate, China's prison population would work out to 1,740 per 100,000 of population, compared to 486 in the United States and 95 in Britain.[40] This is an unusually high figure considering the crime rate in China and seems to indicate that many people are incarcerated simply to provide the state with cheap labor. Supporting this view, according to Wang Mingdi, head of the "Labor Reform Bureau" under the Ministry of Justice, 50 percent of prison inmates are under twenty-five years of age. Eighty percent are less than thirty-five years old. Wang disclosed this fact at a ceremony while accepting magazines donated by the Communist Youth League and the National Federation of Youth. Referring to the youthful inmate population, Wang said, "Labor reform and labor education are a special kind of youth work."[41] (See Appendix 3.)

## Selling Organs of Executed Prisoners

One of the most disturbing categories of news concerning the violation of human rights in the People's Republic of China in 1993 and 1994 involved allegations of the sale of death-row inmates' organs for use in medical transplants. This practice was not new; it had been reported before and vehemently denied by the government.[42] During the period under review, however, more reports surfaced, including many documented by human rights groups and corroborated by eyewitnesses.

In the way of background, by the late 1980s, the organ selling practice had become a lucrative trade. It catered mainly to foreigners who were willing to pay a hefty fee for an organ they could not get elsewhere easily or quickly. Patients from Hong Kong, Thailand, Taiwan, Indonesia, and Malaysia needing organs paid as much as HK$400,000 (U.S.$51,000) for a kidney transplant at well-equipped hospitals in Guangdong in southern China. The whole operation was organized very efficiently. Doctors would wait at the execution grounds and remove organs from prisoners right after execution in a makeshift operating tent or in the back of a military truck and then rush the organs to the hospital to the waiting patient on the operating table. In some cases, reports said, organs such as kidneys and corneas, were taken from prisoners the day before the scheduled execution.

On April 22, 1993, the Tokyo *Mainichi Shimbun* quoted a surgeon from a hospital in Guangdong Province in southern China as saying that his hospital performed an average of 100 kidney transplant operations a year, with most kidneys coming from executed prisoners. He estimated that as many as 2,000 kidney transplants were done annually in China. The doctor told *Mainichi Shimbun* that the cost of a transplant operation was so high that the ordinary citizen in China could not afford it. Consequently, organs of executed prisoners were sold to rich foreign patients or powerful high officials. The paper cited a sixty-six year-old woman from Hong Kong who had received a kidney transplant operation at a Guangdong hospital. The kidney was from an executed prisoner. She reported that during her stay at the hospital, sixteen similar transplant operations were performed there. *Mainichi Shimbun* said the fees varied greatly for such operations, depending on the medications used and the level of care the patient received. They ranged from HK$150,000 (U.S.$20,000) to HK$400,000 (U.S.$51,000), astronomical figures for the average Chinese citizen.[43]

The New York-based human rights group Asia Watch said in an August 1994 report that as many as 2,000 to 3,000 organs, mainly kidneys and corneas, were removed from death-row prisoners annually in China for transplants. It said executed prisoners had become "a principal source for organ transplants" in

China in a system where there was no prior consent from the condemned or judicial safeguards against abuse.[44]

Asia Watch added that high officials were first in line for the organs and that the remaining organs went for high prices to foreigners and overseas Chinese, mainly from Hong Kong. According to Chinese laws, removal of organs was supposed to be based on the consent of the prisoner or his family. Given the situation in China, however, where arrests and imprisonments are made at will, authorities apparently ignore the law or claim that the prisoners "willingly donated the organs." In many cases, organs are even removed without the knowledge of the prisoner or his family. In other cases, the family would receive a partial payment before the removal, and if the family refused to grant permission, it was threatened by the police or hit with a big bill for the prisoners' room and board during incarceration up to the day of execution. The bills even included the cost of the execution bullet and cremation charges.[45]

Asia Watch said it had also received reports on removal of organs before execution for optimum freshness. In some cases, executions were deliberately delayed to fit transplant operation schedules at the hospital. The human rights group quoted a former doctor from Guangdong who was ordered to remove kidneys from prisoners the day before their execution.[46]

The Asia Watch reports were corroborated by two eyewitnesses now residing in New York: Lao Gui, a former reporter for Beijing's official *Legal Daily*; and Liu Qing, who had spent ten years in prison because he was a dissident student leader. While covering a story in Nanchang, the capital of Jiangxi Province, Lao Gui recalled he once stayed at the armed police guest house where a remorseful policeman had told him of his participation in the execution of a political prisoner named Zhong Haiyuan. He had also witnessed the removal of her kidneys.

Lao Gui's subsequent investigation uncovered the following grisly tale. Zhong was a primary school teacher in Ganzhou, Jiangxi Province, who was imprisoned because she had spoken out in defense of a colleague accused of counterrevolutionary activities. Four months after her friend was shot, she was also sentenced to death. At this time, at the No. 92 Field Hospital in Nanchang, an air force pilot, the son of a high official, was dying of kidney failure and in urgent need of a transplant. Doctors at the hospital told the officers in charge of the execution of Zhong not to kill her instantly so as to save a "live" kidney for the privileged patient. On the day of the execution, Zhong was first injected under her ribs with a solution to "preserve" her kidneys. Later, she was shot only once in the right side of her back and apparently did not die right away. She was rushed to a makeshift operating table on the back of a military truck near the execution grounds where her kidneys were taken out.[47]

Liu Qing told the story of his college schoolmate Yang Liangrong, who worked for the Academy of Architecture in Jiangsu Province. Seriously ill with kidney failure, Yang was able to buy a kidney for 5,000 yuan (U.S.$600) from a death-row prisoner through his family connections. A hospital ambulance was at the execution grounds to take the executed prisoner back to the hospital for the kidney removal, Liu reported.[48]

Chinese authorities denied the practice in November 1994, calling the reports by foreign media "sheer fabrication." Officials at a government agency contacted by the Hong Kong-based China Information Agency said that under Chinese law, organ donation must be based on the consent of the donor and that this rule applies to both convicts and ordinary people. "Such instances are extremely rare," Chinese officials insisted. They declared: "The claims that 90 percent of executed prisoners have had their organs removed by hospitals are completely groundless." Furthermore, they called reports that organ transplant needs had caused a sharp increase in the number of executed convicts "a slanderous attack on China's judicial system."[49]

## China Accounts for Most of World's Executions

The total number of executions carried out in China in any given year is a secret, but it is generally agreed that China is responsible for the lion's share of executions in the world. Amnesty International counted 1,079 in 1992.[50] It said there were more than 1,400 in 1993, and it believed that many more were not recorded or publicized.[51] Amnesty said the number of executions in 1993 was the highest it had ever recorded for a single year. Though the Chinese government does not issue figures, the press does report executions from time to time, mainly as a crime deterrent measure. Local newspapers and official publication of law-enforcement authorities such as *Legal Daily News* often print news of executions for domestic consumption that are in turn picked up by foreign wire services. To publicize the success of major campaigns against crime or to underscore a renewed government determination to fight it, leading Party organs such as *People's Daily* or the Supreme People's Court in Beijing sometimes take the unusual step of publicly announcing death sentences.

The following compilation consists of cases gleaned from a variety of sources. Understandably, it represents only a small percentage of the actual number of cases and should be viewed as merely a sampling of the wide range of types of "criminals" put to death in China. It includes, for example, the case of a man who had robbed passengers at a train station of belongings worth a total of about U.S.$300 and that of a small-time repeated burglar whose loot amounted to a mere U.S.$145. More often than not, as the cases below demonstrate, it was those who were least able to defend themselves who ended up receiving capital punishment while the high and mighty, particularly high party officials and their families, got off free even if they may have committed much more serious crimes. These cases are arranged in chronological order and whenever possible, details such as the name of the offender, the nature of the crime, the sentencing court, and the reporting agency are provided.

The *World Journal* reported in a dispatch on December 31, 1992 that in a year-end "cleanup" fourteen train robbers and thieves were executed in Changsha, the capital of Hunan Province. The report said most of the executed criminals were former inmates of labor camps who continued to rob trains and steal from freight cars after release their from the camps. The report gave the following details: Xu Weidong, who robbed a passenger at a train station and raped a woman there in the early morning hours of April 12, 1992; Hou Jianhui, a former labor camp inmate, who robbed passengers several times at Zhuzhou train station of cash totaling over 2,500 yuan (U.S.$300); Yang Shilin, Fu Jianguo, Long Tieniu, He Shiluo, and twenty others, all former labor camp inmates, who had stolen goods repeatedly from freight trains on the Hunan-Guizhou lines.

In the southern Chinese city of Shenzhen in the first days of January 1993, officials announced death sentences at mass rallies then executed the prisoners on the spot. At one rally, held at a vast square in front of the Shenzhen theater, Li Hao, Shenzhen's Communist Party secretary, told a crowd of some 10,000 people gathered there that the "law and order" situation in the district was severe and that strong measures were necessary to maintain order and to bolster the confidence of foreign investors. Twenty-two executions were handed down during this spate.[52] Shenzhen, across from Hong Kong, is the largest center of foreign investment in southern China.

Associated Press (AP) reported from Beijing on January 10, 1993 that as part of the customary sweep before the Chinese New Year, the government executed fifty-nine criminals in one day, including six in Shanghai and fifty-three in various cities in Guangdong Province in southern China. The AP dispatch quoted an official newspaper as saying that the six in Shanghai had belonged to a crime group that robbed trains throughout twelve provinces. During a three-year period, they committed thirty-two robberies, looting passengers of belongings worth more than 650,000 yuan (U.S.$80,000). According to *Yangcheng Evening News* in Guangzhou on January 9, of these executed in Guangdong Province, nineteen were convicted of thievery, seventeen of armed robbery, nine of murder or rape, six of highway robbery, and two of unspecified "economic crimes." On the day of the execution, various courts in Guangdong also announced the sentences of more than 10,000 criminals, including nearly 300 death, death with reprieve, and life sentences.[53]

Agence France Presse (AFP) reported on March 3, 1993 in a dispatch from Beijing the execution of twenty-one criminals in Sichuan Province to "insure (sic) political stability." Quoting the *Chongqing Legal News*, AFP said the executed criminals had been robbers, rapists, and gangsters who were repeat-offenders. They included a woman named Shih Tingyuan who had murdered the six-year-old son of her former lover. The executions were carried out on February 23 after a mass meeting attended by more than 4,000 people in Chongqing, the provincial capital. Speaking at the mass meeting, Tan Qinglin, the city's deputy mayor, called the executions a "very important move to insure Chongqing's social order and political stability." "Resolute actions" in dealing with crime were particularly necessary in the economic reforms, he told the gathering.[54]

In a March 7, 1993 dispatch from Nanning, the capital city of Guangxi Zhuang Autonomous Region, the China News Agency reported the execution of eighteen criminals in six of the region's major cities. Officials at the Guangxi High People's Court were quoted as saying that rape and the sale of women and children were on the rise in Guangxi. Since 1991, various courts in the region had handled a total of 871 cases of abduction and selling of women and children and sentenced eleven to death. During the same period, the courts tried 2,517 rape cases and handed down forty-seven death sentences.[55]

A man named Ren Jixuan was executed in Xi'an, Shaanxi Province on March 23 for poisoning seven people to death, according to the official Xinhua News Agency. A retired mechanic, he had rented out part of his house to Xu Zhongliang, a food peddler. In January, when the two got into a dispute, the landlord accused the tenant of not paying water and electricity bills. On the night of February 22, according to the report, Ren put insect pesticide into Xu's food. Thirty-two unsuspecting people ate the food and seven died of poison. On March 16, Ren was sentenced to death by the Xi'an Intermediate People's Court.[56]

The Guangzhou Intermediate People's Court sentenced ten drug traffickers to death at a mass rally on March 26, 1993. Their executions were carried out immediately, the official China News Agency reported. Among those executed was a Hong Kong citizen named Lin Guomin who had bought more than 130,000 grams of heroin in China between January 1988 and June 1989 for smuggling to Europe and North America.[57]

The Shanghai High People's Court on April 2, 1993 upheld the death penalty for a man who had splashed his former lover with acid. Li Huaxing, angered by his girlfriend Pan Ping's decision to end their relationship, poured sulfuric acid over her face and body on the night of September 24, 1992, causing severe burns. The case was widely publicized and Li was arrested and sentenced to death by the Shanghai Intermediate People's Court on February 20, 1993.[58] Under Chinese law, the decision of the appeals court is final.

The Fujian High People's Court handed down twelve death sentences for piracy on April 20, 1993 and ordered the immediate execution of nine of the convicted criminals, with a two-year reprieve for the remaining three. Nine others were given life sentences. The Hong Kong-based China Information Agency said that over a two-year period, the pirates had looted eleven fishing boats and freighters along the Fujian coast, scuttled five of them, and killed thirty-three crew members.[59]

The Zhangzhou Intermediate Court in Fujian Province sentenced three drug traffickers to death and one to life in prison on April 28, 1993. The four were Lin Zhengquan and Zheng Songzhi, who were given death sentences; Chen Shaoxiong, who received death with a two-year reprieve; and Gao Quancheng, who was given a life prison sentence. In one of the largest drug cases in the province, police caught the four selling 1,898 grams of heroin in June 1992.[60] Also in Fujian Province, six people were executed on April 29 after being convicted of robbery, murder, and rape. The sentences were handed down by the Intermediate People's Court at a mass rally in the coastal city Xiamen and were followed by immediate executions.[61]

Xu Liangtong, deputy presiding judge of the Guangdong High People's Court, told a press conference in Guangzhou on May 8, 1993 that forty-eight drug traffickers, including several from other countries, had been sentenced to death by various courts of the province in April. He named two Thai women, known by their Chinese names as Zhang Shihui and Huang Huijuan, as among them. Zhang, in fact, had already been executed when this information was released. The official China News Agency said later that Zhang was among the first foreign drug traffickers to be put to death in China.[62]

On April 21, 1993, China News Agency reported the execution of eighteen robbers and rapists in Foshan city of Guangdong Province. The report said the eighteen were among 140 prisoners convicted of major crimes including robbery, killing, and rape. In one case, two robbers stabbed a policeman and then held his head under water in a ditch, drowning him. In another case, five bandits committed thirteen armed robberies, killing five of their victims and gang-raping three women.[63]

The police chief of Longan County of Guangxi Zhuang Autonomous Region was executed for molesting a child on May 21, 1993, according to the pro-Beijing *Wen Hui Bao* in Hong Kong. Lu Shichang, the report said, joined the public security police in 1954 and rose to the head of the county public security bureau in the late 1980s. He had allegedly molested eleven women over the years but had been able to get away with this for some time because of his position and power. However, on the afternoon of October 30, 1991, he went to a nursery and tried to molest two teachers there. When the teachers fled, he grabbed a little girl named Chen and raped her. He was caught in the act and arrested.[64]

Two peasants were executed in Guangzhou on May 30, 1993 for selling the skin of a panda to a Hong Kong smuggler for profit, according to the China Information Agency. The two peasants, fifty-three-year-old Deng Tianshun and a forty-eight-year-old woman named Zhu Xiuying, went to Jiangyu in Sichuan Province in May 1989 and bought the skin of the giant panda for 11,000 yuan (U.S.$1,375). When they took the skin to Guangzhou, they were caught in a hotel. The two had previously sold panda skins on two occasions, according to investigation findings.[65] It is noteworthy that the two were put to death not for illicit trade in endangered animals but rather for profiteering.

The New York *Shih-chieh Jih-pao*'s Mainland China News Center reported on June 12, 1993 that a peasant from Sichuan Province was sentenced to death for selling more than a dozen women, including his own mother, wife, and three-year-old daughter. The report said that the twenty-seven-year-old peasant named Liu from Lingshui, Sichuan Province had, in five years, lured more than a dozen women from his home village and sold them. He then took his wife to Shandong Province and sold her to a local farmer for 1,400 yuan (U.S.$175). Later, he took his three-year-old daughter from home, telling her that she was going to see her mother, and sold her for 450 yuan (U.S.$56). Then, one day, he took his mother to a Beijing suburb and sold her to a farmer for 1,200 yuan (U.S.$150).[66]

Marking International Anti-Drug Day on June 26, 1993, the China Central Television reported in the evening news that mass rallies were held in four provinces to sentence seventy drug-related offenders to death or life imprisonment, including twenty-eight criminals in Yunnan Province and twenty-eight in Fujian Province.[67] In Guizhou Province, according to a China News Agency report, local police handled 289 drug-related cases from January to May 1993, arresting 561 traffickers and 886 addicts and seizing unspecified amounts of heroin and opium. The report said that the government had allocated more than 4 million yuan (U.S.$500,000) to build twenty additional rehabilitation centers in the province.[68] Meanwhile, the English-language *China Daily* reported on June 26, 1993, that there were many underground factories in Guangdong and Fujian provinces turning out amphetamine for export.[69] The paper said that more than 650 kilograms of amphetamine were seized by police in 1992.[70]

In Shenzhen, the new southern city across from Hong Kong, thirteen criminals, mostly drug offenders, were executed on International Anti-Drug Day, according to a *Shih-chieh Jih-pao* report. In the inland city of Xi'an in Shaanxi Province, the city's Intermediate People's Court sentenced several drug traffickers to death, a China News Agency dispatch said, including a peasant named Tong Zhutang who was convicted of selling 10,750 grams of opium.[71]

On July 2, 1993, the Shanghai Intermediate People's Court sentenced to death eight people who had been convicted of murder, rape, and armed robbery and ordered the immediate execution of four of them because of the particular viciousness of their crimes, *Shih-chieh Jih-pao* reported. Among those executed was Liu Xueli, a repeated offender from Harbin, a city in northern China, who robbed a Shanghai home on the afternoon of July 9, 1992. When the homeowner returned home with his son and confronted the robber, the robber stabbed both in the head and chest with a sharp knife causing serious injuries.[72]

The Hong Kong-based China Information Agency reported in a dispatch from Guangzhou on July 9, 1993 the sentencing of 230 drug offenders in the first five months of 1993 saying "many serious offenders" were put to death. Quoting official sources, the dispatch said that during the five-month period, a total of 963 cases were cracked, resulting in the seizure of 69,214 grams of heroin, 51,740 grams of morphine, and 1,525 grams of opium. Nearly 10,000 people were arrested, including 8,000 addicts. In one particularly serious case in Guangzhou, police in the Zhuhai district of the city arrested twenty-one traffickers in March, netting 38,520 grams of heroin destined for distribution to inland areas.[73]

In a dispatch from Guangzhou on July 13, 1993, the official China News Agency reported simultaneous mass rallies in five cities in the province. At the rallies "stiff sentences" (possibly including death sentences) were announced by the local intermediate people's courts for criminals convicted of selling women into prostitution.[74] Most of the victims were innocent young women from rural areas who had swarmed into coastal cities in search of factory jobs and presumably a better life. They became easy prey for crime syndicates. In one typical case, a young woman from the village who worked as a maid in a barber shop was kidnapped, gang raped, and then sold to another crime gang by her tormentors for 600 yuan (U.S.$75).[75] Xu Liangdong, deputy presiding judge of Guangzhou High People's Court, noted that many crime groups were from other provinces. They operated out of hotel rooms and temporarily rented houses with little police surveillance and were part of the so-called "floating population," estimated to number 100 million along coastal cities, that formed an explosive underclass in many boom towns. "It is clear that we have lost control of the population in many areas," Judge Xu said.[76]

The official *Guangming Daily* reported on July 14, 1993 that a dismissed actor was sentenced to death for murdering his own daughter and selling her body. Quoting the paper, a Reuters dispatch from Beijing said the man, named Wang, decided to kill his eleven-year-old daughter and sell the corpse because he had learned that an unmarried young man had died and the young man's family would offer 1,000 yuan (U.S.$174) for a dead girl for him to "marry." (Many superstitious peasants believe that an unmarried man will become a vicious devil. Thus, families often find a girl who has recently died for the deceased to "marry" in order to avoid the curse.) Wang strangled his daughter to death and pretended that she had been killed in a car accident.[77]

The Chongqing Intermediate People's Court in Sichuan Province sentenced ten robbers to death on July 29, 1993 and ordered their immediate execution. The ten highway bandits, most of them peasants, preyed on long-distance buses, robbing and killing passengers. In one case in May, three bandits stopped a bus at night, killed one passenger, wounded three, and made away with a loot of 3,600 yuan (U.S.$450). The youngest of the executed peasant-bandits was only nineteen years old.[78]

On August 11, 1993, the Shanghai Intermediate People's Court sentenced thirteen people to death and ordered the immediate execution of nine of them, according to a Chinese Information Agency dispatch from Shanghai. The sentenced criminals were convicted of murder, rape, robbery, and theft.[79] On August 18, seven criminals were executed in Xiamen, Fujian Province, after their death sentences were upheld by the Fujian High People's Court, the *Xiamen Daily* reported. They were convicted of robbery, embezzlement, theft, and aggravated battery.[80]

In this wave of executions, another 15 criminals were shot in Guangzhou and Fanyu of Guangdong Province on August 24 following sentences announced at mass rallies. They were described as murderers and thieves, all young male, including one who specialized in robbing people at public toilets.[81]

The Yunnan High People's Court at a sentencing rally held in Kunming on August 26, 1993 announced the death sentence of a man convicted of manufacturing and selling fake famous-brand cigarettes, according to a broadcast of the Yunnan People's Radio. The case attracted national attention not only because of the large volume of cigarettes produced and marketed but also because the scandal involved units of the People's Liberation Army. Han Shulin, the ringleader of the crime group, was said to have used forged papers to fake the identity of an army officer in order to avoid taxes. He marketed his fake Hongtashan brand cigarettes (the nationally famous brand from Yunnan and one of the province's top revenue-earners) to several provinces, signing contracts to supply 1.8 million cartons of cigarettes worth 96 million yuan ($12 million). He collected advance payments of 7.94 million yuan (U.S.$982,000) before he was caught.[82] In a broadcast on the day of his execution, the Yunnan People's Radio denounced his criminal activities as having "seriously impaired the reputation of Yunnan's famous brand names, undermined the interests of state enterprises, seriously disrupted the social and economic order and impeded the socialist market economy."[83]

China News Agency in a dispatch from Beijing on August 26, 1993 reported the execution of three men in Sichuan, Yunnan and Anhui Provinces for profiteering through fraudulence. Wang Lingang, an unemployed man from Sichuan, sold more than 400 tons of industrial chemicals to unsuspecting peasants as fertilizer, ruining more than 3,000 acres of crops. He pocketed 120,000 yuan (U.S.$15,000) in profit. In Yunnan, Han Shulin was the ringleader of a group specializing in making and marketing cheap cigarettes under famous brand names. He signed contracts with prospective buyers in five provinces, netting a profit of more than 3,000,000 yuan (U.S.$375,000). The worst case was that of a peasant in Anhui named Bai Songwu, who bought a batch of expired controlled drugs, put new labels on the vials, and sold them as antibiotics, causing three deaths. Liu Jiachen, deputy head of the Supreme People's Court, spoke of this case as a new form of crime, bred by the economic reforms. In the transition from the earlier socialist "command" economy to a socialist "market" economy, Liu said, unprincipled people took advantage of the confusion for personal gains with no concern for public good. Noting that in some areas, both individual entrepreneurs and employees of state-run enterprises and sometimes even smugglers from other countries were involved, he pledged that the government would strike at the criminals without mercy.[84]

On August 27, 1993, the official *People's Daily* reported that four government officials were sentenced to death and two others to life imprisonment and fourteen years, respectively, for corruption. The sentences were handed down by the Beijing Intermediate People's Court. The four sentenced to death were middle-level officials in state-run enterprises, including one director in the huge State Minerals Import and Export Company. They were convicted of either fraud or embezzlement. In its report, *People's Daily* quoted President Jiang Zemin's pledge to "execute a number of people" to underscore the government's determination to curb rampant official corruption.[85]

In a dispatch from Shanghai on September 14, 1993, China News Agency reported the death sentences and immediate execution of seven people who had repeatedly preyed on taxi drivers. The Shanghai Intermediate People's Court, which announced the sentencing at a mass rally, also sentenced four others to life or long prison terms. The report said all eleven offenders were young. Their average age was twenty and the youngest was only seventeen. Nine of them were "floaters" from other parts of China, including Xinjiang in the far west and Guizhou in southwestern China. They committed many crimes, sometimes three robberies in one night. They not only took money and valuables but often viciously killed the victims, the report said.[86]

In an anti-corruption drive in September 1993, several middle-level government officials were executed in the coastal region, where official corruption was rampant due to the vibrant economy. On September 7, the Yangjiang Municipal Intermediate People's Court in Guangdong Province sentenced the manager of a municipal housing corporation to death for corruption. Zhang Tiehan, during his tenure as general manager from January 1986 to December 1989, embezzled public funds and took kickbacks from contractors totaling 1,790,000 yuan (U.S.$237,000), according to a *Shih-chieh Jih-pao* dispatch from Guangzhou.[87] On September 11, a former public security chief of Huizhou, a city in Guangdong Province, was sentenced to death for smuggling and taking bribes. In a verdict decided by the Huizhou Intermediate People's Court, Hong Yonglin, the powerful head of the city's public security bureau, was convicted of various abuses of power, including smuggling seventy-five automobiles into China for huge profits and illegally authorizing people to move to Hong Kong for a fee. Upon his conviction, more than HK$4 million (US$500,000) in personal assets and cash were confiscated because he failed to account for them.[88]

In Fujian Province, according to a dispatch of the China News Agency from the provincial capital of Fuzhou on September 16, courts in four cities handed down five death sentences and one life imprisonment for "economic crimes." Wu Zhaonan, a forty-year-old warehouse clerk, who was convicted of embezzling 140,000 yuan (U.S.$17,500) in government funds by illegally selling public property, and then killing five whistle blowers, was immediately executed upon sentencing. The others were accountants, auditors, and book-keepers in state-run enterprises convicted of embezzlement of public funds from 240,000 Yuan (U.S.$30,000) to 1,130,000 yuan (U.S.$141,200).[89]

In Shanghai, according to a dispatch by the China News Agency on September 21, the local Intermediate People's Court sentenced two persons to death and seven others to life or long prison terms for corruption and embezzlement. The same news agency in another dispatch from Hangzhou, Zhejiang Province, on the same day said that in that coastal province, ninety-nine government officials had been arrested from January to August for various "economic crimes." The report said that although a few of them were factory directors or managers or public security police, most were middle- or low-level employees who occupied "strategic" positions as accountants, bookkeepers, buyers, or warehouse clerks. As such, they could easily abuse their powers for personal gain.[90]

On September 25, 1993, courts in several cities in Guangdong Province handed down sentences on sixteen criminals, including five death sentences for kidnapping and murder, according to a *Shih-chieh Jih-pao* dispatch from Hong Kong. The kidnapping and murder cases were particularly serious. According to the report, Su Shaolun, Su Jiansong, and So Guoqiang ambushed a motorcyclist in a Guangdong suburb in June, killed him by pounding his head with bricks, and then stuffed the body in an abandoned oil barrel on the roadside. Later, in another grisly case, the trio kidnapped two cousins for ransom, a nine-year-old boy and a seven-year-old girl. When the family could not come up with the money on time, they strangled the two children with their scarves and buried their bodies.[91]

### Mass Executions Greet National Day in Many Provinces

Marking National Day on October 1, courts in Jiangxi Province announced more than 80 death sentences in a series of mass rallies held in many cities, reported the China Information Agency on September 28 from Nanchang, the provincial capital. Many of the condemned were unemployed urban youths convicted of robbing homes or buses, according to the report. Some were "floating" people from other provinces; others were ex-convicts who could not find jobs. Meanwhile, in Fuzhou, Fujian Province, the same news agency reported the execution of seven prisoners for murder, robbery, theft, and "economic crimes." Eight others, convicted of similar crimes, were given death with reprieve sentences or life or long prison terms.[92] All this would seem to confirm the prevailing cynicism in the popular saying that in fighting "economic crimes," the government "strikes not at the tigers, but at the flies."

The pre-National Day execution record was set in Hunan Province. Quoting *Hunan Daily*, a Reuters report from Beijing said public sentencing rallies were held on September 25 in 119 cities and towns of the province. Some 2,900 criminals received sentences, and of these, about 360 were given the death penalty or life imprisonment. Most of the death sentences were carried out immediately after the public rallies. *Hunan Daily* proudly proclaimed, "Gunshots of justice rang through the province."[93] The same Reuters report also listed pre-National Day executions in other provinces, including twelve in Shenzhen special economic zone in Guangdong, nine in Xinjiang, and eight in Qinghai.[94]

In October 1993, many cases were reported in Guangdong and Yunnan. Twenty-two drug offenders were executed. On October 23, two traffickers, one a Chinese from Hong Kong named Lin Guoming, were executed in Guangzhou, according to the China News Agency. Lin teamed up with Xie Jianping, an unemployed youth in Guangzhou, to buy narcotics in China and ship the drugs to Hong Kong for distribution to other parts of the world. Between January 1988 and June 1989, the two managed to smuggle a total of 134,000 grams of heroin to Hong Kong. They were sentenced to death by the Guangzhou Intermediate People's Court and executed immediately afterward.[95]

In Kunming, Yunnan Province, the Kunming Intermediate Court sentenced twenty offenders to death and carried out the death sentences after a mass rally, the China Information Agency reported on October 28. The twenty were convicted of trafficking heroin ranging in amount from 187 grams to as much as 14,360 grams. Three of the executed criminals were women.[96] In Guangdong Province, many rehabilitation centers were set up by local authorities and private charities to combat the growing drug problem. A China Information Agency report on October 27 said most addicts treated at the centers were unemployed youths or individual entrepreneurs. The youngest was a fourteen-year-old. At the Yangjiang City Drug Rehabilitation Center, for example, of the 357 addicts taken in during the first six months of 1993, over 90 percent were under thirty years old.[97]

In Guangxi, three low-level officials were executed for corruption and a fourth was given the death sentence with a two-year reprieve, according a China News Agency report from Nanning, capital city of Guangxi Autonomous Region. The three executed were Wu Jihong, a cashier at a food company in Liuzhou; Deng Hanfeng, an accountant at a sugar refinery in Nanning; and Huang Sanming, an acquisitions clerk at Guangxi University. The three were all convicted of embezzling public funds ranging from 170,000 yuan (U.S.$21,250) to 290,000 yuan (U.S.$36,250).[98] Meanwhile, Tang Anbang, deputy presiding judge of Guangxi High People's Court, told a press conference that from January to September 1993, courts in Guangxi had handled 869 cases of "economic crime," including corruption, bribery, smuggling and counterfeiting. A total of 1,590 people were arrested and 27 were sentenced to death. Tang said economic crimes were growing more serious, citing one case that involved as much as 120,000,000 yuan (U.S.$15,000,000). The majority of offenders were managers and officials in finance and accounting, Tang said.[99]

Sixteen people were executed for "economic crimes" and other offenses in various cities in Guangdong on October 29, 1993, according to a *Shih-chieh Jih-pao* dispatch from Huizhou. Among the executed were two high local officials: Hong Yonglin, the former public security chief of Huizhou; and Chen Binggeng, the former head of the housing bureau of Shenzhen. Both were convicted of taking huge amounts of money through bribes and embezzlement.[100]

The *Hubei Daily* reported on November 14, 1993 that sixty criminals had been sentenced to death in the province over a period of several days. The report said the death sentences, announced at public rallies held in eleven cities, were meted out for murder, armed robbery, rape, theft, the selling of women and children, the killing of farm animals, and the disruption of farm production. One person who turned himself in after committing an armed robbery was still sentenced to death, according to the report.[101]

Five low-level employees at state-run enterprises were executed in Yunnan, Guangdong, Fujian, and Zhejiang provinces in November 1993 for embezzling public funds, according to a China News Agency dispatch from Beijing quoting an official source at the Supreme People's Court in the capital. These cases reached the highest court in the land because of their seriousness, each involving embezzling funds of more than a million yuan (U.S.$125,000), the report said. All were offenses committed by low-level officials who either handled large amounts of public funds or were otherwise in a position to abuse their power for personal gain.

In the Yunnan case, the embezzlers were two women: Li Lanzhen, head of the retail department of a food corporation, and Liu Guifeng, a weighing clerk at a meat processing plant. They teamed up well, with Liu under-reporting the amount of meat that passed through her scale at the plant and Li selling off the "excess" meat at her retail outlets to line their own pockets. Over the years, the two netted over 3,740,000 yuan (U.S.$470,000), the report said. In another case, Jiang Jiaxu, an accountant at a textile factory in Fujian, embezzled more than 1,110,000 yuan (U.S.$137,500) by cooking the books to pay off his gambling debts. In still another case, Li Qiang, a clerk at a light industry plant in Shenzhen, simply made off with 8,400 grams of company gold and fled to other parts of the country to sell his loot.[102] The fact that these cases reached the nation's highest court suggests the prevalence and seriousness of official corruption. In addition, the fact that only low-level officials were punished cannot but continue to foster cynicism among the population.

The anti-crime drive continued through the remaining months of 1993 in south China. On November 24, the Haikou Intermediate People's Court of Hainan sentenced eight common criminals to death and nineteen others to prison terms ranging from three to seventeen years.[103] On November 30, ten others, convicted of murder or armed robbery, were executed in Guangzhou following mass rallies held in several districts of the city.[104]

In an unusual case, three border patrol officers and a gang ringleader specializing in smuggling people out of the country were sentenced to death in Beijing on December 3, 1993. The case was unusual because the smugglers operated in the nation's capital at Beijing International Airport. The three border patrol officers, an army major named Zhao Donghe and two first lieutenants, Li Jianhui and Wang Lingang, were inspectors at the airport. The ringleader, Xu Ping, better known as a "snake head," managed to get over 120 persons out of China from Beijing airport between 1988 and 1991 by making fake travel documents stamped by the "cooperative" inspectors with the crucial approvals. During this three-year period, the officers received bribes totaling 1,600,000 yuan (U.S.$200,000) part of it in U.S. dollars, according to a *Shih-chieh Jih-pao* dispatch from Beijing.[105]

Thirteen drug traffickers were executed on December 10, 1993 in several cities in Guangxi following sentencing at mass rallies, a China News Agency dispatch from Nanning, capital of Guangxi, reported. Huang Jianming, deputy head of Guangxi High People's Court, said the thirteen were involved in several major cases of drug trafficking. Ta Zhuling, one of the traffickers, was caught in June 1992 driving back to Guangxi from Yunnan with 2,250 grams of heroin in his car. Yang Tingying, another trafficker, was described as the leader of a smuggling ring which was responsible for distributing some 7,670 grams of heroin.[106]

Three people were executed on December 11, 1993 for publicly molesting women in broad daylight, a Xinhua News Agency dispatch reported from Guangzhou. The dispatch said the incident took place on October 11 on Shahe Street in Guangzhou when six hooligans chased down several women including one who was pregnant, stripped them, and fondled them in public. The men were quickly arrested, and three of them were sentenced to death on October 27 by the Guangzhou Intermediate People's Court. On December 11, their appeals were turned down and they were executed on the same day.[107] On December 24, 1993, twenty common criminals were executed in five towns in Guangdong Province, according to the pro-Beijing *Wen Hui Bao* in Hong Kong. The twenty were all convicted of murder, armed robbery, and kidnap for ransom. They were executed following sentencing rallies in townships under the jurisdiction of Nanhai and Zhuhai.[108]

The year 1994 saw little change in the rising crime and the continued use of capital punishment. On January 17, three common criminals were executed in Guangzhou. Two of them were sentenced to death by the Guangzhou Intermediate Court for murder, and the third was put to death for theft, according to a *Shih-chieh Jih-pao* dispatch from Guangzhou. One of the murders, Li Lun, had killed seven people in three robberies, the report said.[109] On January 22, thirty people were executed in Kunming, Yunnan Province, after being convicted for murder, drug trafficking, and selling women and children, according to a *Shih-chieh Jih-pao* dispatch from the capital city. The executions took place after a mass rally at a sports stadium attended by more than 4,000 people.[110] On January 27, in the first large round of executions in Guangzhou, 30 common criminals were shot for armed robbery, rape, murder, and theft. The executions took place after sentences were announced in mass rallies held in many districts of Guangzhou city, the China News Agency reported. One of the executed, Lu Guiqiang, had in his possession ten Russian-made pistols, two grenades, and 138 rounds of ammunition at the time of his arrest, the report said.[111]

The period prior to the Chinese Lunar New Year in mid-February, officially known as the Spring Festival, is the traditional time for house-cleaning, which in recent years has meant waves of executions. The year 1994 was no exception. An Agence France Presses (AFP) dispatch from Beijing on February 8 said that media reports showed that more than 200 people had been executed since New Year's Day for murder, rape, armed robbery, drug-trafficking, and corruption.[112]

Six drug-traffickers were executed in Guangzhou on March 18, 1994, according to a China News Agency dispatch from the capital city of Guangdong Province. The six were involved in shipping large quantities of heroin from southwestern China to Guangzhou. One of them, Ma Zuohua, helped to transport 12,000 grams of heroin to Guangzhou from Chengdu, Sichuan Province, by air in 1989 and received 50,000 yuan (U.S.$6,250) in "commission," the report said. Two other traffickers, Ma Wengui and Ma Guoying, brought in 4,900 grams of heroin from Yunnan in April 1991 and were caught in a hotel a month later while negotiating a deal.[113]

Meanwhile, in Fujian, security police in Chuanzhou reported on March 18 that they had cracked a major drug ring in the province. The case involved smugglers from Taiwan and Hong Kong. In what Fujian officials described as the largest drug seizure in the province in history, police took in ninety-six "heroin bricks" bearing the "Twin-Lion Globe" trade mark, with a total weight of 36 kilograms. Police said the ring had twenty-two members, including eight from Taiwan and four from Hong Kong, and that the crime group's funds mainly came from Taiwan. From September 1992 to March 1993, the group managed to transport some 70 kilograms of heroin to Taiwan by fishing boat.[114]

The Central News Agency reported on April 1, 1994 that the Shaanxi

High People's Court had sentenced eight corrupt government officials to death, three to life imprisonment, and sixteen others to prison terms ranging from three to fifteen years. Among those sentenced to death was Liu Huimin, department head of the Xi'an Farmers Bank. Liu embezzled 6,150,000 yuan (U.S.$770,000) in government funds. Another official, an accountant at a ceramics and earthenware company named Li Zhiqing, made off with 133,300 yuan (U.S.$16,600) in company funds.[115]

Also on April 1, 1994, a China Information Agency dispatch from Nanchang, capital of Jiangxi Province, reported the execution of a peasant couple for kidnapping and selling ten children. The couple, Li Wenchu and Luo Lanzhen, from a village near Pingxiang, had kidnapped ten children ranging in age from four to eight in nearby villages and sold them in Fujian Province between August 1989 and April 1993, netting some 36,000 Yuan (U.S.$4,500), the report said. Their executions were ordered by the Jiangxi High People's Court.[116]

Kidnapping of women and children has been a persistent problem in the vast rural areas. In Guangxi Autonomous Region in the southwest, the problem was so serious that the government set up an "Office to Combat Kidnapping and Selling Women and Children." A spokesman for the office said in April 1994 that Guangxi ranked second in the nation in the number of women and children kidnapped annually, next only to the populous Sichuan Province, which had the highest number. Since 1991, he said, security police had rescued more than 1,000 kidnap victims every year. In 1993, police smashed 292 kidnapping rings and arrested 1,289 offenders, rescuing 997 women and 72 children. The spokesman made the disclosure as an eighteen-year-old girl was returned to her village in Guangxi from her fifty-seven-year-old "husband" in Inner Mongolia several thousand miles from her home.[117] On April 22, the *Legal Daily News* reported in Beijing the cracking of a large-scale human-trafficking ring operating in central China and the arrest of 66 operators. The report said most of the 120 women held by the group came from four rural counties in Hubei Province in central China. "Twenty women were gang-raped, 11 had been held for a long time, and four were crippled through torture," the report said. The going price for a woman was 3,800 yuan (U.S.$480).[118]

On April 4, 1994, the *China Procurators News* reported the death sentences for five people on drug-related charges in Gansu Province. Those sentenced included the son of the former public security chief of the province, according to an AFP dispatch from Beijing. Chuan Xiaoyang, the son of the former police chief, was a railway security policeman when he became the head of a seventeen-member drug ring. He was first arrested and sentenced to death with a two-year reprieve by the Lanzhou Intermediate People's Court in 1992. According to the report, there was an outcry of favoritism after the sentencing because four of his accomplices were immediately executed. To placate popular resentment, a committee was named and, after an eighteen-month investigation, it recommended immediate execution.[119] In publicizing the case, the *Legal Daily News*, the organ of the judicial authorities, tried to convey the impression of equal justice in China.

The head of a $100 million pyramid scheme was put to death on April 11, 1994, according to both Xinhua and China News Agencies. His accomplice was sentenced to twenty years in prison. The case, regarded as the largest financial scandal in the history of the People's Republic and allegedly involving some of the most powerful families in the country, attracted wide attention both at home and abroad. Shen Taifu, head of Great Wall Enterprises, was charged with illegally raising funds from potential investors by promising high returns. Established in February 1993, the company saw meteoric growth and, within a few months, it attracted more than 200,000 investors, widely rumored to include families of some top Party and government leaders. It garnered more than 1 billion yuan (U.S. $120,000,000) in funds and set up more than 120 branches throughout the country before it collapsed. Shen's chief accomplice, Li Xiaoshi, was formerly the deputy head of the state scientific commission, a cabinet post. In publicizing the punishments that the culprits in the scandal received, the official organs made no mention of any powerful investors or supporters, even though it was widely believed that the Great Wall would not have come into existence in the first place without them.[120]

### Drug Traffickers Work with Taiwan Counterparts

With the opening up of contacts between mainland China and Taiwan in recent years, drug and gun smugglers on both sides of the Taiwan Strait in increasing numbers teamed up to ship narcotics and firearms to Taiwan, where demand was on the rise in the newly affluent society. On April 27, 1994, six Taiwanese were sentenced to death or given life or long prison terms by the Xiamen Intermediate People's Court in Fujian Province for gunrunning, the China News Agency reported. In 1989 and 1990, six Taiwan businessmen and fishermen, including Wu Wenxin and Gan Qingzhi, bought more than 2,200 Chinese guns and some 49,000 rounds of ammunition in several deals, the report said. Wu and Gan were sentenced to death.[121]

Meanwhile, in the south of Taiwan, a counterfeiting operation was cracked by police in the city of Tainan on April 25. The plant printed a large amount of fake Chinese currency intended for use in China to buy narcotics. Five offenders were nabbed in the raid, together with finished and half-finished bills totaling over 300 million yuan (U.S.$37,500,000) at face value. Investigators said the suspects had confessed that they had used fake money to buy narcotics in China and brought the drugs in by fishing boat.[122]

On April 28, 1994, a *Shih-chieh Jih-pao* dispatch from Shenzhen, the southern China special economic zone, reported the sentencing of 106 common criminals. Nine were executed, and the remaining ninety-seven were given death with reprieve or life or long prison terms. The executed were guilty of armed robbery, murder and rape. Two others convicted of stealing eleven motorcycles were given life in prison.[123]

Four people were executed in Sichuan on May 9, 1994 for corruption and embezzlement, according to a Xinhua News Agency dispatch from Chengdu, the provincial capital. All four were sentenced to death by the Sichuan High People's Court for abusing their positions for personal gain. Yang Ciqing, general manager of a state-owned electronics corporation, took 385,000 yuan (U.S.$48,100) in kickbacks in marketing color television sets and embezzled another 400,000 yuan (U.S.$50,000) in company funds for personal use. Shih Furen, deputy director of a regional college entrance examination commission, took 411,300 yuan (U.S.$51,400) in bribes from the families of some 400 examination candidates, the report said. The other two included a bank teller and an insurance company clerk who likewise embezzled company funds.[124]

On May 10, twenty common criminals were executed in various cities for murder, rape, armed robbery and theft at railroad depot and oil fields, Liu Jiachen, deputy head of China's Supreme People's Court, told a press conference in Beijing. Meanwhile, two Filipino citizens were given the death sentence with a two-year reprieve in Fuzhou for drug trafficking, according to separate dispatches of the China News Agency. The fact that the nation's highest court took the unusual step of announcing the executions was meant to underscore both the serious crime problem and the government's determination to fight crime. Liu condemned the criminal activities as "very harmful to public security, social stability, state property, and the smooth building of the national economy" and pledged "resolute and forceful struggle" against such activities.[125]

Among the sixteen executed in Guangzhou were Min Qianbo and Yang Chunming, who on May 22 murdered an attendant at a hotel in Guangzhou. They stuffed the body under a bed and took his keys to other rooms to loot hotel guests. Seven others, including Liu Xiaoguang and Zhang Guobin, were guilty of stealing from Daqing oil fields in northern China equipment and materials worth 520,000 yuan (U.S.$65,000), the report said. The two Filipino nationals went to Xiamen, Fujian Province, under the guise of tourists on October 9, 1991 and were caught a week later at the airport with a large quantity of illegal amphetamine, which they had received from their Chinese accomplice. They were tried by the lower courts and the conviction was upheld by the Fujian High People's Court as the first drug case involving the death sentence for foreign nationals.[126]

On May 14, 1994, *Beijing Daily* reported the execution of four people "guilty of the most heinous crimes" and death sentences for eleven other criminals, with offenses ranging from murder, looting, and trafficking in guns and ammunition to "acting indecently." Among the executed was one named Peng Lipeng who, while on medical parole, had committed three burglaries and made away with a total of 1,160 yuan (U.S.$145) worth of loot. The report did not explain the crime of "acting indecently."[127]

Xinhua News Agency on May 16, 1994 reported the execution of two bootleggers in Sichuan. The two, Liu Bangyun and Huang Kaihong, mixed industrial-use alcohol with water to make some 20 tons of "white wine" for sale in October 1993, causing four deaths and ten cases of poisoning. Liu was a food store employee; Huang was an unemployed former inmate of a labor camp.[128]

A *Shih-chieh Jih-pao* dispatch on May 27, 1994 from Guangzhou in southern China reported that ten criminals were executed and twenty-two others given life or long prison terms for murder, kidnapping, car theft, and robbery in Guangdong Province. The executions were carried out in Zhuhai following several mass rallies. In one case, He Junwei killed a resident from Macao, dismembered the body, and hid the pieces in a sewer. Two kidnapping cases involved ransoms of nearly 3 million yuan (U.S.$375,000), the report said.[129]

Four cigarette smugglers were executed on May 29, 1994 in two provinces. They included a deputy battalion commander of the border patrol force in Guangdong—whose official duty was fighting smuggling—and two ranking public security officials in the coastal city of Weihai in Shandong Province. In announcing the executions, deputy head of the Supreme People's Court, Zhu Mingshan, said in Beijing that smuggling had reached "crisis proportions." He condemned local officials who protected one another from prosecution.[130] "Local protectionism and departmental coverups are an important root of the malignant and prevailing crime," Zhu said. Pointing to the executions, he warned that "those still adhering to such ideas will swallow what they have sown."[131]

Yang Mingji, the border patrol commander, colluded with a businessman to smuggle large quantities of cigarettes into China from Macao. In March and April 1993, according to official reports, he brought in 2,300 cases of cigarettes, valued at more than 5.1 million yuan (U.S.$637,500), using armed police under his command to guard the smuggling operation. On the day when his death sentence was announced by the Zhuhai Intermediate People's Court, 500 armed police were assembled to witness the execution. The two public security officials executed for smuggling cigarettes in Shandong were Fan Zhanwu, a political commissar of the border patrol force under the Weihai Public Security Bureau, and Li Ning, a deputy department head. Their accomplice, Liu Qishan, commissioner of business of Rushan city, was also executed.[132]

On May 21, 1994, six common criminals were executed in Luancheng, Hebei Province after a public trial, according to *Hebei Daily*. They were convicted of murder and armed robbery as "members of a bus marauding and waylaying gang."[133] On June 23, the Huaiyin Intermediate People's Court in

Jiangsu Province sentenced two thieves to death and several others to long prisons terms, the Nanjing *Xinhua Daily* reported on July 3. The court ordered the immediate execution of the theft ringleader, Sun Wei, an unemployed man who had stolen 128 cars and seven motorcycles from April 1989 to February 1993.[134]

A wave of executions took place on the eve of the International Anti-Drug Day on June 26, 1994. As many as ninety-five people were shot on drug-related charges in different localities from Fujian on the east coast to Xinjiang in the far west, according to the "Night News" on Beijing Central Television. These executed included fourteen drug offenders in Sichuan, ten in Fujian, fourteen in Shaanxi, forty-six in Guangdong and eleven in Xinjiang. Many more were given life or long prison sentences.[135] Six of the drug traffickers were from Taiwan and five were from Hong Kong.[136] An incomplete check of press reports through the end of June 1994 also showed death sentences for fourteen prisoners in Guangxi, five in Guizhou, and twenty-three in Yunnan.[137]

Two former executives of state-run enterprises were executed on July 4, 1994 in Beijing for corruption, according to Xinhua News Agency. The two were Guo Ziwen, fifty-two, former general manager of the China Coal Sales and Transportation Company who was convicted of taking bribes worth 468,000 yuan (U.S.$58,000) and obtaining 1 million yuan (U.S.$125,000) in profits by illegally selling foreign currency; and Hu Cong, thirty-eight, a former department head of the China Rural Development Trust and Investment Company who took 1.4 million yuan (U.S.$175,000) in bribes and approved bad loans totalling 64.5 million yuan (U.S.$8,062,000).[138]

Also on July 4, 1994, eleven criminals in Guangdong Province and seven criminals in Hainan Province were executed for murder and armed robbery, according to the China News Agency. The executions took place immediately following several mass rallies at which the death sentences were announced by the Intermediate People's Courts of Guangzhou and Haikou. Three of the executed in Hainan were gun smugglers from Taiwan.[139]

In a typical case of "catching the flies but not the tigers," the Shanghai Intermediate People's Court on July 7 ordered the execution of a refrigerator plant salesman, Ni Desheng, for embezzling 160,000 yuan (U.S.$20,000) in company funds.[140] On July 17, the Hohhot Intermediate People's Court in Inner Mongolia sentenced seven people to death for murder, rape, robbery, and theft, according to a report in a local newspaper. They were executed on the same day. Among the seven were two petty thieves, Wang Wancheng and Li Qingxiang, who had committed more than fifty thefts from January 1989 to November 1991, with loot worth a total of 250,000 yuan (U.S.$31,200).[141]

On July 22, the Shanghai Municipal Intermediate Court sentenced three to death on charges of rape and robbery and ordered the immediate execution of two other robbers previously sentenced to death, a radio broadcast in Chinese said. It reported that among the criminals sentenced or executed by the court, more than 70 percent were from outside Shanghai and 25 percent were repeat offenders.[142] On July 25, the Hong Kong *Wen Hui Bao* reported that six officials in Guangxi had been sentenced to death for corruption, according to a Central News Agency dispatch from Hong Kong. One of them, a county official named Tang Maorong who had taken 130,000 yuan (U.S.$16,250) in bribes, was immediately executed.[143]

Fuzhou, Shenzhen, and Guangzhou saw the executions of three major "economic criminals" on July 28, 1994 a Xinhua broadcast in Chinese said. To underscore the seriousness of the cases, and to sound a warning around the nation, the Supreme People's Court announced the executions in Beijing. The three were Zhang Jianping, a section head of the China (Fujian) Foreign Trade Center; Liu Jianyi, a clerk at the Shenzhen City Development Company; and Luo Rulong, a bookkeeper at the Guangdong Ceramics Company. These low-ranking employees at state-run companies were guilty of embezzlement and graft involving up to several million dollars. The Supreme People's Court attributed the crimes to the failure of the "leaders of some enterprises" to observe laws and regulations and to exercise supervision, but let those in charge go free with only a perfunctory admonition that they "should take these problems seriously."[144]

An AFP dispatch from Shanghai on August 1, 1994 reported that the authorities had sentenced twenty-one railway bandits to death and executed twelve of them. Lengthy jail terms were handed down to another thirty-two criminals convicted of railway-related offenses. The fifty-three bandits, operating as two gangs, had stolen a total of 1.36 million yuan (U.S.$156,000) worth of goods from freight cars, the report said.[145] On the same day, the Lieling Intermediate People's Court in Liaoning Province sentenced a peasant to death for killing six villagers by putting pesticide in their food, the *Liaoning Daily* reported on August 14.[146]

Several cases of mass executions were monitored in Hong Kong between August 1 and August 14, 1994. The *People's Court News* reported on August 11 that two men had been executed in Henan Province for stealing 36 cows and some small items of agricultural machinery worth a total of 9,300 yuan (U.S.$1,160)[147] On August 9, the Guangzhou Intermediate People's Court sentenced fifteen criminals to death for larceny, robbery, murder, and other crimes and executed them immediately. One of the fifteen condemned was Chen Haifeng, who on July 12, 1993, hijacked a BMW sedan and killed its driver, according to a Guangdong People's Radio broadcast monitored in Hong Kong.[148] On July 28 in Nanchang, Jiangxi province, the Railway Transport Intermediate Court sentenced thirty-four inmates to death or long prison terms for railway-related crimes and immediately executed twelve of them, according to a Jiangxi Radio broadcast on July 31. In Shenyang in the northeast, the city's Intermediate People's Court sentenced twenty-six people to death for bank robbery and murder on July 31, a dispatch of the China News Agency said.[149]

A Beijing radio broadcast on August 11 reported that four people had been sentenced to death for brewing toxic liquor in Sichuan and Hubei. Two of them were immediately executed. They made the toxic liquor by mixing industrial alcohol with water and white spirits and sold it for huge profits. Of fourteen people who suffered acute methanol poisoning after drinking the brew, four died and seven lost vision in both eyes, the broadcast said.[150]

The Fuzhou Intermediate People's Court sentenced fifteen criminals to death or long imprisonment on August 16 for crimes in rural areas including murder, rape, and robbery and ordered the immediate execution of four of them, according to the Hong Kong–based China Information Agency.[151] On August 18 and 19, *Beijing Daily* reported the executions of seven convicted criminals for murder and robbery. Among the murder victims were a Beijing University professor and his wife.[152] On August 19, the Shenyang Intermediate People's Court sentenced thirty-four to death or long prison terms for various crimes and immediately executed twenty-six of them, according to the Beijing *Legal Daily News.[153]*

On August 20, six criminals were executed in Fujian for robbery, murder and theft following sentencing rallies in eight cities in the province, according to the China News Agency. In another report, the agency said two leaders of a human trafficking ring were sentenced to death. The ring, consisting of nine members, kidnapped and sold twenty-two women from March 1989 to May 1992, the agency reported.[154] On August 22, Xinhua News Agency reported from Shenyang in Liaoning province that three officials had been executed for corruption. The three, Gui Bingquan, Zhao Fu, and Hu Yuzhang, were all officials at a county grain bureau who were found guilty of illegally selling public goods, defrauding the government, and taking bribes.[155]

Xinhua reported on August 26 that the Beijing Intermediate People's Court sentenced seven to death for gun-smuggling, armed robbery, and murder and ordered the immediate execution of two of them, Li Chunyou and Zhang Baochang. Li and Zhang had committed armed robbery nine times between April 1992 and November 1993, court papers said. Two other condemned, Liu Baosong and Yu Shuijun, had killed a taxi driver and a traffic policeman while hijacking the taxi.[156]

The Chongqing Intermediate People's Court held a mass rally on September 2, 1994 to announce the sentencing of thirteen economic criminals. Five were sentenced to death and the rest were given life or long imprisonment. The five who received the death sentences had each embezzled more than 300,000 yuan (U.S.$37,500) in government funds, the China News Agency reported.[157]

The China News Agency reported from Haikou the execution of five leaders of a crime ring in Hainan Province and the death penalty or life sentences for five others on September 9. According to the Hainan Intermediate People's

Court, the group terrorized the villages between 1988 and 1994, killing one person and wounding more than a dozen others, including a security policeman.[158] On September 13, the Central News Agency reported from Beijing that the Beijing Intermediate People's Court had sentenced four drug traffickers to death and ordered the immediate execution of two of them. One of the condemned was a woman, the report said.[159] On September 14, the Guangdong People's Radio reported that ten human traffickers including a woman, had been sentenced to death in Lufeng, Guangdong Province. The broadcast said that from January to July 1993, Wen Mali, Song Yangqing, and others had abducted thirty-eight women and sold them at prices ranging from 800 yuan (U.S.$100) to 2,000 yuan (U.S.$250).[160] In a dispatch from Beijing on September 16, Xinhua News Agency reported that two people had been sentenced to death by the Beijing Intermediate People's Court for publishing and selling pornographic materials. Gu Jieshu and Zhang Jun printed and sold twelve kinds of pornographic publications totaling more than 830,000 copies and the sales amounted to more than 4 million yuan (U.S.$500,000), the report said.[161]

A Shandong People's Radio broadcast from Jinan, the provincial capital, reported on September 20, 1994 that three people had been sentenced to death for embezzlement and four others were sentenced to death for theft and rape. The three embezzlers were all low-ranking bank employees who converted some 5.47 million yuan (U.S.$709,000) of public funds to unauthorized uses and directly embezzled 24,000 yuan (U.S.$3,000). The four thieves, one of them a middle-school student, were said to have broken into ten houses from July to December 1993, taking more than 20,000 yuan (U.S.$2,500) worth of goods. During the break-ins, they beat up thirty-eight persons and raped nine women, the radio broadcast said.[162]

In a wave of executions in September and October, dozens of common criminals were executed in major coastal cities, including Beijing, Shanghai, and Guangzhou as well as inland cities such as Wuhan and Nanchang. On September 21, the Shanghai Municipal Intermediate Court sentenced nineteen defendants to death or long prison terms and carried out fifteen death sentences immediately. Their crimes included murder, robbery, rape, and embezzlement, according to a Shanghai People's Radio broadcast.[163] On September 23, a radio broadcast from Nanchang, Jiangxi Province reported that courts in the province had announced sentences on 538 criminals and that "a number of criminals" who had committed "heinous crimes" had been executed. The broadcast said those executed included "thugs, murderers, thieves, and embezzlers."[164]

## Executions Continue Throughout Fall 1994

On September 24, 1994, the central China city of Wuhan in Hubei

Province carried out the largest number of executions since 1983 when forty-five convicted criminals were taken to the execution grounds and shot by firing squads for murder, rape, and robbery, according to *Hubei Daily*. Many of those executed were repeat offenders and one was a woman who had murdered her husband by strangulation and then dumped his body on a rail carriage, the paper said. A separate story in the paper noted, "the crowds along the road cheered on seeing the criminals being taken to the execution grounds."[165]

Also on September 24, the Beijing Intermediate People's Court executed ten people who had been sentenced to death for murder and robbery, the *Beijing Daily* said.[166] On the same day, the China News Agency reported the sentencing of "a number of criminals" in Guangzhou and the execution of "several culprits" who had committed such serious crimes as robbery and murder.[167] On September 26, the Maoming Intermediate People's Court in Guangdong Province sentenced eight to death for stealing firearms and ordered their immediate execution, according to a Guangdong radio broadcast.[168] Xinhua News Agency reported the execution of three in Zhengzhou, Henan Province on September 27 for stealing rail freight. The three, Ma Shichen, Lu Erguo, and Wang Junbin, were sentenced to death by the Zhengzhou Railway Intermediate Court for stealing goods from rail freight worth 180,000 yuan (U.S.$22,500) from May 1992 to January 1993.[169] On the same day, the Shenzhen Intermediate Court in Guangdong province executed eleven criminals after handing down their death sentences for robbery and rape, according to the China News Agency.[170] The Fuling Intermediate People's Court in Sichuan Province sentenced three drug traffickers to death and one to life in prison on October 21, the *Sichuan Daily* reported in the provincial capital. The three had been involved in buying and selling more than 900 grams of heroin in October and November 1993.[171] On October 22, the Xining Intermediate People's Court in the remote western province of Qinghai called a mass rally to pronounce death sentences on eight people for murder, battery and looting, according to a report in the *Qinghai Daily*.[172]

Xinhua News Agency reported one of the largest rounds of sentencing of criminals in Guangzhou on October 25. Forty-four people were executed and 228 others were either sentenced to death with a two-year reprieve, given life imprisonment, or assigned more than five years in prison. Xinhua said fourteen persons guilty of organizing prostitution rings and thirty guilty of drug trafficking were executed. Fourteen others were sentenced to death with reprieve. Thirty-one were given life imprisonment. Since the beginning of 1994, Xinhua said, a total of 912 criminals had been convicted in the province on pornography, drug, and gambling charges and 66 percent of them had been sentenced to death or to prison terms of more than five years.[173]

On October 27, Liu Jiachen, the deputy head of the Supreme People's Court, announced in Beijing the execution of six economic criminals in different parts of China. According to the China News Agency, Liu said the executions were designed to check the wave of economic crimes, including counterfeiting, embezzlement, and fraud throughout China. He cited the cases of low-level tax officials in Jiangsu and Zhejiang provinces who had swindled the government of huge sums of public funds through a variety of schemes, including making bogus government documents. In one case in Jiangsu, he said, a tax bureau clerk issued sixty-four false special value-added tax invoices to thirteen enterprises in Guangdong with total sales in the amount of more than 337,450,000 yuan (U.S.$42,175,000) and pocketed 60,000 yuan (U.S.$7,500) for his services.[174]

Also on October 27, the Hong Kong *Ta Kung Pao* reported that the Kunming Intermediate Court in Yunnan Province had sentenced fourteen drug-traffickers to death at a mass meeting in the provincial capital. More than 4,800 grams of heroin were seized.[175] Earlier, two security policemen were killed and three badly wounded during exchanges with armed drug traffickers in Yunnan. The Hong Kong *Ming Pao* reported  on October 27 that the deaths and injuries had been caused by grenades, which also killed a trafficker. Some 19.3 kilograms of drugs were found on the scene, as well as another grenade.[176]

The Haikou Intermediate People's Court in Hainan Province sentenced eighteen criminals to death at a mass rally and executed eight of them immediately afterward. The eight were convicted murderers who had committed their crimes in particularly vicious and senseless ways, the China News Agency said. In two cases, minor arguments had resulted in the deaths of the victims, whose bodies were subsequently dismembered. In a third case, two bandits killed a victim while robbing him of 25,000 yuan (U.S.$3,150).[177]

A bank manager in Inner Mongolia was sentenced to death for embezzlement on November 12, according to a radio broadcast from the capital city Hohhot. Liu Yuyong, the bond section chief of the People's Bank of Ulan Hot, helped himself to bonds and cash in the bank safe totaling more than 5 million yuan (U.S.$625,000) in September 1992 and November 1993. He was sentenced to death by the Hinggan League Intermediate People's Court as an "extraordinarily serious embezzler."[178] On November 16, the Jinan Intermediate People's Court in Shandong Province sentenced a person to death in a vicious murder case. Wu Lixin, an oil refinery employee, had killed his lover in an argument on July 21, cut her body into twenty-eight pieces and dumped the head and some limb parts near a railroad track, according to the *Dazhong Daily* (Mass Daily) in Jinan.[179] On November 17, the Hong Kong *Ta Kung Pao* reported that the Guangzhou Intermediate People's Court had executed three criminals after sentencing them to death for murdering seven people in several robberies in August and November of 1992.[180]

The *China Local Administration Inspection News* reported the execution of a hospital administrator in Henan Province on November 8 for selling forged tubal ligation certificates. Yuan Jianan, deputy director of Linzhou

City No. 2 People's Hospital, sold 448 ligation certificates complete with the forged signatures of hospital physicians to people for a total of 195,725 yuan (U.S.$24,460). Equipped with such certificates, women presumably could evade detection by the birth control offices when they violated the one-child policy. Yu was sentenced to death by the Anyang Intermediate People's Court and several of his accomplices were given up to fifteen years in prison. Yu was executed on October 18.[181]

On November 17, a radio broadcast from Guangxi reported the execution of nineteen criminals in an anti-crime campaign in the autonomous region in southwestern China. It appeared that those executed were mostly involved in petty offenses. In the Beisi prefecture, the broadcast said, police "inspected 148 roadside shops, cracked 68 prostitution cases, caught 103 lawbreakers and closed down 13 gambling dens" in the anti-crime drive. The local authorities "raised the quality of law enforcement work" by introducing the "mechanism of competition and rewards," thus "raising the initiatives of police officers," the report said.[182] On November 30, Beijing executed six people and sentenced nine to death for murder, rape, and armed robbery, according to the *Beijing Evening News*. The Beijing Intermediate People's Court condemned the "hooligan activities" that seriously damaged public order, the paper said.[183]

The Beijing Intermediate People's Court executed six criminals and sentenced nine others to death on December 1, 1994 for serious crimes including murder and rape, according to the China News Agency. One of the executed, Ma Hongyan, raped more than fifty girls between seven to twelve years old from May 1992 to October 1994, court papers said.[184] On December 7, Xinhua News Agency reported the execution of four people for train robbery and rape. The Beijing Railway Transport Intermediate Court which sentenced the four to death, also handed down life prison terms to three others. From January to July 1993, according to the report, Niu Dun, an unemployed man from Beijing, and his accomplices robbed many Chinese passengers on the international trains between Beijing and Moscow and raped several Chinese women. In all, they robbed trains on the Beijing-Moscow run fourteen times during the six-month period, targeting Chinese passengers. To underscore the government's determination to combat this latest type of crime, the announcement of the execution was made by the Supreme People's Court in Beijing.[185] Also on December 7, a Hunan radio broadcast quoted a high party official of the province as saying that a number of serious criminals had been executed in a year-end anti-crime sweep. Wu Xiandong, party secretary of the province's law and politics commission, said in the three-month campaign from September to November, 6,795 "major and exceptionally big crime cases" had been unearthed and 2,350 "criminal gangs" destroyed.[186] On December 8, an AFP dispatch reported that two peasants from the same province had been sentenced to death for stealing 66 cows worth 60,000 yuan (U.S.$7,500). Six accomplices received prison sentences, including several for life. The same dispatch also reported the execution of a government construction company executive in Sichuan province for embezzling 860,000 yuan (U.S.$107,500) in public funds.[187]

Xinhua News Agency reported on December 19 from Beijing that four people had been executed in three provinces for selling liquor made of industrial alcohol or methanol. More than 120 people who drank the spirits were poisoned, fifteen of them died, and many became blind. In one case, a grocery in Sichuan Province bought 351 kilograms of methanol from a local chemical plant, mixed it with water, and sold the solution as liquor, causing widespread poisoning in the villages. Tests by local public health stations showed that the methanol content in the liquor was 130 times higher than the permissible amount, the report said. In another case, a director of a chemical plant in Henan Province sold 3,800 kilograms of methanol as potable alcohol to a farmer who in turn used it to make a large quantity of liquor for retail sale.[188]

A Reuters dispatch from Beijing reported on December 20 that five people were sentenced to death for killing elephants in Yunnan Province. The report said that the five poachers, including two policemen, killed sixteen protected Asian elephants and wounded another four in the jungles of the Xishuangbanna region in southern Yunnan using machine-guns and semi-automatic rifles. They got over 180 kilograms of ivory for illegal export.[189]

Reporting one of the most serious cases of human trafficking in many years, *Shih-chieh Jih-pao* said in a dispatch from Beijing on December 21 that courts in Anhui Province handed down severe sentences on forty-eight people. Thirteen culprits were sentenced to death, four to life in prison, and thirty-one to long prison terms of more than nineteen years. The dispatch quoted a magazine entitled *Chinese Women* as saying that the traffickers abducted 102 young women from thirty-two counties in Sichuan Province and sold them far away from home to peasants in Anhui, Shanxi, and Inner Mongolia as wives at prices ranging from 800 yuan (U.S.$100) to 4,000 yuan (U.S.$500). Of the forty-eight human traffickers sentenced, seventeen were women, the magazine said.[190]

On December 22 and 23, courts in Guangzhou and Shenzhen in Guang-dong Province executed twenty criminals for murder, rape, robbery, embezzle-ment, and corruption. Twelve of the executed were unemployed job-seekers from other provinces, including one from far away Xinjiang who was sentenced to death for robbing a jewelry store.[191]

Three people were sentenced to death in Guangxi on December 26 for blowing up an explosives warehouse, killing eighty-two people and wounding ninety-one. According to a report by the China News Agency, the three were fired demolition workers who committed the crime as an act of revenge. The warehouse, located near a mine pit, was illegally built and at one time housed more than 11 tons of high explosives with few safety precautions and no guards on site, the news agency said.[192] On December 30, three were sentenced to death in Wuhan, Hubei Province, for embezzlement, according to the *Changjiang Daily*. The three were bank tellers who in two separate cases embezzled more than 3.5 million yuan (U.S.$425,000).

### Endnotes

1. Cited in "China's Secret Economy," *Economist*, October 2, 1993, p. 33.

2. Cited in "Death and Disorder," *Economist*, November 13, 1993, p. 36.

3. Cited in Patrick E. Tyler, "Top Chinese Judge Warns of Serious Problems in Rural Areas," *New York Times*, May 23, 1994, p. A8.

4. Patrick E. Tyler, "China Reports Slaying of 24 From Taiwan," *New York Times*, April 19, 1994, p. A9; "Chien-tao Lake Tragedy: Premeditated Murder," *Shih-chieh Jih-pao*, April 11, 1994, p. A13; B.J. Cutler, "Taiwan Blames China for Tourists' Deaths," *New Haven Register,* April 18, 1994, p. A8.

5. Yu Hsin, "More Than 2,000 People Executed Before Spring Festival," *Reference News*, cited in *Cheng Ming* (Hong Kong), No. 185, March 1, 1993, p. 20, in Foreign Broadcast Information Service (FBIS)-CHI-93-045, March 10, 1993, p. 14.

6. "Anti-Crime and Anti-Drug Drive Ordered in China," *Shih-chieh Jih-pao* (World Journal) (New York), November 13, 1993, p. A19.

7. Ibid.

8. "5 Tons of Drugs Seized in Yunnan in 1993," *Shih-chieh Jih-pao*, March 22, 1994, p. A17.

9. "More Than Two Tons of Drugs Seized This Year in Mainland China," *Shih-chieh Jih-pao*, April 28, 1994, p. A19.

10. "Public Security Ministry Urges Greater Anti-Drug Efforts Along Southwestern Borders," *Shih-chieh Jih-pao*, June 23, 1994, p. A17.

11. "Yunnan Police Seize 1,000 Guns and 2,000 Pounds of Narcotics in Raids," *Shih-chieh Jih-pao*, January 8, 1993, p. 7.

12. "Guangxi 'Double Strike' Campaign Deals Blow at Drug and Gun Traffickers," *Shih-chieh Jih-pao*, December 3, 1993, p. A19.

13. Ibid.

14. "Wave of Executions Reported in China on Anti-Drug Day," *Shih-chieh Jih-pao*, June 25, 1994, p. A19.

15. "Drug Offenders Punished in Tibet, One Executed," *Shih-chieh Jih-pao*, June 27, 1994, p. A17; "Drug Trafficker in Tibet Executed, Others," Beijing Xinhua in English, June 26, 1994, in FBIS-CHI-94-124, June 28, 1994, p. 78.

16. "Drug Addicts Reach 250,000 in Mainland China," *Shih-chieh Jih-pao*, December 14, 1993, p. A10.

17. "Restaurants Spike Foods with Opium-Poppy Shells to Entice Patrons," *Shih-chieh Jih-pao*, November 10, 1993, p. A21.

18. "Courts Handle More Than Two Million Cases in Five Years," *Shih-chieh Jih-pao*, March 23, 1993, p. 15.

19. Ibid.

20. "Ren Jianxin Urges Bold Measures to Combat Economic Crimes," *Shih-chieh Jih-pao*, June 7, 1994, p. 19.

21. Patrick E. Tyler, "Top Chinese Judge Warns of Serious Crime Problem in Rural Areas," *New York Times*, May 23, 1994, p. A8.

22. "Law and Order Situation Worsening in Rural Areas," *Shih-chieh Jih-pao*, October 7, 1994, p. A21.

23. "Use of Torture on the Rise," *Shih-chieh Jih-pao*, October 16, 1993, p. A19.

24. Ibid.

25. Ibid.

26. Ibid.

27. "Death and Disorder," *Economist*, December 11, 1993, p. 36.

28. "China's Secret Economy," *Economist*, October 2, 1993, p. 33.

29. "Illegal Chinese Prison Goods Continue to Enter the U.S.," *Shih-chieh Jih-pao*, May 18, 1993, p. A2.

30. "Chinese Prison-Made Artificial Flowers Sold in U.S.," *Shih-chieh Jih-pao*, September 30, 1994, p. A18.

31. "Harry Wu Says Export of Prison Goods Has Not Stopped," *Shih-chieh Jih-pao*, May 19, 1994, p. A2.

32. See "China's Secret Economy."

33. George J. Church, "Twisting Off the Hook," *Time*, May 30, 1994, p. 41.

34. Bruce Gilley, "Evidence Uncovers Chrysler Link to Prison Labor," *Eastern Express* (Hong Kong), December 19, 1994, p. 8, in FBIS-CHI-94-243, December 19, 1994, p. 13.

35. Bruce Gilley, "Article Views Auto Makers' Links with Labor Camp," *Eastern Express*, (Hong Kong) August 25, 1994, p. 1, in FBIS-CHI-94-166, August 26, 1994, p. 8.

36. Nicholas D. Kristof, "Exports of Prison Goods Seems to Continue," *New York Times*, July 19, 1993, p. A9.

37. Ibid.

38. "Get Serious About Chinese Prison Labor," *New York Times*, July 21, 1993, p. A16.

39. "Over 3,000 Counter-revolutionaries in Prison," *Shih-chieh Jih-pao*, October 16, 1993, p. A18.

40. See "China's Secret Economy."

41. "Majority of Prison Inmates Are Young People," *Shih-chieh Jih-pao*, November 13, 1993, p. A19.

42. See Ta-ling Lee and John F. Copper, *The Bamboo Gulag: Human Rights in the People's Republic of China, 1991–1992* (Baltimore, MD: University of Maryland School of Law Occasional Papers/Reprint Series in Contemporary Asian Studies, 1994), pp. 75–76.

43. "Many Transplant Organs Come from Executed Prisoners," *Shih-chieh Jih-pao*, April 23, 1993, p. 19.

44. Patrick E. Tyler, "Abuse of Rights Persist in China Despite U.S. Pleas," *New York Times*, August 29, 1994, p. A1.

45. "Asia Watch Details Organ Removals from Prisoners in China," *Shih-chieh Jih-pao*, August 29, 1994, p. A1.

46. Ibid.

47. "Lao Gui Tells of Grisly Story of Kidney Removal—From a Living Person," *Shih-chieh Jih-pao*, August 30, 1994, p. A18.

48. Ibid.

49.

50. See "Death and Disorder."

51. "Over 1,400 Executed in China Last Year," *Shih-chieh Jih-pao*, May 5, 1994, p. A2.

52. "22 Executed in Shenzhen Since New Year," *Shih-chieh Jih-pao*, January 16, 1993, p. 2.

53. "59 Executed in Shanghai and Guangdong Before New Year," *Shih-chieh Jih-pao*, January 11, 1993, p. 1.

54. "Chongqing Woman Entrepreneur Executed with Other Criminals," *Shih-chieh Jih-pao*, March 3, 1993, p. 15.

55. "Guangxi Executed 18 for Rape and Selling Women and Children," *Shih-chieh Jih-pao*, March 8, 1993, p. 15.

56. "Retired Worker Executed for Poisoning Seven People to Death," *Shih-chieh Jih-pao*, March 25, 1993, p. 17.

57. "Guangzhou Court Sentences 10 Drug Traffickers to Death," *Shih-chieh Jih-pao*, March 27, 1993, p. 17.

58. "Spurned Lover Sentenced to Death for Injuring Girl Friend With Acid," *Shih-chieh Jih-pao*, April 3, 1993, p. 17.

59. "Nine Pirates Executed in Fujian," *Shih-chieh Jih-pao*, April 28, 1993, p. 17.

60. "Major Drug Case reported in Zhangzhou, Ringleaders Given Death Sentences," *Shih-chieh Jih-pao*, May 4, 1993, p. A17.

61. "Xiamen Executes Six Criminals," *Shih-chieh Jih-pao*, May 4, 1993, p. A17.

62. "48 Drug Traffickers Put to Death in Guangdong," *Shih-chieh Jih-pao*, May 9, 1993, p. A14.

63. "18 Criminals Shot in Foshan," *Shih-chieh Jih-pao*, May 22, 1993, p. 19.

64. "Police Chief Executed in Guangxi for Raping a Child," *Shih-chieh Jih-pao*, May 24, 1993, p. A15.

65. "Two Peasants Executed for Selling Panda Skin," *Shih-chieh Jih-pao*, May 31, 1993, p. A16.

66. "Peasant Sentenced to Death for Selling Wife, Daughter and Mother," *Shih-chieh Jih-pao*, June 12, 1993, p. A19.

67. "Dozens of Drug Offenders Sentenced to Death in Four Places," *Shih-chieh Jih-pao*, June 27, 1993, p. A2.

68. Ibid.

69. Ibid.

70. Ibid.

71. "13 Criminals Executed in Shenzhen," *Shih-chieh Jih-pao*, June 28, 1993, p. A17.

72. "Shanghai Hits Criminals, Sentencing 8 to Death," *Shih-chieh Jih-pao*, July 3, 1993, p. A19.

73. "Serious Drug Problem Reported in Guangdong," *Shih-chieh Jih-pao*, July 10, 1993, p. A19.

74. The wording of the announcement suggested there were death penalties, but it did not say that specifically.

75. "Guangzhou Courts Severely Punish Gangsters Who Force Women into Prostitution," *Shih-chieh Jih-pao*, July 14, 1993, p. A19.

76. Ibid.

77. "Dismissed Actor Sentenced to Death for Killing Daughter," *Shih-chieh Jih-pao*, July 15, 1993, p. A19.

78. "10 Highway Robbers Executed in Chongqing," *Shih-chieh Jih-pao*, July 30, 1993, p. A17.

79. "Shanghai Sentences a Group of Criminals," *Shih-chieh Jih-pao*, August 13, 1993, p. A19.

80. "Seven Criminals Executed in Xiamen," *Shih-chieh Jih-pao*, August 21, 1993, p. A19.

81. "Guangdong Puts Another 15 to Death in Anti-Crime Drive," *Shih-chieh Jih-pao*, August 24, 1993, p. A19.

82. "Fake Cigarette Dealer Given Death Penalty in Yunnan," Kunming Yunnan People's Radio Network in Mandarin, August 26, 1993, in FBIS-CHI-93-169, September 2, 1993, p. 55.

83. "Yunnan Radio on Execution of Cigarette Dealer," Kunming Yunnan People's Radio Network in Mandarin, August 26, 1993, in FBIS-CHI-93-173, September 9, 1993, p. 63.

84. "Three Executed for Making Fake Goods," *Shih-chieh Jih-pao*, August 27, 1993, p. A19.

85. "Four Government Officials Sentenced to Death for Corruption," *Shih-chieh Jih-pao*, August 28, 1993, p. A1.

86. "Seven Taxi Robbers Executed in Shanghai," *Shih-chieh Jih-pao*, September 15, 1993, p. A19.

87. "Guangdong Housing Company Manager Sentenced to Death for Corruption," *Shih-chieh Jih-pao*, September 10, 1993, p. A19.

88. "Former Huizhou Public Security Chief Sentenced to Death for Corruption," *Shih-chieh Jih-pao*, September 12, 1993, p. A14.

89. "Six 'Economic Criminals' Sentenced in Fujian," *Shih-chieh Jih-pao*, September 17, 1993, p. A19.

90. "Nearly 100 Officials Nabbed in Zhejiang Anti-Corruption Drive," *Shih-chieh Jih-pao*, September 22, 1993, p. A19.

91. "16 Criminals Sentenced in Guangdong," *Shih-chieh Jih-pao*, September 25, 1993, p. A19.

92. "Over 80 Criminals Sentenced to Death in Jiangxi," *Shih-chieh Jih-pao*, September 29, 1993, p. A19.

93. "Hunan Sentences 3,000 in Pre-National Day Rallies," *Shih-chieh Jih-pao*, October 1, 1993, p. A19.

94. Ibid.

95. "Hong Kong Drug Trafficker Lin Guoming Executed in Guangzhou," *Shih-chieh Jih-pao*, October 24, 1993, p. A7.

96. "20 Offenders Executed in Kunming," *Shih-chieh Jih-pao*, October 28, 1993, p. A19.

97. Ibid.

98. "Four Officials Sentenced to Death in Guangxi for Corruption," *Shih-chieh Jih-pao*, November 5, 1993, p. A21.

99. Ibid.

100. "Guangdong Executes 16 in Anti-Crime Drive," *Shih-chieh Jih-pao*, October 29, 1993, p. A19.

101. "60 Criminals Put to Death in Hubei," *Shih-chieh Jih-pao*, November 15, 1993, p. A17.

102. "Execution of Economic Criminals Reported in Yunnan, Fujian and Guangdong," *Shih-chieh Jih-pao*, November 28, 1993, p. A16.

103. "Haikou Executes Condemned Criminals," *Shih-chieh Jih-pao*, November 25, 1993, p. A18.

104. "10 Common Criminals Executed in Guangzhou," *Shih-chieh Jih-pao*, December 1, 1993, p. A19.

105. "Border Patrol Officers and Snake Head Sentenced to Death," *Shih-chieh Jih-pao*, December 5, 1993, p. A14.

106. "Guangxi Deals Severely with Drug Traffickers," *Shih-chieh Jih-pao*, December 12, 1993, p. A14.

107. "Guangzhou Executes Three Hooligans," *Shih-chieh Jih-pao*, December 13, 1993, p. A19.

108. "Common Criminals Executed in Nanhai and Zhuhai," *Shih-chieh Jih-pao*, December 25, 1993, p. A18.

109. "Guangzhou Executes Three Criminals," *Shih-chieh Jih-pao*, January 17, 1994, p. A19.

110. "30 Executed in Kunming After Mass Rally in City Sports Stadium," *Shih-chieh Jih-pao*, January 30, 1994, p. A14.

111. "30 Criminals Executed in Guangzhou," *Shih-chieh Jih-pao*, January 28, 1994, p. A19.

112. "More Than 200 Criminals Executed Before Spring Festival," *Shih-chieh Jih-pao*, February 9, 1994, p. A19.

113. "Six Drug Traffickers Executed in Guangzhou," *Shih-chieh Jih-pao*, March 19, 1994, p. A19.

114. Ibid.

115. "Shanxi Punishes Corrupt Officials," *Shih-chieh Jih-pao*, April 1, 1994, p. A17.

116. "Jiangxi Peasant Couple Executed for Kidnapping Children," *Shih-chieh Jih-pao*, April 2, 1994, p. A19.

117. "Large Number of Kidnapped Women and Children Rescued in Guangxi," *Shih-chieh Jih-pao*, April 11, 1994, p. A17.

118. "Large Woman-Kidnap Ring Smashed in Central China," *Shih-chieh Jih-pao*, April 23, 1994, p. 14.

119. "Five Drug Offenders Executed in Gansu," *Shih-chieh Jih-pao*, April 4, 1994, p. A17.

120. "Head of Great Wall Enterprises Executed," *Shih-chieh Jih-pao*, April 12, 1994, p. A19.

121. "Taiwan Gun Smugglers Sentenced to Death in Fujian," *Shih-chieh Jih-pao*, April 28, 1994, p. A19.

122. "Counterfeit Money Made in Taiwan to Buy Mainland Drugs," *Shih-chieh Jih-pao*, April 26, 1994, p. A13.

123. "Nine Common Criminals Executed in Shenzhen," *Shih-chieh Jih-pao*, April 29, 1994, p. A17.

124. "Four Executed in Sichuan for Corruption," *Shih-chieh Jih-pao*, May 10, 1994, p. A19.

125. Zhang Sutang, "Six 'Law Offenders' Executed 10 May Following Trial," Beijing Xinhua Domestic Service in Chinese, May 10, 1994, in FBIS-CHI-94-091, May 11, 1994, p. 20.

126. "20 Criminals Executed in Guangzhou and Beijing," *Shih-chieh Jih-pao*, May 11, 1994, p. A19.

127. "Beijing Executes Criminal Offenders," *Beijing Ribao* (Beijing Daily) in Chinese, May 14, 1994, pp. 1, 4, in FBIS-CHI-94-099, May 23, 1994, p. 82.

128. "Two Bootleggers Executed in Sichuan," *Shih-chieh Jih-pao*, May 17, 1994, p. A19.

129. "10 Executed, 22 Given Severe Sentences in Zhuhai," *Shih-chieh Jih-pao*, May 28, 1994, p. A21.

130. "Four Officials Executed for Cigarette Smuggling," *Shih-chieh Jih-pao*, March 30, 1994, p. A19.

131. "Beijing Executes Official, Three Police Officers," Beijing Xinhua in English, May 29, 1994, in FBIS-CHI-94-104, May 31, 1994, p. 26.

132. See Zhang Sutang, "Six 'Law Offenders' Executed."

133. "Hebei County Executes Six Criminals," Shijiachuang *Hebei Ribao* (Hebei Daily) in Chinese, June 3, 1994, p. 2, in FBIS-CHI-94-114, June 14, 1994, p. 68.

134. "Major Criminals Executed, Imprisoned in Jiangsu," Nanjing *Xinhua Ribao* (Xinhua Daily) in Chinese, July 3, 1994, p. 3, in FBIS-CHI-94-141, July 22, 1994, p. 2.

135. "Executions in Provinces," Beijing Central Television Program One Network in Mandarin, June 25, 1994; "Guangdong Gives Death Sentences," Beijing Xinhua Domestic Service in Mandarin, June 25, 1994; "Xinjiang Gives Death Sentences," Urumqi Television Network in Mandarin, June 25, 1994, all in FBIS-CHI-94-123, June 27, 1994, pp. 37–38.

136. "Crime and Punishment in the PRC for 18–30 June," FBIS-CHI-94-129, July 6, 1994, p. 20.

137. Ibid., pp. 21, 22.

138. "Two Former Officials Executed for Corruption," Beijing Xinhua in English, July 4, 1994, in FBIS-CHI-94-128, July 5, 1994, p. 42.

139. "18 Criminals Executed in Guangzhou and Haikou," *Shih-chieh Jih-pao*, July 6, 1994, p. A19.

140. "Shanghai Reports Execution of Salesman for Embezzlement," Shanghai People's Radio Network in Mandarin, July 8, 1994, in FBIS-CHI-94-132, July 11, 1994, p. 43.

141. "Inner Mongolia Sentences Several Convicts to Death," Hohhot *Neimenggu Ribao* (Inner Mongolia Daily) in Chinese, July 17, 1994, p. 1, in FBIS-CHI-94-147, August 1, 1994, p. 81.

142. "Shanghai Executes Murderers, Robbers," Shanghai People's Radio Network in Mandarin, July 22, 1994, in FBIS-CHI-94-142, July 25, 1994, p. 59.

143. "Guangxi Sentences Six Corrupt Officials," *Shih-chieh Jih-pao*, July 25, 1994, p. A19.

144. "Fuzhou, Shenzhen, Guangzhou Scene of Executions," Beijing Xinhua Domestic Service in Chinese, July 28, 1994, in FBIS-CHI-94-146, July 29, 1994, p. 13.

145. "Twelve Railway Bandits Executed in Shanghai," Hong Kong AFP in English, August 1, 1994, in FBIS-CHI-94-147, August 1, 1994, p. 70.

146. "Liaoning Sentences to Death Criminal Accused of Poisoning," Shenyang *Liaoning Ribao* (Liaoning Daily) in Chinese, August 14, 1994, p. 1, in FBIS-CHI-94-165, August 25, 1994, p. 63.

147. "Crime, Punishment Report for 1–14 August," FBIS-CHI-94-159, August 17, 1994, p. 22.

148. Ibid., p. 25.

149. Ibid., p. 27.

150. "Two Executed in Sichuan for Selling Poisonous Liquor," Beijing Central People's Radio Network in Mandarin, August 11, 1994, in FBIS-CHI-94-157, p. 39.

151. "Four Criminals Executed in Fuzhou," *Shih-chieh Jih-pao*, August 17, 1994, p. A17.

152. "Two Executed by Shooting for Beijing Murders," *Beijing Ribao* (Beijing Daily) in Chinese, August 18, 1994, p. 3, in FBIS-CHI-94-167, August 29, 1994, p. 81; "Beijing Executes 5 Criminals by Firing Squad," *Beijing Ribao* (Beijing Daily) in Chinese, August 19, 1994, p. 1, in FBIS-CHI-94-168, August 30, 1994, p. 59.

153. "Shenyang Executes 26 Criminals," Beijing *Fazhi Ribao* (Legal Daily News) in Chinese, September 15, 1994, p. 2, in FBIS-CHI-94-190, September 30, 1994, pp. 41–42.

154. "Six Criminals Executed in Fujian," *Shih-chieh Jih-pao*, August 21, 1994, p. A14.

155. "Three Grain Officials Executed in Liaoning," Beijing Xinhua Domestic Service in Chinese, August 22, 1994, in FBIS-CHI-94-169, August 31, 1994, p. 39.

156. "Beijing Severely Punishes Criminals," *Shih-chieh Jih-pao*, August 27, 1994, p. A19.

157. "Chongqing Sentences 5 to Death for Economic Crimes," *Shih-chieh Jih-pao*, September 3, 1994, p. A21.

158. "Five Ringleaders Executed in Hainan," *Shih-chieh Jih-pao*, September 10, 1994, p. A19.

159. "Beijing Executes Drug Criminals," *Shih-chieh Jih-pao*, September 14, 1994, p. A19.

160. "Death Sentence for 10 Traffickers in Women," Guangzhou Guangdong People's Radio in Mandarin, September 14, 1994, in FBIS-CHI-94-190, September 30, 1994, p. 37.

161. "Beijing Gives Death Sentence to 2 Pornography Publishers," Beijing Xinhua Domestic Service in Chinese, September 16, 1994, in FBIS-CHI-94-183, September 21, 1994, p. 77.

162. "Shandong to Execute Prisoners for Economic Crimes," Jinan Shandong People's Radio Network in Mandarin, September 20, 1994, in FBIS-CHI-94-183, September 21, 1994, p. 64.

163. "Shanghai Sentences, Executes Accused Murderers, Thieves," Shanghai People's Radio Network in Mandarin, September 21, 1994, in FBIS-CHI-94-186, September 26, 1994, p. 57.

164. "Jiangxi Executes Criminals," Nanchang Jiangxi People's Radio Network in Mandarin, September 23, 1994, in FBIS-CHI-94-190, September 30, 1994, p. 41.

165. "Largest Number of Executions Since 1983," Wuhan *Hubei Ribao* (Hubei Daily) in Chinese, September 24, 1994, p. 1, in FBIS-CHI-94-190, September 30, 1994, p. 41.

166. "Beijing Court Executes 10 Felons on September 23," *Beijing Ribao* (Beijing Daily) in Chinese, September 24, 1994, pp. 1, 4, in FBIS-CHI-94-196, October 11, 1994, p. 77.

167. "Guangzhou Executes Robbers, Murderers," Beijing Zhongguo Xinwen She (China News Agency) in Chinese, September 24, 1994, in FBIS-CHI-94-190, September 30, 1994, p. 39.

168. "Maoming Executes Firearms Offenders," Guangzhou Guangdong People's Radio Network in Mandarin, September 26, 1994, in FBIS-CHI-94-190, September 30, 1994, p. 39.

169. "Three Executed for Stealing Rail Freight," Beijing Xinhua Domestic Service in Chinese, September 27, 1994, in FBIS-CHI-94-189, September 29, 1994, p. 74.

170. "Shenzhen Executes 11 Criminals," Beijing Zhongguo Xinwen She (China News Agency) in English, September 27, 1994, in FBIS-CHI-94-190, September 30, 1994, p. 39.

171. "Sichuan Sentences Drug Traffickers to Death," Chengdu *Sichuan Ribao* (Sichuan Daily) in Chinese, November 10, 1994, p. 3, in FBIS-CHI-94-232, December 2, 1994, p. 17.

172. "Xining Court Sentences Eight to Death for Murder, Looting, Injury," Xining *Qinghai Ribao* (Qinghai Daily) in Chinese, October 23, 1994, p. 1, in FBIS-CHI-94-222, November 17, 1994, p. 27.

173. "Criminals Executed in Guangdong," Beijing Xinhua in English, October 25, 1994, in FBIS-CHI-94-207, October 26, 1994, p. 43.

174. "Six Executed for Economic Crimes," *Shih-chieh Jih-pao*, October 28, 1994, p. A19; "Various Provinces Execute Six for Value-added Tax Invoices Offenses," Beijing *Fazhi Ribao* (Legal Daily News) in Chinese, October 28, 1994, p. 1, in FBIS-CHI-94-222, November 17, 1994, p. 22 .

175. "14 Drug Traffickers Sentenced to Death in Kunming," *Shih-chieh Jih-pao*, October 28, 1994, p. A19.

176. "Two Policemen Killed in Duel with Drug-Traffickers in Yunnan," *Shih-chieh Jih-pao*, October 27, 1994, p. A21.

177. "Haikou Executes Eight for Violent Crimes After Mass Rally," Hong Kong Zhongguo Tongxun She (China Information Agency), November 4, 1994, in FBIS-CHI-94-222, November 17, 1994, p. 26.

178. "Inner Mongolia to Execute Embezzler," Hohhot Inner Mongolia People's Radio Network in Mandarin, November 12, 1994, in FBIS-CHI-94-221, November 16, 1994, p. 40.

179. "Shandong's Jinan Court Sentences Murderer to Death," Jinan *Dazhong Ribao* (Mass Daily) in Chinese, November 17, 1994, p. 5, in FBIS-CHI-94-229, November 29, 1994, p. 63.

180. "Three Murderers Executed in Guangzhou," Hong Kong *Ta Kung Pao* in Chinese, November 17, 1994, p. 4, in FBIS-CHI-94-232, December 2, 1994, p. 17.

181. "Henan Smashes Forged Ligation Certificate Ring, Leader Executed," Beijing *Zhongguo Jijian Jiancha Bao* (China Local Administration Inspection News) in Chinese, November 19, 1994, p. 2, in FBIS-CHI-94-232, December 2, 1994, p. 15.

182. "Guangxi's Beisi Prefecture Steps Up Anti-Crime Campaign, Executes 9," Nanning Guangxi Regional People's Radio Network in Mandarin, November 17, 1994, in FBIS-CHI-94-232, December 2, 1994, p. 16.

183. "Six Criminals Executed, Nine Sentenced to Death in Beijing," Hong Kong AFP in English, November 30, 1994, in FBIS-CHI-94-232, December 2, 1994, p. 17.

184. "Beijing Severely Punishes 15 Criminals," Beijing Zhongguo Xinwen She (China News Agency) in Chinese, December 1, 1994, in FBIS-CHI-94-241, December 15, 1994, p. 17.

185. "Four Executed in Beijing for Robbery and Rape," Beijing Xinhua Domestic Service in Chinese, December 7, 1994, in FBIS-CHI-94-238, December 12, 1994.

186. "Hunan Cracks Down on Criminal Gangs, Executes Serious Criminals," Changsha Hunan People's Radio Network in Mandarin, December 7, 1994, in FBIS-CHI-94-241, December 15, 1994, p. 20.

187. "Hunan Executes Two Peasants for Stealing 66 Cows," Hong Kong AFP in English, December 8, 1994, in FBIS-CHI-94-241, December 15, 1994, p. 20.

188. "Court Orders Execution of Liquor Producers," Beijing Xinhua in English, December 19, 1994, in FBIS-CHI-94-244, December 20, 1994, pp. 20–21.

189. "Five Poachers Sentenced to Death in Yunnan," *Shih-chieh Jih-pao*, December 20, 1994, p. A21.

190. "Anhui Executes Human Traffickers," *Shih-chieh Jih-pao*, December 21, 1994, p. A19.

191. "Guangzhou, Shenzhen Execute Criminals," *Shih-chieh Jih-pao*, December 23, 1994, p. A19; "Shenzhen Court Executes 12 Criminals," *Shih-chieh Jih-pao*, December 24, 1994, p. A19.

192. "Three Sentenced to Death for Guangxi Explosion," *Shih-chieh Jih-pao*, December 27, 1994, p. A19.

# Chapter 6

## China's Foreign Policy and Human Rights, I

Don't smile and don't hug Jiang in Public.

—Representative Nancy Pelosi (D-Calif.) to President Clinton.[1]

A lot of Chinese people now say the United States has retreated (on human rights), that it's defeated.

—Wei Jingsheng.[2]

China cannot ignore the international pressure.

—Fang Lizhi.[3]

### Introduction

During 1993, China continued to be the target of foreign criticism and diplomatic pressure for its human rights abuses as has been the case since the 1989 Tiananmen Massacre, when China lost its edge on the human rights issue.[4] Yet, contrary to the popular view, China was still not as much under the microscope as many other countries in the world and foreign human rights groups as well as foreign governments still lacked detailed and in many cases reliable information on China's human rights condition.

The United States, and to a lesser extent Western European countries, remained China's most vocal critics. In the case of the United States, most favored nation (MFN) status was, as had been the case for several years, linked to

China's human rights record, which was at various times the focus of both official and public attention. Beijing was also the subject of pointed criticism about its arms exports policies and its "proliferation" of nuclear know-how and technology. Though usually not judged to be specifically a human rights issue, these problems were often linked to human rights abuses in China by the media, in public criticisms by Western leaders, and in the public mind.

Chinese leaders in many instances responded in a positive way to external complaints and criticism. Clearly, some political prisoners benefited. (See Chapter 3 for further details.) Chinese citizens were no doubt better off due to foreign charges and complaints. Yet, Beijing also became more aggressive in its responses, and in many cases, retaliated with its own complaints about the motive of those assessing China and their human rights records. Meanwhile, Chinese leaders sought to redefine human rights using its own definitions while at the same time trying to build an Asian consensus on the issue of the meaning, significance and role of human rights to counter what PRC leaders considered unfair Western charges.

## Foreign Criticisms of China's Human Rights Record

In the 1993 "country reports" on human rights published by the State Department, the authors said that Beijing's human rights practices "remained repressive, falling far short of internationally accepted norms." The report criticized and vilified China specifically on a number of issues. (See Appendix 6.) It asserted there had been essentially no progress toward improved human rights in China and concluded by giving China low marks for its human rights performance. Under-secretary of State Patricia Diaz Dennis told the press that in the case of China's human rights record, "there is no upward trend line."[5]

In February, the Washington-based human rights group International Campaign for Tibet distributed a secret speech delivered by Tibet Communist Party secretary Chen Kuaiyuan at a meeting of provincial Communist Party members. In the speech, Chen stated, "Though the class enemy, as a class, has been eliminated, these people are still there and their children are trying to restore the old system."[6] The human rights group also said that Chen had brought several hundred Chinese officials with him when he recently assumed his position in Tibet. This was a setback for local autonomy and meant fewer promotions of Tibetans to higher government positions. The action, according to International Campaign for Tibet, also represented part of a failed effort by the Chinese government to create a "class" loyal to Beijing.[7] This conclusion confirmed reports that the government, in putting down pro-independence riots, was becoming even more repressive than it had been in the past. The governor of Tibet had recently said that authorities had "put down many riots and incidents of troublemaking in Lhasa [and] crushed the evil plots of splittists at home and abroad to split the motherland."[8]

Meanwhile, the London-based Tibet Information Network reported that the first protest by Buddhist nuns in Tibet occurred on February 25. This demonstration and others that followed were the first in Lhasa since October 1992. Tibet Information Network also said that Chinese police had arrested eighteen people.[9] At this same time, it was reported that middle-school students had put up posters and shouted pro-independence slogans in the rural town of Nyemo west of Lhasa. In response security forces fired tear gas at the protestors and then opened fire with rifles, wounding at least one student.[10]

Amnesty International released a report on April 16 asserting that torture was systematic in China, "endemic in many places of detention," and far more common than ten years earlier—notwithstanding claims by the PRC that it had taken effective measures to stop the practice.[11] Estrellita Jones, from the Amnesty International office in Washington, D.C., subsequently told the U.S. Congressional Human Rights Caucus, "There is a human rights crisis in China." She went on to say that the use of the death penalty and the torture of prisoners had increased in frequency and had become "more barbaric" over the past decade. (For related details see Chapter 5.) Furthermore, she asserted, the victims are usually minority ethnic and religious groups.[12] Zhao Haiqing, president of the National Committee on Chinese affairs, speaking at the same meeting, said that China's release of prisoners and its many human rights reports were only "cosmetic gestures" to impress foreigners.[13]

On April 19, the International Campaign for Tibet released a report citing numerous accounts of illness and death among Tibetans living near the city of Ninth Academy, where, according to Chinese officials, the world's largest deposits of uranium lie. (China has been mining and processing uranium and producing weapons at the site.) The report, the first comprehensive analysis of its kind, included tests on soil samples and other materials.[14]

Reflecting U.S. concern, President Bill Clinton met the Dalai Lama on April 27 and discussed human rights problems in Tibet. Clinton said that his administration "continues to urge Beijing to revive the dialog" with Tibet and "will press China to address human rights abuses" there.[15] However, there were no immediate actions taken in follow-up to President Clinton's comments. Some time later, at a performance by composer Marvin Hamlisch, cellist Yo-Yo Ma, and singers Roberta Flack and Richie Havens organized to draw attention to the Tibet situation, the Dalai Lama spoke and lamented that he had failed in his fourteen-year-long effort to discuss Tibet's future with China.[16]

After his visit in the United States the Dalai Lama traveled to London to further promote the cause of human rights in Tibet. The Dalai Lama told an audience in England that Tibet was suffering from "cultural genocide" and called on the world to help. He spoke of China pursuing a policy of "bloodless ethnic cleansing" and noted that Tibetans accounted for less than one-third of the population of Lhasa because of the influx of Chinese. The Dalai Lama subsequently called on the world community to save his country from "cultural death."[17]

In May, the Tibet Information Network reported that there were more than 300 political prisoners in Tibet and that the number had increased more than one-third in the past year. The organization said that 60 percent of these prisoners were being held without trial in detention centers or "reform through education" centers.[18] A list of political prisoners was published in London, and British Foreign Secretary Douglas Hurd assured the Dalai Lama that Britain would "continue to pursue our dialog on human rights with Chinese authorities at every opportunity."[19]

Several days later, Amnesty International reported that more than 100 Tibetans were arrested in Lhasa shortly after the arrival of twelve European ambassadors who had supported a resolution passed by the European Parliament in late 1992 expressing concern about human rights abuses in Tibet. According to Amnesty International, the arrests were made to prevent Tibetan dissidents from making contact with the group.[20]

The Press Trust of India in June reported that more than 100 Tibetans had staged a demonstration in Lhasa calling for "Chinese to get out of Tibet" and praising the Dalai Lama. Police, the report said, broke up the demonstration.[21] At this time, the Tibet Information Network in London said that a number of Tibetans had been arrested for demonstrating, carrying Tibetan flags, and shouting anti-Chinese and pro-independence slogans.[22]

Meanwhile, the Dalai Lama's exiled government published a report entitled "Tibet: Proving Truth from Facts." This report described how Beijing was increasing its use of Tibet for nuclear testing, nuclear weapons manufacturing, and nuclear waste dumping and said that Beijing had placed nuclear missiles at bases south of Lake Kokonor, at Nagchukha, Delingha and Dhashu and had put its first intercontinental ballistic missiles, the DF-4, at Haiyan. It also cited Beijing for setting up weapons manufacturing centers at Dhashu and Tongkhor (renamed Huangyuan by the Chinese government). The report, in addition, charged that Chinese authorities were in the process of eliminating the Tibetan religion and culture, that 1.2 million people had died as a result of human rights violations between 1951 and 1979, and that 80,000 were in exile.[23] The report also sought to refute a Chinese government "White Paper" on Tibet published the previous year by the Chinese government.

At the Vienna World Conference on Human Rights in June, the New York–based Human Rights in China group sent a delegation to protest China's abuses of its citizens. The group was headed by Liu Qing and included Li Shuxian, the wife of Fang Lizhi. The delegation presented a report on China's human rights record and a letter smuggled out of prison written by dissident Liu Gang.[24]

At the same meeting, the Austrian government condemned the pressure Beijing had employed to prevent the Dalai Lama from speaking at the conference. Three hundred conference delegates staged a demonstration to protest the United Nations' decision not to invite the Dalai Lama to address the meeting. Some carried banners reading: "Let the Dalai Lama speak," "No to U.N. ban," and "Save Tibet." The opening session of the meeting was boycotted by fourteen Nobel Peace Prize winners because of the exclusion of the Dalai Lama (a Nobel Peace Prize winner himself). [25]

The Tibet Information Network reported in July that Beijing had launched a "political re-education campaign" in Tibetan monasteries and planned to crack down on nuns who demonstrated on human rights issues. This effort to dampen the human rights issue in Tibet was spearheaded by a "work team" called a "political education unit," made up of members of China's Political Consultative Conference (an organ of government designed to collect various views on political issues and promote democratic practices).[26]

In August, the U.S. House of Representatives passed a resolution opposing China's candidacy for the Olympic Games in the year 2000, noting that the bid was signed by former Beijing Mayor Chen Xitong who had been among those that ordered the bloody crackdown in Tiananmen Square in June 1989.[27] Subsequently, sixty U.S. senators, citing human rights abuses in China, sent a letter to members of the International Olympic Committee asking that they deny China the right to host the upcoming games. Senator Bill Bradley of New Jersey, who led the effort, said, "Holding the games in China would confer upon China's leaders a stamp of approval by the international community which they clearly do not deserve."[28]

At almost this same time, the United States and Hong Kong protested the treatment and deportation of labor activist Han Dongfang, who tried to return to China after receiving medical treatment in the United States. A representative of the Hong Kong government noted that Beijing had violated Article 13 of the Universal Declaration of Human Rights, which states that all persons have a right to return to their own country.[29] (See Chapter 3 for more on Han and China's policy of exiling dissidents.)

The Tibetan government-in-exile, meanwhile, issued a report saying that Chinese authorities in Tibet had arrested 190 persons in late June when police encountered a crowd of 1,000 rock-throwing Tibetan peasants. The report detailed other protests and arrests. It also said that Chinese troops had taken over the Tibetan township of Kyimshi south of Lhasa after pro-independence demonstrations there and had set up machine gun posts to control the town.[30] On the heels of the report, Tibetan Information Network representatives expressed dismay that the United Nations Subcommission on Human Rights had rejected a resolution on human rights in Tibet saying that it constituted an attack on "China's territorial integrity."[31]

The Tibetan government-in-exile accused the Chinese government in September of lying when talking about Tibetan problems. Specifically the Dalai Lama said that Beijing declared that it was always open to negotiations and Tibetans were not, which was not so. Coinciding with the Dalai Lama's statement, the Tibet Information Network issued a press release saying that it had a list of 467 political prisoners in Tibet and that it constituted an increase compared to 1992 and came not from rising demonstrations and protest but rather from greater police "efficiency and determination."[32]

In October, the Tibet Information Network reported that in July there had been a wave of arrests of Tibetans in Qinghai Province—China's "gulag." The arrests were made before and during Communist Party General Secretary Jiang Zemin's visit to the area. Those arrested had or were planning to distribute pro-independence leaflets. Not long after this it was reported that the Chinese military had been sent to a city in Xinjiang Autonomous Region to protect Chinese from Muslim separatists there protesting against a Chinese book offensive to Muslims.[33]

Also during October, the Dalai Lama visited France. Here he spoke to 600,000 Buddhists, saying that China had stepped up the "population transfer" of Chinese to Tibet even though the Chinese population (because of this policy) already outnumbered Tibetans. The Dalai Lama also declared that there were 7 million Chinese in Tibet and only 6 million Tibetans. He further asserted that this policy was decided in a secret meeting in May and its intent was to "drown out attempts at rebellion by Tibetans." He called this population transfer policy "cultural genocide."[34]

At the November Asia-Pacific Economic Cooperation (APEC) meeting in Seattle, President Bill Clinton reportedly lectured Jiang Zemin on human rights abuses in China. Prior to the meeting 270 members of Congress publicly called for the United States to take a tough stand with China on human rights, trade, and other issues.[35] Clinton subsequently raised human rights concerns in five areas: (1) access to prisons for the Red Cross, (2) release of political prisoners, (3) dialog with the Dalai Lama on Tibet, (4) investigations by customs officials of prison-made goods exported to the United States, and (5) freedom for families of dissidents to emigrate. Outside the meeting, members of the Tibetan Rights Campaign demonstrated.[36]

After the Seattle meeting, which represented the highest-level contacts between the United States and China since the Tiananmen Massacre, President Clinton told reporters, "We continue to have differences on (human rights) issues." Clinton's remarks seemed to indicate that he had gotten no positive response from Jiang. Secretary of State Warren Christopher confirmed this, saying that "no specific commitments" had come out of the meeting.[37]

In December, Assistant Secretary of State for Human Rights John Shattuck said that the Clinton administration had begun to tie foreign aid and economic benefits to human rights performances and seemed to suggest a tougher policy toward the PRC. However, he also noted that other countries permitted worse abuses than China, though human rights problems were systemic in China in a massive way. Sending confusing signals, he said also that he was "impressed with the depth of reform potential."[38]

## Most Favored Nation Status and Arms Sales Issues

When the Clinton administration took office, President Clinton immediately made issue of China's most favored nation trade status (MFN) with the United States. Newly appointed Secretary of State Warren Christopher said that the new administration would not wait until June to deal with the issue of China's human rights and weapons proliferation. He went on to say that the Clinton administration would encourage a "broad, peaceful revolution" in China and would use other leverage on the human rights issue.[39] Beijing responded by sending a warning to the United States not to meddle in China's internal affairs. The Foreign Ministry subsequently issued a statement calling for friendly ties but also pointed out that the communiqués (between the United States and China) contained provisions for mutual respect and noninterference in each others internal affairs.[40]

This response, however, may have been little more than posturing for the benefit of the international community or for public consumption at home. Clinton had made rather tough statements about China's poor human rights record during the campaign and Chinese leaders had at that time retaliated in kind. Nevertheless, China made a large purchase of wheat from the United States after Clinton won the election. Subsequently, President-elect Clinton said that he expected progress in relations with China and supported President Bush in efforts to improve Sino-American relations before he left office.[41]

The MFN issue became a highly sensitive one again in May pending the U.S. decision to renew China's status. Prior to making a decision on the matter, Assistant Secretary of State for Asia and the Pacific Winston Lord visited China and made a number of requests for improvements in China's human rights record, including the establishment of a joint U.S.-China commission on human rights and the release of Christian and political dissidents from jail.[42] Despite little or no progress, however, the Clinton administration granted the renewal. President Clinton said at the time, "I want to support modernization in China. But I want to make it clear to them that there has to be some progress on human rights and the use of prison labor."[43] Clinton went on to say, "I hope they understand that the United States can't turn its back on the abuse of lots of people, and especially the use of prison labor and just choking people off when they say their piece."[44] Senator George Mitchell and Representative Nancy

Pelosi at this time introduced legislation making progress on human rights a prerequisite to renewal of MFN status, but their efforts seemed designed primarily to force President Clinton to make demands for progress.[45]

According to observers, President Clinton approved extending MFN status in order to promote U.S. exports, keep China's vote in the United Nations Security Council to restrain North Korea, and to get China to stick to its agreements on Hong Kong. Assistant Secretary of State for East Asia and the Pacific Winston Lord said later, "What we are doing is trying to strike a balance between firm, credible goals and what the Chinese should be able to achieve in the course of the year, not create conditions China can't fulfill."[46]

However, Beijing did make some important concessions: It sent buying missions to the United States to purchase $2 billion in cars and aircraft, released dozens of Catholic priests and dissidents, and used tear gas instead of bullets to break up demonstrations in Tibet. On the other hand, Chinese officials refused to acknowledge a list of prisoners presented by U.S. Ambassador Stapleton Roy.[47]

Immediately before the U.S. decision on MFN was announced, Beijing said it "firmly opposed" any conditions. It subsequently announced the demobilization of 64,000 army officers, however, and the release of one of its longest-held political prisoners, Xu Wenli.[48] Beijing also made the case that MFN was not really a privilege or a special favor but rather an aspect of free trade. An article in *Beijing Review* made this point while arguing that MFN should be granted according to provisions in the General Agreement on Tariffs and Trade (GATT). Specifically, the piece stated, "There is an article in GATT that states when a party applies the most favorable duty rate to a product imported from one member state, it should also apply the same duty to like products imported from other member states."[49] China also cited U.S. leaders who noted that MFN is given to most countries, including South Africa, Syria, and Iraq. It specifically quoted Senator Max Baucus (D-Mont.) who stated, "If the United States wants to do business with China on a fair and reasonable basis, China should be given the same non-discriminatory treatment without exception."[50] In other words, MFN, according to the Chinese argument, is a part of a free trade system.

Beijing also made the point that Washington's annual examination of China's MFN status is discriminatory and out-of-date—a leftover from the Cold War. A Chinese writer, reflecting the government's position, said that China is one of the few countries subject to scrutiny each year, and that this practice is "itself a form of discrimination against China." This same writer also noted that denying MFN status is based on Cold War legislation in the United States that was aimed at the Soviet bloc, which no longer exists, and other "non-market economies," a term that no longer describes China.[51]

After President Clinton announced the renewal of MFN, Chinese leaders denounced the decision to link it in the future to improvements in human rights, saying that this policy had "seriously impaired" relations between the two countries. Xinhua declared that if the Clinton administration "should insist on its own way, it can only seriously impair Sino-U.S. relations." There was no mention of retaliation, however, and the statement seemed generally pro forma.[52] The Ministry of Foreign Affairs subsequently issued a note opposing the conditions placed on MFN, saying that tying other matters to China's trade status violated principles set forth in the three Sino-U.S. joint communiqués. The note also asserted, "The American public and people of vision are increasingly supportive of the unconditional renewal of China's MFN status and the maintenance and expansion of Sino-U.S. relations."[53] This response seemed a very measured or mild one. Beijing's statements were also contradicted by a front-page story in *China Daily* that said that trade officials expressed "guarded pleasure" over Clinton's statement.[54]

The issue of China's exports of arms and nuclear know-how and its violations of arms agreements also came up periodically during 1993. The criticism came mostly from the United States, which in some ways linked the issue to MFN. In early May, a U.S. official said that the United States had a "mounting pile of information" about China's "illegal" exports of weapons, including surface-to-surface missiles that had been purveyed to Pakistan notwithstanding a pledge two years earlier to desist. Another official said that satellite photographs of the port of Karachi revealed that China had not stopped shipments of M-11 missiles to Pakistan that began in the fall of 1992. Assistant Secretary of State for Asia and the Pacific Winston Lord said that talks were in progress with Beijing on such issues.[55]

Chinese leaders responded in July to President Clinton's call for a ban on nuclear testing by saying that China had always exercised restraint and advocated a complete ban on nuclear tests. The Foreign Ministry declared that, among the five nuclear powers, China had conducted the fewest number of nuclear tests. On July 21, Beijing repeated a promise to abide by international agreements restricting arms sales after the United States threatened economic sanctions if China continued to ship missiles to Pakistan in violation of the agreement. U.S. officials said that China had violated the Missile Technology Control Regime. Chinese officials denied the charge.[56] On July 25, Secretary of State Warren Christopher, in his first meeting with Chinese Foreign Minister Qian Qichen, talked about the seriousness of the missile sales and called for specific talks on the issue. Meetings, the subject of which was not reported, followed.[57]

Serious differences between the United States and China surfaced in August when U.S. military planes and ships shadowed the Chinese vessel *Yinhe* for several days saying that the ship was carrying the ingredients for chemical weapons that were being shipped to a Middle Eastern country. The United States stopped the ship in international waters but did not find incriminating evidence. Beijing reacted in a very hostile manner to the incident, saying that Washington was acting as a "self-appointed international policeman" and had displayed "overbearing behavior."[58]

Only days later, the United States imposed sanctions on China and Pakistan after concluding that both countries had violated the Missile Technology Control Regime. U.S. State Department officials said they had repeatedly raised the question of China selling M-11 missiles to Pakistan and were never given a satisfactory reply. The sanctions included terminating sales of sensitive high-tech items to China worth $400 million to $500 million annually.[59]

China again assailed the United States over its search of the *Yinhe* in September. Chinese officials called the United States the "world cop" and said it had behaved in an irresponsible manner and "in contempt of the norms governing international relations." Beijing demanded that the United States take immediate steps to do something about the "adverse consequences of its false intelligence," make a public apology, and pay compensation for the financial losses incurred.[60]

On October 5, in defiance of an international moratorium and pleas from President Clinton, China conducted an underground nuclear test. Clinton, in response, directed the Energy Department to prepare for the possible resumption of U.S. tests. Boris Yeltsin subsequently said he would have to review Russia's position on testing. A host of other countries condemned China's test. Beijing said that the "conditional moratorium" was designed to maintain nuclear superiority and was of limited significance and that international scrutiny of its "relatively small" nuclear program was unfair.[61]

During the APEC meeting in November, Secretary of State Christopher said in a speech at the University of Washington, "On human rights, unless there is overall significant progress, the president will not be able to renew China's Most Favored Nation status."[62] President Jiang Zemin at this same time met with workers at Boeing Corporation and told them that China had made massive purchases of airplanes from the company—in fact, was the biggest buyer in the world—and that if MFN were not renewed China would retaliate by purchasing planes elsewhere—implying that the workers might lose their jobs.[63]

## China's Response to Human Rights Criticisms

Beijing responded with both anger and concessions to foreign criticisms of its human rights practices during 1993. Whether China's response was a hard or soft one depended in part upon the nature of the criticism, it source, and the domestic political situation in China at the time. Beijing's answers to human rights criticisms were more functional and thought out than in the past. In fact, this gave rise to what some called China's "human rights diplomacy."

In reaction to Secretary of State Warren Christopher's statements made soon after he assumed office, Beijing warned the Clinton administration not to meddle in China's internal affairs. A Foreign Ministry spokesman said, in a much milder statement than previous ones that the three Sino-U.S. communiqués contain principles of mutual respect noninterference in each other's internal affairs.[64]

Reacting to the U.S. State Department's human rights report on China published in January, the Foreign Ministry declared it was "firmly opposed to any interference in its internal affairs under the pretext of human rights." The ministry's statement went on to say that the "so-called human rights report contains irresponsible comments on and distortions of China's domestic situation, and attacks against China on the human rights issue. This is entirely unjustifiable."[65]

In February, however, Beijing released two prominent political prisoners and gave visas to two others. Wang Xizhe, who was sentenced to fourteen years in prison in 1981 for his part in the 1979 Democracy Wall movement, was released. Gao Shan, who had worked for Bao Tong, the highest official to be imprisoned after the Tiananmen Massacre, was also let go. A few days later several others were released, including a Catholic priest and China's previously most-wanted student leader. In fact, this step brought to an end the incarceration of student protestors involved in the Democracy Movement of early 1989.[66] (For further details, see Chapter 3.) Diplomats felt that the releases were made to deflect human rights criticisms and to please newly inaugurated president, Bill Clinton. This view was ostensibly confirmed by a statement made at this time by Premier Li Peng calling for improved Sino-U.S. ties.

In reaction to a barrage of criticism of the human rights situation in Tibet, the Chinese government continued its series of articles in *Beijing Review*, focusing on the human rights situation in Tibet in the past. One article described the former Tibet as a region in the early stages of feudalism with "many features of a slave society still in evidence." Tibet's system of serfdom, the article said, was "more brutal and darker than that of medieval Europe."[67] The unequal distribution of land, forced child labor, and cruel punishments employed by serf owners were documented. The illustrations included a picture of a man whose eyes had been gouged out, presumably a Tibetan serf victimized by his owner.[68] The purpose of the pieces was to debunk the claim of the Dalai Lama that Tibetan society had been among the "holiest and the most wonderful."[69] Another article mentioned that the Chinese Constitution protects religious freedom in Tibet, while citing the Dalai Lama's earlier statements, noting that freedom of religion had indeed been put into effect.[70] In yet another article, a reporter cited the 17-Article Agreement with Tibet in 1951, which promised human rights, and described how these rights had been fulfilled. Beijing had protected escaped slaves, redistributed land to help former serfs, and ended the practice of forced labor, the article said.[71]

Chinese officials in March rejected any call for talks with the Dalai Lama, saying that he was trying to "undermine the national unity of China."[72]

In April, Beijing criticized President Clinton for "playing host" to the Dalai Lama, saying that the Dalai Lama is not just a religious person but "a political figure that engages in activities opposed to China with the aim of splitting China."[73]

In response to demonstrations and violence in Tibet in the spring, the Chinese government asserted that "it was within its rights to crack down on protests in Tibet" and that this "should have no bearing on its trade status or its application to host the 2000 Olympics." Government spokespersons said that the matter was an internal affair, and that China's actions were justified to stop lawbreaking and maintain order, and that the concerns of foreign countries were "not necessary."[74]

Beijing reported in June that "thousands of peasants" had rioted in Sichuan Province over taxes and that there had been incidents of peasants beating officials, burning vehicles, and engaging in other acts of violence.[75] Officials mentioned government actions to put down the disorder but did not offer any justification—apparently perceiving that Western governments would not make issue of the tax question, especially since there were protests in Western governments over taxes that were much higher than in China. Later, however, the government did order taxes cut and some fees canceled in rural areas.[76] (See Chapter 2 for further details.)

In reply to criticisms of its actions at the Vienna Conference on Human Rights and comments by U.N. Secretary General Boutros Boutros-Ghali and U.S. Secretary of State Christopher that human rights are not just a domestic matter, *People's Daily* asserted that Western nations were trying to impose their ideology and version of democracy on others and that this constituted a "major obstacle" to the realization of human rights and "may lead the international human rights activities astray." The paper cited the United States for racial discrimination that triggered the Los Angeles riots and said that "xenophobia and neo-Nazism are on the rise in some countries." It went on to say that Western countries emphasize only individual and citizens' rights and "belittle" economic, cultural, and social rights while denying the rights of subsistence and development."[77]

At the conference, Vice Foreign Minister Liu Huaqiu accused foreign governments of using human rights as a pretext for interfering in China's domestic affairs. "Some countries showing no respect for the sovereignty of other countries, try to use the human rights issue to serve certain political interests and interfere in the internal affairs of other countries," he said. Articles subsequently appeared saying essentially the same thing in the *People's Daily* and in *Outlook*.[78] A few days later, Premier Li Peng, in his first public appearance since suffering a heart attack in April, made a similar statement, assailing countries that "impose certain concepts of democracy and human rights" on others. A press analysis of his comments on this subject was also released.[79]

(For more on the releases, see Chapter 3.)

During the November APEC meeting, President Jiang Zemin was asked if he gave President Clinton any guarantees on human rights. He said, "When the leaders of two of the largest countries in the world get together, we should talk about bigger problems."[80] After the meeting, Jiang traveled to Cuba, which some saw as an intentional slap at the United States in view of poor U.S.-Cuban relations.[81] Responding to President Clinton's criticism of China's human rights problems in Tibet, Foreign Minister Qian Qichen said, "Even the United States recognizes that Tibet is part of China and that Beijing will negotiate with the Dalai Lama only after he states that Tibet cannot become independent from China."[82]

### China Promotes Its Views on Human Rights

During the year, China made energetic efforts to redefine human rights and make its own view known and accepted as a way of countering Western human rights criticisms. In fact, it experienced some noteworthy successes in this effort.[83] Beijing was most successful in pushing its definition of human rights during and after a meeting of Asian leaders in Bangkok to discuss a United Nations General Assembly resolution calling for a world conference on human rights. The meeting closed with the issuance of the "Bangkok Declaration," which set forth Asian thinking on the issue of human rights. This "Asian view" was also in large part China's view. The document made the following main points: (1) The promotion of human rights must be done in the context of international cooperation; (2) The current codification of human rights stresses just one category of human rights; (3) The principles of sovereignty and non-interference in the internal affairs of nations must be respected when discussing human rights; (4) The use of double standards and politicization of human rights must be avoided; (5) The right of development must be considered a fundamental human right; (6) International norms must coincide with the development of a just world order; (7) Economic and social progress facilitates the growth of democracy and the advancement of human rights; (8) Education and training are vital to improving human rights. (See Appendix 1.) Clearly the points set forth in this document were influenced by Beijing and were generally in accord with China's view.[84]

The Bangkok Declaration also recommended that human rights not be made a condition for development assistance; that human rights not be used as a means of political pressure; that regional differences be considered when assessing human rights; that cultural and religious backgrounds be considered when discussing human rights; that economic, social, cultural, and civil rights be regarded as interdependent; that poverty be seen as an obstacle to enjoying human rights; and that regional arrangements be established to promote human rights. These points fit even more into Beijing's ideas about human rights.

In fact, the Bangkok Declaration, which was to a large extent inspired by China, may be considered a victory for Beijing. After the publication of the declaration, Chinese officials and the Chinese press frequently cited the document.[85] Chinese leaders were also able to quote a number of participants at the conference who made statements that sounded similar to Beijing's criticism of Western attacks on China's human rights record. The Malaysian delegate to the conference said: "It should be clear there is no let-up in the drive of the North to continue its political, economic and cultural hegemony of the South." Thailand's foreign minister noted, "Western human rights activists can be self-righteous and censorious." And Burma's Win Mra told the conference, "Asian countries with their own norms and standards should not be dictated to by a group of countries who are far distant geographically, politically, economically and culturally."[86]

When Malaysia's Prime Minister Mahathir Mohamad visited China in June, Premier Li Peng met him and said, "Each country must define its own concept of human rights." Another Chinese official quoted Mahathir when he said,"Democracy is not an end but a means." Li, again taking a swipe at the West, said, echoing the Bangkok Declaration, "The imposition of certain concepts of democracy and human rights from outside should be opposed."[87]

Meanwhile, in several official publications Beijing continued to make the case that the right of subsistence is the most important human right and that Asia has a tradition of promoting human betterment and human rights. (See Appendix 1 and Appendix 2.)

Further reflecting the importance Beijing accorded the task of propagating its own view on human rights in June, Vice Foreign Minister Liu Huaqiu headed China's delegation to the World Conference on Human Rights in Vienna to commemorate the forty-fifth anniversary of the signing of the Universal Declaration of Human Rights. In his speech, Liu cited progress in human rights, mentioning the elimination of colonialism, apartheid, and massive gross violations of human rights as a result of foreign invasion and occupation and the safeguarding of the rights of small and weak countries to self-determination and the right of developing countries to develop—major tenets of China's definition of human rights. Liu also pointed out that, in preparation for the conference, the nations of Africa, Latin America and Asia had each held regional meetings and passed the Tunis Declaration, the San Jose Declaration and the Bangkok Declaration, respectively. He averred that these documents represent the "concerns of the developing countries" and the "views of the overwhelming majority of the world's population."[88] (See Appendix 4.)

Liu went on to set forth four proposals to be discussed at the meeting: (1) The international community should give primary attention to gross human rights violations resulting from foreign aggression and occupation and regional conflicts; (2) World peace and stability should be sought and preserved and hegemony and power politics must be eliminated (3) The right of developing countries to develop must be respected and guaranteed to gradually narrow the differences between North and South; (4) The right of each country to formulate its own policies on human rights must be protected.[89] These issues were discussed at the meeting.

In reply to China's efforts, former Senator Timothy Wirth (D-Colo), head of the U.S. delegation, said, "China is at the forefront of a handful of renegade nations trying to slow down or stop the process of drafting a meaningful final document." John Shattuck, the Department of State's human rights officer and deputy head of the U.S. delegation, said that the members of the team would "not hesitate to crack heads with our opponents and isolate those who are being most obstructive." Shattuck assailed China in particular for rejecting the principle of universality and for leading Iran, Bangladesh, Syria, and Malaysia in opposing the creation of a U.N. commissioner for human rights.[90] It was reported, however, that China had the support of seventy countries for its arguments.[91]

Coinciding with this controversy and to help promote China's human rights position, Xinhua in mid-June carried a long piece on China's contributions to safeguarding human rights, an article that was carried as a headline piece in *People's Daily*. The piece observed that China had sent representatives to the working groups that drafted the Declaration on the Right to Development; the U.N. Convention on the Rights of Children; the International Convention on the Protection of the Rights of Migrant Workers and their Families; and the Declaration on the Protection of the Rights of Persons Belonging to National, Ethnic, Religious and Linguistic Minorities. It further noted that China had acceded to eight international conventions on human rights and has conscientiously fulfilled its duties under the conventions it has signed and has submitted progress reports. The article also noted that China published a white paper on human rights in 1991, which advanced for the first time the right of subsistence. Finally the author declared that China, together with other developing countries, had put up strong resistance to the practices of hegemonism and power-politics by Western nations in using human rights as an instrument to bully other nations and impose their political systems and values. (See Appendix 5.)

### Endnotes

1. Cited by Paul Quinn-Judge, *Boston Globe,* November 19, 1993, p. 1.

2. Cited in *South China Morning Post*, December 5, 1993, p. 6.

3. Cited in Central News Agency released of June 7, 1993 from Brussels.

4. For details on China's earlier "edge" regarding human rights, see Roberta Cohen, *People's Republic of China: The Human Rights Exception* (Baltimore: University of Maryland School of Law, 1988).

5. Cited in "Government Seeks U.S. Friendship," *Asian Bulletin*, March 1993, p. 72.

6. "Tibet Party Official Orders Purge," *Asian Bulletin*, April 1993, p. 71.

7. Ibid.

8. From Governor Gyaincain Norbu's speech printed in *Tibet Daily* and cited in Ibid.

9. "Tibetan Pro-Independence Protesters Arrested," *Asian Bulletin*, May 1993, p. 79.

10. Ibid.

11. "Human Rights Conditions Criticized; Ramos Pays Visit," *Asian Bulletin*, June 1993, p. 80.

12. Ibid.

13. Ibid., p. 81.

14. "U.S. Urges Peking to Revive Talks on Tibet," *Asian Bulletin*, June 1993, p. 82.

15. Ibid.

16. "Peking Clamps Down on Large-Scale Demonstrations in Lhasa," *Asian Bulletin*, July 1993, p. 74.

17. Ibid.

18. Ibid.

19. Ibid.

20. Ibid., p. 75.

21. "Peking Assails Universal Human Rights; Tibet Remains Tense," *Asian Bulletin*, August 1993, p. 75.

22. Ibid., p. 76.

23. Ibid., p. 76.

24. Daniel Kwan, "Dissidents Face Battle at Human Rights Forum," *South China Morning Post*, June 11, 1993, p. 10.

25. Ibid., p. 77.

26. "First Tibetan Delegation in a Decade Visits Peking," *Asian Bulletin*, September 1993, p. 85.

27. Stephen Wilson, "Human Rights Issue Hanging over Vote," *Los Angeles Times*, September 19, 1993, p. C10.

28. "Row with U.S. over Arms Sales and Human Rights Issues," *Asian Bulletin*, October 1993, p. 75.

29. Ibid., p. 76.

30. Ibid., p. 77.

31. Ibid., p. 78.

32. "Peking Tightens Control over Tibet," *Asian Bulletin*, November 1993, p. 77.

33. "Crackdown on Muslims, Tibetan Dissent Reported," *Asian Bulletin*, December 1993, p. 87.

34. Ibid., p. 88.

35. Paul Quinn-Judge, "Rights Issue Is Raised as China Leader Arrives in U.S.; Clinton Urged to Take Tough Line," *Boston Globe*, November 19, 1993, p. 1.

36. Ann McFeatters, "U.S. Pushes China on Human Rights," *Ottawa Citizen*, November 20, 1993, p. A6. Also see "CCP Central Committee Announces Blueprint to Step Up Economic Reforms," *Asian Bulletin*, January 1994, p. 22. It is worth noting that President Jiang did not have the authority to agree to the demands made by President Clinton and thus his demands were seen as mainly for domestic consumption in the United States.

37. Carl P. Leubsdorf, "Clinton Prods China About Human Rights; But Differences Continue After Leaders Meet," *Dallas Morning News*, November 20, 1993, p. 1A.

38. "'Toughest' Human Rights Challenge for U.S., State Department Official Says," *BNA International Trade Daily*, December 10, 1993, p. 1.

39. "Government Seeks U.S. Friendship," *Asian Bulletin*, March 1993, p. 71.

40. Ibid.

41. See Nicholas D. Kristof, "Beijing Awaits Decision on Trade," *New York Times*, January 15, 1993, p. A16.

42. Nicholas D. Kristof, "Clinton Aide Ends China Trip with No Sign of Accord," *New York Times*, May 13, 1993, p. A10.

43. Steven Greenhouse, "Renewal Backed for China Trade," *New York Times*, May 28, 1993, p. A5.

44. Ibid.

45. Keith Bradsher, "Clinton Aides Propose Renewal of China's Favored Trade Status," *New York Times*, May 25, 1993, p. A1.

46. Frank Gibney, Jr., Kari Huus, and Jane Whitmore, "China Nods at Human Rights—But Abuse Goes On," *Newsweek*, June 7, 1993, p. 26.

47. Ibid.

48. "U.S. Renews Most-Favored-Nation Status," *Asian Bulletin*, July 1993, p. 73.

49. Sun Zhengao, "China's MFN Also a Benefit to the United States," *Beijing Review*, May 24–30, 1993, p. 8.

50. Cited in Ibid.

51. Ibid.

52. Ibid.

53. "China Protests Clinton's MFN Deal," *Beijing Review*, June 6–13, 1993, p. 4.

54. Sheryl WuDunn, "China Denounces Terms of Clinton's Trade Deal," *New York Times*, May 30, 1993, p. A12.

55. "U.S. Renews Most-Favored-Nation Status," *Asian Bulletin*, July 1993, p. 72.

56. "Austerity Plan Unveiled to Cool Overheated Economy; U.S. Opposes Missile Sales," *Asian Bulletin*, September 1993, p. 84.

57. Ibid., p. 85.

58. "Row with U.S. Over Arms Sales and Human Rights Issues," *Asian Bulletin*, October 1993, p. 75.

59. Ibid., p. 76.

60. "Cargo Ship Incident Dampens U.S. Ties; Olympic Bid Fails Despite Release of Dissidents," *Asian Bulletin*, November 1993, p. 74.

61. "Nuclear Tests Bring International Criticism; Measures Taken to Curb Corruption," *Asian Bulletin*, December 1993, pp. 84–85.

62. Jeff Sommer, "Human Rights Barrier; U.S., China Are Still at Odds as Talks Begin," *Newsday*, November 18, 1993, p. 1.

63. UPI report of November 13, 1993, dateline Seattle.

64. "Government Seeks U.S. Friendship," *Asian Bulletin*, March 1993, p. 71.

65. See Xinhua, January 21, 1993, cited in Foreign Broadcasting Information Service (FBIS), January 21, 1993, p. 1.

66. "Pro-Democracy Activists Released," *Asian Bulletin*, April 1993, p. 70.

67. "Did the People of Old Tibet Have Human Rights?" *Beijing Review*, February 15–21, 1993, pp. 22–24.

68. Ibid., pp. 23 and 24.

69. Ibid., p. 2.

70. "No Religious Freedom for Tibetans?" *Beijing Review*, February 22–28, 1993, p. 18.

71. "How the Tibetans Won Basic Human Rights," *Beijing Review*, March 15–31, 1993, pp. 18–20.

72. "Tibetan Pro-Independence Protestors Arrested," *Asian Bulletin*, May 1993, p. 79.

73. "U.S. Urges Peking to Revive Talks on Tibet," *Asian Bulletin*, June 1993, p. 82.

74. "Peking Clamps Down on Large-Scale Demonstrations in Lhasa," *Asian Bulletin*, July 1992, p. 76.

75. "Tiananmen Quiet as Rural Peasants Revolt over Inequalities," *Asian Bulletin*, August 1993, p. 74

76. Ibid., p. 75.

77. "China Says West Twists Human Rights Dialogue," Reuters, June 15, 1993.

78. Daniel Kwan, "Dissidents Face Battle at Human Rights Forum, " *South China Morning Post*, June 11, 1993, p. 10.

79. "Cargo Ship Incident Dampens U.S. Ties; Olympic Bid Fails Despite Release of Dissidents," *Asian Bulletin*, November 1993, p. 75.

80. Cited in Carl P. Leubsdorf, "Clinton Prods China About Human Rights; But Differences Continue After Leaders Meet," *Dallas Morning News*, November 20, 1993, p. 1A.

81. UPI report of November 13, 1993, dateline Seattle.

82. Edward Epstein and Susan Yaochum, "Clinton, Jian Discuss Human Rights, Markets," *San Francisco Chronicle*, November 20, 1993, p. A1.

83. For background, see John F. Copper, "Peking's Post-Tiananmen Foreign Policy: The Human Rights Factor," *Issues and Studies*, October 1994, pp. 49–73.

84. This is evidenced by the fact it was published in China's major government-controlled news magazine. See "Bangkok Declaration," *Beijing Review*, May 31–June 6, 1993, pp. 9–11.

85. See, for example, "Asia's Major Human Rights Concerns," *Beijing Review*, April 19–25, 1993 (which was published before the Bangkok meeting); "China's View on the Final Document," *Beijing Review*, May 31–June 3, 1993; "Proposals for Human Rights Protection and Promotion," *Beijing Review*, June 28–July 4, 1993; and Dong Yunhu, "Fine Traditions of Human Rights in Asia," *Beijing Review*, June 28–July 4, 1993.

86. See *Asian Wall Street Journal* editorial of April 21, 1993, reprinted in *Asian Bulletin*, June 1993, p. 92.

87. "Tiananmen Quiet as Rural Peasants Revolt over Inequalities," *Asian Bulletin*, August 1993, p. 75.

88. "Proposals for Human Rights Protection and Promotion," *Beijing Review*, June 28–July 4, 1993, pp. 8–11.

89. Ibid., p. 10.

90. "Peking Assails Universal Human Rights; Tibet Remains Tense," *Asian Bulletin*, August 1993, p. 78.

91. Ibid.

# Chapter 7

# China's Foreign Policy and Human Rights, II

Aren't the Chinese putting their thumb in his (Clinton's) eye by allowing the human rights condition to deteriorate after Clinton decided to de-link the issue of human rights and trade with Beijing?

—Reporter's question to Dee Dee Myer[1]

Once divided by ideology, we are now drawn together by shared economic interests.

—Ron Brown, Secretary of Commerce[2]

I don't mean to say that the human rights situation is perfect here. But tremendous progress has been made in human rights. If you look at China's history, this is the best period in our history.

—Zhu Muzhi, President, China Society for Human Rights Studies[3]

### Introduction

Throughout 1994, the People's Republic of China remained the object of widespread human rights criticism in the United States and Western Europe. However, China was labelled a serious violator of human rights to a noticeably lesser extent in other countries and was cited only infrequently in Third World nations. In short, the gap between the West's view of China's human rights abuses and that of the rest of the world widened. In fact, in response to Western attacks, Beijing made increased efforts to win the support of Third World countries for its human rights views. Chinese leaders also issued more direct replies and criticism of human rights abuses in the U.S. in order to blunt or stop the Western attacks.

The decision by the Clinton administration to de-link human rights from most favored nation status for China attracted considerable attention. Critics argued that Clinton should not have made this decision and cited convincing evidence that it had resulted in increased human rights abuses in China and that many political prisoners, who might otherwise have been released or been given better treatment, suffered because of the decision. The president's decision also appeared to demoralize some human rights activists and dissidents in China.

Meanwhile, however, human rights issues in China, even more than in 1993, during 1994 reflected division in the leadership about how to respond to foreign criticism and about dealing with human rights as an issue of foreign policy. The Chinese government responded to some pleas for leniency and requests to release certain prisoners. At other times it adopted a tough approach. It continued to use crackdowns to preclude embarrassing demonstrations or incidents that might affect its reputation internationally.

### Foreign Criticism of China's Human Rights

The year began with the U.S. government criticizing China for its human rights record in the annual Department of State report. (See Appendix 12) According to the report, China continued to hold hundreds, perhaps thousands, of political prisoners. Mentioned specifically was the fact that "thousands of people" detained during the military crackdown in Tiananmen Square in 1989 were not accounted for. It also asserted that "fundamental human rights provided for in the Chinese Constitution frequently are ignored in practice. Still the critique was mixed. The report said that, in the realm of human rights generally, China had made "positive moves," but it said China still "fell far short" in terms of internationally recognized norms. The report pressured Beijing, and some said this was in part intended, to show improvements in human rights, some said, to make it easier for the U.S. to renew China's MFN status in June.[4]

Asia Watch published a report on February 20 entitled "Detained in China and Tibet." The 664-page report detailed worsening human rights abuses and political repression, stating that prisoners are released in a timely fashion for maximum political effect in what it called "hostage politick." It went on to say that Western governments then use the release of political prisoners as evidence of improvements in China's human rights condition while ignoring tens of thousands who have not benefited from international attention.[5] In short, the report suggested that the West is duped into believing there are better human rights conditions in China. Supporting Asia Watch's criticism, Amnesty International reported that Buddhist nuns in Tibet had recently been sentenced to prison terms ranging from two to seven years for attempting to demonstrate in public. Amnesty elaborated, saying the nuns had been taken to Drapchi prison outside of Lhasa which held Tibet's most serious political prisoners.[6] Supporters of the Dalai Lama confirmed this report and noted that nuns had even been imprisoned for composing a song praising the Dalai Lama.[7]

Amnesty International, in another report, said that Chinese police had detained seven foreign Christians from the United States, Indonesia, and Hong Kong and called for their release. The U.S. Embassy subsequently confirmed the report but said that the Americans had been released.[8] Meanwhile, a federal judge in the United States ruled that victims of China's birth control policies (meaning the one-child policy that has led to many forced abortions) were entitled to asylum in the United States, even though the Clinton administration had expelled some. The judge declared that involuntary sterilization as practiced in China is an "egregious infringement on the fundamental right to procreate" and that "to bear children is held to be a basic human right." The case involved a Chinese couple from Fujian Province who had fled as a result of a government order that they be sterilized, after which their property was confiscated and their home destroyed.[9]

John Shattuck, assistant secretary of state for human rights, visited China in March and talked to China's most famous dissident, Wei Jingsheng, who had been released from prison in September 1993. Shattuck also discussed other human rights issues with Chinese officials. After his visit, however, more dissidents were arrested—including Wei. Shattuck, who apparently felt betrayed by the actions, said before departing from Hong Kong, "I am disturbed to learn of the new reports of detentions in China." President Clinton, when he heard the news, said he strongly disapproved of what was done. The Department of State then issued a statement saying that it "would look with particular gravity upon any decision by the Chinese government to subject Wei to additional suffering." Subsequently, Secretary of State Christopher expressed a "strong distaste" over the harassment of dissidents.[10]

U.S. Department of State spokesperson Mike McCurry in April said the United States regretted that China arrested Wei again. American diplomats also met with Chinese diplomats in Beijing to talk about the issue, but they did not issue a formal protest. U.S. officials said at the time that, in their view, Wei had done nothing more than express opinions about conditions in China, an activity that is protected under the Universal Declaration of Human Rights, which they noted China says it adheres to.[11] (For more on Wei and other dissidents, see Chapter 3.)

The London-based Tibet Information Network said on April 18 that thirteen nuns and monks had been arrested in Lhasa for taking part in pro-independence demonstrations. Some had called for religious freedom, others for "Chinese to leave and go back to China."[12]

In May, the Dalai Lama met with President Clinton and Vice President Gore. Clinton voiced support for the Dalai Lama's proposal to discuss problems in Tibet with Chinese officials. Upon returning to India, the Dalai Lama said that he might seek a referendum on Tibet's future if China continued to ignore his offers. He also said that he felt his moderate efforts since 1959 to resolve the Tibet problem had failed. "In the past 14 years of talks with the Chinese, I have adopted a midway approach," he said. "I believed this would help in a meaningful negotiation. But, unfortunately, there has been no progress." He stated further that a referendum may be the only way to go and that the Chinese "are full of deceit."[13]

The Tibet Information Network reported in late May that Chinese police had arrested more Tibetans, this time over protests about tax increases. Shopkeepers reportedly closed their shops in protest over a 20 to 100 percent increase in business taxes.[14]

In June, demonstrators greeted Premier Li Peng when he visited Austria to conclude a trade deal with the Austrian government. The demonstrators, who protested Li's role in the Tiananmen Massacre, however, were kept at a distance by the Austrian government. A few days later, when Li visited Germany, he was presented with a statement signed by twenty-six prominent members of Chancellor Helmut Kohl's Christian Democratic Union that stated that Tiananmen "is not forgotten, especially the contemptible role personally played by Li Peng."

Amnesty International took credit for subsequent protests in Berlin, Munich, and Bonn. In Berlin, Li cut short his visit because of protestors who carried banners saying, "Mass murderer Li Peng," "Butcher of Tiananmen," and "Freedom for Tibet." When Li visited playwright Johann Wolfgang von Goethe's home, a protester wearing a T-shirt saying "Li go home" threw himself in front of the cars in Li's group and had to be dragged away by police. Li subsequently canceled a number of other activities or changed his agenda while in Germany because of being heckled.[15]

Amnesty International at this time also issued its annual report. It stated that the Chinese government continued to use arbitrary powers of arrest and detention and that hundreds had been detained recently because of their religious views or for taking part in unauthorized religious activities. The report documented dissidents who had been arrested in Shanghai, including Democracy Movement leader Fu Shenqi.[16]

Chinese police surrounded a rural nunnery in Tibet in July following anti-Chinese demonstrations. Coinciding with this action, Western diplomats, attending a conference on the Tibetan economy also attended by President Jiang Zemin, said that the plans, if carried out, would lead to a further erosion of

Tibetan culture in the region. They also noted that most of the jobs created by the development plan under discussion for Tibet would go to Chinese.[17]

Amnesty International reported in August that more Chinese dissidents had been arrested. The human rights organization attributed this to the government's fear of social unrest, particularly among impoverished peasants and laid-off workers who had been "left out of the economic boom." Amnesty declared that the Chinese government had "acted swiftly to repress all potential sources of dissent."[18] It also reported that more Tibetans had been given harsh sentences, up to fifteen years in jail, for independence activities and that others had been arrested for carrying the Tibetan flag.[19]

In September, the French government banned demonstrations during President Jiang Zemin's visit, prompting human rights activists there to threaten to defy the ban. Cai Zongguo, spokesman for the Federation for Democracy in China said it was the first time a Western country had banned such demonstrations. He also said that in the future "the Chinese government will despise the French government even more for its lack of dignity." Gerard Fuchs of the opposition Socialist Party described the decision as "unworthy of France." French Foreign Minister Alain Juppe, however, said later that he had "achieved a few results" on the human rights issue and had presented Jiang with a list of thirty dissidents being held in jail and expressed concern about their fate.[20]

Meanwhile, Amnesty International reported that more dissidents were being detained in China without charges being made or trials scheduled, in gross violation of international human rights standards. Specifically mentioned was Tong Yi, an assistant to Wei Jingsheng, China's best-known dissident.[21]

U.S. Secretary of State Christopher, meeting his Chinese counterpart at the November APEC meeting in Djarkata, said that the United States intended to retain some sanctions against China "in light of various actions the Chinese have taken in the past." Meanwhile, a number of human rights organizations condemned the Chinese government for the secret sentencing of journalist Gao Yu. The New York–based Committee to Protect Journalists said the sentencing violated "all international standards of due process of law." Human Rights Watch–Asia said that the sentencing violated China's Criminal Procedure Law.[22]

Elsewhere, in Australia pro-Tibetan protestors disrupted ceremonies welcoming Politburo member Qiao Shi at the Parliament Building. They accused Qiao of bearing the responsibility for the killing of 150 unarmed Tibetans in 1989 in Lhasa. (Qiao headed the Chinese People's Armed Police at that time.) A motion had been made in the Australian parliament condemning the government for "inviting this "merciless butcher" to Australia."[23]

In December, the Dalai Lama called on Western countries to limit commercial deals with China in an effort to bring about greater democracy there. Meanwhile, the United Nations condemned China for violating international human rights laws in detaining thirty-two political prisoners in Tibet and called for their release. The U.N. Working Group on Arbitrary Detentions, according to observers, embarrassed Beijing by its report on this matter.[24]

## Most Favored Nation Status and Arms Transfers Issues

Human rights issues continued to dog U.S. and Chinese trade negot-iators in 1994. The renewal of China's most favored nation status each year drew attention to the human rights situation and each year resulted in some concess-ions by Beijing and usually the release of some political prisoners and dissidents. (See Chapter 3 for further details.) President Clinton de-linking the two issues in the summer thus fanned the flames of the debate and focused attention on U.S. China policy in an unprecedented fashion.

In early January, apparently anticipating that there would be difficulties when renewal came up later in the year, or wanting to show some mettle in dealing with Beijing and avoid the appearance of weakness in the Clinton admin-istration's handling of the situation, U.S. Secretary of the Treasury Lloyd Bentsen criticized Beijing as doing too little about human rights and said pointedly that he was "not satisfied." He warned that Beijing must do more if it expects the United States to renew most favored nation status.[25]

Bentsen may have been laying the groundwork for a major Clinton administration policy change on this issue. A few days later, Senator Max Baucus (D-Mont.) said that withdrawing MFN would be like dropping "the equivalent of a nuclear bomb" in terms of its economic and political impact. He recommended that the annual debate on most favored nation status for China be ended and a permanent policy enacted. Baucus appeared to seek to win his party's support for this opinion. The Clinton administration, having gone on record supporting it in principle, may have sought Baucus's help on the issue and, trying to help the Clinton administration, Baucus took the lead. In any event, Bentsen then said that if China would meet the administration's human rights conditions laid out in June 1993, the United States might end the issue once and for all.[26] Robert Rubin, director of the National Economic Council, echoed this view a few days later in a meeting with journalists, echoed this view.[27]

Beijing was not fully cooperative, however, or it had become an issue of such salience in the left-right struggle that the Left made renewed efforts to provoke the United States to cancel MFN or at least not make it permanent. In early March, after Wei Jingsheng and a number of other dissidents were arrested, Secretary of State Christopher said that this and the security sweep in China would have a "negative effect" upon his upcoming March visit and on the U.S. review of China's most favored nation trade status. During a subsequent meeting between Christopher and Chinese officials, there were apparently sharp and bitter exchanges. Christopher said after one session, "I wish the meeting had been as good as the lunch."[28] Chinese leaders reportedly told Christopher that they would never accept "U.S. dictates" on how to behave toward their own citizens. Premier Li Peng flatly rejected President Clinton's statement that MFN status could be renewed only if China showed "overall, significant progress" on human rights. He said that China "will never accept the United States' human rights concept" and declared that if the United States discontinued China's MFN trade status, it "would suffer no less than China" and that the U.S. "will lose its share of the big Chinese market." Foreign Minister Qian, who accused Christopher of disrespect during his visit, said afterward that for twenty-three years prior to President Nixon's opening up of relations, there was no trade whatsoever between China and the United States. He added, "I think you lived quite well. And so did we." Qian went on to say that he thought that President Clinton had "enmeshed himself in a web of his own spinning" over the June deadline for China to "make overall significant progress" in human rights.[29] The unfriendly Chinese response seems to have been generated by pressure from the Left and the military in the context of China's succession problem. Alternatively, Chinese leaders may have been feeling the heat of increased U.S. pressure for improvements in China's human rights record because the debate now centered on the possibility that the United States would revise its policy and end the annual debates on the topic by granting MFN status to China permanently.

Before he left Beijing, however, Christopher received several concessions. He obtained a written agreement codifying the right of U.S. diplomats to inspect prisons suspected of exporting goods made by prisoners. He also said Chinese leaders confirmed China's support for the Universal Declaration of Human Rights, agreed to talks about Red Cross visits to prisons and meetings with individual prisoners, and promised to provide an accounting of 235 prisoners held for political crimes in China and a similar accounting for Tibet.[30]

The Clinton administration tried to put a good face on the Christopher visit while shifting gears on U.S. China policy (regarding MFN status). He stressed in a news conference that the United States was holding Beijing to "strict standards."[31] Nevertheless, there were reports that top officials in various agencies of the U.S. government opposed Clinton's decision to grant China permanent MFN status. A number of previous foreign policy makers, including former secretaries of state Henry Kissinger, Lawrence Eagleburger, and Cyrus Vance opposed Clinton's action.[32] A.F.L.-C.I.O. head Lane Kirkland opposed renewal even for a year, saying that China "has not met the most minimum conditions for satisfying the requirements."[33]

On April 19, while debate in the U.S. was flaring, Chinese police interrupted a meeting between news reporters and dissident Wang Dan and detained all of them for a short time. Chinese officials seemed to want to temporarily block any news about China's human rights record, fearing it would embarrass the government at a time when the MFN issue was being discussed in the United States. (Ironically Wang had told NBC representatives at the time that he supported MFN's extension.)

U.S. officials said May 1 that Secretary of State Christopher believed that China had not made sufficient progress in human rights to warrant complete renewal of MFN. Some U.S. officials, however, said that they favored a "targeted approach"—meaning that private Chinese companies would be given MFN status but state-run industries would not. Yet, they conceded that it is often impossible to discern which companies are which and that this approach would not fulfill President Clinton's pledge not to "coddle China's aging dictators." But, they said, it would have appeal in Congress.[34]

The next day President Clinton met with China's vice premier Zou Jiahua and told him that China's human rights situation must improve or it would imperil U.S.-China relations, though he also said that he did not want to see China's MFN status changed. Zou, in the first high-level meeting between President Clinton and a top Chinese leader, reportedly told Clinton that the United States should not interfere in China's internal affairs.[35] Reporters questioned whether the two had also discussed China's continued nuclear testing. China's Foreign Ministry issued a statement at the time saying it had no knowledge of any plans for tests.[36] The Chinese government officials subsequently stated, in what appeared to be a friendly gesture, that they appreciated President Clinton's remarks—ignoring threats included in those remarks and the June 3 deadline for China to improve its human rights situation. Some Western diplomats said at the time that Chinese officials felt they did not need to take any action thinking they had Clinton's support and that MFN was "in the bag."[37]

In ensuing days, China rearrested some dissidents and passed an amendment to the Code on Public Order stiffening laws on disturbing the peace. However, Beijing also released some religious dissidents and some protestors jailed after the 1989 Democracy Movement. The most famous of these was Wang Juntao.[38] One might think from these seemingly contradictory responses that policy was being driven by disputes between Left and Right wings of the Chinese Communist Party. Clearly there were indications that some leaders wanted to make concessions to the United States and others did not, and some of the latter wanted to anger the United States so that it would not grant MFN status.

Clinton administration officials said in mid-May that the United States had launched secret negotiations to decide the MFN issue and would not talk about the matter. Subsequently it was reported that Michael Armacost, former U.S. ambassador to Japan and under-secretary of state and now an envoy to China, had recently told Chinese officials what conditions they must meet for MFN to be renewed. Two of these were allowing Red Cross access to prisons and ending the jamming of Voice of America broadcasts. A Chinese Foreign Ministry official admitted at the time that talks were going on concerning these issues.[39]

A few days later, Secretary of State Christopher told Clinton that China had met the two conditions the president had included in an executive order in 1993 (cooperation on ending the export of prison-made goods to the United States and in allowing close family members of certain dissidents to leave the country). Christopher, however, did not say that China had made "overall, significant progress" which has been the key phrasing in talking about the human rights situation in China. In fact, observers were saying that China had not made progress in other important areas: taking steps to begin adhering to the Universal Declaration of Human Rights; releasing and accounting for political prisoners; ensuring humane treatment of prisoners by allowing, for example, access by international organizations; protecting Tibet's religious and cultural heritage; and permitting international radio and television broadcasts into China.[40] Christopher, in fact, did not report on these issues.

At a press conference on May 29, President Clinton announced that MFN status would be renewed for China, and furthermore, that MFN status and human rights would henceforth not be linked. He stated that the linking of the two had been constructive, but that it had reached the end of its usefulness. He declared, without specifically saying why, that the two issues should not be tied and that it was "time to take a new path toward the achievement of our constant objectives." "We need," he said, "to place our relationship into a larger and more productive framework." President Clinton also cited China as the world's fastest growing economy, mentioning $8 billion in U.S. exports to China that supported over 150,000 jobs, and noted U.S. problems with North Korea's nuclear program. He said, in this context, that he wanted to "intensify and broaden" America's engagement with China.

Elsewhere in his speech, President Clinton said that he concurred with Secretary of State Christopher's recommendation, which concluded that China had not achieved "overall progress" in all of the areas outlined in the Executive Order relating to human rights. Nevertheless, he said, there was progress made in important areas, including the resolution of all emigration cases, the establishment of a memorandum of understanding with regard to prison labor issues, China's adherence to the Universal Declaration of Human Rights, and some other matters.

President Clinton also declared that in view of the continuing human rights abuses, he was extending sanctions imposed by the United States as a result of the events in Tiananmen Square and was banning the importation of munitions, principally guns and ammunition, from China. He also said he would support an American "program" to support those in China working to advance human rights and democracy there, which would include broadcasts of Radio Free Asia and other measures.

Secretary of State Christopher subsequently declared that the U.S.

scrutiny of human rights violations in China would continue and human rights dialogues would intensify. Clinton administration officials meanwhile tried to repudiate charges of caving in to China by calling on U.S. businesses to develop principles for doing business with China even though the business community in general was opposed to doing this. Christopher also declared that China had promised greater progress on human rights if there were no MFN linkage.[41]

Two New York–based human rights groups, Human Rights in China and Human Rights Watch–Asia, issued a report in July asserting that they had detected a new and intensified pattern of arrests since President Clinton's decision. They attributed it to the absence of international pressure on China, which they said prompted the Chinese government to "tighten the noose on all forms of dissident activity."[42]

In August, a bill proposed by Representative Nancy Pelosi (D-Calif.) to deny MFN status to products made or exported by the Chinese army, defense trading companies, and state-owned enterprises was defeated in the House of Representatives by a vote of 270-158. This seemed to end the debate about imposing sanctions on China for human rights abuses and about President Clinton's May 29 decision. The Clinton administration said the bill was unworkable because of the problems associated with distinguishing between products made by state-owned companies and others.[43]

Almost coinciding with this report, Robin Munro of Human Rights Watch–Asia noted that China had just held the most prominent trial of political dissidents since the Tiananmen "incident" and had handed down harsh sentences to a number of known protesters and human rights activists. He said, "There is Bill Clinton's answer for you." Others noted that the news of the trials started just as Commerce Secretary Ron Brown began a visit to China. The scheduling was explained as singularly an effort to embarrass the United States and to express China's displeasure at being denied the honor of hosting the Olympic Games in 2000. Wang Dan, one of the best-known dissidents of the Democracy Movement was arrested just hours before Brown arrived.[44]

In September, the Chinese government reported that it rejected calls for China to end nuclear testing, saying that most of China's nuclear weapons factories had been closed or had stopped operations and that China had shifted most of its nuclear research to peaceful uses. Officials noted that China had conducted only one test for every twenty-five done by the United States and that although it would participate in negotiations for a comprehensive test ban, it would test until such a treaty was in place.[45]

Secretary of State Christopher said in early October that the United States would lift the trade sanctions that had been placed on China because of alleged missile technology transfers to Pakistan. Christopher asserted that Beijing had agreed not to export ground-to-ground missiles to Pakistan with a range beyond 300 kilometers and a payload of 500 kilograms or more. He did not say how the agreement would be verified and stated that not all economic sanctions against China would be canceled.[46]

China conducted its second nuclear test of 1994 only a few days later. Australian Acting Foreign Minister Gordon Bilney condemned China for the test, saying that Beijing was "out of step" with negotiations for a Comprehensive Test Ban Treaty. Chinese officials responded that, among the nuclear states, China had conducted the fewest tests.[47]

On October 16, U.S. Secretary of Defense William Perry visited China, becoming the first U.S. defense head to visit since the Tiananmen Massacre in 1989. Perry had promised, before leaving, to raise the issue of human rights during his visit. He did, but only perfunctorily. Perry tried instead to bolster relations, saying during the visit that he had taken advantage of a historic opportunity to "reestablish warm relations between the two military establishments."[48] Subsequently, the director of the U.S. Arms Control and Disarmament Agency reported that the United States and China had "moved closer to common ground."[49]

## China Responds to Foreign Human Rights Criticisms

China responded with both harsh rebukes and concessions to foreign criticism of its human rights abuses in 1994 as it has in previous years. Again, both types of responses seemed very calculated to elicit the best reaction from the West, though each seemed as well to reflect the mood of Chinese leaders at the time and internal disputes between the Right and the Left in the Chinese Communist Party and the government. Generally, the hard-line Left preferred a tougher response; the reformist Right favored concessions more often. China's reactions also appeared to reflect the succession problem discussed in Chapter 2.

Beijing's first response during the year to foreign comments about China's human rights condition came even before the criticism was published. In January President Jiang Zemin told a congressional delegation visiting China that Beijing was "going to make an effort" in the months ahead to satisfy President Clinton's concerns about China's human rights record.[50] Jiang's comments came just prior to the publication of the Department of State's country reports on human rights and may have been intended to blunt the criticism of China in that report. It also came during important talks with the United States on textile imports and may have been a concession designed to favorably influence those talks, since a considerable amount of money was at stake for China. Jiang's comments similarly coincided with an agreement reached with the United States allowing inspection visits to thirty Chinese prisons suspected of exploiting prison labor to make products for export.[51]

Less than a month later, Xinhua News Agency announced that three prisoners arrested in connection with the Democracy Movement demonstrations in 1989 had been released. Chinese government authorities told American human rights advocate John Kamm at this time that the prisoners would be given their freedom because of the Lunar New Year (when debts and bad deeds are tradition-ally forgiven). An alternative explanation was that they were let go in antici-pation of the U.S. debate on China's most-favored-nation trade status, which was already in progress.[52] Beijing also released some Tibetan prisoners and started serious discussions with the Red Cross about allowing this organization to visit political prisoners and providing a list of these prisoners.[53]

In what one might suggest was a more leftist response, however (per-haps elicited by the concessionary statements made by Jiang and Xinhua News Agency, or perhaps in anger over the Department of State's report), a few days later *People's Daily* published a stinging attack on the U.S. Department of State's report on human rights in China. It said it constituted an "unprovoked attack on a different society." The paper also described the report as reflecting "hegemonism and strong-arm tactics" that have not disappeared from inter-national life and said that it constituted "foreign interference." It also said Westerners were equating rights with property and "shooting themselves in the foot," because the report would "accomplish the exact opposite of what they hope."[54]

The Foreign Ministry joined the hard-liners, when on February 17, it issued a statement saying that foreign Christians had been detained because they had conducted illegal religious activities and violated a ban on foreign missionary activities.[55] Later in the month, the ministry called both the Amnesty Inter-national and Asia Watch reports full of bias toward China. It said that ordinary life in China has never been better after fifteen years of market reforms and continued efforts to build a modern, democratic legal system. It accused both groups of "harboring prejudices toward China" and of "not understanding the human rights situation in China."[56]

Two months later, Chinese officials criticized the Japanese government for allowing the Dalai Lama, who made a ten-hour stopover in Japan, to visit there and carry out "illicit political activities." Days later, Chinese officials blasted the U.S. president and vice president for meeting with the Dalai Lama, accusing them of "serious interference" in China's internal affairs and charging the United States with "not living up to its commitment concerning recognizing Tibet as Chinese territory" and "hurting the feelings of the Chinese people."[57]

The Chinese government accused the Dalai Lama in May of blocking reconciliation talks by refusing to abandon his plans for Tibet's independence. In response to the Dalai Lama's suggestion of holding a referendum, Beijing said this "so-called referendum" was "yet another trick for his splittist activities." A spokesman for the Foreign Ministry said, "the question of holding a referendum on the future of Tibet does not exist."[58] China seemed to be on a tough policy binge.

During U.S. Secretary of Commerce Ron Brown's visit to China in August, *China Daily* carried an article written by Yu Quanyu, vice president of the China Society for Human Rights Studies, saying that "an all around comparison will show that China is in many fields ahead of the United States in human rights protection." Yu declared that using indicators ranging from the number of children living in one-parent homes, to murder and rape rates, the number of homeless people, the number of prisoners, the number of repeat offenders, and measures of sexual equality, China has done a great deal and has "done better than the United States." (See Appendix 10.)

However, at this same time Commerce Secretary Brown reported that China had agreed to resume talks with the United States on human rights policies. More specifically, China agreed that Foreign Minister Qian would meet with Assistant Secretary of State for Human Rights John Shattuck when he visited the United States in September. Some interpreted this as a concession aimed at getting support for China's bid to join GATT.[59]

Politburo member Li Tieying visited Tibet soon after this, apparently to draw attention to infrastructure projects started after the Tibet conference. The Chinese media reported that forty of the sixty-two planned projects were underway and that Li had decided while on his visit to install fire and burglary prevention equipment in Lhasa's three major monasteries at a cost of U.S. $750,000. Observers, however, described Li as using the "carrot and stick approach," in view of Beijing's simultaneous tough policies toward Tibet.[60] Beijing, however, also provided a list of Tibetans who were imprisoned in response to an inquiry made earlier by U.S. Secretary of State Warren Christopher.[61]

Regional officials in China said in September that "cliques" loyal to the Dalai Lama had infiltrated the Tibetan countryside and had used religion to stir up separatist feelings. Laba Pincou, vice chairman of the Tibet Autonomous Regional People's Government, said, "They do not wish to see the development of Tibet, stability in Tibet, and everything they do is damaging to the basic interests of the Tibetan people."[62] Zhou Dunyou, a member of the Tibetan Regional Nationalities Affairs Commission, declared that Tibetans had full freedom of religion and that since 1984 the Tibetan Buddhist Institute had trained 3,000 monks and nuns.[63] Several days later, Xinhua News Agency reported that four well-known Tibetans had been released from jail for medical treatment. Robin Munro of Human Rights Watch–Asia said that the releases were intended to "fend off the Americans" at the Asia-Pacific Economic Conference in Djarkata where President Clinton was to meet President Jiang Zemin.[64]

In November, the Foreign Ministry invited Abdelfattah Amor, the first U.N. investigator on religious intolerance to visit China. Amor made few comments after the visit and issued no report. Some observers said it set a positive precedent; others thought it was a handled visit and a whitewash.[65]

## China Pushes Its Human Rights View

As has been more and more noticeable in recent years, during 1994 China made many and often loud proclamations of its own position on human rights. It also promoted an Asian and Third World view of human rights, which it often equated with its own. This appeared to be a way of parrying or challenging the West,or at least dealing in a different and more innovative way with Western criticism of China's human rights record.

In January, China's most popular news magazine published an article entitled "Establishing a New International Order on the Five Principles of Peaceful Coexistence" written in December 1988 by Deng Xiaoping. Focusing on a conversation with Indian Prime Minister Rajiv Gandhi, the piece discussed apprehension about the division of the world into North and South camps. Deng observed that all countries are adopting new policies relating to the establishment of a new international order, noting that "hegemonism, bloc politics and pact organizations will no longer work." He suggested a new world order based on the Five Principles of Peaceful Coexistence that formed the basis of Sino-Indian relations in the 1950s, which, he asserted, have stood the test of time.[66] (The Five Principles, it is worth noting, emphasize respect for other countries' sovereignty, domestic affairs, and the like.) In short, Deng sought to emphasize China's right of sovereignty and to reemphasize the argument that human rights problems belong in the realm of domestic politics and do not invite foreign involvement.

Days later the *Beijing Review* carried another article promoting China's views and definition of human rights. Quoting Zhu Muzhi, president of the China Society for the Study of Human Rights, the author noted that different countries follow different human rights practices just as they have different histories, social systems, economies, cultures, and religions. Sovereign rights must be respected in deciding how to safeguard human rights; otherwise, "there would be worldwide turmoil." He went on to say that some conventions on human rights passed by the United Nations "could not be forced upon all countries." He suggested that the right of subsistence is the most basic human right and that China, as a socialist democracy, stresses this right.[67] Perhaps not by coincidence, next to this article was a report of China's economic growth in 1993, which was 13 percent together with a prediction of 10 percent growth in 1994. (For a summary of this interview, see Appendix 11.)

In an interview in this same magazine a few weeks later," human rights specialist" Fan Guoxiang, commenting on the human rights issue, stated that it was used during the Cold War as a tool in the East-West confrontation. He went on to assert that the human rights issue is now taken up by some as an "instrument of power politics" to "force other nations to accept their human rights formula as a so-called common standard." He compared this to religious groups in the past proselytizing and efforts by some of those groups to promote claims that "some nationalities were superior to others." Following through with this argument, he stated, "In history, the religious fanatics and those who advocated ethnic superiority were proved wrong." Making an argument that this proves there cannot and should not be an international standard of human rights, because the world is "multicolored," he concluded that any attempt to impose a single standard on the world would "lead nowhere."[68]

Regarding the issue of whether there can be a universal standard, which seems to put China at odds with the U.N. view, Fan commented that human rights is a matter that is "universally significant," but this "cannot be twisted to claim there is only one standard." He went on to say, "The concept of universal values for human rights is quite different from that of a common standard of human rights." He suggested that countries should "exchange views...rather than resorting to attacks and charges against each other. He concluded saying: "The only reasonable and feasible way to promote human rights is, as stipulated by the UN Charter, through international cooperation."[69]

In another article meant for international consumption, China argued against the Western view that its population control policy violates human rights and personal freedom. China's position, it said, is that the right of development is the most basic right and "traditional concepts such as the idea that a son is essential to carry on the family line still exists, so education is required." The author stated that China opposes coercion, but this does not mean it must take a laissez-faire approach. He went on to say that China's family planning combines the principle of state guidance with the will of the people and pointed out that the World Population Planning Act also advocates that couples select the number of children and space births "with a responsible attitude." In addition, he cited the Law on the Protection of the Rights and Interests of Women, which stipulates that women's rights in the areas of reproduction are protected by law, contradicting in many instances the desire to carry on the family line—thus justifying state involvement.[70]

An October article in the government-run *Beijing Review* entitled "China Leads the U.S. in Human Rights" compared aspects of China's human rights situation with that of the United States and concluded that China was better off. The author of the article pointed out that in 1990, 9.37 of every 100,000 people in the United States were murdered, while in China the number was less than 2 per 100,000. Three hundred people were injured in attempted murders in the United States; in China the figure was 7. Rapes: 70 per 100,000 in the United States annually; 4 in China. The number of homeless people in the United States (according to the U.S. government) was 7 million; in China it was 150,000. In the United States 455 per 100,000 are in jail—a world's record;

in China it is 99. And the death rate of prisoners in the United States, it said, was higher. The number of repeat offenders is 41 percent in the United States; in China it is 8 percent. The author also stated that the U.S. government has admitted that the status of American women is not as good as that of women in China, adding that in China women have made up 20 percent of the deputies in the people's congresses, whereas in the U.S. Congress the highest it has been is 18.4 percent. He also noted that the United States has not yet subscribed to the International Treaty Eradicating All Forms of Racial Discrimination, the International Treaty of Prohibiting and Punishing Racial Segregation, and the Treaty Eradicating All Forms of Discrimination Against Women, yet China has signed on and complies with all. He concluded that China is more advanced in the realm of human rights than the United States.[71] (See Appendix 10.)

In December, one of the Beijing correspondents of the *New York Times* interviewed Zhu Muzhi, head of the China Human Rights Society, an interview published in the *Beijing Review* for external consumption. In the interview, Zhu, drawing on his own experience, spoke of the improvements in human rights in China, mentioning the bad situation during the period of Japanese occupation. He also noted that in the most basic right, of subsistence, China has made big strides—feeding 22 percent of the world's population on 7 percent of the land. He went on to explain why China appears to have a bad human rights record. This reputation comes, he said, from attacks by Western countries and is based on a lack of knowledge about China. He averred that few countries criticize China in inter-national meetings and almost all of the criticism of China comes from a few Western countries. Following up on this point, Zhu said that human rights "by and large fall under the sovereignty of an individual country" and, "owing to differences in historical background, cultural tradition, social customs and habits, religious beliefs and economic development, situations in different countries vary greatly." Finally, he said, China has experienced expanded freedoms in the areas of speech because of the economic boom—suggesting further improvements may accompany further economic growth and that using economic leverage against China to engender better human rights will be counterproductive.

## Endnotes

1. Reuters North American Wire, August 29, 1994.

2. *Washington Post*, August 31, 1994, p. 3.

3. Cited in Philip Shenon, "Want to Sell China's Record on Human Rights? Get Mr. Smooth," *New York Times*, August 28, 1994, Section 4, p. 7.

4. "Human Rights Conditions Criticized in Annual Reports; Foreign Religious Activities Curtailed," *Asian Bulletin*, April 1994, p. 19.

5. Ibid., p. 20.

6. Ibid.

7. Ibid.

8. Ibid.

9. Robert Pear, "Victims of China's Birth-Control Policy Are Entitled to Asylum, a U.S. Judge Says," *New York Times*, January 21, 1994, p. A4.

10. "Leaders Reject U.S. Views on Human Rights; Dissidents Detained," *Asian Bulletin*, May 1994, p. 24.

11. "Leading Dissidents Detailed; Premier Embarks on Central Asian Tour," *Asian Bulletin*, June 1994, p. 25.

12. "More Tibetan Demonstrators Arrested; Dalai Lama Meets U.S. President," *Asian Bulletin*, June 1994, p. 27.

13. Ibid., p. 29, citing the Times *of India* (no date or page given).

14. *Ibid., p. 30.*

15. *"Li Peng Ducks German Protestors During State Visit: Human Rights Policy Again Under Attack," Asian Bulletin,* September 1994, pp. 25–26.

16.  See Amnesty International's 1994 report cited in Ibid., p. 26.

17.    "Tibetan Culture Further Threatened by Peking," *Asian Bulletin*, September 1994, p. 27.

18.    "Premier Sounds Warning over Economy; Human Rights Concerns Remain as U.S. Official Pays Visit," *Asian Bulletin*, October 1994, p. 16.

19.    "Peking Initiates New Policy in Tibet; More Arrests Reported," *Asian Bulletin*, October 1994, pp. 19–20.

20.    "Advances in Foreign Relations Claimed; Jiang Allies Win Key Posts," *Asian Bulletin*, November 1994, pp. 18–19.

21.  Ibid., p. 20.

22.    "Peking Presses for GATT Membership; U.S. Sanctions to Remain," *Asian Bulletin*, January 1995, p. 22.

23.  "Australians Protest Qiao Visit; U.N. Official Tours Tibet," *Asian Bulletin*, January 1995, p. 25.

24.    "Tibetan Unrest Admitted; U.N. Group Criticizes Detentions," *Asian Bulletin*, February 1995, p. 30.

25.    Thomas L. Friedman, "Bentsen Says China Isn't Doing Enough on Rights," *New York Times*, January 20, 1993, p. A6.

26.  Thomas L. Friedman, "Senator Asks End to Threats Against China," *New York Times*, January 27, 1994, p. A11.

27.  "U.S. Urged to Shift China Policy on Trade," *New York Times*, January 30, 1994, p. A3.

28.    "Leaders Reject U.S. Views on Human Rights; Dissidents Detained," p. 25.

29.  Patrick E. Tyler, "Beijing Says It Could Live Well Even if U.S. Trade Was Cut Off," *New York Times*, March 21, 1994, p. A1.

30.  Ibid.

31. Douglas Jehl, "Clinton Stresses China Rights Goal," *New York Times*, March 25, 1994, p. A12.

32. Elaine Sciolino, "Christopher Is Drawing Fire in Washington on China Visit," *New York Times*, March 18, 1994, p. A1.

33. Catherine S. Manegold, "A.F.L.-C.I.O. Leader Urges End to China's Current Trade Status," *New York Times*, April 14, 1994, p. A6.

34. "Dissidents Released in Run-up to Clinton's Decision on MFN Status," *Asian Bulletin*, July 1994, p. 23.

35. Douglas Jehl, "Clinton Makes No Progress with Beijing," *New York Times*, May 3, 1994, p. A8.

36. "Dissidents Released in Run-up to Clinton's Decision on MFN Status," p. 23.

37. Ibid., p. 24.

38. Ibid., p. 25.

39. Ibid., p. 27.

40. Elaine Sciolino, "White House Gets Progress Report on Rights in China, " *New York Times*, May 24, 1994, p. A1.

41. "Dissidents Released in Run-up to Clinton's Decision on MFN Status," p. 28.

42. "Li Peng Ducks German Protestors During State Visit; Human Rights Policy Again Under Attack," p. 27.

43. "Premier Sounds Warning over Economy; Human Rights Concerns Remain as U.S. Official Pays Visit," p. 17.

44. Ibid.

45. "Advances in Foreign Relations Claimed; Jiang Allies Win Key Posts," *Asian Bulletin*, November 1994, p. 21.

46. "Commitment to Deng's Policies Reaffirmed; Ties with Washington on Mend," *Asian Bulletin*, December 1994, p. 22.

47. Ibid.

48. Ibid., p. 23.

49. "Peking Presses for GATT Membership; U.S. Sanctions to Remain," p. 21.

50. Patrick E. Tyler, "China Promises U.S. to Try to Improve Its Human Rights," *New York Times*, January 16, 1994, p. A1.

51. Thomas L. Friedman, "U.S. Inspections of Jail Exports Likely in China," *New York Times*, January 21, 1995, p. A1.

52. "Human Rights Conditions Criticized in Annual Reports; Foreign Religious Activities Curtailed," *Asian Bulletin*, April 1994, p. 19.

53. Thomas L. Friedman, "With a Close Embrace, U.S. Seeks to Budge China," *New York Times*, January 23, 1994, p. 10.

54. "Human Rights Conditions Criticized in Annual Reports: Foreign Religious Activities Curtailed," p. 19.

55. Ibid., p. 20.

56. Ibid., p. 21.

57. "More Tibetan Demonstrators Arrested; Dalai Lama Meets U.S. President," *Asian Bulletin*, June 1994, p. 28.

58. "Tibetan Refugees in India State Protest over Chinese Rule," *Asian Bulletin*, July 1994, p. 29.

59. Ibid.

60. "Peking Initiates New Policy in Tibet; More Arrests Reported," *Asian Bulletin*, October 1994, p. 20.

61. "List of Tibetan Prisoners Released; Dalai Lama Concedes Dissent Among Supporters," *Asian Bulletin*, November 1994, p. 21.

62. Ibid., p. 25.

63. Ibid.

64. "Peking Presses for GATT Membership; U.S. Sanctions to Remain," *Asian Bulletin*, January 1995, p. 21.

65. "Australians Protest Qiao Visit; U.N. Official Tours Tibet,", p. 25.

66. Deng Xiaoping, "Establishing a New International Order on the Five Principles of Peaceful Coexistence," *Beijing Review*, January 17–23, 1994, p. 9.

67. "Standpoint on Human Rights Aired," *Beijing Review*, January 10–16, 1994, pp. 6–7.

68. "International Cooperation on Human Rights: A Reasonable and Practical Choice," *Beijing Review*, March 14–20, 1994, p. 9.

69. Ibid., p. 10.

70. *Beijing Review*, August 1–8, 1994, p. 12.

71. Yu Quanyu, "China Leads the U.S. in Human Rights," *Beijing Review*, October 3–9, 1994, p. 24.

# Chapter 8

## Conclusions, Trends and Forecasts

An academic analysis of two years of China's record of human rights abuses, problems and policies does not, of course, tell a complete story. However, what happened in the realm of human rights in the People's Republic of China during 1993 and 1994 that is reported here is instructive and certain generalizations can be made. So too, changes in China's human rights policies and its treatment of its citizens that are assessed in the above chapters are worthy of some final comments in the order of trends and forecasts.

One thing that conditions and possibly distorts any look at human rights in China, including this study, is the fact that expectations for progress in human rights were higher. By 1993, China had experienced fifteen years of rapid, some say miracle, economic growth. In other countries, as is widely known, economic growth has usually had a positive impact on human rights. In Taiwan and South Korea, after a decade an a half of rapid economic development, there was a marked improvement in human rights. China, some say, should have followed suit. Why was this not the case?

China has also been under much more scrutiny about its human rights situation than before 1989. And there has been considerable outside pressure, especially from the West, to improve. Outside concern and pressure have evoked positive change in other countries. Again, why not China?

One reason the human rights condition did not improve, of course, is that the People's Republic of China has had to make a difficult transition from totalitarianism to authoritarianism and in so doing to a less oppressive system that intrudes into people's lives less often. This was required by progressive changes in the economy. China's leaders thus perforce had to consider political change in the direction of democracy prematurely or before the proper foundation had been laid and maybe did not want to in any case. Taiwan and South Korea moved from authoritarianism to democracy; that was easier.

Since Mao's death, after which China's political system underwent very deep and marked change and totalitarianism was discarded, some of the traits of totalitarianism have reappeared periodically. It is obvious 1993 and 1994 were years when this was true. The importance given to ideology was one barometer of this trend. In the best case it was distracting. In fact, it seemed much more than that—with Deng's works assuming some of the role Mao's writings once did. Reading Deng's books took the place of reading other things. Understanding what Deng said and wrote overshadowed learning, or caring about, human rights. In the worst case, ideological correctness crowded out concerns for making human rights a more important political concern much less an institutionalized part of the polity.

Even more important was the fact that political succession was on the minds of top leaders during this period. Specifically, they were preoccupied with Deng's health. Speculation was rampant about when he was going to die and what this might do to China politically. Succession had not been smooth the last time. Who was going to succeed Deng was a very serious matter. Jiang Zemin seemed to be chosen to be Deng's heir; but would that stick? Deng's earlier chosen heirs were no longer around. They had fallen from power. Would Deng change his mind about Jiang? Many wondered. Would other leaders organize or conspire against Jiang? Would there be a collective leadership? Human rights could not make progress in this milieu.

The struggle between left and right "factions" in the top echelons of the Chinese Communist Party and the government had a similar effect. In the past, power struggles were devastating to the cause of human rights. The reason is not difficult to understand: When top leaders' overriding concern is their personal survival and that of their faction, which in the case of China is generally synonymous, human rights get short shrift. That was generally the situation during 1993 and 1994. And, whereas the Right seemed dominant during the period and this seemed auspicious for at least broadening civil and political rights and a more decentralized political system and perhaps a less oppressive government not to mention the continuation of the process abandoning totalitarianism, in some other ways the dominance of Deng and the rightist reformers was not all good. They, it seemed clear, enjoyed and wanted to keep unchallenged power. In addition, the rightist reformers were apprehensive, even afraid, of the revival of the left. This certainly made them reluctant to tolerate opposition.

Thus, while there was considerable progress in human rights in the realms of the rights of association, travel and movement, and while the vast majority of the Chinese population saw progress in terms of their right to express their feelings and opinions by reading what they wanted, picking different forms of entertainment and spending their money on things they wanted, and most important of all many more were out of poverty, this was offset to some degree by increases in corruption (which was already an extremely serious problem). Corruption in the party, government and the military and in business as well, in fact, corruption permeating society, caused rules to take a back seat. Without rules of conduct and behavior there could be little progress in human rights.

The unevenness of economic gains was another factor contributing to human rights not making much progress. Some people had made very impressive gains in their standards of living, while others had made little or no gains. This continued to be the case during 1993 and 1994. The widening disparity between rich and poor meant that a concept of equality before the law and in the government and elsewhere did not evolve. Likewise there was a callous disregard in many ways by officials in the government and the Chinese Communist Party for the vast majority of Chinese who live in rural China. Too much attention and concern was given to the industrial and export sectors of the economy, which are centered in the cities. The cities are also the loci of opportunity, money making, deal making, progress in science and technology and education and advances in social services and in many other realms; rural China was left out. The peasants protested, but of little avail.

Similarly, changes in the political and legal systems, which might forecast future improvements in civil and political rights, did not indeed suggest this. Or it was minimal. Political instability overshadowed improvements in the polity. There were, of course, advances in the legal system in certain realms which made doing business easier and faster. Whether and when there might be a spinoff effect was difficult to say. Efforts made to make the legal system generally more efficient were mainly to facilitate better law enforcement and these changes were made almost exclusively in reaction to the problem of increasing crime. The additional attention given to the legal process, even if the top leadership did not intend to extend rights or make the system fairer, may be auspicious; but that is clearly too soon to say.

Meanwhile, some new (actually much expanded) kinds of human rights problems appeared. The practice of selling human organs from those executed for a crime was astonishing in terms of both its newness and the rapid increases in this practice. It also constituted a quandary for many people outside of China inasmuch as organ transplants saved many lives and those who needed organs, especially foreigners who went to China to buy one, did not seem to care where they came from. Thus, if China was doing something wrong, there were many co-conspirators. Meanwhile, some Western observers opined that this was a good way for those who have committed a crime against society to pay their debt which few do in the West now. Others said this simply reflected Chinese capitalism. Yet it had its appalling side.

Likewise, China's continued use of abortions to control population growth. Late term abortions remained a widespread practice. Many human rights groups in the West were reluctant to say as much about this as other human rights abuses. Them seemed convinced that China had a population problem that was so acute that this was justified. This was true even though party members and minorities were still often exempt and huge numbers of women were victimized. Western leaders likewise did not have a good reply when Chinese officials told them the practice could be stopped if a sizeable number of Chinese were welcomed as immigrants.

The treatment of women in other respects, as well as the status of minorities, religious advocates, intellectuals and some other groups remained serious concerns. So did Tibet. Because human rights abuses in these realms remained fairly constant during the period under review and there were few headline-creating events or drastic increases in the numbers of victims or problems that came to the attention of the Western media, they were not noticed as much as other issues.

Dissidents did not fare well during the 1993-94 period even though they attracted considerable attention from the Western media. In fact, their treatment was very much a mixed bag. Well-known dissidents did better. The vast majority did not. The government to a large extent regressed to its totalitarian mode of coping with the problem of dissidents: make them non-persons. Yet it was clear this was less possible, with China now open to the world in terms of doing business and much more. And, since the Tiananmen Massacre in 1989, dissidents have become a focus of human rights concern and something people elsewhere seemed to care about. To fend off criticism, the government sent the message that China was prospering and this was good the nation and for most Chinese. But it also declared that opposition to the government would disrupt the economic development process and would cause instability and was therefore not welcome. Hence, officials advised that opponents of the government would not be treated kindly. At other times government officials intimated that when China made further advances economically, political and civil rights, and human rights in general, would make progress. (They even mentioned the recent history of Taiwan and South Korea in this respect.) But, when or even whether, this was going to happen, was a matter of guessing.

Another message the government conveyed was that China is too big, too little subject to pressure from the West, too independent, and too much determined to do things its own way to be pressured to do as Taiwan has done. In other words, China would change the world; the world would not change China. And in many respects this seemed to be the case. Chinese leaders, in fact, sought to change the meaning of human rights and were in some measure successful. To some degree the West was isolated or at least put on the defensive by China when Beijing advanced a new concept of human rights and won many supporters in Asia and the Third World. Will Chinese leaders continue to succeed in this realm? It may be that other Asian countries and Third World countries strongly agree with Beijing's concept of sovereignty and the Westphalian system, and therefore will continue oppose the West imposing its human rights standards on others. On the other hand, it may be only that these countries want to express for a while and to a limited extent their ill-feeling with having been told what to do and how to behave by the West in the past and that their opposition to Western standards and support of China's views will soon pass.

Clearly the West was on the horns of a dilemma in dealing with China, not only in this way but also as to how to treat China in terms of using, or not using, economic pressure to get China to change. Many in the West favored it. It seemed to work often enough not to dismiss it as ineffectual. On the other hand, China appeared (and in some respects this was irrefutable) to be making progress due to economic development. So, why do anything to slow China's successful economic expansion, especially when it was doing it using free market capitalism—which has been the avenue for others to improve the human rights condition? Others, however felt that this was a short sighted view and that gains in one area were setbacks in another. Some also, it seemed, sought to use the human rights lever to impede China's development, seeing it as threatening.

The Clinton administration, by de-linking human rights from most-favored-nation trading status appeared to solve one problem or at least a controversy. It won kudos from the business community. But, it did not look good in terms of earlier statements about concern for human rights abuses in China and the evidence that many benefitted from trade privileges and human rights being connected.

The two years studied here may turn out to be in the minds of future historians a turning point in terms of China once again being given an edge in terms of criticism of its human rights abuses and/or in terms of China being able to change global public opinion about what human rights means. Chinese leaders clearly demonstrated that China is not simply another nation in terms of human rights or simply a bigger problem because there are more people whose rights can be violated in China than any other nation.

# Appendix 1

# Bangkok Declaration

The Ministers and representatives of Asian States, meeting at Bangkok from 29 March to 2 April 1993, pursuant to general Assembly resolution 46/116 of 17 December 1991 in the context of preparations for the World Conference on Human Rights,

Adopt this Declaration, to be known as "The Bangkok Declaration", which contains the aspirations and commitments of the Asian region:

Emphasizing the significance of the World Conference on Human Rights, which provides an invaluable opportunity to review all aspects of human rights and ensure a just and balanced approach thereto,

Recognizing the contribution that can be made to the World Conference by Asian countries with their diverse and rich cultures and traditions,

Welcoming the increased attention being paid to human rights in the international community,

Reaffirming their commitment to principles contained in the Charter of the United Nations and the Universal Declaration of Human Rights,

Recalling that in the Charter of the United Nations the question of universal observance and promotion of human rights and fundamental freedoms has been rightly placed within the context of international cooperation,

Noting the progress made in the codification of human rights instruments, and in the establishment of international human rights mechanisms, while expressing concern that these mechanisms relate mainly to one category of rights,

Emphasizing that ratification of international human rights instruments, particularly the International Covenant on Civil and Political Rights and the International Covenant on Economic, Social and Cultural Rights, by all States should be further encouraged,

Reaffirming the principles of respect for national sovereignty, territorial integrity and noninterference in the internal affairs of States,

Stressing the universality, objectivity and non-selectivity of all human rights and the need to avoid the application of double standards in the implementation of human rights and its politicization,

Recognizing that the promotion of human rights should be encouraged by cooperation and consensus, and not through confrontation and the imposition of incompatible values,

Reiterating the interdependence and indivisibility of economic, social, cultural, civil and political rights, and the inherent interrelationship between development, democracy, universal enjoyment of all human rights, and social justice, which must be addressed in an integrated and balanced manner,

Recalling that the Declaration on the Right to Development has recognized the right to development as a universal and inalienable right and an integral part of fundamental human rights,

Emphasizing that endeavors to move towards the creation of uniform international human rights norms must go hand in hand with endeavors to work towards a just and fair world economic order,

Convinced that economic and social progress facilitates the growing trend towards democracy and the promotion and protection of human rights,

Stressing the importance of education and training in human rights at the national, regional and international levels and the need for international cooperation aimed at overcoming the lack of public awareness of human rights,

1.  Reaffirm their commitment to the principles contained in the Charter of the United Nations and the Universal Declaration of Human Rights as well as the full realization of all human rights throughout the world;

2.  Underline the essential need to create favorable conditions for effective enjoyment of human rights at both the national and international levels;

3.  Stress the urgent need to democratize the United Nations system, eliminate selectivity and improve procedures and mechanisms in order to strengthen international cooperation, based on principles of equality and mutual respect, and ensure a positive, balanced and non-confrontational approach in addressing and realizing all aspects of human rights;

4. Discourage any attempt to use human rights as a conditionality for extending development assistance;

5.  Emphasize the principles of respect for national sovereignty and territorial integrity as well as non-interference in the internal affairs of States, and the non-use of human rights as an instrument of political pressure;

6.  Reiterate that all countries, large and small, have the right to determine their political systems, control and freely utilize their resources, and freely pursue their economic, social and cultural development;

7.  Stress the universality, objectivity and non-selectivity of all human rights and the need to avoid the application of double standards in the implemen-

tation of human rights and its politicization, and that no violation of human rights can be justified;

8. Recognize that while human rights are universal in nature, they must be considered in the context of a dynamic and evolving process of international normsetting, bearing in mind the significance of national and regional particularities and various historical, cultural and religious backgrounds;

9. Recognize further that States have the primary responsibility for the promotion and protection of human rights through appropriate infrastructure and mechanisms, and also recognize that remedies must be sought and provided primarily through such mechanisms and procedures;

10. Reaffirm the interdependence and indivisibility of economic, social, cultural, civil and political rights, and the need to give equal emphasis to all categories of human rights;

11. Emphasize the importance of guaranteeing the human rights and fundamental freedoms of vulnerable groups such as ethnic, national, racial, religious and linguistic minorities, migrant workers, disabled persons, indigenous peoples, refugees and displaced persons;

12. Reiterate that self-determination is a principle of international law and a universal right recognized by the United Nations for peoples under alien or colonial domination and foreign occupation, by virtue of which they can freely determine their political status and freely pursue their economic, social and cultural development, and that its denial constitutes a grave violation of human rights;

13. Stress that the right to self-determination is applicable to peoples under alien or colonial domination and foreign occupation, and should not be used to undermine the territorial integrity, national sovereignty and political independence of States;

14. Express concern over all forms of violation of human rights, including manifestations of racial discrimination, racism, apartheid, colonialism, foreign aggression and occupation, and the establishment of illegal settlements in occupied territories, as well as the recent resurgence of neo-nazism, xenophobia and ethnic cleansing;

15. Underline the need for taking effective international measures in order to guarantee and monitor the implementation of human rights standards and effective and legal protection of people under foreign occupation;

16. Strongly affirm their support for the legitimate struggle of the Palestinian people to restore their national and inalienable rights to self-determination and independence, and demand an immediate end to the grave violations of human rights in the Palestinian, Syrian Golan and other occupied Arab territories including Jerusalem;

17. Reaffirm the right to development, as established in the Declaration on the Right to Development, as a universal and inalienable right

and an integral part of fundamental human rights, which must be realized through international cooperation, respect for fundamental human rights, the establishment of a monitoring mechanism and the creation of essential international conditions for the realization of such right;

18. Recognize that the main obstacles to the realization of the right to development lie at the international macroeconomic level, as reflected in the widening gap between the North and the South, the rich and the poor;

19. Affirm that poverty is one of the major obstacles hindering the full enjoyment of human rights;

20. Affirm also the need to develop the right of humankind regarding a clean, safe and healthy environment;

21. Note that terrorism, in all its forms and manifestations, as distinguished from the legitimate struggle of peoples under colonial or alien domination and foreign occupation, has emerged as one of the most dangerous threats to the enjoyment of human rights and democracy, threatening the territorial integrity and security of States and de-stabilizing legitimately constituted governments, and that it must be unequivocally condemned by the international community;

22. Reaffirm their strong commitment to the promotion and protection of the rights of women through the guarantee of equal participation in the political, social, economic and cultural concerns of society, and the eradication of all forms of discrimination and of gender-based violence against women;

23. Recognize the rights of the child to enjoy special protection and to be afforded the opportunities and facilities to develop physically, mentally, morally, spiritually and socially in a healthy and normal manner and in conditions of freedom and dignity;

24. Welcome the important role played by national institutions in the genuine and constructive promotion of human rights, and believe that the conceptualization and eventual establishment of such institutions are best left for the States to decide;

25. Acknowledge the importance of cooperation and dialogue between governments and non-governmental organizations on the basis of shared values as well as mutual respect and understanding in the promotion of human rights, and encourage the non-governmental organizations in consultative status with the Economic and Social Council to contribute positively to this process in accordance with Council resolution 1296 (XLIV);

26. Reiterate the need to explore the possibilities of establishing regional arrangements for the promotion and protection of human rights in Asia;

27. Reiterate further the need to explore ways to generate international cooperation and financial support for education and training in the field of human rights at the national level and for the establishment of national infrastructures to promote and protect human rights if requested by States;

28. Emphasize the necessity to rationalize the United Nations human rights mechanism in order to enhance its effectiveness and efficiency and the need to ensure avoidance of the duplication of work that exists between the treaty bodies, the Sub-Commission on Prevention of Discrimination and Protection of Minorities and the Commission on Human Rights, as well as the need to avoid the multiplicity of parallel mechanisms;

29. Stress the importance of strengthening the United Nations Centre for Human Rights with the necessary resources to enable it to provide a wide range of advisory services and technical assistance programmes in the promotion of human rights to requesting States in a timely and effective manner, as well as to enable it to finance adequately other activities in the field of human rights authorized by competent bodies;

30. Call for increased representation of the developing countries in the Centre for Human Rights.

**Source:** *Beijing Review*, May 31-June 6, 1993

# Appendix 2

# Right To Subsistence Should Be Given Priority

*Renmin Ribao*, China's leading newspaper, published an article entitled "The Development of the Concept of the Right to Subsistence Is a Great Contribution to the Theory of Human Rights" on May 31. The main points of this article are excerpted as follows.

by Lui Fenzhi

For years China has stressed at many international conferences and meetings on human rights that the right to subsistence and the right to development are the most fundamental of human rights, especially for developing countries. The white paper Human Rights in China issued by the Information Office of the State Council in November 1991 pointed out that the right to subsistence is the most important of all human rights. This stand by China has aroused wide attention at home and abroad and many developing countries have expressed agreement.

The right to subsistence includes the following four aspects:

First, the right to subsistence is the most important of human rights. *Human Rights in China* pointed out that "for any country or nation, the right to subsistence is the most important of all human rights, without which other rights are out of the question." No matter how many rights people enjoy, people must first subsist and live.

In the developing countries, where three quarters of the world's population live, the majority of whom still face the problem of subsistence, it is imperative to ensure their rights to subsistence. And the problem of subsistence also exists for many people in developed countries.

Second, state sovereignty is the basis for the right to subsistence. The white paper stressed that "without national independence, there would be no guarantee for people's lives." Therefore, the people must win national independence before they can gain the right to subsistence.

State sovereignty means that the state has the supreme right to independently handle domestic and international affairs, without any foreign interference. State sovereignty is the basis for and the guarantee of the human rights of individuals.

Chinese representatives again and again stressed at the 49th session of the United Nations Commission for Human Rights and the regional meeting in Asia for the World Conference on Human Rights that the World Conference on Human Rights held this month should reaffirm the principles of the United Nations Charter and international law concerning the respect for state sovereignty. Only when the state sovereignty is fully respected can human rights be guaranteed.

Third, the right to subsistence includes the guarantee of life. The white paper pointed out that "national independence has protected the Chinese people from being trodden under the heels of foreign invaders. However, the problem of the people's right to subsistence can be truly solved only when their basic means of livelihood is guaranteed." That is to say, our concept of human rights not only refers to the right to security including the right to life, health and other personal rights, but also to guaranteeing basic living conditions. The state has an obligation to improve the people's living standards through development of economic, social and cultural spheres.

To guarantee and improve basic living conditions, China and other developing countries have attached great importance to the right to development. They have listed both the right to subsistence and the right to development as human rights priorities. The World Conference on Human Rights should reaffirm the right to development as an inalienable right, work out effective measures insuring this right and consider setting up an institution to supervise implementation of this right.

Fourth, the right to subsistence is the right of individuals as well as collectives. The white paper *Human Rights in China* clearly pointed out that "the Chinese government pays great attention to safeguarding and realizing the right to state, national and individual development in economics, culture, society and politics."

To ensure the right to collective subsistence of a nation, China and other developing countries consider the rights of independence, national self-determination, subsistence and development to be collective human rights and the right to subsistence in a broad sense.

The development and perfection of the concept of the right to subsistence is a great contribution to the theory of human rights, because it deals with the fundamental question of the right to human subsistence. This is the highest standard of human rights.

The right to subsistence is an ancient concept. This idea was conceived by the newly born bourgeoisie in the struggle against feudal autocratic system and became a powerful ideological weapon against feudalism. A review of history proves that the right to life and subsistence was an important component of the bourgeois idea of human rights.

On the one hand, the right to subsistence is generally acknowledged by most of the world, yet on the other it is belittled and rejected by the Western world. This is a contradictory phenomenon in the current status of international human rights.

Some in the West first held high the banner of the right to subsistence when they considered it useful, and then abandoned and trampled on it when they found it of little use to them.

As a class, the bourgeoisie has not only possessed the means of production, but it has also enjoyed a rich livelihood. It has controlled state power, so the right to subsistence has lost its urgent significance. Furthermore, the capitalist system cannot fully guarantee the right to subsistence for the broad masses of the laboring people. The capitalist world is the paradise of the rich and cannot be the paradise of the poor. The capitalist system is not able to solve social problems such as polarization between the rich and poor, the high rates of unemployment and crime and racial discrimination. As a consequence, it cannot possibly guarantee the right to subsistence for the majority of people.

Western human rights theory has one-sidely stressed the political rights of individuals and citizens while belittling their economic, cultural and social rights; it one-sidely stresses the human rights of individuals while belittling or even rejecting the human rights of collectives.

In terms of the rights of individuals, Western theory pays attention only to a number of so-called "political dissidents" while ignoring the right to subsistence by the majority of people.

Such politicalization of human rights is aimed at promoting the "democratic politics" of the Western world so as to gradually change political and social system which are not the same as their own.

The right to subsistence is the lifeline of the broad masses of people in the developing countries of Asia, Africa and Latin America. In their long struggle for the right to subsistence these countries have raised the banner of the right to subsistence.

After World War II, national-liberation movements in Asia, Africa and Latin America vigorously developed and finally overthrew colonial rule. Such movements address themselves to the right to subsistence.

The national-liberation movement of the developing countries and their struggles for the right to independence, subsistence and development have injected fresh meaning into the theory and practice of human rights.

At present, the international situation is becoming more turbulent, and conditions in the developing countries are becoming grave. Certain international forces are pursuing "human rights diplomacy" as part of hegemonism and power politics. The unreasonable, old international economic order has not changed; the gap between the North and the South continues to widen. People's lives in many countries have not been guaranteed. Under such a situation, the people of various countries, developing countries in particular, are demanding world peace, development, social progress, economic prosperity and the improvement of living standards. The World Conference on Human Rights should conform to this international trend, meet the demands of the world's people, pay full attention to the right to subsistence, with which people are especially concerned, and give it priority in deliberation, so as to ensure that international human rights activities develop in a healthy direction.

**Source:** *Beijing Review*, June 21-27, 1993, pp. 9–10.

# Appendix 3

# Fine Traditions of Human Rights in Asia

by Dong Yunhu

In the field of international human rights, the contributions of the people of Asia cannot be ignored.

Asia, a major birthplace of world civilization, has a long and splendid cultural tradition. In ancient times Asian people created a brilliant civilization, made technological inventions and formed major religions, leaving rich cultural and spiritual treasures for mankind. Thus, Asian people have made an indelible contribution to world civilization and the development of human rights and fundamental freedoms.

These cultural achievements brought a unique concept and tradition of human rights to Asia. Although the human rights concept centering on individuals originated in the West, the humanitarian spirit, such as the value of human dignity in India and Confucian humanism in China, has long been a part of Asia's cultural tradition. In these humanitarian traditions, humanism and kind-heartedness were regarded as the natural features of man. The idea that "the aged should be well supported, children should be brought up, the able-bodied should be given an opportunity to bring his ability into full play, and the disabled should be helped," also encouraged people to be concerned about society and others before themselves.

Individuals should enjoy their own rights on the basis of these principles. The cultural tradition of respect for individual rights while guaranteeing the state, social, family and other collective rights has played an important role in promoting economic and social progress in the region and will continue to promote its further revitalization.

In view of this cultural tradition and modern experience, Asia found a unique way to promote human rights. In modern times Asian countries, with the exception of Japan, were all invaded by Western powers one after another, and became colonies or semi-colonies. Under these miserable conditions, every one linked their own destiny with national independence. So, the right to state independence and national self-determination became a precondition for the enjoyment of human rights. As a Philippine jurist said, national rights and individual rights complement each other; in fact, if community rights are not recognized, individual rights cannot be guaranteed either.

Therefore, to guarantee individual rights on the precondition of maintaining state and national rights became the basic way Asian countries strived for human rights. The tradition of treasuring national and state destiny encouraged Asian people to oppose external oppression and colonial rule, and finally win their independence. Billions of Asians broke away from imperialist rule, and this in itself was a major contribution to the development of human rights.

After independence, Asian countries faced poverty and backwardness left by a long-time colonial rule. Under this situation, in order to enable their people to enjoy full rights, they gave priority to developing the national economy and realizing modernization. Without social and economic development individuals cannot enjoy full human rights. Therefore, promoting the individual enjoyment of human rights and fundamental freedoms on the basis of socioeconomic development has become the basic model for Asian countries. Former Singapore Prime Minister Lee Kuan Yew said that it was undoubtedly more suited to Asian countries to set up a society which emphasizes social interests rather than American style individualism.

Asian countries stress state responsibility for maintaining social stability, promoting economic development and improving living standards. This collective humanitarian tradition is helpful for Asia and has promoted a high economic growth rate and the improvement of living standards. At present, most Asian countries are experiencing an economic take-off. Despite difficulties, the situation in Asia is optimistic.

After the end of the Cold War Western countries witnessed economic recession, and their inherent human rights problems have become more evident. Those countries which followed Western democratic and human rights model have also seen national separation, social instability and deteriorating living standards Compared with this, the Asia-Pacific region is enjoying good times. Political stability promotes socio-economic development and improves living standard, which, in turn, guarantees political stability.

The facts show that it is fruitful for Asian nations to promote human rights on the basis of keeping a balance between individual rights and social interests. Malaysian Prime Minister Mahathir Mohamad once pointed out that ASEAN countries attempt to balance individual rights with social needs so as to realize political stability, and this enables them to make great social and economic progress.

**Source:** *Beijing Review*, June 28-July 4, 1993

# Appendix 4

# Proposals for Human Rights: Protection and Promotion

The following is a speech made by Vice-Foreign Minister Liu Huaqiu, head of the Chinese delegation to the World Conference on Human Rights held in Vienna, on June 15.

The World Conference on Human Rights is convened on the occasion of the 45th anniversary of the Universal Declaration of Human Rights. This is a noteworthy event in the international community today. We hope that this conference will contribute positively to strengthening international cooperation in the field of human rights and promoting full human rights and fundamental freedom of people of all countries.

In the wake of World War II and victory over the brutal fascist forces, the United Nations worked out the Charter of the United Nations and the Universal Declaration of Human Rights which give expression to the longing desire of people across the world for the respect and protection of human rights and fundamental freedoms. It has, through relentless efforts, scored many achievements in safeguarding and promoting human rights. During this period, nearly a hundred countries broke down the shackles of colonialism and won independence successively, which culminated in the total collapse of the centuries-old evil colonial system. All this has created prerequisites and opened up broad vistas for the realization of basic human rights for people of all countries in the world. The United Nations and the international community have done a great deal of work in terms of eliminating colonialism, racism, apartheid, massive gross violations of human rights as a result of foreign invasion and occupation, safeguarding the rights of small and weak countries to self-determination and the right of developing countries to development, and helping people of all countries to obtain the basic human rights. All these represent a major development of the Universal Declaration of Human Rights. Moreover, the series of programmatic documents such as the Proclamation of Tehran and the Declaration of the Right to Development adopted successively by the United Nations have further enriched the contents of and defined the objectives and guiding principles for international activities in the field of human rights. In preparation for this conference, Africa, Latin America and Asia convened regional preparatory meetings which passed respectively the Tunis Declaration, the San Jose Declaration and the Bangkok Declaration. These important instruments on human rights have identified some pressing issues of concern to the developing countries which make up the overwhelming majority of the world population and put forward their practical and feasible principled propositions, thus further enriching and expanding the contents of human rights protection and promotion.

The issue of human rights has attracted universal attention in the international community as it bears on the basic rights and vital interests of the world's people. In recent years, the international situation has undergone drastic changes. The world has entered a historical juncture whereby the old pattern is giving way to a new one. The international community has before it difficulties and challenges on the one hand, and hopes and opportunities on the other. In the international human rights field, the pressing task facing the people of all countries is to sum up experience and set the correct direction and principles for the future course in light of the changing situation, with a view to effectively protecting and promoting basic human rights. This World Conference on Human Rights is an important conference linking the past and future. Its success will undoubtedly be of great significance to the realization of this objective

We should also be soberly aware that the serious consequences of colonialism, racism, apartheid, foreign invasion and occupation are great to be fully removed. People in countries still under foreign occupation or apartheid have not yet enjoyed basic human rights and freedom. Though the Cold War, characterized by confrontation between the two military blocs has come to an end, the world today is far from tranquil as is evidenced by increasing factors of de-stabilization and emergence of new hot spots. People in some regions are still struggling for survival. Many developing countries find themselves in greater economic difficulties and impoverishment. Over one billion people in the world are still living below the poverty line, suffering from starvation, diseases and shortages. These, no doubt, are the stumbling blocks in the way to the realization of universal human rights. Therefore, to remove these obstacles and carry out international cooperation in this connection should be given top priority by the international community in its efforts to promote the cause of human rights.

The concept of human rights is a product of historical development. It is closely associated with specific social, political and economic conditions and the specific history, culture and values of a particular country. Different historical development stages have different human rights requirements. Countries at different development stages or with different historical traditions and cultural backgrounds also have different understanding and practice of human rights. Thus, one should not and cannot think the human rights standard and model of certain countries as the only proper ones and demand all other countries to comply with them. It is neither realistic nor workable to make international economic assistance or even international economic cooperation conditional on them.

The concept of human rights is an integral one, including both individual and collective rights. Individual rights cover not only civil and political rights but also economic, social and cultural rights. The various aspects of human rights are interdependent, equally important, indivisible and indispensable. For the vast number of developing countries, to respect and protect human rights is first and foremost to ensure the full realization of the rights to subsistence and development. The argument that human rights is the pre-condition for development is unfounded. When poverty and lack of adequate food and clothing are commonplace and people's basic needs are not guaranteed, priority should be given to economic development. Otherwise, human rights are completely out of the question. We believe that the major criteria for judging the human rights situation in a developing country should be whether its policies and measures help promote economic and social progress, help people meet their basic needs for food and clothing and improve the quality of their life. The international community should take actions to help developing countries alleviate economic difficulties, promote their development and free them from poverty and want.

The rights and obligations of a citizen are indivisible. While enjoying his legitimate rights and freedom, a citizen must fulfill his social responsibilities and obligations. There are no absolute individual rights and freedom, except those prescribed by and within the framework of law. Nobody shall place his own rights interests above those of the state and society, nor should he be allowed to impair those of others and the general public. This is a universal principle of all civilized societies. Moreover, to maintain social stability and ensure the basic human rights to citizens do not contradict each other. The practice of the international community has proved once and again only when there is justice, order and stability in a country or society, can its development and the well-being as well as basic human rights of all its citizens be guaranteed.

According to the UN Charter and the norms of international law, all countries, large or small, strong or weak, rich or poor, have the right to choose their own political system, road to development and values. Other countries have no right to interfere. To wantonly accuse another country of abuse of human rights and impose the human rights criteria of one's own country or region on other countries or regions are tantamount to an infringement upon the sovereignty of other countries and interference in the latter's internal affairs, which could result in political instability and social unrest in other countries. As a people that used to suffer tremendously from aggression by big powers but now enjoys independence, the Chinese have come to realize fully that state sovereignty is the basis for the realization of citizens' human rights. If the sovereignty of a state is not safeguarded, the human rights of its citizens are out of the question, like a castle in the air. The views that the human rights question goes beyond boundary and that the principle of non-interference in other's internal affairs is not applicable to it and actions on these premises are, in essence, a form of power politics. They run counter to the purposes and principles of the UN Charter and to the lofty cause of the protection of human rights.

China believes that the protection of human rights, like the promotion of development, requires international cooperation and a peaceful and stable international environment. For the purpose of strengthening international cooperation in the field of human rights and promoting activities in the protection of human rights in the whole international community, the Chinese delegation hereby puts forth the following principled proposals and wishes to discuss them with you.

1. The international community should give its primary attention to the massive gross violations of human rights resulting from foreign aggression and occupation and continue to support those people still under foreign invasion, colonial rule or apartheid system in their just struggle for national self-determination. It should also commit itself to the elimination of the massive gross violations of human rights ensued from regional conflicts.

2. World peace and stability should be enhanced and a favorable international environment created for the attainment of the goals in human rights protection. To this end, countries should establish a new type of international relationship of mutual respect, equality, amicable coexistence and mutual beneficial cooperation in accordance with the UN Charter and the norms of international law. All international disputes should be solved peacefully in a fair and reasonable manner and in the spirit of mutual accommodation and mutual understanding, and consultation on equal footing, instead of resorting to force or threat of force. No country should pursue hegemonism and power politics or engage in aggression, expansion and interference. This is the way to ensure regional and global peace and stability and to prevent armed conflicts which may incur massive violations of human rights.

3. The right of developing countries to development should be respected and guaranteed. To create a good international economic environment for the initial economic development of developing countries, the international community should commit itself to the establishment of a fair and rational new international economic order. Developed countries, in particular, have the responsibility to help developing countries through practical measures in such areas as debt, capital, trade, assistance and technology transfer, to overcome their economic difficulties and develop their economy. This is the way to gradually narrow the gap between the North and the South which may otherwise be widened and finally to bring about common development and prosperity .

4. The right of each country to formulate its own policies on human rights protection in light of its own conditions should also be respected and

guaranteed. Nobody should be allowed to use the human rights issue to exert political and economic pressures on other countries. The human rights issue can be discussed among countries. However, the discussions should be conducted in the spirit of mutual respect and on an equal footing.

It is the sole objective of the Chinese government to serve the Chinese people and work for their interests. Therefore, China has always attached importance and been committed to the guarantee and promotion of the basic human rights of its people. It is known to all that the old China was an extremely poor and backward semi-feudal and semi-colonial society where the Chinese people did not have any human rights to speak of as they were enslaved and oppressed by the imperialists and Chinese reactionary forces. This bitter past was not put an end to until the founding of the People's Republic. Since then, the Chinese people have, for the first time in history, taken their own destiny into their own hands, become masters of their own country and enjoyed basic human rights. According to China's Constitution, all power in the People's Republic of China belongs to the people. The law guarantees that each and every Chinese citizen, regardless of gender, family background, ethnic status, occupation, property status and religious belief, enjoys genuine democracy and freedom, civil and political rights as well as extensive economic, social and cultural rights. China is a unitary multi-national state. To strengthen national unity and safeguard the unification of the motherland accord with the common interests and aspiration of the Chinese people of all nationalities. To handle properly the ethnic question and the relations among different nationalities has all along been of vital importance to the stability, development and equality among all nationalities of the country. The Chinese government, therefore, attaches great importance to the work in this regard. Equality and unity among all nationalities and regional national autonomy are China's basic principles and policies for handling matters concerning nationalities. As a result, people of all nationalities living in the same big family are now marching toward common prosperity. Since China began to implement the policy of reform and opening to the outside world, its economy has been developing vigorously and its democratic and legal system improving steadily. The nearly 1.2 billion Chinese populace of all nationalities, who are united as one, have seen their material and cultural well-being improved considerably. As their basic needs have been more or less met, they are briskly heading toward a fairly comfortable and affluent life. China has made steady progress in promoting and protecting human rights, which has been acknowledged and commended by all fair-minded people in the international community.

China respects and abides by the basic principles of the UN Charter and the Universal Declaration of Human Rights. It attaches importance to and has actively participated in the international exchanges and cooperation in the field of human rights as well as UN activities in this field. China has acceded, one after another, to eight international conventions on human rights and is earnestly honoring the obligation it has thereby undertaken. It is ready to further strengthen exchanges and cooperation with other countries on human rights in the international arena and to contribute its part to the effective promotion and protection of human rights in the international community and to the achievement of the lofty ideal that people throughout the world will be able to fully enjoy the basic human rights.

**Source:** *Beijing Review*, June 28-July 4, 1993

# Appendix 5

# Standpoint on Human Rights Aired

Zhu Muzhi, president of the China Society for the Study of Human Rights, said on December 27, 1993, that different people have different views and practices on human rights.

Just as countries's histories, social systems, economies, cultures and religions differ, so do their points of view and practices on human rights, he said.

Sovereign rights had to be respected, and countries should basically be allowed to decide how to safeguard and promote human rights by themselves. Otherwise, there would be worldwide turmoil.

"I say 'basically' because human rights also have another international aspect," Zhu said. "All countries oppose activities which seriously endanger world peace and security and human rights. Such activities include colonialism, genocide, armed invasion and international terrorism."

He called on the international community to take measures to stop such activities.

He said, some conventions on human rights passed by the United Nations could not be forced upon all countries.

Just as strong and weak countries continued to exist, so did power politics and hegemony under which the weak are bullied.

Therefore, the only way for weak, small and developing countries to defend their human rights is to rely on their sovereign rights, Zhu said.

He said the view that political rights are the most important—or even the only—human rights cannot be justified.

"We hold that human rights consist of several aspects, including the right of subsistence, and the right concerning politics, the economy, development and cultures, which are closely linked," he said.

Zhu said there was a saying in the West that China has a developing economy but no democracy, which implies China attaches no importance to political rights.

This was not a complicated issue, he said. Some people in the West not only regard political rights as the only content of human rights, they also take the Western democracy as the only political model, neglecting other forms of political democracy.

He stressed that China adheres to socialist democracy, which is not only a necessary prerequisite for the right of subsistence but also for the development of its economy and modernization.

The crux of political democracy is letting the people enjoy the right to seek their own interests and happiness, he said.

Whether a government acts in accordance with the aspirations and demands of the majority of the people or not is the fundamental standard by which to judge whether its people enjoy real political democracy or not, he continued.

Currently, the immediate aspirations and demands of the majority of the Chinese people are the maintenance of political stability and unity, and the momentum of progress toward prosperity.

China is now carrying out a basic line with priority on economic construction that is based on the aspirations and demands of the Chinese people, he said.

China has become a major target of attack from Western countries on the issue of human rights. Certain countries often attempt to condemn China with the use of distorted or fabricated information and materials.

These countries have, in disregard of truth, accused China of "invading Tibet and depriving the Tibetan people of human rights." They also attempt to encourage resolutions which aim to dismember China by intervening in its internal affairs.

However, China has won support from all just countries, especially from the developing countries, thwarting the plots of those countries with ulterior motives.

Zhu also talked about his views on the prospects for human rights.

He said the world today is not a peaceful place and the two major problems of peace and development have yet to be resolved, so the issue of human rights will remain a focal point of world struggles.

This is because some countries always want to use human rights as a means to put pressure on other countries in a bid to realize their own objectives. Obviously this is not conducive to peace and development, he added.

Zhu said he believed it is normal for different countries to have different ways of understanding and implementing human rights.

"To reach the goal of mutual understanding and mutual promotion, we favor dialogue," said Zhu.

All the parts in the dialogue should respect facts, he noted. Dialogue is not possible based on fiction, inaccuracies, gossip, groundless accusations, or distorted or fabricated information.

Meanwhile, countries must treat each other as equals. Only on an equal basis is dialogue possible.

And scientific and factual attitude should be adopted. "Neither can we rely on idealism nor force our own mode on others," Zhu said.

**Source:** *Beijing Review*, January 10–16, 1994, pp. 6–7.

# Appendix 6

## China Human Rights Practices, 1993
## U.S. Department of State January 31, 1994

The People's Republic of China (PRC) remains a one-party state ruled by the Chinese Communist Party through a 21-member Politburo and a small circle of officially retired but still powerful senior leaders. Almost all top civilian, police, and military positions at the national and regional levels are held by party members. Despite official adherence to Marxism-Leninism, in recent years economic decisionmaking has become less ideological, more decentralized, and increasingly market oriented. Fundamental human rights provided for in the Constitution are frequently ignored in practice, and challenges to the Communist Party's political authority are often dealt with harshly and arbitrarily. Security forces, comprised of a nationwide network which includes the People's Liberation Army, the Ministry of State Security, the Ministry of Public Security, the People's Armed Police, and the state judicial, procuratorial, and penal systems, are poorly monitored due to the absence of adequate legal safeguards or adequate enforcement of existing safeguards for those detained, accused, or imprisoned. They are responsible for widespread and well-documented human rights abuses, including torture, forced confessions, and arbitrary detentions.

A decade of rapid economic growth, spurred by market incentives and foreign investment, has reduced party and government control over the economy and permitted ever larger numbers of Chinese to have more control over their lives and livelihood. Despite significant income disparities between coastal regions and the interior, there is now a growing "middle class" in the cities and rural areas as well as a sharp decline in the number of Chinese at the subsistence level. These economic changes have led to a de facto end to the role of ideology in the economy and an increase in cultural diversity. An example of this is the media, which remains tightly controlled with regard to political questions, although it now is free to report on a wider variety of other issues.

The Government took some positive steps on human rights issues during 1993. It released some prominent political prisoners early or on medical parole; many had served long terms in prison. The Government still has not provided a full or public accounting of the thousands of persons detained during the suppression of the 1989 democracy movement, when millions of students, workers, and intellectuals defied the Government and participated in public demonstrations. Most of these detainees appear to have been released, however, some after serving periods of detention without charges having been brought and some after having completed their prison sentences. The Government says it has released the remaining imprisoned or detained Vatican loyalists among the Catholic clergy. Although it continues to restrict the movements and activities of some elderly priests and bishops, the Government announced in November that two priests, whose movements had been restricted, were free to return to their homes. The authorities also allowed a number of prominent political dissidents to leave China in 1993. In November the Government announced it would give positive consideration to a request from the International Committee of the Red Cross (ICRC) to visit China.

Nevertheless, the Government's overall human rights record in 1993 fell far short of internationally accepted norms as it continued to repress domestic critics and failed to control abuses by its own security forces. The Government detained, sentenced to prison, or sent to labor camps, and in a few cases expelled from the country, persons who sought to exercise their rights of freedom of assembly and speech. The number of persons in Chinese penal institutions considered political prisoners by international standards is impossible to estimate accurately. In 1993 hundreds, perhaps thousands, of political prisoners remained under detention or in prison. Physical abuse, including torture by police and prison officials persisted, especially in politically restive regions with minority populations like Tibet. Criminal defendants continue to be denied legal safeguards such as due process or adequate defense. In many localities, government authorities continued to harass and occasionally detain Christians who practiced their religion outside the officially sponsored religious organizations.

RESPECT FOR HUMAN RIGHTS

Section 1 Respect for the Integrity of the Person, Including Freedom from:

a. Political and Other Extrajudicial Killing

There were accounts of extrajudicial killings by government officials in 1993. A few cases resulted in severe punishment for the officials involved and were widely publicized as admonitory examples. Local officials beat to death an Anhui farmer in February after he protested the level of taxes and fees. Those found directly responsible for the beating, including a local public security official, received long prison terms and, in one case, a death sentence. Other officials were dismissed or disciplined. Also, in another well-publicized case, the powerful local Communist party secretary of a village near Tianjin was sentenced in August to 20 years in prison for obstruction of justice and other offenses related to a December 1992 beating death. Those who actually took part in the beating also received long prison terms.

The official responses to other cases served to cover up abuses, however. Credible reports indicated that a Shaanxi man beaten by public security officials in March, during a raid on an unauthorized Protestant gathering, died as a result of his injuries and the lack of timely medical care while in police custody. An official autopsy ascribed the death to an unrelated illness.

Because the Government often restricts access to such information, it is impossible to determine the total number of such killings. However, according to a credible report issued in 1993 by a human rights group, at least 12 persons died in 1992 as a result of torture while in police custody.

b. Disappearance

There were no reported cases in 1993 in which persons who disappeared were suspected to have been killed by officials, however, the Government has still not provided a comprehensive, credible public accounting of all those missing or detained in connection with the suppression of the 1989 demonstrations.

c. Torture and Other Cruel, Inhuman, or Degrading Treatment or Punishment

Cases of torture and degrading treatment of detained and imprisoned persons persisted. Both official Chinese sources and international human rights groups reported many instances of torture. Persons detained pending trial were particularly at risk as a result of weaknesses in the legal system, including the emphasis on obtaining confessions as a basis for convictions and the lack of access to prisoners, even by family members, until after formal charges are brought, a step that can be delayed for months. Former detainees have credibly reported the use of cattle prods and electrodes, prolonged periods of solitary confinement and incommunicado detention, beatings, shackles, and other forms of abuse against detained women and men.

While generally refusing to allow impartial observers to visit prisoners, officials stated that internal monitoring and laws to prevent and punish abuses continue to be strengthened. Procurator General Liu Fuzhi said in March that 2,800 procuratorate offices had been set up in jails and detention centers to safeguard the welfare of detainees. In response to a call by the Chairman of the National People's Congress (NPC), a national-level procuratorial conference held in Shanghai in early April focused on measures to improve the Procuratorate's supervision of law enforcement personnel and government officials who violate the civil rights of citizens. In August the Guangdong provincial public security bureau issued a regulation forbidding police torture during interrogations. In

April China told the U.N. Committee Against Torture that 339 cases of torture to extract confessions were investigated during 1992, 209 cases were reported to the Procuratorate with a view to prosecution, and 180 prosecutions were brought. No information on convictions or punishments was provided. While Chinese officials said in December that 23 prison officials had been punished in serious cases of mistreatment of prisoners, the number of actual incidents of torture and ill-treatment by government officials is almost certainly far greater than this number.

Conditions of imprisonment for political prisoners vary widely. Some prisoners, including the student leader Wang Dan, who was released in February, have stated they were treated reasonably well. Credible reports indicate others have been abused. Political prisoners are often intermingled with common criminals. Credible reports persisted in 1993 that Liu Gang, a political prisoner held at a Liaoning labor camp, suffers ill health as a result of beatings and other mistreatment, and that prison officials instigated some beatings by cellmates. Officials strongly denied these allegations and arranged for an interview with Liu and his jailers, which was published in August by a Chinese English-language journal. They declined repeated requests by foreign groups to allow access to the jailed dissident by independent observers.

There was limited evidence that, at least in a few cases, detained dissidents have been incarcerated in psychiatric institutions and treated with drugs. The lack of independent outside access to such persons made it impossible to verify the reports. Shanghai dissident Wang Miaogen was detained by public security officials in May and committed to a mental institution after he attempted to protest the holding of the East Asia games. Wang had earlier chopped off four of his fingers in a protest over alleged persecution. Wang Wanxing, detained in 1992 while attempting to stage a one-man protest on Tiananmen Square, continued to be held in a Beijing-area mental hospital.

Conditions in Chinese penal institutions are generally harsh and frequently degrading, and nutritional and health conditions are sometimes grim. Medical care for prisoners has been a problem area, despite official assurances that prisoners have the right to maintain good health and receive prompt medical treatment if they become ill. In 1993 political prisoners who reportedly had difficulties in obtaining timely and adequate medical care included Wang Juntao, Chen Ziming, and Ren Wanding. Medical paroles may be granted to ailing prisoners, and 1989 detainee Li Guiren was released in January to obtain medical treatment. Working conditions for prisoners in many facilities are similar to those in ordinary factories, but some prisoners working in penal coal mines and at other sites must endure dangerous conditions (see Section 6.c.).

Political prisoner Qi Dafeng continued to serve a 2-year sentence in a coal mine in Anhui, where he had been sent under the nonjudicial "reeducation through labor" program in late 1992.

d. Arbitrary Arrest, Detention, or Exile

China's Criminal Procedure Law proscribes arbitrary arrest or detention, limits the time a person may be held in custody without being charged, and requires officials to notify the detainee's family and work unit of the detention within 24 hours. These provisions are subject to several important exceptions, including the sweeping provision that notification may be withheld if it would "hinder the investigation" of a case. Senior judicial officials acknowledged in 1993 that limits on detention are frequently ignored in practice or circumvented by various informal mechanisms. In numerous cases, the precise legal status or location of detainees is unclear. Public security authorities often detain people for long periods of time under mechanisms not covered by the Criminal Procedure Law. These include unpublished regulations on "taking in for shelter and investigation" and "supervised residence" as well as other methods not requiring procuratorial approval. According to the Chinese media, close to 1 million detentions under "shelter for investigation" have been carried out annually in recent years. No statistics were available to indicate the usual length of these detentions, but at least some lasted several months. Links between local officials and business leaders have resulted in scattered detentions as a means of exerting pressure in economic disputes. The legality of detentions may be judicially challenged under the Administrative Procedures Law, but such challenges are rare and there is little evidence that this is an adequate or timely remedy for improper actions. There is no judicially supervised system of bail, but at the discretion of public security officials some detainees are released pending further investigation.

Political dissidents are often detained or charged for having committed "crimes of counterrevolution" under Articles 90 through 104 of the Criminal Law. Counterrevolutionary offenses range from treason and espionage to spreading counter-revolutionary propaganda. These articles have also been used to punish persons who organized demonstrations, disrupted traffic, disclosed official information to foreigners, or formed associations outside state control. Detention and trial of dissidents on other charges is also possible. People participating in unauthorized religious organizations may be charged with criminal offenses such as receiving funds from abroad without authorization or changing such funds on the black market. Legal provisions requiring family notification and limiting length of detention are often ignored in political cases. Liao Jia'an, a university student in Beijing detained in 1992 for peaceful expression of his political views, was held for a year before being formally arrested in mid-1993 for counterrevolutionary crimes.

A well-documented estimate of the total number of those subjected to new or continued arbitrary arrest or detention for political reasons is not possible due to the Government's tight control of information. Individuals reported detained are sometimes released without charge after several days or weeks of interrogation. There were several reported lengthier detentions of dissidents, including Sun Lin, Wang Miaogen, and Zhang Xianliang, in Shanghai during 1993. Sun was released in August after 5 months in detention. Democracy activists Qin Yongmin, Yang Zhou, and Zheng Xuguang were detained in November in connection with the formation of a group called the "Peace Charter." Yang Zhou was released from detention on December 31, but the authorities had not provided information on the status or location of the other peace charter detainees. Several dozen Tibetans were also reported to have been detained after participation in proindependence demonstrations or activities (see Section 5). Gendun Rinchen, a Tibetan tour guide who had been detained in May 1993, was released on January 14, 1994

e. Denial of Fair Public Trial

Officials insist that China's judiciary is independent but acknowledge that it is subject to the Communist Party's policy guidance. In actuality, party and government leaders almost certainly predetermine verdicts and sentences in some sensitive cases. According to the Constitution, the court system is equal in authority to the State Council and the Central Military Commission, the two most important government institutions. All three organs are nominally under the supervision of the National People's Congress. The Supreme People's Court stands at the apex of the court system, followed in descending order by the higher, intermediate, and basic people's courts.

Due process rights are provided for in the Constitution but are often ignored in practice. Both before and after trial, prisoners are subject to severe psychological pressure to confess their "errors." Defendants who fail to "show the right attitude" by confessing their crimes are typically sentenced more harshly. Despite official media and other reports that indicate coerced confessions have led to erroneous convictions, a coerced confession is not automatically excluded as evidence. According to judicial officials, however, confessions without corroborating evidence are an insufficient basis for conviction.

Accused persons are given virtually no opportunity to prepare a defense in the pretrial process, during which the question of guilt or innocence is essentially decided administratively. Defense lawyers may be retained only 7 days before the trial. In some cases even this brief period has been shortened under regulations issued in 1983 to accelerate the adjudication of certain serious criminal cases. Persons appearing before a court are not presumed innocent; despite official denials, trials are essentially sentencing hearings. Conviction rates average over 99 percent. There is an appeal process, but initial decisions are rarely overturned, and appeals generally do not provide meaningful protection against arbitrary or erroneous verdicts. Like the initial court verdict, the judgment of the Appeals Court is subject to Communist Party "guidance."

Under the Criminal Procedure Law, persons "exempted from prosecution" by procurators are deemed to have a criminal record, despite the lack of a judicial determination of guilt. Such provisions can be applied in "counterrevolutionary crimes" as well as for ordinary criminal offenses. In August Shanghai activists Sun Lin, Yao Tiansheng, and Han Lifa were "exempted from prosecution" for counterrevolutionary offenses and released.

Some officials have acknowledged that trials in China are conducted too rapidly. These officials state that China's 70,000 lawyers, most of whom are engaged in commercial law, are insufficient to meet the country's expanding legal needs and point to the Government's intention to increase this number to at least 150,000. Knowledgeable observers report that defense attorneys appear in only a small number of criminal trials. Under Chinese law, there is no requirement that the court appoint a defense attorney for the defendant unless the defendant is deaf, dumb, or a minor. When attorneys do appear, they have little time to prepare a defense and rarely contest guilt; their function is generally confined to requesting clemency. Defense lawyers, like other Chinese, generally depend on an official work unit for employment, housing, and many other aspects of their lives. They are therefore often reluctant to be viewed as overzealous in defending persons accused of political offenses.

The need for adequate, independent legal aid is increasingly understood in legal circles and within the Government. In many cities, law firms are being organized outside the framework of established government legal offices. These firms are self-regulating and do not have their personnel or budgets determined directly by the State. The Minister of Justice announced in October that China would gradually increase the number of autonomous law firms from the current total of 410.

The Criminal Procedure Law requires that all trials be held in public, except those involving state secrets, juveniles, or "personal secrets." Details of cases involving "counterrevolutionary" charges, however, have frequently been kept secret, even from defendants' relatives, under this provision. The 1988 Law on State Secrets affords a ready basis for denying a public trial in cases involving "counterrevolution."

Lack of due process is particularly egregious when defendants receive the death sentence. Chinese officials refuse to provide comprehensive statistics on death sentences or executions, but hundreds of executions are officially reported annually. The actual numbers may be much higher. All death sentences are nominally reviewed by a higher court. Reviews are usually completed within a few days after sentencing and consistently result in a perfunctory confirmation of sentence. However, no executions for political offenses are known to have occurred in 1993.

In addition to the formal judicial system, government authorities can assign persons accused of "minor" public order and "counterrevolutionary" offenses to "reeducation through labor" camps in an extrajudicial process. In 1990 Chinese officials stated that 869,934 Chinese citizens had been assigned to these camps since 1980, with about 80,000 assigned each year. Chinese officials reported 120,000 prisoners were undergoing "reeducation through labor" at the end of 1993. Other estimates of the number of inmates are considerably higher. Terms of detention run from a normal minimum of 1 year to a maximum of 3 years. The "labor reeducation" committee which determines the term of detention may extend an inmate's sentence for an additional year. Under a State Council regulation issued in early 1991, those sentenced to "reeducation through labor" may ask the committee to reconsider their decision. Since 1990, "reeducation through labor" sentences may also be judicially challenged under the Administrative Procedures Law. While some persons have gained reduction or withdrawal of their sentence after reconsideration or appeal, in practice these procedures are rarely used, and short appeal times, lack of access to lawyers, and other problems weaken their potential assistance in preventing or reversing arbitrary decisions.

The system of "reeducation through labor" sometimes is used by security authorities to deal with political and other offenders without reference to even the nominal procedures and protections the formal criminal process offers. In Shanghai, Fu Shenqi and Zhang Xianliang were given 3-year "reeducation through labor" sentences in July for "provoking incidents" and "inciting trouble" which disturbed public order.

Government officials deny that China has any political prisoners, asserting that persons are detained not for the political views they hold, but because they have taken some action which violates the Criminal Law. The number of persons in Chinese penal institutions considered political prisoners by international standards is impossible to estimate accurately. Hundreds, perhaps thousands, of political prisoners remained imprisoned or detained. Estimates by some foreign researchers of the number of political prisoners are much higher. Many if not most people held for political offenses are charged as counterrevolutionaries. Chinese officials said in December there were 3,172 persons serving sentences for counter-revolutionary crimes, down from a figure of 3,317 given to an American human rights monitor in October. As part of the October figure, officials also indicated that 560 persons convicted of counterrevolutionary crimes had been paroled. Those convicted of counterrevolutionary crimes make up 0.2 percent of the total prisoner population of 1.22 million, but they are about 5 percent of total parolees. As recently as November 1992, an Australian delegation was told there were 4,000 in prison for counterrevolutionary crimes. All these estimates almost certainly include a substantial number of persons convicted of espionage or other internationally recognized criminal offenses. At the same time, the figures exclude many political prisoners detained but not charged, persons held in labor reeducation camps and an undetermined number of persons sentenced for criminal offenses due solely to their nonviolent political or religious activities.

Many prominent activists, including Chen Ziming, Wang Juntao, and Liu Gang (all three held since 1989), remained imprisoned in 1993. Some persons detained for political reasons were released on parole before the end of their sentences. Those released early included longtime political prisoners Wei Jingsheng, Wang Xizhe, and Xu Wenli, and Tiananmen-related detainees Wang Dan, Gao Shan, Zhai Weimin, Wu Xuecan, and Guo Haifeng. Shanghai activist Fu Shenqi was released in March but reimprisoned on other charges in June. Even after release, such persons have a criminal record, and their status in society, ability to be employed, freedom to travel, and numerous other aspects of their lives are often severely restricted. Economic reform and social change have somewhat diminished these problems, but some people continue to experience serious hardships. For example, the families of political prisoners sometimes encounter difficulty in obtaining or keeping employment and housing. Zhang Fengying, wife of imprisoned activist Ren Wanding, remained in poor housing conditions in 1993. Zhang and her teenage daughter were evicted from their apartment in 1992. Ren's work unit owns the apartment. While the work unit asserted it wanted to reassign the housing to another worker, the apartment reportedly has remained vacant.

f. Arbitrary Interference with Privacy, Family, Home, or Correspondence

The authorities extensively monitor and regulate personal and family life, particularly in China's cities. Most persons in urban areas still depend on their government-linked work unit for housing, permission to marry or have a child, approval to apply for a passport, and other aspects of ordinary life. The work unit, along with the neighborhood watch committee, is charged with monitoring activities and attitudes. However, changes in the economic structure, including the growing diversity of employment opportunities and the increasing market orientation of many work units, are undermining the effectiveness of this system. Search warrants are required by law before security forces can search premises, but this provision is often ignored. In addition, both the Public Security Bureau and procuracy apparently can issue search warrants on their own authority.

The 1982 Constitution states that "freedom and privacy of correspondence of citizens ... are protected by law," but, according to a Western expert on Chinese law, legislation for this purpose does not exist. In practice, some telephone conversations are recorded, and mail is frequently opened and censored. The Government often monitors and sometimes restricts contact between foreigners and Chinese citizens, particularly dissidents.

The Government has continued its effort to control citizens' access to outside sources of information, selectively jamming Chinese language broadcasts of the Voice of America (VOA) and the British Broadcasting Corporation. Despite the effort made to jam VOA, the effectiveness of the jamming varies considerably by region, with audible signals reaching most parts of China. A small but rapidly growing segment of the population has access to satellite television broadcasts. Authorities issued new regulations on the installation and operation of satellite dishes in October, requiring permits for operation and banning private ownership and operation except under limited circumstances. However, China has not been very successful in implementing past regulations restricting the use of satellite dishes. Satellite television dishes are widely available for sale, and a licensing scheme which nominally controls purchase of the equipment is loosely enforced.

China's population has roughly doubled in the past 40 years to nearly 1.2 billion people, over a fifth of all humanity. In the 1970's and 1980's China adopted a comprehensive and highly intrusive family planning policy. This policy most heavily affects Han Chinese in urban areas. For urban couples, obtaining permission, usually issued by their work units, to have a second child is very difficult. Numerous exceptions are allowed for the 70 percent of Han who live in rural areas. Ethnic minorities are subject to less stringent population controls. Enforcement of the family planning policy is inconsistent, varying widely from place to place and year to year.

The population control policy relies on education, propaganda, and economic incentives, as well as more coercive measures, including psychological pressure and economic penalties. Rewards for couples who adhere to the policy include monthly stipends and preferential medical and educational benefits.

Disciplinary measures against those who violate the policy include stiff fines, withholding of social services, demotion, and other administrative punishments, including, in some instances, loss of employment. Unpaid fines have sometimes resulted in confiscation or destruction of personal property. Because penalties for excess births may be levied against local officials and the mothers' work units, many persons are affected, providing multiple sources of pressure.

Physical compulsion to submit to abortion or sterilization is not authorized, but Chinese officials acknowledge privately that there are still instances of forced abortions and sterilizations in remote, rural areas. Officials maintain that, when discovered, abuses by local officials result in discipline or retraining. They admit, however, that stronger punishment is rare and have not documented any cases where punishment has occurred. A sharp reported drop in fertility rates in 1991-92 sparked concern about a possible upturn in incidents of coercion. One cause for worry about such increased pressures was a policy change in early 1991 making local political officials more directly responsible for success in meeting family quotas. There was strong evidence, however, that the magnitude of the reported fertility drop was sharply exaggerated, in part because the policy change intensified strong existing incentives for officials and families to underreport births.

At least five provincial governments have implemented regulations with eugenics provisions, beginning with Gansu in 1988. These regulations seek to prevent people with severe mental handicaps from having children. National family planning officials say they oppose such legislation, but the Government has taken no action to overturn these local laws.

Section 2  Respect for Civil Liberties, Including:

a. Freedom of Speech and Press

Freedom of speech and self-expression remain severely restricted, although there has been an easing of the limits imposed during the post-Tiananmen crackdown. Citizens are not permitted to publish or broadcast criticism of senior leaders or opinions that contradict basic Communist Party doctrine which provides for a Socialist state under the party's control, or to make speeches which contain such criticism or opinions.  The Government interprets the Communist Party's "leading role" as circumscribing the various individual rights guaranteed in the Constitution.  People who violate these quidelines are warned and often punished.  Gao Yu, a former writer of a now banned periodical, was charged in October with "leaking state secrets abroad" in connection with articles published in Hong Kong.  Xi Yang, a Hong Kong reporter, was detained in September for "stealing" financial secrets in connection with articles published in Hong Kong.

Domestic television and radio broadcasting and the press remain under party and government control and are used to propagate the currently acceptable ideological line.  A more lively tabloid sector continued to expand in 1993, and the circulation of major propaganda-oriented dailies continued to slip.

Radio talk shows also flourished and, although they generally avoided politically sensitive subjects, they provided some opportunity for Chinese to discuss, and sometimes question officials about, public issues, including corruption.  Under official pressure, the film "Farewell My Concubine," which caused controversy because of its implicit criticism of the cultural revolution and portrayal of a homosexual relationship, was withdrawn from distribution in July after showings in Beijing and Shanghai.  After further editing, it was rereleased in September.

The Government has continued to impose tight controls on colleges, universities, and research institutes.  However, Beijing University and Shanghai's Fudan University stopped sending students to a full year of training and ideological indoctrination at military camps, a requirement imposed in 1989.

The heavy ideological control of academic institutions and media censorship continued to force Chinese journalists and scholars to exercise caution in 1993. Many scholars, including some of China's most prominent, have been deterred from exercising free speech and have declined opportunities to publish or present papers on subjects that they fear could be construed as sensitive. On some less sensitive but still controversial subjects, such as economic policy, legal reform and even civil rights issues, the Government has tolerated more vigorous public discussion. Some authors who were considered politically unacceptable after 1989, such as legal scholar Yu Haocheng, were able to overcome bans and regain at least limited ability to get articles published in 1993.

b. Freedom of Peaceful Assembly and Association

While the Constitution provides for freedom of peaceful assembly and association, these rights are severely restricted in practice. The Constitution provides, for example, that such activities may not infringe "upon the interests of the State," and in practice protests against the political system or its leaders are proscribed. Demonstrations involving expression of dissident political views are denied permits and suppressed if held. Qin Yongmin was briefly detained several times when he attempted to leave his native Wuhan for Beijing to protest against the capital's bid to host the Olympic Games in the year 2000 (see Section 1.d). However, some small-scale demonstrations on nonpolitical grievances are tolerated in practice. In February there were two small demonstrations at the gate of the Zhongnanhai leadership compound in Beijing by women laid off from a state steel firm. In August authorities also tolerated generally peaceful demonstrations in several provinces by Muslims, sometimes numbering in the thousands, who were protesting a book they found offensive. The book was subsequently banned. Demonstrators protesting the same book in Qinghai in October, however, were met with force when Muslim demonstrators threatened to take their protest to Beijing. According to credible reports, there were at least nine deaths.

Public security forces acted with more restraint than in the past to demonstrations in Lhasa in May, which began with a small protest on economic grievances but attracted hundreds of additional participants, including many who shouted proindependence slogans and some who threw rocks. Several dozen persons were believed to have been at least briefly detained in the wake of the protests, but reports of a handful of deaths or serious injuries from the impact of tear gas projectiles appeared to be erroneous. According to human rights organizations, smaller scale protests were reported to have occurred frequently in the Tibetan capital and resulted in swift detention for the participants. Gendun Rinchen and Lobsang Yonten were detained in May, apparently because of alleged proindependence activities, and they were held through the remainder of the year before being released in January 1994. Tibetan political prisoners like Yulo Dawa Tsering, Ngawang Pulchung, and Jempel Tsering remained imprisoned in 1993. While repression continued, there was at the same time a continuation of limited dialog on Tibet with representatives of the Dalai Lama.

The Communist Party organizes and controls most professional and other mass associations. All organizations are required by 1990 regulations to be officially registered and approved. Ostensibly aimed at secret societies and criminal gangs, the regulations also deter the formation of unauthorized political or labor organizations. They have also been used to disband groups, such as unregistered house churches, deemed potentially subversive. Security forces maintain a close watch on groups formed outside the party establishment.

c. Freedom of Religion

Religious freedom in China is subject to restrictions of varying severity. While the Constitution affirms toleration of religious beliefs, the Government restricts religious practice outside officially recognized and government-controlled religious organizations. The management and control of religion is the responsibility of religious affairs bureaus, which are staffed by officials who rarely are believers in religion. Communist Party officials state that party membership and religious belief are incompatible. This places a serious limitation on religious believers, since party membership is required for almost all high positions in government- and state-owned businesses.

The Government, after forcefully suppressing all religious observances during the 1966-76 cultural revolution, began in the late 1970's to restore or replace confiscated churches, temples, mosques, and monasteries. The official religious organizations administer more than a dozen Catholic and Protestant seminaries, nine institutes to train imams and Islamic scholars, and institutes to train Buddhist monks. Students who attend these institutes must demonstrate "political reliability," and all graduates must pass an examination on their theological and political knowledge to qualify for the clergy. The Government permitted Catholic seminarians from several cities to go to the United States in 1993 for additional religious studies. There have also been increased contacts between China and the Vatican.

The Government supervises the publication of religious material for distribution to ensure religious and political conformity. Religious books are not permitted in ordinary bookstores, and there are persistent complaints that the number of Bibles and amounts of other religious materials allowed to be printed fall far short of demand. Religious proselytizing is officially restricted to government-registered and sanctioned places of worship. Unauthorized proselytizing is proscribed and sometimes punished, although some discreet proselytizing and distributing of religious texts outside official channels is tolerated. Local authorities have confiscated private property under the guise of searching for illegal religious materials. Officially sanctioned religious organizations are permitted to maintain international contacts as long as these do not entail foreign control, but proselytizing by foreign groups is forbidden by law and regulation.

Buddhists are by far the largest body of religious believers in China. The Government estimates that there are 100 million Chinese Buddhists, most of whom are from the dominant Han ethnic group. Other Buddhists belong to Tibetan, Mongolian, and other ethnic groups. Han Buddhist leaders generally cooperate with the Government, and there have been few complaints of government restrictions.

In Tibet, however, where Buddhism and Tibetan nationalism are closely intertwined, relations between Buddhists and secular authorities continued to be tense in 1993. The Government tightly controls Tibetan Buddhism and does not tolerate religious manifestations that advocate Tibetan independence.

The Government condemns the Dalai Lama's political activities and his leadership of a "government in exile," but recognizes him as a major religious figure and has tolerated the open veneration of the Dalai Lama by Tibetans. The Government has spent large amounts of money on reconstruction of the main sacred sites, including the Potala Palace and a grand stupa to house the remains of the 10th Panchen Lama. Chinese officials have also publicly asked the Dalai Lama to assist in the process of finding the reincarnation of the 10th Panchen Lama, who died in 1989.

The practice of religion in Tibet is hampered, however, by the limits the Government imposes on religious education and on the number of monks in the religious community compared to traditional norms. Monks at some Tibetan monasteries known for their opposition to Chinese rule face severe travel restrictions and intense monitoring.

According to government figures, there are 17 million Muslims in China. In some areas with large Muslim populations, there continues to be concern regarding restrictions on the building of mosques and the religious education of youths under 18. Following the 1990 unrest in Xinjiang, the authorities issued regulations further restricting religious activities and teaching. China permits Muslim citizens to make the hajj to Mecca, and the number of those making the hajj has significantly increased in recent years. Nongovernment sources indicate that about 5,000 Chinese made the hajj in 1992.

The number of Christians has grown rapidly in recent years, albeit from a small base. Only those Christian churches affiliated with either the Catholic Patriotic Association or the (Protestant) Three-Self Patriotic Movement, which the Government established in the 1950's to eliminate perceived foreign domination of Christian groups, may operate openly. Active unofficial religious movements pose an alternative to the state-regulated churches. The unofficial,

Vatican-affiliated, Catholic Church claims a membership far larger than the 3.7 million registered with the official Catholic church, though actual figures are unknown. In addition to the 5 million persons who are officially counted as following Protestantism, a large number of Protestants worship privately in "house churches" that are independent of government control.

Sporadic repression in some areas has reflected official concern over the Government's inability to control the rapid growth of membership in Christian groups. There continued to be credible reports in 1993 of efforts by authorities in some areas to rein in activities of the unapproved Catholic and Protestant movements, including raiding and closing a number of unregistered churches. In March public security officials disrupted a Protestant religious gathering in Shaanxi, beating many of those present. One man beaten later died, apparently of wounds suffered in the incident (see Section 1.a.). However, authorities in many areas tolerate the existence of unofficial Catholic and Protestant churches as long as they remain small and discreet. In some parts of China, official and underground churches seem to coexist and even cooperate. The Guangzhou House Church of Pastor Samuel Lamb (Lin Xiangao) continued to operate openly, although with frequent harassment by authorities.

A number of religious activists remained imprisoned in 1993, but others were released. There was some evidence that authorities have increasingly used short-term detentions, rather than long prison terms when dealing with unauthorized religious activities. Some of those released from penal detention were apparently placed under house arrest or other restrictions. The number of Catholic clerics in penal detention dropped sharply in 1992 and 1993, although the whereabouts of some reported to have been released could not be confirmed, and others remained under some restrictions. Catholic Gansu bishop Casimir Wang Milu and Hebei priest Pei Ronggui were released from long-term imprisonment during the year. Ministry of Public Security officials told a visiting U.S. official in October that there were no Catholic clerics remaining in detention. In November Bishop Peter Chen Jianzhang and auxiliary bishop Cosmas Shi Enxiang were reportedly released from either prison or house arrest in "old people's homes."

d. Freedom of Movement Within the Country, Foreign Travel, Emigration, and Repatriation

The Government uses an identification card system to control and restrict individual residence location within the country. This system's effectiveness has eroded during China's shift to a more market-oriented economy. The need for a supplemental work force in the areas of fastest economic growth has led to official tolerance for a large itinerant population which is not in compliance with formal requirements to obtain permission to change residence. However, because this itinerant population lacks official status, access to housing, schooling, and the full range of employment opportunities can be restricted.

Some former inmates have been denied permission, under the "staying at prison employment" system, to return to their homes, a provision applicable to those incarcerated in both the "reform through labor" and the "reeducation through labor" systems. For those assigned to camps far from their residences, this constitutes a form of internal exile. The number of prisoners subject to this restriction is unknown. A Vice Minister of Justice told a British human rights delegation in late 1992 that no former prisoners were subject to such restrictions.

The Government routinely permits legal emigration and most foreign travel but has placed obstacles in the way of foreign travel by a few citizens on political or other grounds. Legal scholar Yu Haocheng continued to be unable to obtain permission to travel abroad. These obstacles extend to some dissidents' family members who have not themselves been active politically or accused of any wrongdoing by the Government. Other dissidents, including Hou Xiaotian, Li Honglin, and Qian Liyun, were eventually able to obtain the passports and exit permits needed to leave the country.

Regulations issued in 1990 require those college and university graduates who received free postsecondary education to repay the cost of their education to the State by working for 5 years or more before being eligible for passports to go abroad to study. For those who have overseas Chinese relatives or have not yet graduated, the regulations provide a sliding scale of tuition reimbursement exempting them from the work requirement. Implementation of these regulations has varied from place to place, and most students wishing to go abroad still managed to obtain passports. Persons subject to the regulations on study abroad appear to have had little trouble obtaining passports to visit relatives overseas. Political attitudes, however, are still a major criterion in selecting people for government-sponsored study abroad.

The Government has made a concerted effort to attract back to China persons who have studied overseas. To reassure them, Chinese citizens who return from overseas were exempted in 1992 from re-exit formalities, which had involved Public Security Bureau clearances. However, official media have stated that, before returning home, people who have joined foreign organizations viewed by the Government as hostile to China should quit them and refrain from activities that violate Chinese Law. Procurator General Liu Fuzhi warned in 1992 that people wanted by the public security authorities were not covered by the official assurances extended to other overseas scholars.

Some dissidents, such as Dai Qing and Liu Xiaobo, reentered China without incident in 1993. In August labor activist Han Dongfang, who had been allowed to leave for medical treatment in the United States in 1992, was expelled shortly after he returned. Han's passport was subsequently revoked by Chinese authorities on the grounds that he had engaged in activities hostile to China while overseas. Chinese border officials frustrated Han's several subsequent attempts to return to China. Another labor activist, Lu Jinghua, was refused entry in June when she arrived at the Beijing airport. Lu had fled China in 1989 before she could be arrested. A handful of prominent dissidents overseas continued to have difficulty extending or renewing passports.

The Government accepts the repatriation of citizens who have entered other countries or territories illegally. In 1993, in addition to the routine return of Chinese illegal immigrants found in Hong Kong, China accepted the return of several large groups of illegal immigrants from other countries, including Mexico, Honduras, and the Marshall Islands. Citizens illegally smuggled to other countries are often detained for a short time after their return to China to determine their identity and any past criminal record or involvement in smuggling activities. As a deterrent and to recover repatriation costs, authorities in some areas levy a fine of about $1,000 equivalent on returnees.

China does not have legislation in place that would allow it to grant refugee status and, with the exception of Vietnamese refugees of Chinese ancestry, has generally repatriated persons of other nationalities seeking to be recognized as refugees. The Ministries of Foreign Affairs, Public Security, and Civil Affairs, in collaboration with the United Nations High Commissioner for Refugees (UNHCR), are writing legislation that would allow China to honor its obligation as a party since 1982 to the 1967 protocol relative to the status of refugees.

Although the Government denies having tightened its policy on accepting Vietnamese refugees, in recent years very few such refugees have actually been resettled in China. According to the UNHCR, from 1989 to 1992 China granted admission and provided resettlement to about 130 Vietnamese refugees who came to China to reunite with their families and gave temporary refuge to 35 Vietnamese who subsequently settled in third countries. There were credible reports that larger numbers of Vietnamese have remained in China without official harassment. China has cooperated with Hong Kong to reduce the flow of Vietnamese refugees into the colony. China has not participated in the Comprehensive Plan of Action negotiated at the International Conference on Indochinese Refugees in 1989 but generally has abided by its principles.

Section 3  Respect for Political Rights: The Right of Citizens to Change Their Government

Citizens lack the means to change their government legally and can not freely choose or change the laws and officials that govern them. Citizens vote directly only for county-level people's congress delegates. People's congress delegates at the provincial level are selected by county-level people's congresses, and in turn provincial-level people's congresses select delegates to the National People's Congress. According to the 1982 Constitution, the National People's Congress (NPC) is the highest organ of state power. It elects the President and Vice President, decides on the choice of the Premier, and elects the Chairman of the Central Military Commission. The election and agenda of the NPC are under the tight control of the Communist Party.

In some elections, voters are offered more candidates than positions, allowing a modest degree of choice among officially approved candidates. There were credible reports in 1993 that the candidates most favored by authorities were defeated in a handful of county-level elections and in at least two elections of governors by provincial people's congresses.

As is the case with the NPC, the election and agenda of people's congresses at other levels also remain under tight control by the Communist Party, the paramount source of political authority in China. The Constitution was amended in 1993 to ratify the existence of small "democratic" parties, but these play only a minor consultative role at most, and all pledge allegiance to the Communist Party. Thus, the Communist Party retains an explicit monopoly on political decision-making. The requirement that associations register and be approved makes it difficult for independent interest groups to form and affect the system. Within the Communist Party, a closed inner circle of a few senior leaders reserves the right to set ultimate policy directions. Some hold key positions within the standing committee of the Politburo, the Central Military Commission, or other organs, while others who are nominally retired wield great influence on at least selected issues.

Reversing previous moves to separate the party and government apparatus, at the National People's Congress in April General Secretary Jiang Zemin and several other senior party members were named to hold concurrent government positions.

Section 4    Governmental Attitude Regarding International and Nongovernmental Investigation of Alleged Violations of Human Rights

There are no independent Chinese organizations that publicly monitor or comment on human rights conditions in China. The Government has made it clear it will not tolerate the existence of such groups. Authorities in Shanghai took no action on a March application by several persons to register a proposed "human rights association." Public criticism of the Government's human rights record can be interpreted as "counterrevolutionary" activity and punished accordingly.

Limited academic study and discussion of concepts of human rights have been promoted since 1991. Research institutes in Shanghai and Beijing, including the Chinese Academy of Social Sciences, have organized symposia on human rights, established human rights research centers, and visited other nations to study human rights practices in these countries. Such activities appear to have originated in a desire to improve China's image abroad and strengthen the Government's ability to respond to criticism of its human rights record. Whatever the motivation, this process of study and dialog has exposed more Chinese to international standards and concepts of human rights. Three official White Papers on human rights subjects were published in 1991 and 1992. While the reports stridently defended Chinese practices and glossed over fundamental problems, they sparked a limited debate among academic experts on human rights problems in China that continued in 1993.

Despite the Government's professed adherence to the United Nations Charter, which mandates respect for and promotion of human rights, Chinese officials accept only in theory the principle that human rights are universal. They argue that each nation has its own concept of human rights, grounded in its political, economic, and social system and its historical, religious, and cultural background. China was active in international forums, including the World Conference on Human Rights in June and the annual U.N. Commission on Human Rights meeting in February, in support of this view and to deflect attempts to discuss China's human rights record. China remains reluctant to accept criticism of its human rights situation by other nations or international organizations. Its officials often criticized reports by international human rights monitoring groups, as well as past Department of State reports on human rights practices in China. By and large, Chinese officials continue to insist that criticism of China's human rights practices constitutes interference in China's internal affairs. Nevertheless, in 1993 Chinese authorities expanded their dialog with foreign governments on human rights issues in talks with a number of visiting delegations from the United States and other countries and also during visits abroad by Chinese leaders.

Chinese authorities have refused most requests by foreign human rights delegations to meet with political prisoners but did allow U.S. human rights officials to visit Yulo Dawa Tsering in Drapchi prison in Lhasa in October. Representatives of some international human rights groups visited China in 1993 but did so in an individual capacity and did not engage in an official dialog with the Government. A private American human rights monitor, however, did meet with midranking government officials on several occasions to discuss specific human rights cases.

Finally, while China has continued to engage in a human rights dialog with foreign critics, it has consistently taken the position that human rights practices should be assessed not on the basis of universal principles but rather in the context of local economic, political, and cultural conditions. The Government also maintains that human rights issues are internal matters and that external intervention on human rights issues constitutes interference with its sovereignty.

## Section 5 Discrimination Based on Race, Sex, Religion, Disability, Language, or Social Status

While laws exist to protect minorities and women, in practice discrimination based on ethnicity, sex, and religion has persisted. Minorities, however, do benefit from an official policy of "privileged treatment" in marriage policy, family planning, university admission, and employment, as well as from disproportionate infrastructure investment in some minority areas.

### Women

The 1982 Constitution states that "women in the People's Republic of China enjoy equal rights with men in all spheres of life" and promises, among other things, equal pay for equal work. In fact, most women employed in industry work in lower skilled and lower paid jobs. Women hold relatively few positions of significant influence within the party or government structure. Persistent problems have remained with regard to the status of women, who have often been the unintended victims of reforms designed to streamline enterprises and give workers greater job mobility. Many employers prefer to hire men to avoid the expense of maternity leave and child care.

Reports by women of discrimination, sexual harassment, unfair dismissal, demotion, and wage cuts have continued. In 1992 the NPC enacted legislation on the protection of the rights and interests of women designed to assist in curbing these types of sex-related discrimination. While the gap in the education levels of men and women is narrowing, men continue to constitute the majority of the educated class, particularly the highly educated.

The Government continued in 1993 to condemn strongly and take steps to prevent and punish the abduction and sale of women for wives and prostitutes, abuse of female children, violence against women, and female infanticide. It has severely punished a number of people accused of such crimes. No nationwide statistics were available on the extent of physical violence against women. A May study on family violence reported that in Shanghai from 29 to 33 percent of domestic disputes from 1991-92 involved physical violence. In another 1993 study on the social status of women, 21.2 percent of urban wives and 31.4 percent of rural wives said there was frequent or occasional violence during family quarrels. The abduction of women remains a serious problem in some areas where local officials have resisted efforts of central authorities to stop it. Many discriminatory practices are rooted in traditional rural attitudes which highly value boys as prospective earners and as future caretakers for elderly parents. A number of provinces have sought to reduce the perceived higher economic value of boys in providing old age support by establishing or improving pensions and retirement homes.

In many areas, the ready availability of sonograms has facilitated selective abortion of female fetuses, contributing to a growing gap in the ratio of reported male and female births. Insistence that local units meet population goals exacerbates the problem, since traditional-minded parents often wish to ensure they have one or more sons without incurring official penalties. The Government has condemned sex-selective abortion and stated it is tightening access to sonogram results.

## Children

China does not condone violence against children, and physical abuse can be grounds for criminal prosecution. In January 1992, China passed a national law on the protection of juveniles. According to Chinese media, China's infant mortality rate has declined to 45 per 1,000 live births, severe malnutrition among children under 5 years of age has been "virtually eliminated," 95 percent of children have received immunizations, and primary school enrollment is at 97 percent. In January an English-language magazine reported on the problem of child abuse, noting that physical punishment was widespread, citing four cases from 1992 where children died from abuse. According to one study from Zhejiang province, 60 percent of 200 children surveyed said they would be beaten if they did not do well in school. In addition, Chinese officials indicated in October that there were about 200,000 homeless children in China out of a total of 300 million children under age 18.

## National/Racial/Ethnic Minorities

The 55 designated ethnic minorities constitute just over 8 percent of China's total population. Most minority groups reside in areas they have traditionally inhabited, with standards of living often well below the national average. Government development policies have helped raise minority living standards but have at the same time disrupted traditional living patterns. The Dalai Lama continued to state his concern in 1993 that the Government's plan to develop Tibet's economy would lead to a massive influx into Tibet of Han Chinese. Tens of thousands of non-Tibetan entrepreneurs without residence permits have come to Lhasa, capital of Tibet, to engage in business.

In some instances, the Government has tried to adopt policies responsive to minority sensitivities but in doing so has encountered the dilemma of how to respect minority cultures without damaging minority educational and economic opportunities. In Tibet and Xinjiang, for example, there are two-track school systems using standard Chinese and minority languages. Students may choose which system to attend. One acknowledged side effect of this policy to protect and maintain minority cultures has been reinforcement of a segregated society. Under this separate education system, those graduating from minority schools are at a disadvantage in competing for jobs, which require good spoken Chinese, in government and business. These graduates must take remedial language instruction before attending universities and colleges.

The Communist Party has an avowed policy of boosting minority representation in the Government and the party, and a few members of minorities occupy local and national leadership positions. However, ethnic minorities are effectively shut out of most positions of real political and decisionmaking power. Some minorities resent Han officials holding key positions in minority autonomous regions. Ethnic minorities in Tibet, Xinjiang, Qinghai, and elsewhere have demonstrated against Han Chinese authority, but central authorities have made it clear that they will not tolerate opposition to Beijing's rule in minority regions.

People with Disabilities

There is no legislation to ensure that buildings, even new ones, are accessible to those with handicaps. A State Council committee was established in October to coordinate policy toward the disabled under China's 1990 law on the handicapped. The results of the eighth 5-year plan for handicapped people, which ended in 1992, were discussed in October; schools for the disabled increased from 400 in 1988 to 1,000 in 1992, and special education increased six-fold. But according to the Disabled Person's Federation, only 6 percent of disabled school-age children are receiving primary education. There are 40,000 welfare enterprises nationwide providing work for the handicapped, and 1.26 million have benefited from rehabilitation projects. Concern that the disabled will lose jobs as enterprises emphasize productivity has led to the creation of a pilot project in which all state enterprises will be required to hire a certain number of disabled workers. The handicapped still suffer from social isolation, especially in rural areas, and some handicapped children are given to orphanages. At the end of December, the Government announced plans to adopt a new law on eugenics, but specifics of the law were not available at year's end.

Section 6 Worker Rights

a. The Right of Association

China's 1982 Constitution provides for "freedom of association," but the guarantee is heavily diluted by references to the interest of the State and the leadership of the Chinese Communist Party. The country's sole officially recognized workers' organization, the All-China Federation of Trade Unions (ACFTU), ostensibly independent, is in fact controlled by the Communist

Party. Independent trade unions are illegal. Though union officials recognize that workers' interests may not always coincide with those of the Communist Party, the Union Law passed by the National People's Congress in March 1992 states that the union is a party organ and its primary purpose is to mobilize workers for national development. The 1993 revised Trade Union Law requires that the establishment of unions at any level be submitted to a higher level trade union organization for approval. The ACFTU is the highest such organization, and it has not approved the establishment of any independent unions. While the foreign press has reported that some exist, because of severe repression they operate only deep within the shadows. The vast majority of workers have no contact with any union other than the ACFTU. There are no provisions allowing for individual workers or unofficial worker organizations to affiliate with international bodies.

The ACFTU's primary attention remains focused on its traditional constituency, state sector workers. The Trade Union Law mandates that workers may decide whether to join the union in their enterprise. By official estimate, 10 percent of workers in collectively and state-owned enterprises have chosen for their own reasons not to join. There have been no reports of repercussions for workers who have not joined ACFTU unions. Diversification of enterprise types over the last decade of reform has vastly increased the number of workers outside this traditional sphere of the ACFTU. In fact, over half of China's nonagricultural work force is now largely nonunion and outside the state industrial structure--in collectives, village and township enterprises, private and individual enterprises, and foreign-invested enterprises. In township and village enterprises, one of the fastest growing sectors of the economy, only one-tenth of 1 percent of workers are unionized. Unemployed workers are not considered union members.

Workers in companies with foreign investors are guaranteed the right to form unions, which then must affiliate with the ACFTU. According to Ministry of Labor national statistics, 30 percent of foreign-invested companies now have unions. Other official estimates show that about 10,000 trade unions with a total of 500,000 members have been established in the nearly 20,000 foreign-funded companies in Guangdong province. However, a 1993 embassy survey of foreign-invested ventures in Beijing indicated the unionization rate diminished from 60 percent in 1991 to 40 percent in 1993.

The right to strike, which had been included in China's 1975 and 1978 constitutions, was not retained in the 1982 Constitution. In general, the union law passed in 1992 assigned unions the role of mediators or go-betweens with management in cases of work stoppages or slowdowns. Nonetheless, well-documented work stoppages occurred in several locations in China during 1993. There were two highly visible strikes in Guangdong's Zhuhai City, namely a 3-day strike over wages at a joint-venture camera factory and a work stoppage at a joint-venture electrical components factory. Ministry of Labor officials broke with their past practice of denying the existence of strikes in China by giving details about recent strikes in Tianjin and Xian. Strikes in 11 foreign-invested enterprises in Tianjin were widely reported in the Chinese press. One particularly high profile case involved a foreign-owned footwear factory at which 1,200 workers struck over poor working conditions and alleged mistreatment of several of the workers by the management. The 11 enterprises were held up as examples of disregard for local regulations by foreigners and indications of the need to establish unions in foreign-invested enterprises. Strikes were uniformly resolved in favor of workers, and enterprises were required to bring facilities up to regulatory standards. Ministry of Labor officials have not provided any statistics on how many strikes occurred in 1993, but one Hong Kong newspaper reported that in the first half of 1993 there were 190 strikes and protests across China involving about 50,000 workers. It is not possible to determine the validity of this estimate.

Credible reports by foreign human rights organizations indicate that the Government has attempted to stamp out all clandestine union activity and that independent unions and worker groups feature prominently in lists of illegal organizations. In May four men were detained and later formally arrested for the crime of organizing a counterrevolutionary organization, the Shanghai Autonomous Workers Federation. Two of these men were released in early September. As noted in Section 2.d., labor activists Han Dongfang and Lu Jinghua have been refused reentry to China. The International Confederation of Free Trade Unions (ICFTU) alleges that in May and June of 1992 the Public Security Bureau (PSB) secretly arrested activists of the clandestine China Free Trade Union Preparatory Committee and appeared to have dismantled this organization. On May 15 another clandestine union group, the Free Trade Union of China, issued a manifesto. Preemptive arrests took place just before the June 4 Tiananmen anniversary. These included seven members of the clandestine Liberal Workers Union detained by the PSB to prevent them from circulating commemorative leaflets. Accurate figures on the number of Worker Autonomous Federation detainees still being held after the 1989 Tiananmen Square demonstrations are not available. The ICFTU alleges that hundreds of workers are still being held.

In response to an ICFTU complaint, the Governing Body of the International Labor Organization (ILO) in March requested that the Government modify "many provisions" of the Trade Union Act that are contrary to the principle of freedom of association, expressed concern at the severity of sanctions pronounced by the courts against members or leaders of Workers' Autonomous Federations, and asked that detained workers be released.

b. The Right to Organize and Bargain Collectively

Under a 1988 law and current regulations, collective bargaining is permitted only by workers in private enterprises (which employ less than 3 percent of workers). There have been no reports of collective bargaining actually taking place. Most private enterprises are small and nonunionized. Thus far, without legal status as a collective bargaining body, the ACFTU's role has been limited to consultations with management over wages and regulations affecting labor and working conditions and efforts to serve as a conduit for communicating workers' complaints to the management of enterprises or municipal labor bureaus. The ACFTU has shown itself concerned with protecting workers' living standards in areas such as unemployment insurance.

Before wage reform, workers' salaries were set according to a uniform national scale based on seniority and skills. Following wage reforms, a total wage bill for each collectively and state-owned enterprise is set by the Ministry of Labor according to four criteria: 1) As a percentage of profits, 2) as a contract amount with the local labor bureau, 3) for money losing enterprises, according to a state-set amount, and 4) as an enterprise-set amount subject to ministry review. Individual enterprises determine how to divide the total among the workers, a decision usually made by the enterprise manager in consultation with the enterprise party chief and the union representative. Worker congresses have mandated authority to review plans for wage reform, though these bodies serve primarily as rubber stamp organizations. Wages are generally equal for the same type of work within enterprises. Incentives are provided for increased productivity.

The old permanent employment system is giving way to a more flexible contract-based system. However, the percentage of workers laboring under contract is still low, approximately 40 percent nationwide in state enterprises. Under the Labor Contract System, individual workers may negotiate with management over contract terms. In practice, only the very few workers with highly technical skills are able to negotiate effectively on salary and fringe benefits issues.

Worker congresses, held periodically in most Chinese enterprises, theoretically have the authority to remove incompetent managers and approve major decisions affecting the enterprise, notably wage and bonus distribution systems. However, worker congresses generally take place once a year and serve essentially to rubberstamp agreements worked out among factory managers, party secretaries, and union representatives. In smaller enterprises it is not unusual to find these three posts held by the same person.

A dispute settlement procedure has been in effect since 1987. The procedure provides for two levels of arbitration committees and a final appeal to the courts. Of the 50,000 cases brought for arbitration in 1992, most were resolved at the first or second level, with less than 5 percent reaching the courts. According to Labor Ministry officials, most arbitration cases are filed by contract workers or their employers, an indication, they assert, that the new contract system provides a clearer set of ground rules which both sides can attempt to enforce.

Laws governing working conditions in China's special economic zones (SEZ's) are not significantly different from those in the rest of the country. However, wages in the SEZ's are significantly higher than in other Chinese enterprises. Unskilled laborers can expect much higher pay in southern China generally, but highly skilled workers are the main beneficiaries of the wage discrepancy.

The 1982 Trade Union Law prohibits antiunion discrimination and specifies that union representatives may not be transferred or terminated by enterprise management during their term of office. Unionized foreign businesses generally report pragmatic relations with ACFTU representatives. The ACFTU's stated goal is to establish unions in all foreign-funded enterprises within 2 to 3 years.

c. Prohibition of Forced or Compulsory Labor

Chinese penal policy emphasizes "reform first, production second," but compulsory labor is an integral part of the system both to rehabilitate prisoners and to help support the facilities. Almost all persons the courts sentence to prison, including political prisoners, are required to work, usually for little or no compensation. China also maintains a network of "reeducation through labor" camps (see Section 1.e.), the inmates of which generally must work. Reports from human rights organizations and released prisoners demonstrate that at least some persons in pretrial detention are also required to work. The number of workers in prison for nonviolent labor-related activity is not known. (See Section 1.e.) According to prison authorities, prisoners in labor reform institutions work a full 8-hour day and must also engage in both ideological and basic literacy and skills training. Justice officials have stated that in labor reeducation facilities there is a much heavier emphasis on education than on labor. Most reports conclude that work conditions in the penal system's light manufacturing factories are similar to those in ordinary factories, but conditions on farms and in mines can be harsh. As is the case nationwide, safety is often neglected, putting prisoners at risk, but there were no available figures for casualties in prison industry.

Some penal facilities contract with regular industries for prisoners to perform light manufacturing and assembly work. In 1992 Chinese newspapers reported that Chinese prison labor is used for many types of production (examples in parentheses), including heavy industry (coal, steel), light manufacturing (clothing, shoes, small machine tools), and agriculture (grain, tea, sugar cane). In 1991 the Chinese Government published a reiteration of its regulations barring the export of prison-made goods. On August 7, 1992, the U.S. and Chinese Governments signed a memorandum of understanding (MOU) prohibiting trade in prison labor products. The U.S. Customs Service has issued detention orders barring a number of products reportedly made by prisoners from entering the United States and detained several shipments of such goods in 1993. Under the MOU the Chinese have provided requested investigation reports on 31 suspected facilities. Five facilities investigated by the Chinese were found to have had prisoners engaged in some aspect of export production at some point in time, though not necessarily to the United States; of these, two with export activities at the time of the investigation reportedly received unspecified administrative sanctions. U.S. officials have conducted on-site visits of three suspected facilities and another facility visit has already been scheduled. The detention orders on two of the visited facilities were lifted, one in December 1993 and one in January 1994. The other case is still under study.

d. Minimum Age for Employment of Children

Regulations promulgated in 1987 prohibit the employment of school age minors who have not completed the compulsory 9 years of education. Press reports indicate that dropout rates for lower secondary schools (ages 12-15 years) in several southern provinces exceed 9 percent (the national average is 2.2 percent). This suggests the booming economy in that region is enticing more children to leave their studies to find jobs. In poorer, isolated areas, child labor in agriculture is widespread. Most independent observers agree with Chinese officials that China's urban child labor problem is relatively minor. No specific Chinese industry is identifiable as a significant violator of child labor regulations. In 1991 the State Council issued regulations imposing severe fines, withdrawal of business licenses, or jail for employers who hire laborers under 16 years of age.

e. Acceptable Conditions of Work

China does not have a labor code. A draft has been circulating since mid-1992. Due to the complexity of incorporating myriad existing regulations into the proposed unified code, it remains unclear if it will be made law. Labor regulations continue to be promulgated at both the national and provincial level, but they are not uniformly enforced.

There is no minimum wage in China. However, the Ministry of Labor is currently drafting minimum wage regulations. Anticipating the issuance of the regulations, some local governments, particularly those in more highly developed east coast areas, have already drafted regulations on minimum wages. On the higher end, in Zhuhai, Guangdong Province, the minimum monthly wage has been set at $62 (350 yuan at the official exchange rate). Generally the levels have been set to provide for a decent standard of living for a worker and his family. Minimum wage figures do not include free or heavily subsidized benefits which employing work units commonly provide in kind, such as housing, medical care, and education. Factories or ministries are required to pay 70 percent of final monthly wages to workers laid off because of a factory closing or reduction in force, but there have been numerous reports of violations of this policy.

The national standard workweek, excluding overtime, is 48 hours with a mandatory 24-hour rest period. In the past, 3 to 12 working hours per week were generally spent in political study or "education" on current social issues. In recent years, many factories have abandoned political study either for regular work or for an additional half day off each week. Starting in 1991, factories (including joint ventures) were allowed to adopt shorter workweeks. Despite laws mandating a standard 8-hour workday throughout the country, there continue to be reports of workers in the SEZ's regularly working 12 hours daily. Occupational health and safety are constant themes of posters and campaigns. Every work unit must designate a health and safety officer and the International Labor Organization has established a training program for these officials. Moreover, while the right to strike is not provided for in the 1982 Constitution, the Trade Union Law explicitly recognizes the right of unions to "suggest that staff and workers withdraw from sites of danger" and to participate in accident investigations. Labor officials reported that such withdrawals did occur sometimes in 1993. Nonetheless, pressures for increased output, lack of financial resources to maintain equipment, lack of concern by management, and a traditionally poor understanding of safety issues by workers have contributed to a continuing high rate of accidents. State prosecutors deal annually with thousands of negligence and accident cases. In November 1992, the Standing Committee of the National People's Congress passed a law on mining safety, which established standards and provided for enforcement, including fines and imprisonment. Labor officials were unable to provide statistics verifying the effects of the law, but they claimed that despite substantially increased across-the-board production in mining output, mine accidents were down in the first half of 1993.

More than 15,000 workers died in industrial accidents in 1992, 63 percent of them miners. Because of the lack of legislation to bring together diverse and often unpublished regulations in other health and safety areas, compliance with existing regulations is haphazard. Official Chinese press reports in July announced the issuance of a State Council circular stressing safety in production following "sharp increases in job accidents in the first half of this year." Officials blame the increases on lax enforcement of safety regulations in the rapidly expanding rural, foreign-funded, and private industry sectors.

As fires and explosions in southern China amply demonstrated in 1993, enforcement of China's safety regulations, particularly in the booming light industry sector, continued to be lax. In late November, 81 workers died in a blaze in a Shenzhen toy factory because safety precautions were not taken and warnings from the local labor ministry office had allegedly gone unheeded.

# Appendix 7

# Draft Text of "Peace Charter"

The "Peace Charter" was drafted by Qin Yongmin of Wuhan and issued in Beijing on November 14, 1993 after a meeting at which it was signed by eight other supporters. The eight included Yang Zhou, head of a human rights group in Shanghai; Zhou Guoqiang and QianYumin, veteran labor activists; Li Hai, a Beijing student leader; Liu Nianchun, brother of jailed Tiananmen student leader Liu Gang; and Chen Lu, Sha Yuguang and Song Shuyuan. In a statement issued after the meeting, the group said it meant to present the draft to the public for discussion and revision before a final version can be worked out. Qin and Zhou were arrested the next day and the other signers were never heard of again.

During the past 10 years and more, great changes have taken place in the structure of the economy of the mainland. We are deeply appreciative of such changes. However, as contemporary history has fully demonstrated, the rapid development of a market economy will inevitably lead to demand for pluralistic democracy. In view of the fact that the Cold War has ended in favor of a new world order and all Chinese are concerned about China's peaceful development in the future, we wish to put forward this charter.

Taking a broad view of the numerous precedents of political change in Chinese and world history, we cannot help but worry about the next stage of change in China. Since pluralistic democracy is the inevitable outcome of this historical process, we must ask the crucial question whether this process will take place in a peaceful or non-peaceful way in China.

We are convinced that leaders of great insight in the government of mainland China are similarly aware of this problem and its urgency. Historical lessons, both positive and negative, particularly those of the former Soviet Union and Eastern Europe, should be sufficient to prompt different parties of opposing views on the Chinese mainland to come to the following consensus:

The historic change from one-party dictatorship to pluralistic democracy can only be accomplished when the government is sincerely committed to it and then proceed to carry it out in an orderly way, thus keeping its negative impact, namely, its destructive effects on the people's social and economic life, to a minimum.

It should be pointed out that the global trends and the strong democratic forces in the world have not only made China's peaceful change a common desire but also provided the necessary conditions for its realization. The international and domestic situation today will not permit a repetition of the June 4th Incident of 1989 (Tiananmen Massacre). At the same time, justice and rationality certainly demand that the uncontrollable situation just prior to the June 4th Incident will never occur again.

The crux of the problem is that the change will inevitably impact the upper class and those with vested interests making them resistant to the change. Meanwhile, those who are victimized under the present system will likely turn radical. These two forces will have considerable negative impact on the process of peaceful and orderly political change.

As to the relations between the two sides of the Taiwan Strait, the question is not when or how the two sides will reach unification; rather, it is on what basis and what shared views will the two sides be unified.

It is against the above-mentioned background that we, a group of Chinese citizen imbued with a strong sense of mission, boldly urge the following upon the whole nation:

Let us follow the principle of "national interests above everything else," forsake past grudges, respect and accommodate one another, jointly delib-erate national issues, reach a grand reconciliation of the Chinese nation, pool our efforts to accomplish the great tasks of political change in mainland China and peaceful unification of the two sides of the Taiwan Strait.

We want to especially remind leaders both in and out of the government that no efforts should be spared at this point to prevent the contradictions in the course of the political change from degenerating into a situation of anarchy and civil war. In particular, the government must begin to take the initiatives now to ease the tension by following the trends of history. Otherwise, it must bear the responsibility for the above-mentioned eventuality.

In order to get out of the vicious cycles of China's political history in the past 100 years and in full consideration of the common and special interests of the people on both sides of the Taiwan Strait, we sincerely recommend the following workable steps to the governments on both sides of the Taiwan Strait and particularly the mainland government, all Chinese people at home and abroad including those in Hong Kong and Macao, and all groups dedicated to the goal of social progress:

First, we hold that the mainland government, representing China as a member of the U.N. Security Council, is obligated to observe all U.N. reso-lutions on human rights and should immediately enact laws and regulations according to contemporary international standards guaranteeing freedom of the person, of speech, of correspondence, of the press, of assembly and association (including lifting the ban on forming political parties), of procession and demonstration, of strike, and the freedom to enter and leave the country. It should also immediately abolish the "counterrevolutionary crime." All this should be carried out under the supervision of international bodies and public opinion.

As a goodwill response, we call on the people to keep their inalienable rights of assembly, procession and demonstration within the present lawful limits for the time being in order to reduce social unrest as the government begins the process of peaceful change.

Second, we call on the mainland government to demonstrate its boldness and vision by taking swift measures to guide the smooth transition from autocracy to pluralistic democracy, making sure that it is always in control of the situation.

Third, assuming that the mainland government accepts the above two points, we call on the Chinese people and all progressive elements at home and abroad to respect and cooperate with the mainland government as the only force capable of guiding the peaceful change on the mainland, making constructive suggestions while setting aside minor differences to work for reconciliation.

Fourth, we urge the mainland government to take the first necessary step toward reconciliation, namely, to reverse the verdict on the June 4th Incident by immediately releasing all political prisoners jailed because of involvement in the incident and providing adequate compensations to the families of the victims in the incident.

We call on the victims and their families to stop pursuing the matter further once the government shows a sincere desire toward reconciliation.

We appeal to the Chinese Communist Party and the government to lift the ban on all political exiles to allow students, scholars, labor activists and others in exile to return home.

We firmly believe that China's problems can only be solved by Chinese on their own soil. We therefore call on all those who are genuinely dedi-cated to the motherland to immediately return home to participate in the econ-omic modernization and political democratization.

The day when a law on association that measures up to international standards is promulgated and the ban on forming political parties is lifted will be the time for all nonviolent political groups at home and abroad to apply for registration according to law and we urge all such groups to do so at that time. For now, we call on everybody to abide by the principles of openness, legality and nonviolence to launch a tactful and measured ideological campaign in order to apply minimal pressure in the quest for human rights and democracy. The same principles should continue to apply when the groups are properly registered under the new law.

Seventh, we call on the governments across of the Taiwan Strait to immediately begin talks on equal footing. We believe the cohesive force of the Chinese nation provides a sufficient foundation for the unification of the mainland and Taiwan. Therefore, we appeal to the mainland government to abandon the use of force, to treat equally Taiwan's Kuomintang (the Nationalist Party), the Democratic and Progressive Party and other political parties and, when the time is ripe, to welcome Taiwan's political parties to come to the mainland, thus accomplishing the social and political integration across the Taiwan Strait.

At the same time, we also appeal to Taiwan's Democratic and Progressive Party to abandon its advocacy of "Taiwan Independence" and to devote itself instead to a democratic and progressive China inclusive of the mainland, Taiwan Hong Kong and Macao.

Eighth, we appeal to the mainland government to fully respect the autonomy of the people of Hong Kong and Macao by adhering to the dual principle of national sovereignty and local self-government, giving the people free choice of social, political and economic systems and their way of life.

Ninth, we call on the people of all nationalities across the land to work for the grand unity of the Chinese nation. At the same time, we appeal to the government to live up to international standards in handling problems concerning minority nationalities, to respect their right of self-determination and to refrain from the use of force to maintain unity.

Tenth, on the basis of the acceptance of the above-mentioned articles by all parties and by the mainland government above all, we propose the convening of a roundtable conference at an early date of leaders of mainland, Taiwan, Hong Kong and Macao and minority nationalities to discuss China's next stage of peaceful change and the peaceful unification across the Taiwan Strait. Depending on needs, bilateral or multilateral preliminary meetings may be held and separate meetings may be held on peaceful change and peaceful unification.

We believe the above proposals are in the fundamental interests of the Chinese people. They also represent a rational demand as China moves on to the next stage of its history. We especially urge that the mainland China under-stand our good intention and accept our appeal for national reconciliation.

We urge all Chinese nationals and all descendants of the Yellow Emperor in the world to join us in a common appeal for a peaceful political transformation on the mainland and a peaceful unification across the Taiwan Strait.

The "Peace Charter" is a free, open and informal body encompassing all Chinese at home and abroad who identify with the goals of this charter. Individually or collectively, it promotes open and lawful activities in the interests of peaceful transition to pluralistic democracy in a unified China.

The "Peace Charter" welcomes the support and participation of people at home and abroad who agree with its viewpoints. It will sponsor signing petitions, publicity campaigns and other activities allowed under the Constitution and other laws.

The "Peace Charter" attaches great importance to the fact that the Chinese Communist government is the only social force capable of leading the mainland's peaceful transition from autocracy to pluralistic democracy. We sincerely hope that it will take up this historic mission and not miss the last opportunity.

The measures proposed in the "Peace Charter" merely represent what in our judgment are possibly some of the feasible steps that can be taken. They are meant to be tentative. However, we are convinced that the essence of our position on peaceful change under the leadership of the present government conforms to the maximal interests of the Chinese people and the mainland government. Moreover, we are equally convinced that it represents the only rational choice for China today.

The signers of the "Peace Charter" come from all walks of life. As initiators, they jointly assume responsibility for the charter. Meanwhile, they have selected three members who will represent the "Peace Charter" in talks with the governments across the Taiwan Strait and serve as spokesmen for the Charter on all public occasions. All official documents issued by the Charter will be signed by the initiators or the spokesmen. All initiators have the obligations to accept signed petitions, take part in activities with the public, carry out designated tasks and share responsibility for the Charter.

Let us join all Chinese in our efforts to effect mainland China's peaceful change and the peaceful unification across the Taiwan Strait!

Source: *China Spring*, February 1994, pp. 68–70. Translated by Ta-ling Lee.

# Appendix 8

# International Cooperation on Human Rights

### A Reasonable and Practical Choice

In a recent interview with our staff reporter Zhang Xiaodong, Chinese human rights specialist Fan Guoxiang gave an analysis of the current distortion of the human rights issue and concluded that international cooperation is the most reasonable and practical way to promote human rights.

**QUESTION: Respect for human rights and fundamental freedom is widely regarded as an important issue by all countries in the world. But unfortunately it has been used by some countries as an excuse to practice power politics. Can the universal significance of human rights be interpreted as a common human rights standard?**

**ANSWER:** The understanding and appreciation of human rights have undergone a historical process. In this century, especially during World War II, the armed aggression against and military occupation of other countries by the German, Italian and Japanese fascists brought about untold sorrow to millions of innocent people. There were no human rights in the occupied countries and regions, and the people in the fascist countries were also stripped of their human rights.

Reflecting on the scourges of war, the Charter of the United Nations solemnly stipulates, "To develop friendly relations among nations based on respect for the principle of equal rights and self-determination of peoples" and "to achieve international cooperation...in promoting and encouraging respect for human rights and for fundamental freedoms for all without distinction as to race, sex, language or religion."

The United Nations has also adopted some other international human rights instruments which have given, for the first time, a number of specifications to human rights.

Respect for and promotion of human rights are significantly important to all countries, in the West or East, developed or developing. However, during the Cold-War period, human rights were used to serve the West-East confrontations.

In recent years, human rights have been further distorted by some countries which have used the human rights issue as an instrument to perform power politics and force other nations to accept their human rights formula as the so-called common standard, turning the universal value of human rights into a uniform and predetermined human rights formula.

Historically, certain religions persecuted and proselytized others in order to spread their rule to the ends of the globe. There were also claims that some nationalities were superior to others. Although powerful political and military forces were exploited to carry out such policies using all kinds of excuses, these blatant violations of human rights were continually cast aside by the people.

The present world is a multicolored one. Different cultures and state systems and government forms co-exist. Insisting that some way of life or specific values should be a common standard and claiming that some governments through certain methods of elections are democratic and others are not have confused the universal significance of human rights with the common standard of human rights. It is designed to force the developing countries to take in the so-called common standard by putting pressures and imposing sanctions on these countries.

In history, the religious fanatics and those who advocated ethnic superiority were proved wrong. At present, any attempt to impose a single human rights standard on the world will also lead nowhere.

Many specialists have pointed out that some people claim to support democracy in other countries, but they are far from being democratic in the international arena. They vigorously support dissidents in other nations, but they are internationally intolerant of different views on human rights, demonstrating their hegemonist behavior.

Human rights is universally significant, but it cannot be twisted to claim that there is only one standard. The concept of universal values for human rights is quite different from that of a common standard of human rights.

**QUESTION: The specific situation of human rights differs from nation to nation. Under such circumstances, how can we embody the universal value of human rights while respecting the diversity of human rights in each country?**

**ANSWER:** For a long time, the human rights issue has been politicized and distorted. It became a political instrument in the Cold-War confrontation. This practice should be cast aside. The only reasonable and feasible way to promote human rights is, as stipulated by the UN Charter, through international cooperation.

Various countries should discuss, exchange views and consult on human rights, rather than resorting to attacks and charges against each other. When a consensus is reached in some areas and conditions mature, international conventions may be signed and the signatories should be legally bound to the stipulations of those documents.

Concrete cooperation may be achieved through bilateral, multilateral, regional and global meetings to exchange the experiences of each country.

Before the 1993 Human Rights Conference was convened in Vienna, there were regional meetings in Asia, Africa and Latin America, which have proved to be beneficial to reflecting the views on the promotion of human rights from different regions.

International cooperation in human rights may encompass a wide range of activities. Discussions between countries may include, inter alia, individual human rights and collective human rights; people's rights and obligations in society; personal freedom and national security; political rights and economic rights; relationships between human rights, development and peace; protection of the rights of minority nationalities and indigenous populations; and protection of the rights of women, children and the handicapped. The discussions may be conducted from different points of views, taking into account divergent historical backgrounds. But it is improper to arbitrarily say someone is 100 percent correct and others totally wrong.

It needs to be noted that discussions should be held with all participants enjoying an equal status. Equality is the basis for cooperation. Although history, tradition and the present situation differ from state to state, each country has made specific contributions to human rights. The developing countries should be aware of the practices in developed countries. At the same time, they can relate their experiences to the developed countries so that both sides can learn from the successes and mistakes of the other. But it is inappropriate to assert that some countries are advanced in promotion of human rights and other backward, and that the former should be the educator and investigator and the latter the educated and investigated.

In the international human rights field there must be a strict distinction between humanitarian assistance and humanitarian intervention.

International armed conflicts, natural disasters and other uncontrollable forces have caused great harm to the people of the affected areas. The United Nations and some other international organizations have provided assistance to the victims so as to ease their misery. This is positive, beneficial and welcome.

But some countries, with their own political motives, have deliberately engaged in humanitarian intervention in the name of rendering assistance, going as far as to send troops to extend so-called aid that finally results in the escalation of war. This runs counter to the original intention and deepens the misery of the victims.

The negative effect of humanitarian intervention has put the United Nations and some other international organizations in a dilemma and their prestige has been damaged. Humanitarian intervention has invited widespread opposition from the international community. More and more people are concerned that, far from promoting human rights and fundamental freedoms, this type of power politics practiced in the name of humanitarianism will bring about more serious international tension and instability. Therefore, humanitarian assistance is welcome and humanitarian intervention should be opposed.

**Source:** *Beijing Review*, March 14-20, 1994, pp. 9–10.

# Appendix 9

# An Appeal From Seven Intellectuals

On March 9, 1994, seven leading intellectuals signed an appeal to President Jiang Zemin and Chairman Qiao Shi of the National People's Congress, calling for respect of human rights and release of all political prisoners. The seven were led by Xu Liangying, a member of the Academy of Sciences, the highest research institute in China. Xu, 74, is a respected historian of science who translated Albert Einstein's collected works into Chinese. Other signers of the appeal were Ding Zilin and Jiang Peikun, philosophy professors whose son was killed during the June 1989 Massacre in Tiananmen; Shao Yanxiang, a poet; Zhang Kangkang, a writer; Liu Liao, a physicist; and Professor Xu's wife, Wang Laide, a historian. All came under surveillance and harassment by public security police after the publication of the appeal.

May 9, 1994

President Jiang Zemin and Chairman Qiao Shi:

Recently, many people in Beijing and Shanghai have been arrested or detained for interrogation because of problems concerning their ideas and speeches. These incidents have caused grave concern in world opinion. People of learning who are concerned with the fate of the nation and dedicated to the modernization of our country are shocked and deeply disturbed and worried.

Looking at human history, it is clear that modern civilization began with the modernization of the people whey they awoke to their destiny and began to struggle to free themselves from under the ideological yoke of ancient and medieval tyranny. They became aware that individuals should have independent identity and dignity and should enjoy certain inalienable and inviolable rights, the foremost of which is the right to freedom of thought and speech. This is at the heart of modern concept of human rights. Therefore, to talk about modernization without mentioning human rights is like "climbing up a tree to look for fish." (Translator's note: "Climbing up a tree to look for fish" or yuanmu qiuyu is a class expression meaning to make a futile effort.)

Two hundred and five years ago, the French Declaration of the Rights of Man and the Citizen clearly stated that "ignorance, neglect and disdain of the rights of man is the sole cause of misfortune of the general public and corruption in government." China's past and present also testify to this everlasting truth.

Following the victory of the antifascist war in the 1940s, striving for and safeguarding of human rights have become a common goal of the people of the whole world. The Universal Declaration of Human Rights, adopted by the United Nations in 1948, states:

> Every one has the rights to life, liberty and the security of person;
> No one should be subjected to arbitrary arrest, detention or exile;
> Everyone has the right to freedom of thought, conscience and religion;
> Everyone has the right to freedom of opinion and expression.

As a founding member of the United Nations and a permanent member of its Security Council, China should be at the forefront in observing all U.N. covenants concerning human rights rather than the target of international criticism because of its domestic human rights problems.

For this reason we appeal to the authorities to summon the courage to end our country's long history of punishing people for their ideas and speeches. Only through respecting human rights and guaranteeing the citizens all their rights can there be a truly stable society. Otherwise, contradictions will only intensify, leading to uncontrollable turmoil.

Xu Liangying

Wang Laidi

Ding Zilin

Jiang Peikun

Shao Yanxiang

Liu Liao

Zhang Kangkang

Source: *Beijing Spring*, May 1994, p. 6. Translated by Ta-ling Lee.

# Appendix 10

# China Leads the US in Human Rights

by Yu Quanyu

China's human rights conditions have fundamentally improved. The people are now the masters of their own country. We have won independence for our nation and realized equality between the sexes and for all ethnic nationalities. People's rights for a decent life and liberty are properly guaranteed, and living standards are rising year by year.

Due to inadequate natural resources and low economic and cultural development, China's human rights conditions are far from satisfactory. There are still shortcomings and problems, and sometimes cases of human rights violations do occur.

However, an all-round comparison will show that China is in many fields ahead of the United States in human rights protection. Although there is a big gap in resources and economic strength between China and the United States, the following illustrates the two nations' human rights records:

**Life security.** In 1990, 9.37 out of every 100,000 people were murdered in the United States, while in China the figure was less than two in 100,000. In the United States, 300 in every 100,000 were injured in attempted murders, while in China the figure was seven in 100,000. More than 70 women in every 100,000 in the United States were raped, while the figure was four in 100,000 in China.

**Homeless people.** In January this year, the US government admitted that there are 7 million homeless people living in the United States, and 3 million of them sleep in the open. We have 150,000 homeless people in China.

**Number of prisoners.** The United States, with a population of 260 million, has 1.1 million people serving jail terms, 455 out of every 100,000, which is a world record. Yet in China the ratio was only 99 to 100,000 in 1990, less than one fourth of that in the United States.

**Death rate of prisoners.** The death rate of Chinese prisoners in 1993 is 2.87 per thousand, and the rate for unnatural death is 0.24 per thousand, much less than that in the United States. This means the management of prisons in China is humanitarian.

**The number of repeat offenders among released prisoners.** The American rate is 41 percent and the Chinese rate is 8 percent. This can be an indicator that China does a better job in educating criminals.

**Equality for all ethnic nationalities.** China advocates not only national equality but also preferential treatment for ethnic minorities.

**Women's status.** The US government has admitted that the social status of female Americans in the United States is not as good as that of women in China. In the people's congresses at various levels, women make up over 20 percent of the deputies, while in the United States, the highest rate for women in the congresses is 18.4 percent.

The United States has not yet subscribed to the International Treaty of Eradicating All Forms of Racial Discrimination, the International Treaty of Prohibiting and Punishing Racial Segregation or the Treaty of Eradicating All Forms of Discrimination against Women. China has subscribed to all of them and faithfully complies with all their obligations.

In short, China has done a great deal for human rights, and in some aspects it has done better than America. Naturally, there is still a lot more for us to do before our ultimate goal is reached. However, the United States cannot resolve its own issues on human rights in a short period.

**Source:** Yu, Quanyu, "China Leads the US in Human Rights," *Beijing Review*, October 3-9, 1994.

# Appendix 11

## Interview with Zhu Muzhi

Philip Shenon, chief Beijing correspondent of the US-based The New York Times, recently interviewed Zhu Muzhi, chairman of the China Human Rights Society. The following presents Zhu's answers to questions posed by Shenon.

**ZHU MUZHI**: I will call on personal experience to answer your question concerning the status quo of human rights in China. I have lived in Beijing since the 1930s and have personally witnessed the tremendous changes taking place in China. About six decades ago, savage Japanese aggression pushed Beijing to the brink of being reduced to a colony. Under brutal of Japanese aggression, Chinese people lacked any guarantee of their lives, let alone the dignity as human beings. Ordinary Chinese living in occupied areas were forced to kowtow to Japanese soldiers, while citizens in unoccupied areas lived from hand to mouth, suffering from hunger and cold. As a result, young Chinese students and hundreds of millions of civilians rose to launch resistance movements. The Declaration of Independence of your country says that all people enjoy certain untransferable rights endowed by the "Creator", including the right to life and liberty, as well as the right to pursue happiness. However, during the dark years of Japanese aggression, Chinese people were deprived of such rights. Today, the conditions of the Chinese people have reversed completely. To eat their fill and dress warmly, a goal cherished by the Chinese people for centuries, have basically been accomplished. Today's China enjoys an unprecedentedly fine situation. Tilling 7 percent of the world's total cultivated land, China has nevertheless succeeded in feeding 22 percent of the world's total population and has basically solved the problem regarding the right to subsistence of the Chinese people. Just think it over how many hundreds of millions of people throughout the world are still not guaranteed the right to subsistence, you will be able to understand how extraordinary the achievements scored by China are. China's effort to improve human rights has also been a great contribution to the development of global human rights undertakings. Of course, it does not mean that China's human rights situation is perfect. In fact, current circumstances of human rights in China fall far short of the lofty goal and demand. There are many aspects requiring us to devote arduous effort to making improvements.

SHENON: Since the US government dissociated human rights from the annual extension of the MFN trade status, do you think China will in the future assume a more intransigent attitude toward the human rights issue in the future?

ZHU: It has nothing to do with intransigence. We respect facts, or, in other words, approach things as they stand.

SHENON: In your opinion, why does China have a poor reputation worldwide in terms of human rights?

ZHU: In my opinion, we must first analyze which countries and who on earth have said that China's human rights situation is undesirable. Judging from the outcome of several international conferences on human rights, countries which oppose and attack China at the meetings are in the minority, with most attacks coming from Western countries. However, those making the most violent attacks against China represent a tiny handful of Western countries. Therefore, you can't say that China has a bad reputation in the world. According to my observations, different circumstances exist with regard to countries which claim that china's human rights status is bad. Some countries have no real knowledge of the reality in China, but they have believed various rumors and slanders. Some have set demands on China in accordance with their own standards. This is what we refer to as a situation in which "the well-fed don't know how the starving suffer", as I told the chief editor of your newspaper's editorial department during his last visit. Still others have an axe to grind, and hence they are truly concerned about the human rights issue in China.

SHENON: You have politely used diplomatic jargon and have not mentioned the United States by name. May I ask whether or not you think the United States has been a thorn for China in regard to the human rights issue?

ZHU: One point in your question is quite important. That is whether the issue of human rights will affect diplomatic relations between China and other countries. We hold that the human rights issue has certain international involvements, but it is essentially a matter within the domestic jurisdiction of a country. Therefore, the human rights issue should not affect relationships between various countries, unless problems regarding human rights endanger international peace and security. Neither China's concept of human rights, nor its practices related to guaranteeing human rights, have done harm to the interests of the United States. If the Sino-US relations are held up because of the human rights issue, it will be harmful to both sides. It is so wise of President Clinton to unhook human rights from the annual extension of MFN trade status. Since then, economic and trade relations between the two countries have witnessed marked progress. It is of great benefit to both, isn't it? Nonetheless, it seems that the United States will hold fast to the issue. I wonder to which direction it intends to lead the relationship between the two countries, and what on earth will benefit the United States by doing so.

SHENON: What would have been the outcome had President Clinton made an opposite decision?

ZHU: An old Chinese saying goes that "a person lifts a rock only to drop it on his own ties". Some Americans have noted that China is a huge market. The United States would lose this vast market if it canceled China's MFN trade status. In case the United States withdraws from the market, other countries would not follow. On the contrary, they would think it an opportunity the United States has given them. Under this scenario, had the United States wanted to re-enter the Chinese market in the future, it would have been by no means as easy as before because most niches would have been filled. That's why I say that President Clinton made a wise decision and refrained from reaping a whirlwind by sowing the wind.

SHENON: What is your opinion on one country commenting on the human rights situation of another country?

ZHU: We hold that the issue of human rights by and large falls under the sovereignty of an individual country. Owing to differences in historical background, cultural tradition, social customs and habits, religious beliefs and economic development, situations in different countries vary greatly. Therefore, the human rights issue is highly complex, and it is far from easy to evaluate correctly and objectively the human rights situation in a given country. The Chinese government has refrained form casually making carping comments on the human rights situations in other countries. However, this does not mean that we show no care for the human rights issue in other countries. Due to differing circumstances, each country has its own merits and shortcomings in terms of human rights. We maintain that various countries should enhance dialogue to promote mutual understanding and draw on the successful experiences of others through exchange of views. This approach will be of greater benefit to the improvement of the human rights situation the world over. The US State Department publishes a report annually, evaluating the human rights situation in 193 countries. In my opinion, the United States might have been too bold by doing so.

SHENON: How do you comment on the human rights situation in the United States?

ZHU: I don't think that the human rights status in the United States is perfect in every respect, with a case in point being racial discrimination. While the United States finds fault with the human rights situation in other countries, in fact it has its own shortcomings.

SHENON: What will China do to improve the human rights situation?

ZHU: The solution to the problem regarding to the right to subsistence and development will remain a major issue in the coming years due to the fact that 80 million Chinese are still living under the line of sufficiency of food and clothing, which is not a small number. Politically, we will further strengthen the construction of socialist democracy and improve the people's congress system. I think the people's congress system is the most suitable for national conditions in China. Hence, China cannot adopt the American political system. The two party system is perhaps the most appropriate for the United States.

SHENON: I've personally witnessed tremendous economic progress in China. In the future, will China advance in terms of freedom of speech?

ZHU: The economic boom in China fully demonstrates that the Chinese people enjoy more political rights and freedom. In fact, Chinese people have full freedom of speech in regard to how to go about building the country. At present, China has more than 7,000 newspapers and periodicals. In China, a saying, which is popular with both the government and the masses goes that "human beings are the decisive factor". This is our code of conduct. Yet another slogan reads, "having faith in the masses, respecting the masses and relying on the masses". It is also known as "following the mass line". Our principle of "from the masses, to the masses". In other words, when making decisions, we must solicit and summarize extensive opinions from the masses. Formulated policies are presented to the masses for test. Simply because China has followed this principle, the Chinese people have supported the policies of the government. Why have China's revolution and construction scored such great success? Why has the Chinese economy witnessed such rapid growth? The answer lies in the fact that the Party and the government have won the endorsement and support of the people. Would the people support the government if they had been restrained and deprived of their democratic rights and if their opinions had not been accepted? This is why I contend that foreign opinions saying that China has scored economic expansion, but has no political freedom, are obviously misguided and do not explain the actual situation in China.

SHENON: The heart of the human rights issue the Americans are concerned about centers on political prisoners. Do you think certain Chinese people have been jailed simply because of their different political viewpoints?

ZHU: I don't think so. In China, only those who violate criminal laws are prosecuted. The counterrevolutionary crimes in China are clearly defined in the criminal code, which include murder, arson and robbery. I hope you will delve in to the aspects related to counterrevolutionary crimes in China's Criminal Law and introduce overseas readers the true reality in China. As far as I now, no country in the world publishes regular reports concerning the status of prisoners, nor does any country submit to demands that the government provide details about a specific prisoner. Demanding such information simply represents an act of disrespect for the sovereignty of other countries.

**Source:** *Beijing Review*, Dec 12-18, 1994.

# Appendix 12

# China Human Rights Practices, 1994
# U.S. Department of State (February 1995)

The People's Republic of China (PRC) is an authoritarian state in which the Chinese Communist Party (CCP) monopolizes decisionmaking authority. Almost all top civilian, police, and military positions at the national and regional levels are held by party members. A 22-member Politburo and retired senior leaders hold ultimate power, but economic decentralization has increased the authority of regional officials. Socialism continues to provide the ideological underpinning, but Marxist ideology has given way to pragmatism in recent years. The party's authority rests primarily on the success of economic reform, its ability to maintain stability, and control of the security apparatus.

The security apparatus comprises the Ministries of State Security and Public Security, the People's Armed Police, the People's Liberation Army, and the state judicial, procuratorial, and penal systems. The Constitution protects fundamental human rights, but they are frequently ignored in practice, and challenges to the CCP's political authority are often dealt with harshly and arbitrarily. Legal safeguards for those detained or imprisoned are inadequate and inconsistently implemented. The Government attaches higher priority to maintaining public order and suppressing political opposition than to enforcing legal norms. As a result, security forces are responsible for numerous human rights abuses, including arbitrary detention, forced confessions, and torture.

More than a decade of rapid economic growth has raised living standards and enabled growing numbers of Chinese to assume greater control over their own lives. The scope for private economic activity has expanded rapidly, and the degree of government and party control over the economy has continued to decline. Although many details remain to be worked out, and the pace of privatization has been uneven, many elements of the old planned economy have already been dismantled. Income disparities between coastal regions and the interior are significant and growing, but overall there has been a sharp drop in the number of Chinese living in absolute poverty. Greater disposable income, looser ideological controls, and freer access to outside sources of information have led to more diversity in cultural life and media reporting. Government control of information media now depends to an increasing extent on self-censorship to regulate political and social content, but the authorities also consistently penalize those who exceed the permissible.

In 1994 there continued to be widespread and well-documented human rights abuses in China, in violation of internationally accepted norms, stemming both from the authorities' intolerance of dissent and the inadequacy of legal safeguards for freedom of speech, association, and religion. Abuses include arbitrary and lengthy incommunicado detention, torture, and mistreatment of prisoners. Despite a reduction during the year in the number of political detainees from the immediate post-Tiananmen period, hundreds, perhaps thousands, of other prisoners of conscience remain imprisoned or detained. The Government still has not provided a comprehensive, credible public accounting of all those missing or detained in connection with the suppression of the 1989 demonstrations. Chinese leaders moved swiftly to cut off organized expressions of protest or criticism and detained government critics, including those advocating greater worker rights. Citizens have no ability peacefully to change their government leaders or the form of government. Criminal defendants are denied basic legal safeguards such as due process or adequate defense. The regime continued severe restrictions on the freedoms of speech, press, assembly and association, and tightened controls on the exercise of these rights during 1994. Serious human rights abuses persisted in Tibet and other areas populated by ethnic minorities.

The human rights situation in 1994 was, however, marked by the same diversity that characterizes other aspects of Chinese life. In several instances, the Government acted to bring its behavior into conformity with internationally accepted human rights norms. These actions included releasing several prominent political and religious prisoners, granting passports to some critics of the regime and their relatives, and adopting a law, which became effective in January 1995, that allows citizens to recover damages from the Government for infringement of their rights. The Government continued to acknowledge the need to implement the rule of law and build the necessary legal and other institutions, but it has not yet significantly mitigated continuing repression of political dissent. In 1994 China also continued a human rights dialog with some foreign critics, and reaffirmed its adherence to the Universal Declaration of Human Rights. Chinese officials provided limited information about the status of several hundred specific cases of international concern.

Respect for Human Rights

Section 1  Respect for the Integrity of the Person, Including
         Freedom from:

a. Political and Other Extrajudicial Killing

It is impossible to determine the number of extrajudicial killings by government officials in 1994 or the adequacy of the government response, since the Government restricts access to such information. There were individual accounts of such killings, including some carried in the Chinese press. Credible reports from international human rights organizations indicate a Tibetan nun died on June 4 in a prison hospital, reportedly as a result of a beating by guards. In May Tibetan officials reported that a former public security official in Tibet was sentenced to 9 years for causing the death of a suspect while torturing him to obtain a confession. In Fujian, a public security official was also prosecuted for torturing a prisoner to death, but no details on his sentence were provided. In December the Chinese press reported that a city police chief in Shanxi province was sentenced to 5 years for malpractice after ordering the detention and beating of two Chinese for allegedly complaining about the police chief's son. One detainee died from his injuries. Two other police officials were sentenced to death and life imprisonment, respectively, for extorting a confession in the same case. Legislators in Guangdong province also reported two cases of death by torture, but there were no details on the disposition of the cases.

### b. Disappearance

There were no reported cases in 1994 in which individuals who disappeared were suspected to have been killed by officials. The Government still has not provided a comprehensive, credible public accounting of all those missing or detained in connection with the suppression of the 1989 Tiananmen demonstrations.

### c. Torture and Other Cruel, Inhuman, or Degrading Treatment or Punishment

Police and other elements of the security apparatus continue to employ torture and degrading treatment in dealing with detained and imprisoned persons. Both official Chinese sources and international human rights groups reported many instances of torture. Persons detained pending trial were particularly at risk as a result of government failure to correct obvious systemic weaknesses in the design and operation of the legal system. These weaknesses include a reliance on confessions as a basis for convictions and the lack of access to prisoners by legal counsel and family members until after formal charges are brought, a step which often takes months. Former detainees have credibly reported that officials used cattle prods, electrodes, prolonged periods of solitary confinement and incommunicado detention, beatings, shackles, and other forms of abuse against detained men and women. There are credible reports that some women detainees in Tibet have been tortured, but female prisoners do not appear to have been targeted for rape.

In March the Supreme People's Procuratorate reported it had investigated 378 cases where torture was used to extract confessions in 1993, but it provided no information on convictions or punishments. The number of actual incidents of torture and ill-treatment by government officials is almost certainly far greater than this number. In one case, a policeman was given a 1-year suspended sentence for beating Yan Zhengxue, an artist who was also a municipal people's congress deputy from Jiaojiang in Zhejiang province. In May legislators in Guangdong province identified 838 cases of police corruption and brutality, but Chinese press accounts reported that only 50 of the cases had been "corrected." According to Chinese officials, the Procuratorate has a total of 748 officials in China's jails, "reform through labor," and "reeducation through labor" facilities. Their responsibility is to supervise prison management and enforce laws on treatment of prisoners. Procuratorial offices or officers are assigned to approximately 94 percent of prisons and labor camps. Another 7,000 officials are responsible for supervising China's detention centers.In January Justice Minister Xiao Yang announced plans to modernize 80 percent of China's prisons and reform through labor facilities by the year 2000.

Conditions in Chinese penal institutions are generally harsh and frequently degrading, and nutritional and health conditions are sometimes grim. Adequate medical care for prisoners continues to be a problem, despite official assurances that prisoners have the right to prompt medical treatment if they become ill. In 1994 political prisoners who reportedly had difficulties in obtaining timely and adequate medical care included Bao Tong, Ren Wanding, and Qin Yongmin. Wang Juntao was allowed to go to the United States for medical treatment in April, and Chen Ziming was released on medical parole in May, although he remains at home under heavy surveillance.

Conditions of imprisonment for political prisoners vary widely. According to credible reports, some detained dissidents continue to be incarcerated in psychiatric institutions and treated with drugs. Dissidents such as Wang Wanxing, Wang Miaogen (who had chopped off four of his fingers in a protest in 1993 over alleged persecution), and Xing Jiandong are reportedly being held in mental hospitals in Beijing and Shanghai. However, the lack of independent outside access to such persons made it impossible to verify their diagnoses or medical treatment or the conditions under which they are being held.

Political prisoners are also often incarcerated with common criminals. Chinese press reports claimed that Zheng Musheng, a Christian, was beaten to death by fellow inmates, who were then arrested. His widow filed suit against local public security officials after Zheng died in custody in early 1994. Unspecified "action" was taken against prison supervisory personnel. There were credible reports that dissident Qin Yongmin was severely beaten twice by fellow inmates in a reeducation through labor facility in June. According to these reports, he failed to receive adequate medical care after the beatings.

China does not permit independent monitoring of prison conditions. The Procuratorate, charged with law enforcement in the corrections system, reported 39,342 law violations in prisons, 17,823 of which were corrected. China held two rounds of talks with the International Committee of the Red Cross in January and April to discuss access to prisoners, but no agreement was reached. In February five American journalists were permitted to visit a Liaoning labor camp where political prisoner Liu Gang is held. The journalists saw Liu through a window but were not allowed to interview him. Reports persist that Liu suffers ill health as a result of beatings and other mistreatment, although Chinese officials have denied these allegations. In February a member of the China Human Rights Society, an organization established primarily to study and defend China's human rights record, was allowed to meet Liu and review his medical records in an attempt to refute reports that he had been mistreated.

### d. Arbitrary Arrest, Detention, or Exile

Because the Government tightly controls information, it is impossible to estimate accurately the total number of people subjected to new or continued arbitrary arrest or detention. According to one Chinese media report from 1992, authorities have carried out close to 1 million detentions annually in recent years under a form of detention known as "shelter for investigation." They released some people without charge after several days or weeks. In some cases, they charged dissidents with "disturbing public order" or "causing social turmoil" and sentenced them to 1 to 3 years of detention without independent judicial review (see Section 1.e.).

Under China's Criminal Procedure Law, officials may hold detainees for up to 10 days before a formal arrest warrant must be approved by the Procuratorate; they must notify the detainee's family or work unit within 24 hours. Exceptions to these provisions include the sweeping provision that notification may be withheld if it would "hinder the investigation" of a case. On May 12, the Government issued revised public order regulations setting out penalties for social groups that fail to register with the proper authorities or for persons on parole or deprived of political rights who "violate regulations," as well as for several other offenses. With some exceptions, violators can be detained for up to 15 days and fined about $23 (RMB200). In 1994 authorities detained dissidents before high-level visits of foreign leaders, but it is not clear whether the new public order regulations were the basis for these detentions. Most of those detained were released shortly after the visits ended. Others were held for longer periods or detained formally.

In practice, authorities often disregard or circumvent limits on detention by using regulations on "taking in for shelter and investigation," "supervised residence," and other methods not requiring procuratorial approval. Dissident Wei

Jingsheng has been held incommunicado in supervised residence since April 1. Credible reports indicate that police detained several other political activists, including Dai Xuezhong, Xiao Biguang, Zhou Qianbing, and Zhu Fuming, for months without filing charges against them. Wang Dan and others were also detained briefly without charge several times during 1994.

Local officials and business leaders frequently conspire to use detentions as a means of exerting pressure in commercial disputes; cases in some areas have reportedly increased 50 percent over 1993. Authorities held Hong Kong business-man Chong Kwee-Sung for 30 months in Henan while his case was being "investigated," then released him in February without charges being filed. Australian businessman James Peng was kidnaped by public security officials in Macao and brought to China, where he was held for several months before being tried in November. Chinese officials said his detention was legal because it was approved by the National People's Congress Standing Committee, which has apparently not been the case in other commercial dispute cases.

In March Procurator General Zhang Siying reported on the problem of prisoners kept in prison past their release dates, noting that 34,432 of 73,416 such cases had been corrected. The legality of detentions can be challenged under the Administrative Procedure Law, but since detainees do not have access to lawyers, they have been unable to use this law to obtain prompt judicial determination of the legality of their detentions. The new State Compensation Law, passed in May, clarified the right of citizens to recover damages for illegal detentions. Even before the law took effect on January 1, 1995, the Chinese press reported a decision by a Beijing lower court awarding damages to a law professor who was illegally detained and beaten by public security officials in May. In June a Fujian court awarded damages in a case of illegal "taking in for shelter and investigation." There is no judicially supervised system of bail, but at the discretion of public security officials, some detainees are released pending further investigation.

e.  Denial of Fair Public Trial

According to the Constitution, the court system is equal in authority to the State Council and the Central Military Commission, the two most important government institutions. All three organs are nominally under the supervision of the National People's Congress (NPC). The Supreme People's Court stands at the apex of the court system, followed in descending order by the higher, intermediate, and basic people's courts. Judges are appointed by the people's congresses at the corresponding level. There are special courts for handling military, maritime, and railway transport cases.

Officials insist that China's judiciary is independent but acknowledge that it is subject to the Communist Party's policy guidance. In practice, party and government leaders use a variety of means to influence court verdicts and sentences. Corruption and conflicts of interest also affect judicial decision-making. In March Supreme Court officials acknowledged problems with local protectionism and failure to conduct fair trials, particularly in economic disputes. The Chinese press publicized a 1993 economic case in which the court told the parties the decision was already written before the parties had finished producing their evidence.

In practice, officials often ignore due process rights granted by the Constitution. Both before and after trial, prisoners are subjected to severe psychological pressure to confess their "errors." Defendants who fail to "show the right attitude" by confessing their crimes are typically sentenced more harshly. Persons appearing before a court are not presumed innocent; despite official denials, trials are essentially sentencing hearings. Confessions without corroborating evidence are insufficient for a conviction under Chinese law, but coerced confessions are not automatically excluded as evidence.

Accused persons are given virtually no opportunity to prepare an adequate defense while their cases are being investigated, a time when the question of guilt or innocence is essentially decided. The law provides that defense lawyers may be retained 7 days before trial. However, in some cases, even this brief period is shortened under regulations issued in 1983 to accelerate the adjudication of certain serious criminal cases. Under Chinese law, there is no requirement that the court appoint a defense attorney for the defendant unless the defendant is hearing impaired or a minor, although the court may appoint defense counsel if it feels an attorney is necessary. When attorneys do appear, they have little time to prepare a defense and rarely contest guilt; their function is generally confined to requesting clemency. The conviction rate is over 90 percent. The court's permission is required before the accused or his representative can interrogate witnesses, produce new witnesses, or review evidence.

In some regions, experimentation with the trial system is underway. Shanghai court officials announced plans in August in some criminal and civil cases to expand an experiment with a more adversarial system, which gives attorneys more responsibility for presenting evidence and arguing the facts during trials.

Chinese officials state that China has insufficient numbers of lawyers to meet the country's growing needs. Knowledgeable observers report that defense attorneys appear in only a small number of criminal trials. As a key element in its legal reform plans, China plans to increase the number of lawyers to 150,000 by the year 2000. As of July, there were 70,515 lawyers working in 5,885 law firms. In many cities, private law firms are being organized outside the framework of established government legal offices. These firms are self-regulating and do not have their personnel or budgets determined directly by the State. At the end of 1993, there were 502 such firms. However, many defense lawyers, like other Chinese, still depend on an official work unit for employment, housing, and other benefits. They are therefore often reluctant to be viewed as overzealous in defending individuals accused of political offenses. In some sensitive cases, relatives of defendants have reportedly found it difficult to hire defense lawyers.

The Criminal Procedure Law requires that all trials be held in public, except those involving state secrets, juveniles, or "personal secrets." Details of cases involving "counterrevolutionary" charges, however, have frequently been kept secret, even from defendants' relatives, under this provision. The 1988 Law on State Secrets affords a ready basis for denying a public trial. Hong Kong reporter Xi Yang's trial in March on the charge of stealing state secrets was not open to the public (see Section 2.a.). In November journalist Gao Yu was sentenced to 6 years in prison for "leaking state secrets," allegedly published in the Hong Kong press. Gao's lawyer and her relatives said they had not been notified of the final trial or sentencing hearing (the case had been returned twice for insufficient evidence). There is an appeals process, but initial decisions are rarely overturned, and appeals generally do not provide meaningful protection against arbitrary or erroneous verdicts. Under the Criminal Procedure Law, persons "exempted from prosecution" by procurators may still be deemed to have a criminal record, despite the lack of a judicial determination of guilt. Such provisions can be applied in "counterrevolutionary crimes" as well as in ordinary criminal offenses.

Lack of due process is particularly egregious when defendants receive the death sentence. Chinese officials refuse to provide comprehensive statistics on death sentences or executions, but hundreds of executions are officially reported annually. The actual numbers may be much higher. All death sentences are nominally reviewed by a higher court. Reviews are usually completed within a few days after sentencing and consistently result in a perfunctory confirmation of sentence. No executions for political offenses are known to have occurred in 1994.

During 1994 new reports revived previous allegations that organs from executed Chinese prisoners are removed and transplanted to patients without the consent of the prisoner or his or her family. These reports have not been verified.

In January 1995, a Ministry of Justice official said there were a total of 1,285,000 prisoners in prisons or reform through labor camps at the end of 1994. Prisoners can be sentenced to these facilities only by the courts. However, government authorities can assign persons accused of "minor" public order offenses to "reeducation through labor" camps in an extrajudicial process. Terms of detention run from a normal minimum of 1 year to a maximum of 3 years. The labor reeducation committee which determines the term of detention may extend an inmate's sentence for an additional year. According to Chinese officials, 153,000 detainees were in reeducation through labor facilities at the end of 1993, up 16 percent over 1992 figures. Other estimates of the number of inmates are considerably higher. Officials said 75,900 were released from reeducation through labor facilities in 1993. Under a State Council regulation issued in early 1991, those sentenced to reeducation through labor may ask the committee to reconsider its decision.

Since 1990 reeducation through labor sentences may also be judicially challenged under the Administrative Procedure Law. While some persons have obtained a reduction in or withdrawal of their sentence after reconsideration or appeal, in practice these procedures are not widely used, and short appeal times, lack of access to lawyers, and other problems weaken their effectiveness in preventing or reversing arbitrary decisions.

Government officials deny that China has any political prisoners, asserting that persons are detained not for the political or religious views they hold, but because they have taken some action which violates the Criminal Law. Political dissidents, however, are often detained or charged for having committed "crimes of counterrevolution" under Articles 90 through 104 of the Criminal Law. Counterrevolutionary offenses range from treason and espionage to spreading counterrevolutionary propaganda. The authorities also used these articles to punish persons who organized demonstrations, disrupted traffic, disclosed official information to foreigners, or formed associations outside state control. In December, 9 of 16 defendants tried in Beijing in July were sentenced to prison terms ranging from 3 to 20 years for leading or participating in "counterrevolutionary groups" or conducting "counterrevolutionary propaganda and incitement." One defendant was sentenced to two years of "supervision," one was excused before trial for medical reasons, and charges against five others were dropped. All 16 defendants had been held in pretrial detention for more than 2 years. In other cases, the system of reeducation through labor is used to deal with political offenders. Qin Yongmin was sentenced to 2 years' reeducation through labor in January for "creating turmoil," apparently for his role as founder of the "Peace Charter" group in 1993. Labor activist Zhang Lin and lawyer Zhou Guoqiang were reportedly sentenced to 3-year terms of reeducation through labor in September, as were activists Bao Ge, Yang Zhou, Li Guotao, and Yang Qingheng in October. Liu Huanwen was sentenced to 2 years' reeducation through labor in August. Shanghai Human Rights Association member Dai Xuezhong was sentenced to 3 years for alleged tax evasion in December. Wei Jingsheng's secretary, Tong Yi, began serving a 2 1/2 year sentence of reeducation through labor in late December for allegedly forging an official stamp. Dissidents such as Fu Shenqi and Zhang Xianliang are also still being held in reeducation through labor facilities and are reportedly in poor health.

In January an official from the Chinese Ministry of Justice said there were 2,678 people serving sentences for counterrevolutionary crimes at the end of 1994. Chinese officials told an American human rights monitor in June that as of the end of March there were 2,935 people serving sentences for counter-revolutionary crimes, down from 3,172 in December 1993. These figures include people convicted of espionage or other internationally recognized criminal offenses but do not include political prisoners detained but not charged; political or religious activists held in reeducation through labor camps; and persons detained or convicted for criminal offenses due solely to their nonviolent political or religious activities.

The Government released on parole during 1994 several Chinese prisoners who were detained for political or religious reasons, including prominent activists Wang Juntao, Chen Ziming, Ding Junze, Yulo Dawa Tsering, and others. Nevertheless, many others, including Wei Jingsheng, Ren Wanding, Bao Tong, and Liu Gang, remained imprisoned or under other forms of detention in 1994. Some of those released in 1994 or earlier, such as Chen Ziming and Wang Dan, remain under close police surveillance and suffer from occasional police harassment, making it difficult for them to live a normal life. Wang Dan, for example, was threatened physically in December by undercover police officers, some of whom continued surveillance outside his home. Fearing physical harm, Wang disappeared from public view for 4 weeks before returning home.

Many political prisoners are subject to "deprivation of political rights" even after their period of parole has expired. This status further limits their rights of free speech and association. With a criminal record, their status in society, ability to be employed, freedom to travel, and numerous other aspects of their lives are often severely restricted, although economic reform and social change have ameliorated these problems somewhat. The families of political prisoners are also adversely affected; sometimes family members encounter difficulty in obtaining or keeping employment and housing. For example, Zhang Fengying, wife of imprisoned activist Ren Wanding, and her teenage daughter were evicted from their apartment, owned by Ren's work unit, in 1992 and remained in poor housing during 1994.

### f. Arbitrary Interference with Privacy, Family, Home, or Correspondence

Changes in the economic structure, including the growing diversity of employment opportunities and the increasing market orientation of many work units, are undermining the ability of the authorities to monitor and regulate personal and family life as closely as in the past, particularly in rural areas. In urban areas, however, most people still depend on their government-linked work unit for housing, permission to have a child, approval to apply for a passport, and other aspects of ordinary life. The work unit, along with the neighborhood committee, is charged with monitoring activities and attitudes.Although the law requires search warrants before security forces can search premises, this provision is often ignored. In addition, both the Public Security Bureau and procuracy apparently can issue search warrants on their own authority. The 1982 Constitution states that "freedom and privacy of correspondence of citizens...are protected by law," but in practice, authorities record some telephone conversations and some mail is opened and censored. Government security organs monitor and sometimes restrict contact between foreigners and Chinese citizens, particularly dissidents. Rules issued in July implementing the State Security Law define "activities of individuals outside the country (including non-Chinese citizens resident in China) who disregard dissuasion and meet with personnel in the country who have endangered state security or who are seriously suspected of endangering state security" as a violation of the State Security Law.

The Government has continued its effort to control citizens' access to outside sources of information, selectively jamming Chinese language broadcasts of the Voice of America (VOA) and British Broadcasting Corporation. The effectiveness of the jamming varies considerably by region, with audible signals of VOA and other broadcasters reaching most parts of China.

China's population has roughly doubled in the past 40 years to 1.18 billion people. In the 1970's and 1980's, China adopted a comprehensive and highly intrusive one-child family planning policy. This policy most heavily affects Han Chinese in urban areas. Urban couples seldom obtain permission to have a second child. However, exceptions are allowed for the 70 percent of Han who live in rural areas, and ethnic minorities are subject to less stringent population controls. Enforcement of the family planning policy is inconsistent, varying widely from place to place and year to year.

The population control policy relies on education, propaganda, and economic incentives, as well as more coercive measures, including psychological pressure and economic penalties. Rewards for couples who adhere to the policy include monthly stipends and preferential medical and educational benefits. Disciplinary measures against those who violate the policy include fines, withholding of social services, demotion, and other administrative punishments, such as loss of employment. Unpaid fines have sometimes resulted in confiscation or destruction of personal property. Because penalties for excess births can be levied against local officials and the mothers' work units, many individuals are affected, providing multiple sources of pressure.

Physical compulsion to submit to abortion or sterilization is not authorized, but Chinese officials acknowledge privately that there are instances of forced abortions and sterilizations. Officials maintain that, when discovered, responsible officials are disciplined and undergo retraining. They admit, however, that stronger punishment is rare. Individuals can also sue officials who have exceeded their authority in implementing family planning policy, but government officials have not provided data on the number of successful suits on these grounds.

Regulations forbid sex-selective abortion, but because of the traditional preference for male children, particularly in rural areas, some families have used ultrasound to identify and abort female fetuses. Use of ultrasound for this purpose was specifically prohibited by the Maternal and Child Health Law passed in October, which prescribes penalties for medical practitioners who violate this provision. The Chinese press has reported that the ratio of male to female births is 114 to 100, based on a nationwide average, while the statistical norm is 106 male births to 100 female. The ratio excludes many female births, especially the second or third in a family, which are unreported to permit the parents to keep trying to conceive a boy, but may also reflect the abuse of sonography. Female infanticide may also be a factor in some areas of China.

At least five provincial governments have implemented regulations seeking to prevent people with severe mental handicaps from having children. In October China passed a national Maternal and Child Care Law calling for pre-marital and prenatal examinations to determine whether couples have acute infectious diseases, certain mental illnesses (not including mental retardation), or are at risk for passing on debilitating genetic diseases. The law goes into effect on June 1, 1995, and implementing regulations defining which diseases or con-ditions will be covered have not yet been completed. The law will be imple-mented by the Ministry of Health, not the State Family Planning Commission, and while it includes provisions for abortion or sterilization in some cases based on medical advice, it provides for obtaining a second opinion and mandates that patients or their guardians give written consent to such procedures. (See also Section 5 on People with Disabilities.)

There were no reported cases of prosecution of parents for teaching their children religion in the privacy of their home.

Section 2  Respect for Civil Liberties, Including:

a. Freedom of Speech and Press

Although the Constitution states that freedom of speech and freedom of the press are fundamental rights enjoyed by all Chinese citizens, the Government interprets the Communist Party's "leading role" as circumscribing these rights. It does not permit citizens to publish or broadcast criticism of senior leaders or opinions that contradict basic Communist Party doctrine, which provides for a Socialist state under the party's leadership. The Government and party main-tained strict control over published expression of dissenting views in 1994. Public security authorities briefly detained several foreign journalists in March, April, and May after they had interviewed or attempted to interview noted dissidents or their relatives. Under China's State Security Law, "official secrets" are broadly defined, and interpretation is left to the Ministries of State Security and Public Security. Hong Kong reporter Xi Yang was convicted of "spying and stealing state secrets" after a closed trial in March. He was sentenced to 12 years' imprisonment and 2 years' deprivation of political rights for allegedly obtaining "financial and economic secrets," including information on China's interest rates and plans to sell gold. Tian Ye, the bank official who allegedly supplied Xi with the information, was sentenced to 15 years' imprisonment and 3 years' deprivation of political rights. After a closed trial, former journalist Gao Yu was sentenced to 6 years' imprisonment in November for "leaking state secrets abroad." (See Section 1.e.)

The party and the Government continue to control print and broadcast media and compel them to propagate the currently acceptable ideological line. In June press guidelines called on reporters to protect state secrets, avoid corruption, and not publicize "sensitive subjects." Despite these admonitions, the lively tabloid sector continued to expand in 1994, while circulation of major propaganda-oriented dailies continued to decline. Radio talk shows remained popular, and, while generally avoiding politically sensitive subjects, they provided opportunities to air grievances about public issues. A small but rapidly growing segment of the population has access to satellite television broadcasts. Satellite television dishes are widely available for sale, and a licensing scheme begun in October 1993, which controls purchase and possession of the equipment, has been implemented at best unevenly.

The Government's ability to control the production and dissemination of publications continued to diminish in 1994. Fierce competition and dwindling government subsidies have increased opportunities for private publishers and booksellers. Some credible estimates hold that, at the end of 1993, as much as one-third of all books were being published through these unsanctioned channels. In April officials announced the number of licensed publications would be frozen at current levels. Shenzhen authorities confiscated a thousand copies of "Tendency Quarterly" and briefly detained its founder in January. In May 45 newspapers and periodicals were banned for illegally reselling their publishing licenses. Seven film directors were banned in March for entering their works in an overseas film festival without going through official channels.

The Government has continued to impose heavy ideological controls on colleges, universities, and research institutes. As a result, many intellectuals and scholars, fearing that books or papers on political topics would be deemed too sensitive to be published, feel compelled to exercise self-censorship. In areas such as economic policy or legal reform, there was greater official tolerance for comment and criticism.

b. Freedom of Peaceful Assembly and Association

While the Constitution provides for freedom of peaceful assembly and association, the Government severely restricted these rights in practice. The Constitution provides, for example, that such activities may not infringe "upon the interests of the State"; protests against the political system or its leaders are prohibited. Although some small-scale demonstrations on nonpolitical grievances are tolerated in practice, demonstrations involving expression of dissident political views are denied permits and suppressed if held. Police detained Zhou Guoqiang and Yuan Hongbing in March, reportedly in part due to their presentation of a petition on human rights and worker rights to the NPC during its annual plenary session. Press reports from a Chinese-controlled service also accused Zhou of planning to sell "political" T-shirts while the NPC was in session.

The Communist Party organizes and controls most professional and other mass associations. Regulations promulgated in 1990 require all organizations to be officially registered and approved. Ostensibly aimed at secret societies and criminal gangs, the regulations also deter the formation of unauthorized political or labor organizations. Authorities in Shanghai refused to allow several individuals to register a proposed "human rights association," and some members of the group were subsequently detained (see Section 4). In March Liu Nianchun was denied permission to register the Association for Protection of Labor Rights; Liu himself was detained in May but released in October. No charges were filed against him.

c. Freedom of Religion

The Government subjects religious freedom to restrictions of varying severity, although the number of believers continues to grow. While the Constitution affirms toleration of religious beliefs, government regulations restrict religious practice to government-controlled religious organizations and registered places of worship. The Government supervises the publication of religious material for distribution. There are persistent complaints that the number of Bibles and other religious materials allowed to be printed falls far short of demand. Religious affairs bureaus, which are staffed by officials who rarely are religious believers, provide "guidance and supervision" over implementation of government regulations on religion. In a Catholic seminary in Chengdu, all the seminarians walked out in April to protest party interference in the operation of the school. Communist Party officials state that party membership and religious belief are incompatible. This places a serious limitation on religious believers, since party membership is required for almost all high positions in government and state-owned businesses.

There are no specific bans on particular religious groups, but the treatment of religious believers and organizations varies widely. Unregistered or "house" church leaders and members are harassed in some regions but tolerated in others. Nonmainstream sects are often singled out. Credible reports indicate members of an evangelical sect known as "Shouters" continued to be harassed, detained, fined, and imprisoned in Henan after the group was deemed "counter-revolutionary" in 1984.

After forcefully suppressing all religious observances during the 1966-76 Cultural Revolution, the Government began in the late 1970's to restore or replace damaged or confiscated churches, temples, mosques, and monasteries. The official religious organizations administer more than a dozen Catholic and Protestant seminaries, nine institutes to train Imams and Islamic scholars, and institutes to train Buddhist monks. Students who attend these institutes must demonstrate "political reliability," and all graduates must pass an examination on their theological and political knowledge to qualify for the clergy. The Government permitted some Catholic seminarians, Muslim clerics, and Buddhist clergy to go abroad for additional religious studies in 1994.

The authorities permit officially sanctioned religious organizations to maintain international contacts as long as these do not entail foreign control. In January China promulgated regulations on religious practices by foreigners and on places of religious activities. The regulations codified many existing rules, including a ban on proselytizing by foreigners, but allow foreign nationals to preach to foreigners, bring in religious materials for their own use, and preach to Chinese in churches, mosques, and temples at the invitation of registered religious organizations. In practice, some discreet proselytizing and distribution of religious texts by foreigners outside official channels is tolerated.

Buddhists are by far the largest body of religious believers in China. The Government estimates that there are 100 million Chinese Buddhists, most of whom are from the dominant Han ethnic group. (A discussion of government restrictions on Tibetan Buddhism can be found in the addendum to this report.)

According to government figures, there are 17 million Muslims in China. In some areas with large Muslim populations, officials continue to restrict the building of mosques and the religious education of youths under 18. Following the 1990 unrest in Xinjiang, the authorities issued regulations further restricting religious activities and teaching. Ningxia authorities issued regulations in July forbidding religious bodies from interfering in administrative affairs, including education, marriage, and family planning.

China permits Muslim citizens to make the hajj to Mecca, and the number of those making the hajj has significantly increased in recent years. About 3,000 officially sponsored Chinese made the hajj in 1993; many more traveled at their own expense.

The number of Christians continues to grow rapidly. Only those Christian churches affiliated with either the Catholic Patriotic Association or the (Protestant) Three Self Patriotic Movement, which the Government established in the 1950's to eliminate perceived foreign domination of Christian groups, may operate openly.

Active unofficial religious movements pose an alternative to the state-regulated churches, although in some areas there is tacit cooperation between official and unofficial churches. The unofficial, Vatican-affiliated, Catholic Church claims a membership far larger than the 4 million registered with the official Catholic Church, though actual figures are unknown. In addition to the 6 million persons who are officially counted as following Protestantism, a large number of Protestants worship privately in "house churches" that are independent of government control.

There continued to be credible reports in 1994 of efforts by authorities in some areas to rein in activities of the unapproved Catholic and Protestant movements, including raiding and closing a number of unregistered churches. Two Protestant house churches in Shenzhen were reportedly closed and their leaders briefly detained. Several Hong Kong-based Christian missionaries were detained for a few days in Henan in February for violating regulations on religious activities by foreigners; several Chinese Christians also detained in connection with the incident were released later. In November, in another town in Henan, a preacher from Taiwan and 152 local Christians were reportedly detained on charges of unauthorized proselytizing by foreigners (under the January religious regulations, Chinese from Hong Kong and Taiwan are covered by the rules governing foreigners). Ten are still in custody; the rest reportedly were released after paying fines of approximately $118 (1,000 RMB). The Guangzhou house church of Pastor Samuel Lamb (Lin Xiangao) continued to operate openly but was subject to limited harassment by the authorities. Elsewhere, authorities tolerate the existence of unofficial Catholic and Protestant churches as long as they remain small and discreet.

A number of religious activists remained imprisoned in 1994. There was some evidence that authorities have increasingly used short-term detentions, rather than long prison terms when dealing with unauthorized religious activities. Pan Yiyuan, leader of a house church in Fujian, was detained in March and released in December. Wei Jingyi was redetained in January in Hebei less than a year after finishing a 3-year sentence to reeducation through labor. Two church members from Anhui were reportedly sentenced to 2 years' reeducation through labor in September, reportedly for contacting "anti-China overseas organizations." Father Gu Zheng was reportedly detained in Xinjiang in October for teaching in an unregistered Catholic seminary. Father Vincent Qin Guoliang was sentenced to 3 years' reeducation through labor in November in Qinghai province. Bishop Su Zhiming was detained briefly in January after meeting with a visiting U.S. Congressman. Authorities in Jiangxi reportedly redetained Bishop Zeng Jingmu in September after holding him for a few days in August. Father Liao Haiqing, also detained in September, was released in November. Several other religious activists were released in 1994, although the whereabouts of some reported to have been released could not be confirmed, and others remained under some restrictions. Pei Ronggui and Jia Zhiguo were released in late January or early February; Zhang Ruiyu, Chen Zhuman, Cui Tai, Yan Peizhi, Xu Zhihe and Zhang Li were released in May. In April a visiting American religious figure was told that Han Dingxiang, Fan Zhongliang, Liu Guangdong, and others had been released. In November the U.N. Special Rapporteur on Religious Intolerance made a 10-day visit to China, including Tibet, at the invitation of the Chinese Government.

### d. Freedom of Movement Within the Country, Foreign Travel, Emigration, and Repatriation

The effectiveness of the Government's identification card system used to control and restrict individual residence location within the country continued to erode in 1994. The "floating population" migrating to China's urban areas from the countryside is estimated at anywhere from 50 to 100 million. In January the Government announced the household registration system would be revamped to adapt to the new situation. However, because this itinerant population lacks official status, access to housing, schooling, and the full range of employment opportunities can be restricted.

Some former inmates have been denied permission, under the "staying at prison employment" system, to return to their homes, a provision applicable to those incarcerated in both the "reform through labor" and the "reeducation through labor" systems. For those assigned to camps far from their residences, this constitutes a form of internal exile. The number of prisoners subject to this restriction is unknown. Others have reportedly been forced to accept jobs in state enterprises where they can be more closely supervised after their release from prison or detention.

The Government routinely permits legal emigration and most foreign travel. There was progress during 1994 in several cases in which the Government had denied passports for political reasons. Legal scholar Yu Haocheng finally obtained a passport and exit permit in May, as did several relatives of dissidents currently residing abroad. Although regulations promulgated in 1990 require college graduates to repay the cost of their free postsecondary education by working for 5 years before going abroad, students wishing to go abroad still manage to obtain passports. The Government continues to use political attitudes as a major criterion in selecting people for government-sponsored study abroad.

The Government continued its efforts to attract persons who have studied overseas back to China. Official media have said that before returning home, Chinese citizens who have joined foreign organizations hostile to China should quit them and refrain from activities which violate Chinese law. The authorities continued to refuse to allow labor activist Han Dongfang to return to China after revoking his passport in 1993 on the grounds that he engaged in activities hostile to China while overseas. In November authorities stopped poet Bei Dao at Beijing Airport and reportedly interrogated him overnight about his position as director of Human Rights in China, a U.S.-based organization. He was then refused entry into China. Some former student leaders who were active in the 1989 Tiananmen demonstrations reportedly continue to have difficulty getting permission to return to China.

The Government accepts the repatriation of citizens who have entered other countries or territories illegally. In 1994, in addition to the routine return of Chinese illegal immigrants found in Hong Kong, the Government permitted the return of several large groups of illegal immigrants from other countries. Citizens illegally smuggled to other countries are often detained for a short time to determine identity and any past criminal record or involvement in smuggling activities. As a deterrent and to recover local costs incurred during the repatriation, the authorities in some areas levy a fine of $1,000 or more on returnees.

Currently there is no law authorizing the authorities to grant refugee status, and they generally repatriate persons of other nationalities seeking to be recognized as refugees. The Ministries of Foreign Affairs, Public Security, and Civil Affairs, in collaboration with the U.N. High Commissioner for Refugees, are writing legislation that would allow China to honor its obligation as a party since 1982 to the Geneva Convention in regard to refugees.

Although the Government denies having tightened its policy on accepting Vietnamese refugees, in recent years very few such refugees have actually been resettled in China. China has not signed the Comprehensive Plan of Action negotiated at the Geneva International Conference on Indochinese Refugees in 1989, but it generally has abided by its principles.

Section 3   Respect for Political Rights: The Right of Citizens to Change Their Government

Citizens lack the means to change their government legally and cannot freely choose or change the laws and officials that govern them. Citizens vote directly only for county-level people's congress delegates. People's congress delegates at the provincial level are selected by county-level people's congresses, and in turn provincial-level people's congresses select delegates to the National People's Congress. According to the 1982 Constitution, the National People's Congress (NPC) is the highest organ of state power. It elects the President and

Vice President, decides on the choice of the Premier, and elects the Chairman of the Central Military Commission. In some elections (but not for the central Government positions chosen by the NPC), voters are offered more candidates than positions, allowing a modest degree of choice among officially approved candidates. There were credible reports that the candidates most favored by authorities were defeated in some local elections, particularly at the village level.

There are no restrictions placed on the participation of women or minority groups in the political process, and women make up 14 percent of Communist Party membership. However, the election and agenda of people's congresses at all levels remain under tight control by the Communist Party, the paramount source of political authority in China. The Constitution was amended in 1993 to ratify the existence of small "democratic" parties, but these play only a minor consultative role at most, and all pledge allegiance to the Communist Party. Thus, the Communist Party retains an explicit monopoly on political decisionmaking.

The requirement that associations register and be approved makes it difficult for independent interest groups to form and affect the system. Several persons who petitioned the NPC calling for greater attention to human rights and workers' rights, including Zhou Guoqiang, Yuan Hongbing, and others, were detained by authorities in March and April. Zhou Guoqiang was sentenced in September to 3 years' reeducation through labor (see Section 1.e.).

Section 4 Governmental Attitude Regarding International and Non-governmental Investigation of Alleged Violations of Human Rights

There are no independent Chinese organizations that publicly monitor or comment on human rights conditions in China. The Government has made it clear it will not tolerate the existence of such groups. In April Shanghai officials denied a request for permission to register by the Chinese Human Rights Association, a group founded by Yang Zhou and other dissidents. The decision was justified on the grounds that the group was not affiliated with an official organization. The authorities subsequently detained most of the members of the group, but it is not clear whether their detentions resulted solely from their involvement in the group. Wang Dan, a 1989 student activist, was repeatedly detained for brief periods in 1994 after announcing his intention to investigate China's human rights situation. (See also Section 1.d.)

The Government has promoted limited academic study and discussion of concepts of human rights since 1991. Research institutes in Shanghai and Beijing, including the Chinese Academy of Social Sciences, have organized symposia on human rights issues, established human rights research centers, and visited other countries to study human rights practices in those nations. In 1993 the Government formed the China Society for Human Rights Studies as a "non-governmental organization"; its efforts have focused largely on improving China's image abroad and responding to criticism of China's human rights record. In June the Society issued comments on the 1993 U.S. State Department Human Rights Report which stridently defended Chinese practices and glossed over fundamental human rights abuses that the Government continues to perpetrate.

The Government reiterated in April that China agrees to abide by the Universal Declaration of Human Rights and other international human rights documents. Despite this public statement, Chinese officials accept only in theory the universality of human rights. They argue instead that a nation's political, economic, and social system and its unique historical, religious, and cultural background determine its concept of human rights. To advocate this non-universal view, and to deflect attempts to discuss its human rights record, China was active in 1994 in international forums, including the annual U.N. Human Rights Commission meeting.

The Government remains reluctant to accept criticism of its human rights practices by other nations or international organizations and often criticized reports by international human rights monitoring groups in 1994. Nevertheless, officials no longer dismiss all discussion of human rights as interference in the country's internal affairs. Chinese authorities continued their limited dialog with foreign governments on human rights issues in talks with a number of visiting delegations from other countries, and also during visits abroad by Chinese leaders. At the request of the U.S. Government in 1993, the Chinese Government provided limited information about the status of several hundred persons believed to be imprisoned for their political or religious beliefs. As noted in Section 2.c., in November the U.N. Special Rapporteur on Religious Intolerance visited China for 10 days at the invitation of the Chinese Government. His visit included a trip to Lhasa, capital of the Tibet Autonomous Region.

Section 5  Discrimination Based on Race, Sex, Religion, Disability, Language, or Social Status

Laws exist that seek to protect women, children, the disabled, and minorities. In practice, social discrimination based on ethnicity, gender, and disability has persisted and the concept of a largely homogeneous Chinese people pervades the general thinking of the Han majority.

Women

The 1982 Constitution states that "women enjoy equal rights with men in all spheres of life," including ownership of property, inheritance rights, and access to education. In 1992 the NPC enacted legislation on the protection of the rights and interests of women which was designed to assist in curbing sex-related discrimination. Women continued, however, to report discrimination, sexual harassment, unfair dismissal, demotion, and wage cuts. Women are sometimes the unintended victims of economic reforms designed to streamline enterprises and give workers greater job mobility. A survey of the All-China Federation of Trade Unions found that women made up 60 percent of those forced to leave their jobs due to enterprise cutbacks or reorganizations in 1993. Many employers prefer to hire men to avoid the expense of maternity leave and child-care, and some even lowered the retirement age for female workers to 40 years of age. Although Chinese law promises equal pay for equal work, a 1990 survey found that women's salaries averaged 77 percent of men's. Most women employed in industry work in lower-skilled and lower-paid jobs.

In June the Government issued a white paper on the situation of Chinese women, spurred by plans to host the Fourth World Conference on Women in Beijing in 1995. According to the white paper, women hold relatively few positions of significant influence within the party or government structure (there are no women in the 22-member Politburo), although 21 percent of national People's Congress delegates and 13 percent of members of the Chinese People's Political Consultative Conference are women. While the gap in the education levels of men and women is narrowing, men continue to constitute the majority of the educated, particularly the highly educated. For example, the white paper reported that in 1992, women made up 33.7 percent of college students, and 24.8 percent of postgraduates. From 1982 to 1993, 4.9 percent of doctoral degrees were awarded to women.

The Government continued in 1994 to condemn strongly and take steps to prevent and punish the abduction and sale of women for marriage or prostitution, violence against women, and female infanticide. It has severely punished and in some cases executed a number of people accused of such crimes. In a case reported in the Chinese press in December, a gang of 48 people in Anhui province received sentences ranging from 19 years to death for abducting, raping, and selling 102 women. The case was the most serious which has become known to date. The abduction of women remains a serious problem, especially in those areas where local officials have resisted efforts of central authorities to stop it. According to figures announced by the Ministry of Public Security in January, there were 15,000 cases of abduction and trafficking in women and children in 1993.

One report from Inner Mongolia blamed part of the problem of abduction and selling of women on a serious imbalance in sex ratios in one county, where there were 115 men for every 100 women. The question of male/female birth ratios and traditional preferences for boys is discussed in Section 1.f. Although Chinese authorities have enacted laws and conducted educational campaigns to eradicate the traditional preference for sons, in many areas this preference remains strong, especially in rural China. A number of provinces have sought to reduce the perceived higher value of boys in providing old- age support for their parents by establishing or improving pensions and retirement homes.

Nationwide statistics on the extent of physical violence against women are not available, but a survey of 2,100 families by the Beijing Society for Research on Marriage and the Family published in March, showed that one-fifth of all wives had been abused by their spouses. One government study indicated 2 percent of urban households and 5 percent of rural ones had serious problems of domestic violence.

### Children

China does not condone violence against children, and physical abuse can be grounds for criminal prosecution. In 1992 China's Law on the Protection of Juveniles was enacted. It forbids infanticide, as well as mistreatment or abandonment of children. The law also prohibits discrimination against handi-capped minors, emphasizes the importance of safety and morality, and codifies a variety of judicial protections for juvenile offenders. The Chinese press continues to report instances of child abuse, for example a December case in which a mother beat her daughter to death despite several prior warnings to stop abusing the child. In one case publicized in the Chinese press, a hospital successfully sued a father for abandoning his infant twin daughters soon after their birth. He was given a 1-year suspended sentence. Female and especially handicapped children represent a disproportionate percentage of those abandoned. Kidnaping and buying and selling of children continued to be a problem in some rural areas. China's extensive health care delivery system has led to a sharp decline in infant mortality rates and improved child health. According to Chinese media, China's infant mortality rate declined to 31 per 1,000 live births in 1994.

### National/Racial/Ethnic Minorities

The 55 designated ethnic minorities constitute just over 8 percent of China's total population. Most minority groups reside in areas they have tradit-ionally inhabited, many of which are in mountainous or remote parts of China. China's minorities benefit from a policy of preferential treatment in marriage policy, family planning, university admission, and employment. While the standard of living for most minorities has improved in recent years, incomes in these areas are often well below the national average. The Government has pro-grams to provide low interest loans, subsidies, and special development funds for minority areas. While these government development policies have helped raise minority living standards, they have also disrupted traditional living patterns.

The central Government has tried to adopt policies responsive to minority sensitivities, but in doing so has encountered the dilemma of how to respect minority cultures without damaging minority educational and economic opportunities. In many areas with a significant population of minorities, there are two-track school systems using standard Chinese and minority languages. Students can choose which system to attend. One acknowledged side effect of this policy to protect and maintain minority cultures has been reinforcement of a segregated society. Under this separate education system, those graduating from minority schools are at a disadvantage when competing for jobs in government and business, which require good spoken Chinese. These graduates must take Chinese language instruction before attending universities and colleges.

The Communist Party has an avowed policy of boosting minority representation in the Government and the party. Many minorities occupy local leadership positions, and a few have positions at the national level. However, in most areas, ethnic minorities are effectively shut out of most positions of real political and decisionmaking power. Some minorities resent Han officials holding key positions in minority autonomous regions. Ethnic minorities in Tibet, Xinjiang, and elsewhere have at times demonstrated against Han Chinese authority. Central authorities have made it clear that they will not tolerate opposition to Communist Party rule in minority regions.

People with Disabilities

In 1990 China adopted legislation protecting the rights of China's 54.64 million disabled. However, as with many other aspects of Chinese society, reality for China's handicapped lags far behind the legal provisions. Misdiagnosis, inadequate medical care, pariah status, and abandonment remain the norm for China's disabled population.

Statistics on education reveal the inequity of resources afforded the handicapped in China: only 6 percent of disabled school children receive primary education. The illiteracy rate among the disabled is 60 percent, and school attendance averages only 20 percent for blind, deaf, or mentally retarded children.

In May the China Welfare Fund for the Handicapped, headed by Deng Pufang, son of retired senior leader Deng Xiaoping, announced plans to raise the employment rate and the education enrollment rate of the disabled to 80 percent by the year 2000, increase vocational training, and promote research on disabilities in China. All state enterprises are required to hire a certain number of disabled workers, but Chinese authorities estimate that 40 percent of disabled people are jobless.

In May China adopted standards for making roads and buildings accessible for the handicapped. The 1990 Law on the Handicapped, however, calls for "gradual" implementation of the standards. A low level of compliance with the regulations to date has resulted in limited access to most buildings for China's physically handicapped.

The new Maternal and Child Health Care Law passed in October postpones the marriage of persons with certain specified contagious diseases or certain acute mental illnesses such as schizophrenia. If doctors find that a couple is at risk of transmitting disabling congenital defects to their children, the couple may marry only if they agree to use birth control or undergo sterilization. The law mandates premarital and prenatal examination for genetic or contagious diseases, and it specifies that medically advised abortion or sterilization require the signed consent of the patients or their guardians.

### Section 6  Worker Rights

#### a.  The Right of Association

China's 1982 Constitution provides for "freedom of association," but this right is heavily diluted by references to the interest of the State and the leadership of the Chinese Communist Party. The country's sole officially recognized workers' organization, the All-China Federation of Trade Unions (ACFTU) is controlled by the Communist Party. Independent trade unions are illegal. Though ACFTU officials recognize that workers' interests may not always coincide with those of the Communist Party, the trade union law passed by the NPC in March 1992 stated that the ACFTU is a party organ, and its primary purpose is to mobilize workers for national development. The 1993 revised Trade Union Law required that the establishment of unions at any level be submitted to a higher level trade union organization for approval. The ACFTU, the highest level organization, has not approved the establishment of independent unions. Attempts to form or register independent unions have been severely repressed (see Section 1.e. and 2.b.). There are no provisions allowing for individual workers or unofficial worker organizations to affiliate with international bodies. The vast majority of workers have no contact with any union other than the ACFTU.

Credible reports indicate that the Government has attempted to stamp out clandestine union activity. In March a petition calling, among other things, for workers to have "freedom from exploitation," the right to strike, and the right to organize nonofficial trade unions was circulated in Beijing. Chinese authorities later detained Zhou Guoqiang, (an associate of Han Dongfang, see Section 2.d.) Yuan Hongbing, and Wang Jiaqi after they presented the petition; Zhou was sentenced in September to 3 years' reeducation through labor, although the charges against him were reportedly not linked to the petition. Accurate figures are not available on the number of Worker Autonomous Federation detainees still being held after the 1989 Tiananmen Square demonstrations.

The ACFTU's primary attention remains focused on its traditional constituency, state sector workers. The Trade Union Law mandates that workers may decide whether to join the union in their enterprise. By official estimate, 10 percent of workers in collectively and state-owned enterprises have chosen for their own reasons not to join. There have been no reports of repercussions for workers who have not joined ACFTU unions. Diversification of enterprise types over the last decade of reform has vastly increased the number of workers outside the traditional sphere of the ACFTU. Over half of China's nonagricultural work force is now largely unorganized and outside the state industrial structure, in collectives, township and village enterprises, private and individual enterprises, and foreign-invested enterprises. In township and village enterprises, one of the fastest growing sectors of the economy, only 0.1 percent of workers are organized in ACFTU affiliates.

Workers in companies with foreign investors are guaranteed the right to form unions, which must affiliate with the ACFTU. According to ACFTU statistics, 60 percent of workers in foreign-invested companies had joined unions by December 1994. Unofficial Embassy surveys suggest a more accurate estimate of unionization of employees in foreign-invested enterprises might be closer to 40 percent. According to press reports, 14 coastal provinces issued regulations requiring all foreign-invested enterprises to establish unions by the end of 1994. Enforcement of these regulations appears to have been haphazard. Guangdong province, recipient of much of China's foreign investment, reported 40-percent unionization of foreign-invested enterprises in December 1994.

The right to strike, which had been included in China's 1975 and 1978 constitutions, was not retained in the 1982 Constitution. In general, the Union Law assigns unions the role of mediators or go-betweens with management in cases of work stoppages or slowdowns. Nonetheless, work stoppages occurred in several locations in China during 1994. One of the largest well-documented cases occurred when 1,300 workers in a foreign-invested enterprise in Shekou in Guangdong province struck over working conditions. Beginning in 1993, the Ministry of Labor no longer officially denied the existence of strikes in China. In 1994 Ministry of Labor officials provided detailed statistics on the number and type of labor disputes. The statistics, based on National Mediation Center and Labor Bureau records, reveal a 50-percent increase in disputes in 1993. Ministry of Labor arbitration bureaus across China recorded 12,358 disputes involving 34,794 workers. Of these, all but 1,173 were initiated by workers. According to the Ministry of Labor, roughly two-thirds of the disputes were settled through mediation or arbitration, 334 were taken to court, and 244 resulted in strikes.

b. The Right to Organize and Bargain Collectively

The long-awaited National Labor Law, passed by the NPC's Standing Committee on July 5, permits workers in all types of enterprises in China to bargain collectively. The law, which will take effect January 1, 1995, supersedes a 1988 law that allowed collective bargaining only by workers in private enterprises. Some high-profile experiments in collective bargaining have been carried out at state enterprises, notably the Shanghai Number Five Iron and Steel Plant. In the past, the ACFTU has limited its role to consulting with management over wages and regulations affecting working conditions and serving as a conduit for communicating workers' complaints to management or municipal labor bureaus. The ACFTU has shown concern about protecting workers' living standards in areas such as unemployment insurance and argued in 1993 that the traditional definition of workers should be expanded to include peasants laboring in China's township and village enterprises.

Before wage reform, workers' wages were set according to a uniform national scale, based on seniority and skills. Since wage reform, a total wage bill for each collective and state-owned enterprise is set by the Ministry of Labor according to four criteria: 1) as a percentage of profits, 2) as a contract amount with the local labor bureau, 3) for money losing enterprises, according to a state-set amount, or 4) as an enterprise-set amount subject to Labor Ministry review. Individual enterprises determine how to divide the total among workers, a decision usually made by the enterprise manager in consultation with the enterprise party chief and the ACFTU representative. Worker congresses (see below) have mandated authority to review plans for wage reform, though these bodies serve primarily as rubberstamp organizations. Wages are generally equal for the same type of work within enterprises. Incentives are provided for increased productivity. Under the new Labor Law, wages may be set according to conditions set out in collective contracts negotiated between ACFTU representatives and management. In practice, only the small number of workers with high technical skills can negotiate effectively on salary and fringe benefit issues.

The old permanent employment system is increasingly giving way to a more flexible contract-based system. Most workers in state-owned enterprises hired in the last 3 years have signed individual contracts--a practice mandated by the new Labor Law--and a number of large enterprises have converted all workers to such contracts. Approximately 40 percent of state sector workers now work under contract, but the proportion of contract workers varies widely according to regional economic development. In Shanghai, 1.5 million workers, or 97.5 percent of all workers in state sector firms, have signed labor contracts. Contract arrangements are more common in township and village enterprises and many types of joint ventures. In collective enterprises below the provincial level, contract workers are a distinct minority. China's new Labor Law provides for workers and employers at all types of enterprises to sign both collective and individual contracts. The former will be worked out between ACFTU or worker representatives and management and will specify such matters as working conditions, wage distribution, and hours of work. Individual contracts will then be drawn up in line with the terms of the collective contract.

Worker congresses, held periodically in most Chinese enterprises, theoretically have the authority to remove incompetent managers and approve major decisions affecting the enterprise, notably wage and bonus distribution systems. However, worker congresses generally take place only once a year and serve essentially to approve agreements worked out among factory managers, party secretaries, and ACFTU representatives. In smaller enterprises it is not unusual to find these three posts held by the same person.

A dispute settlement procedure has been in effect since 1987. The procedure provides for mediation, two levels of arbitration committees, and a final appeal to the courts. Of the 12,358 cases brought for arbitration in 1993, 64 percent were resolved at the first or second level. Less than 3 percent reached the courts. Approximately 40 percent of the cases closed in 1993 were resolved in favor of the worker(s), 20 percent in favor of management; the rest resulted in a compromise. According to Labor Ministry officials, most arbitration cases are filed by contract workers or their employers, indicating, they assert, that the new contract system provides a clearer set of ground rules which both sides can attempt to enforce.

The 1982 Trade Union Law prohibits antiunion discrimination and specifies that union representatives may not be transferred or terminated by enterprise management during their term of office. Unionized foreign businesses generally report pragmatic relations with ACFTU representatives. At its National Congress in October 1993, the ACFTU set the goal of establishing unions in 50 percent of all foreign-funded enterprises by the end of 1994.

Laws governing working conditions in China's special economic zones (SEZ's) are not significantly different from those in the rest of the country. However, wages in the SEZ's, and in southeastern China generally, are significantly higher than in other parts of the country.

c. Prohibition of Forced or Compulsory Labor

In addition to prisons and reform through labor facilities, which contain inmates sentenced through judicial procedures (see Section 1.c.), China also maintains a network of "reeducation through labor" camps, where inmates are sentenced through nonjudicial procedures (see Section 1.e.). Inmates of reeducation through labor facilities are generally required to work. Reports from international human rights organizations and the foreign press indicate that at least some persons in pretrial detention are also required to work. Justice officials have stated that in reeducation through labor facilities there is a much heavier emphasis on education than on labor. Most reports conclude that work conditions in the penal system's light manufacturing factories are similar to those in ordinary factories, but conditions on farms and in mines can be harsh. As is the case in most Chinese workplaces, safety is not a high priority. There are no available figures for casualties in prison industry.

Some penal facilities contract with regular industries for prisoners to perform light manufacturing and assembly work. In 1991 the Government published a reiteration of its regulations barring the export of prison-made goods. On August 7, 1992, the U.S. and Chinese Governments signed a memorandum of understanding (MOU) prohibiting trade in prison labor products. A statement of cooperation detailing specific working procedures for implementation of the MOU was agreed to and signed on March 14, 1994.

### d. Minimum Age for Employment of Children

China's National Labor Law, effective January 1, 1995, forbids employers to hire workers under 16 years of age and specifies administrative review, fines, and revocation of business licenses of those businesses that hire minors. In the interim, regulations promulgated in 1987 prohibiting the employment of school-age minors who have not completed the compulsory 9 years of education continued in force. Enterprise inspection and effective enforcement of labor regulations is expanding. Officials insist that increased diligence in monitoring temporary workers has successfully precluded widespread employment of minors. Labor officials also report that employers were disciplined in 1994 for infringement of child labor regulations, but such reports cannot be verified. In poorer isolated areas, child labor in agriculture is widespread. Most independent observers agree with Chinese officials that, given its vast surplus of adult labor, urban child labor is a relatively minor problem in formal sectors of the economy. Rising dropout rates at secondary schools in some southern provinces and anecdotal reports suggest that children may increasingly be entering unregulated sectors of China's economy. No specific Chinese industry is identifiable as a significant violator of child labor regulations.

### e. Acceptable Conditions of Work

The new Labor Law codifies many of the general principles of China's labor reform, setting out provisions on employment, labor contracts, working hours, wages, skill development and training, social insurance, dispute resolution, legal responsibility, supervision, and inspection. In anticipation of the Law's minimum wage requirements, many local governments already enforce regulations on minimum wages. Generally the wage levels have been set higher than the local poverty relief ceiling but lower than the current wage level of the average worker. Minimum wage figures do not include free or heavily subsidized benefits which employers commonly provide in kind, such as housing, medical care, and education. Unemployment insurance schemes now cover a majority of urban workers (primarily state sector workers). Benefits from these funds are provided to laid off workers according to "local conditions," but unemployment subsidies generally equal 120 to 150 percent of the local hardship relief standard. Regularization of unemployment insurance coverage and administration in 1994 has served to decrease the incidence of nonpayment of severance allowances. Workers are eligible to receive unemployment relief funds for varying lengths of time, up to 24 months, according to length of service.

In February the State Council reduced the national standard workweek from 48 hours to 44 hours, excluding overtime, with a mandatory 24-hour rest period. A system of alternating weeks of 6- and 5-day workweeks began in March, with a 6-month grace period for implementation. The same regulations specified that cumulative monthly overtime could not exceed 48 hours. The Chinese press regularly reported cases of workers forced to work regular 12-and 14-hour days of forced overtime at foreign-invested enterprises, particularly in southeast China and the SEZ's.

Occupational health and safety are constant themes of posters and campaigns. Every work unit must designate a health and safety officer, and the International Labor Organization has established a training program for these officials. The U.S. Department of Labor's Mine Safety and Health Administration is participating actively in this program. Moreover, while the right to strike is not provided for in the 1982 Constitution, the Trade Union Law explicitly recognizes the right of unions to "suggest that staff and workers withdraw from sites of danger" and to participate in accident investigations. Labor officials reported that such withdrawals did occur in some instances during 1994. Nonetheless, pressures for increased output, lack of financial resources to maintain equipment, lack of concern by management, and a traditionally poor understanding of safety issues by workers have contributed to a continuing high rate of accidents. Statistics provided by the ACFTU indicate that 11,600 workers were killed in industrial accidents from January to August of 1993, up 13 percent over the same period of 1992. One credible report indicates there are over 10,000 miners killed in accidents yearly. Fatal factory explosions, fires, and collapsing dormitories have been covered by both the domestic and foreign press. Officials blame 60 percent of accidents on violation of safety regulations, particularly in the rapidly expanding rural, private, and foreign-invested enterprise sectors. In Guangdong, where 1,300 fires killed 329 people and injured 889 in 1993, the authorities announced in February new fines for enterprises that neglect safety precautions. Negligent units will be fined 1 to 5 percent of the total losses they incur in any fire, $3,450 (RMB 30,000) for every worker killed, and $345 to $575 (RMB 3,000 to 5,000) for each worker injured. Many factories using harmful products, such as asbestos, fail not only to protect their workers against the ill effects of such products, but also fail to inform them about the potential hazards.

TIBET

(This section of the report on China has been prepared pursuant to Section 536 (b) of Public Law 103-236. The United States recognizes the Tibet Autonomous Region (hereinafter referred to as "Tibet") to be part of the People's Republic of China. Preservation and development of Tibet's unique religious, cultural, and linguistic heritage and protection of its people's fundamental human rights continue to be of concern.)

Respect for the Integrity of the Person

Because the Chinese Government strictly controls access to and information about Tibet, it is difficult to state precisely the scope of human rights abuse there. It is known, however, that during 1994 Chinese government authorities continued to commit widespread human rights abuses in Tibet, including instances of torture, arbitrary arrest, and detention without public trial, long detention of Tibetan nationalists for peacefully expressing their political views, and rigid controls on freedom of speech and the press, particularly for Tibetans. There are credible reports that authorities in some instances tortured and killed detainees in Tibet. Reports from international human rights organizations indicate that a Tibetan nun died on June 4 in a prison hospital, reportedly as a result of a beating by guards. In May Tibetan officials reported that a former public security official in Tibet was sentenced to 9 years in prison for causing the death of a suspect while torturing him to obtain a confession. The United Nations Working Group on Arbitrary Detentions has concluded that China is arbitrarily detaining 32 Tibetans and has called for their release.

The authorities permit most traditional religious practices except those seen as a vehicle for political dissent, which they ruthlessly suppress. They continue to detain and prosecute monks and nuns who have expressed dissenting political views in public. Legal safeguards for Tibetans detained or imprisoned are inadequate in design and implementation, and lack of independent outside access to prisoners or prisons makes it difficult to assess the extent and severity of abuses and the number of Tibetan prisoners.

According to human rights organizations, small-scale protests were reported to have occurred in Lhasa, the capital, and elsewhere during 1994, resulting in swift detention for participants. According to credible reports, in January, 11 nuns were sentenced to terms of 2 to 7 years' imprisonment for taking part in a pro-independence demonstration in 1993. Another group of 14 nuns reportedly had their prison sentences increased by up to 9 years for singing pro-independence songs. In May a demonstration by Tibetan shopkeepers protesting tax increases took on political overtones, and several dozen Tibetan monks and nuns were detained, apparently for raising independence slogans. Police responded without using excessive force, reflecting better riot control training; no lives were lost. Tibetan political prisoners such as Ngawang Pulchung and Jempel Tsering remained imprisoned in 1994, although Yulo Dawa Tsering and three other Tibetans were released in November.

### Freedom of Religion

In Tibet, where Buddhism and Tibetan nationalism are closely intertwined, relations between Buddhists and secular authorities continued to be tense in 1994. The Government does not tolerate religious manifestations that advocate Tibetan independence, and it has prohibited a large traditional festival which has in the past been used to encourage separatist sentiment. The Government condemns the Dalai Lama's political activities and his leadership of a "government in exile," but it recognizes him as a major religious figure. Government religious authorities in 1994 forbade party and government officials from displaying the Dalai Lama's photograph, including in their homes, and removed his photographs from sale at bazaar shops. His photos remain in prominent positions in most temples in Tibet. The autonomous region government in Tibet also ordered Tibetan officials who have children studying in India to bring them back to Tibet immediately.

In 1994 the Chinese Government continued to take steps to ameliorate damage caused in the 1960's and 1970's to Tibet's historic religious buildings and other aspects of its cultural and religious heritage. The Government has expended substantial sums to reconstruct the most important sacred sites of Tibetan Buddhism. A 5-year project to restore the Potala Palace (the most important Tibetan Buddhist center) in Lhasa was concluded in August 1994 at a cost of $6.4 million. The Government also provided funding in 1994 for the restoration of two other major religious sites in Lhasa, the Jokhang and Ganden monasteries. Ganden had been completely destroyed during the Cultural Revolution. Public contributions also helped to rebuild these and many smaller monasteries. Although the Government denied it, the practice of religion in Tibet continued to be hampered by the limits the Government imposes on the number of resident monks in several of Tibet's main temples. There are 34,000 Buddhist monks and nuns in Tibet, according to official figures, a small number compared to traditional norms. Tibetan Buddhists claim that they are restricted in the numbers and training of religious practitioners, even though limits on resident monks are not strictly observed in practice. Monks at some Tibetan monasteries known for their opposition to Han Chinese domination may still face travel restrictions.

### Economic Development and Protection of Cultural Heritage

Like China's 54 other minority ethnic groups, Tibetans receive preferential treatment in marriage policy, family planning, university admission, and employment. Chinese government development policies have helped raise the living standards of Tibetans, but also have disrupted traditional living patterns. The Government has sought to preserve the Tibetan language, but in doing so has encountered the dilemma of how to preserve the language without limiting educational opportunities. In Tibet primary schools at the village level teach in Tibetan. Many pupils end their formal education after graduating from these schools, which usually only have two or three grades. Those who go on to regional primary schools and beyond, particularly after junior high school, receive much of their education in Chinese, although some areas provide instruction in Tibetan through junior high school. Efforts to expand Tibetan language instruction are hampered by lack of materials and competent teachers at higher levels.

In July 1994, the Chinese Communist Party and the State Council conducted a large-scale work conference on Tibet. The third of its kind since 1980, this work conference was attended by delegations from the CCP and central government organizations, as well as provincial representatives and delegates from certain urban areas. The conference focused on setting economic development goals, pledging to increase economic activity in Tibet by 10 percent a year. The plan included a total of $270 million in investment projects, continuing the government policy of providing substantial budget subsidies to develop Tibet's backward economy. China's leaders also made clear that Tibet would continue to receive central government financial assistance and would retain "special flexibility" in implementing reform policies mandated elsewhere in China. In a speech covered extensively in the Chinese press, President Jiang Zemin reiterated Beijing's willingness to "welcome back" the Dalai Lama to Tibet, so long as "he abandons advocacy of Tibetan independence and ceases activities to split the motherland." Although the work conference approved plans to boost economic development in Tibet, it produced no change in the Chinese Government's policy toward Tibet.

The Dalai Lama continued in 1994 to express concern that development projects and other central government policies encourage a massive influx of Han Chinese into Tibet, which has the effect of overwhelming Tibet's traditional culture and diluting Tibetan demographic dominance in Tibet. Freer movement of people throughout China in recent years, and the prospect of economic opportunity in Tibet, has led to a substantial increase in the non-Tibetan population (including China's Muslim Hui minority as well as Han Chinese) in Lhasa and other urban areas. Most of these migrants profess to be temporary residents, but small businesses run by ethnic Han and Hui peoples (mostly restaurants and retail shops) are becoming more numerous in or near some Tibetan towns and cities. Roughly one-third of the population of Lhasa is Han Chinese. Chinese officials assert that 95 percent of Tibet's officially registered population is Tibetan, with Han and other ethnic groups making up the remainder. Increased economic development will likely mean the transfer to, or temporary duty in, Tibet of a greater number of non-Tibetan technical personnel, and may also increase the number of immigrants from China's large floating population seeking to take advantage of new economic opportunities.

Economic development, fueled by central government subsidies, is changing traditional Tibetan ways of life. While the Chinese Government has made efforts in recent years to restore the physical structures and other aspects of Tibetan Buddhism and Tibetan culture damaged or destroyed during the Cultural Revolution, repressive social and political controls continue to limit the individual freedoms of Tibetans.

# Index

14th Party Congress, 14-15, 86
*93 Hasty Thoughts—Who Are the Ugly Chinese*, 94
*A Showy City*, 95
*A Third Eye Observes China*, 7, 93
abortions, 181, 203, 236, 285
Academy of Sciences, 44, 64, 162
accidents, 254, 303
addicts, 107, 109, 120-121, 125
adolescents, 88
affluence, 8, 97, 100, 106
Africa, 33, 164, 171, 215, 220, 265
Agence France Presse (AFP) 73, 117, 128-129, 134, 139
aggression, 66, 96, 171, 209, 221-222
aging, 68, 73, 93, 186
agriculture, 27, 32-35, 45, 252-253, 302
Ai Bei, 94
AIDS, 109
America, 7, 25, 85-86, 118, 171, 186-187, 215, 220, 236, 265, 270, 285 (See also United States)
American, 6, 28, 51, 57, 59, 61, 84, 90, 112-113, 165, 181, 187, 190, 194, 218, 234, 245, 272, 274, 279, 283, 291
Ammunition, 108, 128, 130, 132, 187
Amnesty International, 9, 56, 69-70, 116, 159-160, 181-183
Amor, Abdelfattah, 191
anarchism, 19, 26

anarchy, 258
Anhui Province, 140, 295
Anti-Drug Day, 108, 120
Anyang Intermediate People's Court, 139
apartheid, 33, 171, 209, 220, 222
appeals, 45, 58, 61, 118, 127, 232-233, 282
April 5th Forum, 57
Arabs, 209
Arbitration, 251, 299, 301
Armacost, Michael, 186
army, 20, 28, 31, 68-69, 73, 87, 94, 106-108, 122, 127, 164, 188 (See also People's Liberation Army.)
arrests, 6, 22, 44, 51, 53, 61, 64, 71-72, 115, 160, 162, 188, 250
arson, 109, 274 (See also fires.)
Asia Watch, 47, 53, 56, 59, 72-73, 114-115, 180-181, 190
Asian Pacific Economic Cooperation (APEC), 72, 162, 166, 169, 183
Asians, 218
Association of Southeast Asian Nations (ASEAN), 218
asylum, 55, 64, 181
attorneys, 233, 281 (See also lawyers)
Australia, 183
Australian, 56, 87, 183, 189, 234, 280
Australian Broadcasting Company, 56
authoritarian, 26, 93
autocracy, 259-260
Bai Songwu, 122

banditry, 109
bandits, 106, 108, 119, 121, 134, 138
Bangkok Declaration, 170-171, 207, 220
Bangladesh, 171
Bao Tong, 47
Bao Ge, 66, 283
Bao Ruowang, 105, 111
Bao Zunxin, 61
Bao Ruowang, 105, 111
Baucus, Max, 164, 184
Beethoven, 29
Beijing Auto Works, 112
*Beijing Bastards*, 92
Beijing Central Television, 133
*Beijing Evening News*, 139
Beijing Foreign Language Institute, 66
Beijing Jeep, 112
*Beijing Review*, 164, 168, 192-194, 211, 216, 218, 224, 226, 266, 270, 274
*Beijing Spring*, 45, 268
Bentsen, Lloyd, 184
Berkeley, 59
Berlin, 182
bibles, 239, 288
Bilney, Gordon, 189
blacklist, 61
*Blue Kite*, 92-93
BMW, 134
Bo Yibo, 18, 20
Boeing Corporation, 167
bombings, 109
books, 7, 86-89, 93-94, 96, 100, 126, 202, 239, 287
bookstores, 86, 239
bourgeois, 14, 100, 215
bourgeoisie, 214-215
Boutros-Ghali, Boutros, 169
Bradley, William 161

bribery, 28, 30, 34-35, 105, 126
bribes, 28, 30, 35, 123, 126-127, 131, 133-135
Britain, 50, 84, 87, 113, 160 (See also England and United Kingdom.)
British, 160, 236, 242, 285
broadcasting, 56, 236-237, 285
Brown, Ron, 179, 188, 191
Buddhism, 240, 289, 305, 307
Buddhist nuns, 159, 181
Buddhists, 162, 240, 289, 305
bureaucracy, 2
bureaucratic, 21-22
bureaucrats, 106
Burma, 170
businesses, 29, 188, 239, 252, 288, 301-302, 307 (See also companies and corporations.)
businessmen, 34, 51,57, 61, 68, 130, 280
cadres, 19-20, 22, 28, 30, 32-33, 74, 90, 99
Cai Zongguo, 183
California, 59
campaigners, 57, 71
campaigns, 8, 23, 116, 254, 260, 296, 303
*Can China's Army Win the Next War?*, 94
cancer, 95
Cannes Film Festival, 93
capital punishment, 8, 116, 128 (See also executions.)
capitalism, 2, 19, 74, 203, 205
capitalists, 14, 26, 215
censors, 7, 83, 88, 91-93
censorship, 7, 86, 89, 92,235, 238, 285
Central Advisory Commission, 18
centralism, 15, 26-27 (See also democratic centralism.)

Changsha, 117
Chen Binggeng, 126
Chen Kuaiyuan, 158
Chen Lantao, 48
Chen Mingzhang, 109
Chen Xitong, 161
Chen Yun, 19
Chen Ziming, 47, 61-62, 64, 230,
    235, 278, 284
*Cheng Ming*, 60
Chengdu, 128, 131, 288
China Alliance Society, 70
China Coal Sales and Transportation
    Company, 133
*China Daily*, 120, 165, 191
*China Digest*, 30
China Free Labor Union, 72-73
China Information Agency, 107, 116,
    118-120, 124-125, 129, 135
*China Local Administration Inspec-
    tion News*, 138
China News Agency, 108, 110, 118-
    128, 130-131, 133, 135,
    137-140
China Progressive Union, 72
*China Quarterly*, 111
China Rural Development Trust and
    Investment Company, 133
*China Youth Daily*, 99, 111
*China's Secret Wars*, 94
Chinese Communist Party (CCP), 4,
    8-9, 1, 14-15, 17-18, 20-21,
    23-27, 30-31, 34, 73, 95,
    186, 189, 202-203, 248,
    259, 298, 306
Chinese People's Political
    Consultative Conference, 24,
    295
Chinese Socialist Democratic Party,
    72-73
*Chinese Women*, 139-140, 295

Chongqing, 117-118, 121, 135
Chongqing Intermediate People's
    Court, 121, 135
Christmas, 56, 113
Christopher, Warren, 51, 64-65, 163,
    166-167, 169, 181, 183-188,
    191
Chrysler Corporation, 112
Chuan Xiaoyang, 129
clergy, 228, 239, 289
clerics, 241, 289
Clinton, William, 5, 50-51, 57, 59,
    61, 65-66, 72, 86, 113, 157,
    159, 162-169, 179-182, 184-
    189, 191, 205, 272-273
Cable News Network (CNN), 68, 87
Cold War, 165, 192, 218, 220, 157
colonialism, 171, 209, 220
Columbia, 64
Commission for Discipline Inspec-
    tion, 27-28, 34
communism, 2, 5, 83-84, 95
communist ideology, 2
Communist Party, 1-9, 14-15, 17-
    18, 20-27, 30-31, 34, 56,
    59, 73, 95, 98, 110, 117,
    158, 162, 186, 189, 202-
    203, 1, 228, 232-233, 237,
    239, 244, 248-249, 259,
    280, 286, 288, 293, 297-
    298, 306 (See also Chinese
    Communist Party.)
Communist Youth League, 99, 113
communists, 22, 52
companies, 16, 30, 87, 89, 93, 112-
    113, 134, 186, 188, 249,
    299 (See also businesses and
    corporations.)
confiscation, 236, 285
consumer, 87, 111
contradictions, 26, 93, 258, 268

corporation, 16, 112-113, 123, 126, 131, 167, 236, 285 (See also businesses and companies.)
counterfeiting, 126, 130, 138
counterrevolutionaries, 234
countryside, 4, 31-35, 73, 93, 95, 191, 291
Cowan, Jeffery, 86
crime syndicates, 107, 121
criminal justice, 3, 8, 105-106, 110, 140
Cui Jian, 92
Cultural Revolution, 16, 18, 57, 73, 91-92, 95-97, 237, 239, 289, 307
customs, 61, 162, 194, 252, 273

Daqing, 131
*Dazhong Daily*, 138
deaths, 69, 122, 132, 138, 238
decentralization, 3, 22, 26
Democracy Wall, 4, 44-45, 57, 167
democratic centralism, 15, 26-27
demonstrations, 6, 34, 58-59, 162, 164, 168, 180, 182-183, 190, 231-232, 238, 250, 276-277, 283, 288, 292, 298 (See also protests.)
demonstrators, 182, 238
Deng Hanfeng, 125
Deng Liqun, 19
Deng Xiaoping, 1-2, 4, 7, 14, 17-20, 23, 30, 33, 44-45, 48-50, 57, 65, 67, 83, 87, 91, 93-96, 98, 110, 192, 297
Dengism, 96-97
Dennis, Patricia Diaz, 158
Department of State (of U.S.), 9, 171, 180-181, 189-190, 245,
Ding Guangen, 89, 97
Ding Junze, 62, 284

Ding Zilin, 65, 68, 162, 268
diplomacy, 167, 215
diplomats, 66, 68, 167, 181-182, 185-186
*Divining Post-Deng Era*, 94
Dong Yunhu, 217
dormitories, 67, 303
downsizing, 2, 21
drug seizures, 107
drugs, 8, 30, 106-109, 118-121, 122, 125, 127-31, 136-138, 230, 278
Dubcek, Alexander, 44

Eagleburger, Thomas, 185
*Eastern Express*, 112
economic reform, 72-74, 90, 93-94, 97-100, 106, 235, 284
*Economic Weekly*, 62
elderly, 228, 246
embezzling, 124-126, 133, 140
emigration, 187, 241-242, 291
employers, 246, 252-253, 295, 300-303
England, 160
English, 96
espionage, 231, 234, 283-284
ethnicity, 246, 294
eugenics, 237, 248
executions, 2, 8-9, 27, 29, 106-108, 115-119, 122, 124-125, 128-129, 131-138, 233, 282 (See also capital punishment.)

factions, 16, 202
factories, 28, 52, 85, 87, 112, 120, 188, 230, 252, 254, 302-303
Fang Lizhi, 87, 157, 161
*Farewell My Concubine*, 7, 25, 91-92, 237
Federation for Democracy in China, 183

Federation of Chinese Civil Groups, 72-73
females, 246-247, 270, 277, 286, 295-296
feudalism, 97, 168, 215
films, 7, 92-93
*Financial Daily*, 99
firearms, 108, 130, 137 (See also guns.)
fires, 254, 303
fishermen, 130
Flack, Roberta, 159
flood, 29
Ford, 86
Foreign Ministry, 86, 163, 165, 167, 186, 190-191 (See also Ministry of Foreign Affairs)
foreigners, 6-7, 9, 56, 68, 85, 114-115, 159, 203, 231, 235, 250, 283, 285, 289-290
fraud, 16, 105, 123, 138
Freedom and Democratic Party, 72
freedom of movement, 6, 10, 241, 291
freedom of speech, 3, 6, 44, 70, 83-84, 237, 274, 276, 286, 304
freedoms, 2-3, 5-6, 14, 22, 24, 31, 98, 207, 209, 217-218, 220, 265, 276, 307 (See also freedom of movement and freedom of speech.)
Fu Jianguo, 117
Fu Shenqi, 47, 56, 182, 234-235, 283
Fuchs, Gerard, 183
Fudan, 237
Fujian High People's Court, 118, 122, 131
Fuzhou Intermediate People's Court, 135
Fuzhou, 124, 131, 134-135

gambling, 57, 86, 126, 137, 139

Gandhi, Rajiv, 192
gangs, 134, 139, 239, 288
gangsters, 117
Gansu Province, 129
Gao Quancheng, 119
Gao Haifeng, 235
Gao Shan, 167
Gao Yu, 183, 237, 282, 287
General Agreement on Tariffs and Trade (GATT), 52, 164, 191
Gellat, Timothy, 53
Geneva, 73, 292
genocide, 160, 162
German, 72, 93, 96
Germany, 66, 69, 105, 111, 182
gerontocrats, 54
*Godfather*, 92
Golan, 209
Golden Globe Award, 25
Golden Triangle, 106-108
Gore, Albert, 182
graft, 27, 29-30, 134
grenades, 107-108, 128, 138
Group to Protect Chinese Human Rights, 73
Gu Jieshu, 136
Guangdong, 29, 107-108, 114-115, 117, 119-120, 122-128, 132-134, 136-138, 229, 249, 253, 277-278, 291, 299, 303
Guangdong People's Radio, 134, 136
*Guangming Daily*, 97, 121
Guangxi High People's Court, 118, 126-127
Guangzhou, 117-119, 121, 123, 125, 127-128, 131-134, 136-138,140, 241, 290
Gui Bingquan, 135
Guizhou, 120, 123, 133

gulag, 2, 48, 162
guns, 62, 69, 106-108, 130, 132, 187
　　(Also see firearms.)
Haifeng, 134, 235
Haikou, 133, 135
Haikou Intermediate People's Court,
　　127, 138
Hainan, 54, 127, 133, 135, 138
Haiyan, 160
Hamlisch, Marvin, 159
Han Shulin, 122
handicapped, 17, 248, 265, 296-298
Hangzhou, 124
hardliners, 49
hardships, 235
Havens, Richie, 159
*Hebei Daily*, 132
hegemonists, 6, 59, 84
hegemony, 170-171
Heilongjiang, 19, 94
*Henan Legal News*, 110
hepatitis, 61
hijacking, 135
Hinggan League Intermediate People's
　　Court, 138
Hohhot Intermediate People's Court,
　　133
homeless (people), 191, 193, 247,
　　272
homosexuality, 7, 25, 91
Honduras, 243
Hong Yonglin, 123, 126
hooligans, 139
household registration system, 22,
　　291
Hu Cong, 133
Hu Yaobang, 17-18, 20, 48
Hua Guofeng, 20, 95
Huang Jianming, 127
Huang Kaihong, 132
Huang Sanming, 125
*Hubei Daily*, 126, 137

human rights edge (China's), 1
Human Rights Watch, 8-9, 112
humanism, 217
humanitarian, 217-218, 265-266, 272
*Hunan Daily*, 125
hunger, 48, 58, 63
Hurd, Douglas 160

ideological education, 24
ideological work, 19, 96
imperialism, 96
imperialists, 223
imprisonments, 115
India, 160, 182, 217, 305
individualism, 19, 218
Indochinese, 243, 292
Indonesia, 114, 181
infanticide, 246, 286, 295-296
inflation, 33-34, 49, 68, 89, 99, 110
*Information and Publishing Journal*,
　　96
intellectuals, 71
intelligence, 166
International Anti-Drug Day, 108,
　　120
International Olympic Committee
　　(IOC), 4, 46-48, 161
International Treaty Eradicating All
　　Forms of Racial
　　Discrimination, 194
interrogate, 281
interrogations, 229
intimidation, 54, 58
intolerance, 191, 276, 291, 294
investment, 28, 33-35, 117, 133,
　　246, 299, 306
investors, 117, 130, 249, 299
Iran, 171
Iraq, 164
Italians, 96

jails, 27, 229, 278

Japan, 66, 69, 84, 87, 113, 186, 190, 217
Japanese, 93, 96, 190, 194
Jerusalem, 209
Jiang Peikun, 65, 162, 268
Jiang Pingchao, 70
Jiangsu Province, 35, 115, 133
Jiangxi High People's Court, 129
Jiangxi Province, 115, 124, 129, 134, 136
jobless, 22, 297
Jones, Estrellita, 159
journalism, 69-70, 90
journalists, 50-51, 54, 57, 63-64, 67-68, 84, 86, 91, 100, 183-184, 238, 279, 286
judges, 119, 121, 126, 181
judiciary, 57, 232, 280
Juppe, Alain, 183
juveniles, 296 (Also see adolescents.)

Kamm, John, 51, 57, 62, 190
Karachi, 165
Keating, Paul, 56
kidnappings, 106, 109, 124, 129, 132
killings, 119, 121, 124, 126, 134, 136, 140, 183, 228, 276
Kirkland, Lane, 185
Kissinger, Henry, 185
Kohl, Helmut, 72, 182
Korea, 10, 84, 164, 187, 201, 204
Kristof, Nicholas, 113
Kunming, 122, 125, 128, 138
Kuomintang (KMT), 259

labor camps, 4, 8, 110-112, 117, 228, 234, 252, 278, 282, 284, 301
Labor Alliance, 52
laborers, 35, 252-253
landlords, 118

Lanzhou, 73, 129
Lao Gui, 115
Laogai Foundation, 111
lawbreaking, 168
lawyers, 53, 62, 282-283 (See also attorneys)
Lee Kuan Yew, 218
leftism, 19
Leftists, 14-15, 190
*Legal Daily News*, 109, 116, 129-130, 135
*Legal News*, 110, 117
legal reform, 3, 22, 238, 281, 287
legislation, 164-165, 235, 237, 243, 246, 248, 254, 292, 295, 297
Leninist system, 96, 98
Li Guohan, 57
Li Jingfang, 43, 72
Li Lun, 128
Li Qiang, 126
Li Qingxiang, 133
Li Sanyuan, 60
Li Tieying, 191
Li Wenchu, 129
Li Xiaoshi, 130
Liang Weimin, 57
Liang Xiaosheng, 94
Liao Gailong, 97
Liao Yiwu, 62
Liaoning Province, 58, 112, 134-135, 230, 279
liberalism, 19
*Liberation Army Daily*, 107
*Liberation Daily*, 26, 89
liberties, 2, 26, 237, 286 (See also freedoms.)
*Life and Death in Shanghai*, 92
life sentences, 107-108, 117-118, 135
Lin Guoming, 125
Lingyuan Labor Reform Camp, 58

Liu Bangyun, 132
Liu Gang, 47, 58, 161, 230, 235, 157, 279, 284
Liu Guifeng, 126
Liu Huaqiu, 169, 171, 220
Liu Huimin, 129
Liu Jianyi, 134
Liu Liao, 65, 162, 268
Liu Shaoqi, 20
Liu Xiaoguang, 131
London, 111, 160
Lord, Winston, 164-165
Lu Erguo, 137
Lu Guiqiang, 128
Lu Shichang, 119
Luanda Yuanyang Bang, 94
Lunar New Year, 8, 107, 128, 190
Luo Lanzhen, 129
Luo Rulong, 134

Ma Shaofang, 54
Ma Shaohua, 73
Ma Yo-Yo, 56
*Mainichi Shimbun*, 114
*Mao Anlong, Son of Mao Zedong*, 88
market economy, 15, 19, 22, 54, 74, 91, 96, 99, 122-123, 157
McCurry, Mike, 181
Military Commission, 20, 232, 244, 280, 293
Min Qianbo, 131
*Ming Pao*, 94, 138
Ministry of Public Security, 87, 107, 241, 295 (See also Public Security Bureau.)
Ministry of Radio, Film and Television, 7, 87, 92
Ministry of State Security, 87 (See also Public Security Bureau.)
Ministry of Foreign Affairs, 165 (See also Foreign Ministry.)
Ministry of Culture, 88, 97

Missile Technology Control Regime, 166
most-favored-nation (trade status for China by U.S.) MFN, 9-10, 51-52, 57, 61, 64-65, 86, 157, 163-165, 167, 180, 184-188, 272-273
Munro, Ross, 43, 47-48, 53, 56, 59, 188, 191
Muse Fengyuan, 95
*My Father Deng Xiaoping*, 17
Myer, Dee Dee, 179

National Economic Council, 184
National Federation of Youth, 113
National People's Congress (NPC), 15, 21, 24-26, 29-30, 35, 52, 54, 61-62, 64, 72-73, 90, 98, 109, 162, 229, 232, 244, 246, 249, 254, 280, 288 292-293, 295, 198,300
National Security Act, 6, 85
National Security Ministry, 60
*New York Times*, 48, 50, 63, 66, 113, 194
New York University, 53
*Newsweek*, 86
No. 1 Reeducation Through Labor Camp, 113
nuclear technology, 10

Olympic Games, 4, 43, 46, 48, 56, 71, 86, 161, 188, 238
organ donors, 9

Pasquallini, Jean, 111
Pelosi, Nancy, 157, 164, 188
Peng Zhen, 18
*People's Court News*, 134
*People's Daily*, 15, 17, 23, 26, 47, 54, 68, 83, 85-86, 90, 116, 123, 169, 172, 190

People's Liberation Army (PLA), 20, 28, 87, 122 (See also army.)
Perry, William, 189
*Piano*, 91
Politburo Standing Committee, 20
political prisoners, 1, 8-9, 43, 46-47, 51, 54-56, 61-62, 70, 73, 113, 158, 160, 162, 164, 180-181, 183-184, 187, 190, 228, 230, 234-235, 239, 245, 252, 259, 162, 274, 278, 283-284, 305
profiteering, 28, 105, 120, 122
Propaganda Department, 7, 14, 18, 25, 84, 87, 89, 94, 96
Public Security Bureau, 54, 57-58, 62, 87, 119, 123, 132, 229, 235, 242, 250, 285 (See also Ministry of Public Security and Ministry of State Security.)
Public Security Leading Group, 34

Qian Qichen, 166, 169
Qiao Shi, 15-16, 24, 26, 183, 162
Qin Yongming, 48, 71-72
Qingdao University, 55
Qinghai Province, 45, 48, 108, 125, 137, 162, 238, 248, 290
*Qinghai Daily*, 137
*Quotations of Chairman Mao*, 96

Radio Asia, 85
Radio Free Asia, 187
Radio Orient, 88
Railway Transport Intermediate Court, 134, 139
rapes, 193
Red Cross, 162, 185-186, 190, 228, 279
Red Guards, 73
reformists, 1, 15, 22

regionalism, 19
Ren Jianxin, 25, 30, 52, 105, 109
Republican Party (of China), 71
residency permits, 35
Roy, Stapleton, 164
Rubin, Robert, 184
Secretariat, 14, 19, 24, 89
Shaanxi High People's Court, 128
Shandong People's Radio, 136
Shandong Province, 55, 98-99, 109, 113, 120, 132, 138
Shanghai mafia, 16, 21
Shanghai Municipal Intermediate Court, 133, 136
Shanghai People's Radio, 136
Shanxi People's Publishing House, 93
Shattuck, John, 51, 61, 163, 171, 181, 191
Shen Taifu, 130
Shenzhen, 117, 120, 125-126, 131, 134, 137, 140, 255, 287, 290
Shih Furen, 131
*Shih-chieh Jih-pao*, 120, 123-124, 126-128, 131, 140
Si Jiuyi, 107
Sichuan High People's Court, 131
So Guoqiang, 124
socialism with Chinese character- istics, 24, 26, 83, 96-97
socialist market economy, 15, 19, 91, 122-123
Society on Party History, 97
Song Ping, 18
*South China Morning Post*, 57, 70
spiritual pollution, 3, 87
Spring Festival, 107, 128
Standing Committee (of National People's Congress), 15, 20, 26, 29, 35, 244, 254, 280, 300

State Council, 5-6, 21, 27-28, 34, 60, 85, 87, 89, 108, 213, 232, 234, 248, 253-254, 280, 283, 303, 306
State Commodity Control Office, 29
sterilizations, 181, 236, 285-286, 298
Su Jiansong, 124
Su Shaozhi, 98
Su Shaolun, 124
subsistence, 169, 171-172, 192, 194, 213-216, 221, 273
Sun Wei, 133
Sun Weiben, 20
Supreme People's Court, 25, 30, 70, 109, 116, 122, 126, 131-132, 134, 137, 139, 232, 281

*Ta Kung Pao*, 138
Ta Zhuling, 127
Taiwanese, 130
Tang Anbang, 125
Tao Siju, 25, 107, 111
*The Snow City*, 95
*The Selected Works of Mao Zedong*, 17
*The Selected Works of Deng Xiaoping*, 17, 23
*The Confession of a Red Guard*, 95
*There is a Snowstorm Tonight*, 95
Third World, 10, 179, 192, 204
Tian Zhuangzhuang, 93
Tiananmen Square, 14, 43, 65, 68, 95, 161, 180, 187, 230, 250, 298
Tianjin, 74, 228, 250
Tibet Information Network, 9, 159-162, 181-182
Tibetan Rights Campaign, 163
*To Live*, 5, 32, 93, 260, 284
Tong Yi, 51, 183, 283

*Too Hard to Call Father*, 94
Treaty Eradicating All Forms of Discrimination Against Women, 194
trials, 22, 43, 46-47, 66, 70-71, 183, 188, 232-233, 281-282

unemployment, 22, 32, 34, 215, 251, 300, 303
United Nations (UN), 10, 110, 161-162, 164, 169, 170, 172, 183, 184, 191, 192, 193, 207-209, 211, 214, 220, 230, 243, 245, 258, 265, 268, 291-292, 294, 304
Universal Declaration of Human Rights, 52, 161, 171, 181, 185, 187, 207-208, 220, 223, 268, 276, 294
University of Washington, 166

Vance, Cyrus, 185
Vienna World Conference on Human Rights, 161

Wang Dan, 4, 43-44, 52, 55, 64, 185, 188, 230, 235, 280, 284, 293
Wang Jiaqi, 52, 62-63, 298
Wang Juntao, 43, 47, 61, 186, 230, 235, 278, 284
Wang Mingdi, 113
Wang Shan, 93
Wang Shijun, 58
Wang Tiancheng, 65
Wang Wancheng, 133
Wang Xizhe, 61, 167, 235
Wei Jingsheng, 4, 43-44, 46, 55, 57, 86, 157, 181, 183-184, 235, 279, 283-284
*Wen Hui Bao*, 89, 119, 127, 134 (See also *Wen Wei Po*.)

*Wen Wei Po*, 59 (See also *Wen Hui Bao*.)
Wirth, Timothy, 171
World Journal, 117
Wu Jihong, 125
Wu Songfa, 57
Wu Wenxin, 130
Wu Zhaonan, 124
Wuhan Polytec College, 58
Xi'an Farmers Bank, 129
Xiamen Intermediate People's Court, 130
Xiao Yang, 98, 113, 278
Xie Jianping, 125
Xinhua (News Agency), 53, 86, 88, 90, 94, 97, 108, 118, 127, 130-137, 139-140, 165, 172, 189-191
Xining Intermediate People's Court, 137
Xu Liangtong, 119
Xu Yiruo, 5, 55, 113
Xu Weidong, 117
Xueshu Yuekan, 91

Yang Chunming, 131
Yang Jingsheng, 66
Yang Minghua, 88
Yang Mingji, 132
Yang Shangkun, 15, 18
Yang Zhou, 66, 71, 232, 157, 283, 293
Yangjiang City Drug Rehabilitation Center, 125
Yangjiang Municipal Intermediate People's Court, 123
Yu Youxian, 89
Yu Zhuo, 58
Yuan Hongbing, 52, 62, 64, 288, 293, 298
Yunnan People's Radio, 122
Yunnan High People's Court, 122

Zhang Guobin, 131
Zhang Jianping, 134
Zhang Jun, 136
Zhang Kangkang, 65, 162, 268
Zhang Mingpeng, 71
Zhang Siqing, 27, 30
Zhang Weiguo, 59
Zhao Haiqing, 159
Zhao Lee, 86
Zhao Ziyang, 17-18, 20, 47, 94
Zhou Guoqiang, 52, 62, 64, 157, 283, 288, 293, 298
Zhou Shaowu, 67
Zhou Yuan, 70
Zhu Muzhi, 179, 192, 194
Zhu Rongji, 16-17, 19
Zhuhai Intermediate People's Court, 132

# About the Authors

John F. Copper is the Stanley J. Buckman Professor of International Studies at Rhodes College in Memphis, Tennessee. He is the author of twenty books on China and Taiwan, including those on human rights in China listed in the preface of this book. His book *China's Global Role* (Stanford: 1980) won the Clarence Day Foundation Award for outstanding research and scholarship. His most recent book is *The Taiwan Political Miracle* (1997).


Ta-ling Lee is Professor of History at Southern Connecticut State University. In addition to the books cited in the preface of this book, he is the author of *Foundations of the Chinese Revolution* (1970) and *The Revenge of Heaven* (1972). He also edited and contributed to several other books and translated part of Wei Jingsheng's autobiography which was published in *The New York Times* in November 1980.